Jackson School Publications in International Studies

Jackson School Publications in International Studies

Senator Henry M. Jackson was convinced that the study of the history, cultures, political systems, and languages of the world's major regions was an essential prerequisite for wise decision making in international relations. In recognition of his deep commitment to higher education and advanced scholarship, this series of publications has been established through the generous support of the Henry M. Jackson Foundation, in cooperation with the Henry M. Jackson School of International Studies and the University of Washington Press.

The Crisis of Leninism and the Decline of the Left: The Revolutions of 1989, *edited by Daniel Chirot*

Sino-Soviet Normalization and Its International Implications, 1945–1990, *by Lowell Dittmer*

Contradictions: Artistic Life, the Socialist State, and the Chinese Painter Li Huasheng, *by Jerome Silbergeld with Gong Jisui*

The Found Generation: Chinese Communists in Europe during the Twenties, *by Marilyn A. Levine*

Rules and Rights in the Middle East: Democracy, Law, and Society, *edited by Ellis Goldberg, Resat Kasaba, and Joel S. Migdal*

Can Europe Work? Germany and the Reconstruction of Postcommunist Societies, *edited by Stephen E. Hanson and Willfried Spohn*

Marxist Intellectuals and the Chinese Labor Movement: A Study of Deng Zhongxia (1894–1933), *by Daniel Y. K. Kwan*

Deng Zhongxia in 1924

Marxist Intellectuals and the Chinese Labor Movement

A Study of Deng Zhongxia (1894–1933)

Daniel Y. K. Kwan

UNIVERSITY OF WASHINGTON PRESS   *Seattle & London*

Library of Congress Cataloging-in-Publication Data

Kwan, Daniel Y. K.

  Marxist intellectuals and the Chinese labor movement : a study of Deng Zhongxia (1894–1933) / Daniel Y.K. Kwan.

      p.   cm. — (Jackson School publications in international studies)

  Includes bibliographical references and index.

  ISBN 0-295-97601-2 (alk. paper)

  1. Teng, Chung-hsia, 1894–1933.   2. Communists—China—Biography. 3. Labor movement—China.   4. General Strike, Canton, China, 1925. 5. General Strike, Hong Kong, 1925.   I. Title.   II. Series.

DS777.488.T45K83   1997

322'.2'092—dc20

[B]   96-27538

                                                                     CIP

The paper used in this publication is acid-free and recycled from 10 percent postconsumer and at least 50 percent preconsumer waste. It meets the minimum requirements of American National Standard for Information Sciences— Permanence of Paper for Printed Library Materials, ANSI Z39.48–1984.

Contents

Illustrations

Foreword

DANIEL KWAN's richly suggestive study of the Communist labor leader Deng Zhongxia engages two important themes. First is Deng Zhongxia himself, May Fourth intellectual radicalized by the labor movement, a major activist in the formation of the Communist Party, and prominent labor organizer who was to lead the crucial Guangzhou–Hong Kong General Strike of the midtwenties. But the story of Deng's life is anything but a simple romantic epic of a successful revolutionary. His execution at the age of thirty-nine was preceded by embroilment in the power struggles of the 1920s within the Communist Party and the Comintern, where competing factions sought sacrificial scapegoats to blame for the tragedy of this first phase of the Chinese Communist revolution. Kwan, while deeply sympathetic to Deng, does not let his sympathies distort his judgment of the sordid politicking of these years.

The second theme of the study is the Shenggang (Guangzhou–Hong Kong) General Strike itself, which was the apogee of the urban revolution in China in the 1920s. Guangzhou (Canton) by the twenties was a backwater compared to Shanghai. Kwan demonstrates that, if Shanghai provided the trigger for the revolutionary movement, it was in Guangzhou that the revolutionary movement gathered momentum, and it was from Guangzhou, with its long-standing worker radicalism, that the revolutionary armies achieved the momentum that would enable the reunification of China by 1928, albeit at the cost of betraying the revolution that had launched them. Kwan's study of the strike is the first thorough investigation of this important event available in English (there have been earlier studies in dissertations). We are in his debt.

The two aspects of the study stand in uneasy relationship to one another. Biography does not easily mesh with social movement; the individual viewed as part of a social movement yields a different portrayal of the past than the social movement viewed as part of individual biography. Kwan has the wisdom to let the tension stand rather than seek to achieve a forced coherence, so that the work presents the past to the reader in its disjunctures as well as its conjunctures. The strategy enables the author to reveal the revolutionary movement in all its contradictions. That between the Comintern and the Communist Party we have long been aware of. But Kwan also brings to the surface contradictions that are often hidden in histories of the Communist revolution. Foremost in this study, enunciated in the title, is the contradiction between the intellectuals and the workers, which, given that the Communist Party leadership consisted mostly of intellectuals, translates also into contradictions between the Party and the working class, which, theoretically, legitimized the Party. No less important is the contradiction between the Party, with its national aspirations and assumptions, and the local Guangdong revolutionary movement, which had a history and a logic of its own. The approach is in line with a growing awareness in studies of the revolution that we should perhaps speak of histories, not just one history, of the revolution.

The study, in its reminder of the radical workers' movement in Guangdong, presents us with the ironies of the Chinese revolutions of the twentieth century. In 1989, the leaders of the Guangdong Revolutionary History Museum were kind enough to invite me to participate in the sixty-second anniversary commemoration of the Canton Commune of December 1927, which was the last, tragic event in the urban revolutionary movement of the 1920s and also of the Shenggang General Strike described here. About sixty to seventy of the participants in the commune were still alive in 1989, the oldest (Tan Tiandu) being ninety-six years of age. Only six months had passed since the tragedy at Tiananmen Square, and the mood in the country was certainly not favorable to memories of the revolution. It was all the more ironic, and not a little touching, to hear one after another of these old revolutionaries, most of them workers (a few of them women), proclaim once again their commitment to the revolution, to solidarity with other oppressed peoples, and to the cause of international revolution, topped off with an enthusiastic rendition of "The International." It was as if they were able to relive once again the glories of "Red Canton," viewed by many in the twenties as the capital of revolutions in Asia. But by this time Guangzhou was a different capital. It was the home of a flourishing capitalism under the new policies and now faced a Hong Kong that was not an imperialist oppressor but a partner in capitalist development. More than the June events in Beijing, it was this new situation that made the commemoration appear as the echo of a distant past rather than a living memory, except to those few in the room. In earlier, more revolutionary days, this commemoration was integral to revolutionary renewal; now even the local Guangzhou paper relegated it to the back pages in a short notice. Daniel Kwan's study is important for bringing to us the events of the 1920s, which, though they may now fire up with enthusiasm only the few old revolutionaries who remain, cast upon the present the irony (or is it tragedy?) of memories of the past.

Arif Dirlik
Duke University

Acknowledgments

LIKE THE FIRST monographs of many other young historians, this book is a revision and extension of my doctoral thesis, which I submitted to the University of London in 1985. Among all those who have helped me at the various stages of this study, I would like first to record my deepest gratitude to my mentor, Charles A. Curwen, for his intellectual guidance in the completion of both my master's and my doctoral degrees. Charles has always been helpful whenever I have encountered problems in my academic studies, or indeed in my personal life; I owe him more than I can express. To Stuart R. Schram, I owe thanks for showing me the techniques of textual analysis of Chinese Communist ideology, and for encouraging me as well as supporting me in my research. I am also grateful to William G. Beasley for directing my attention to the relevance of British diplomatic papers for the study of modern Chinese sociopolitical history.

An early draft of this work was commented on carefully by the late Jian Yingxi, vice-director of the Guangdong Provincial Academy of Social Sciences and a specialist of labor history in south China. Arif Dirlik of Duke University read through the manuscript and provided me with many critical comments and perceptive suggestions. To these two scholars, I would like to extend my sincere appreciation for their intellectual guidance and inspiration. I greatly regret that Professor Jian is not here to see the publication of this work, even though he would probably have disagreed with my pessimistic views on the Chinese Communist revolution.

I am also indebted to the many scholars who have either smoothed the way for my research in Hong Kong and China or shared with me their extensive knowledge of this field. They include Huang Yin of the Guangdong Provincial Academy of Social Sciences, Lu Quan of the Guangdong People's Press, Ni Junming of the Zhongshan Library in Guangzhou, Zhu Yuhe of Qinghua University in Beijing, Wu Dabai of the February Seventh Memorial Hall in Changxindian, and Ming K. Chan at the University of Hong Kong.

Over the years, a number of institutions have offered their support to my research. I am grateful to the Central Research Funds Committee of the University of London, which financed my research trip to the Hoover Institution on War, Revolution, and Peace at Stanford during the initial stage of this study. Thanks are also due to the Hong Kong Baptist University (where I was a faculty member before joining the University College of the Fraser Valley in British Columbia) for offering me a grant which facilitated my research in Guangzhou, Beijing, and Washington, D.C., in the summer of 1989, and for providing me with a six-month sabbatical leave in the fall semester of 1991–92. It was during this sabbatical period that I was able to complete a large portion of my manuscript at Duke University, where I was invited as a Visiting Scholar. I am grateful to Nan Lin and his staff at the Asian-Pacific Studies Institute at Duke for their friendly hospitality and research support during my fruitful stay there.

The following libraries and archives granted me access to their holdings, and I would like to express my appreciation for the assistance extended to me by their staff members: the School of Oriental and African Studies, Guangdong Provincial Academy of Social Sciences, Hoover Institution on War, Revolution, and Peace at Stanford, the Bureau of Investigation in Taiwan, the Library of Congress and the National Archives in Washington, D.C., Qinghua University in Beijing, the February Seventh Memorial Hall in Changxindian, and the University of Hong Kong.

I am grateful to the Henry M. Jackson School of International Studies at the University of Washington for supporting the publication of this work. I am fortunate enough to have been assisted by a highly professional team from the University of Washington Press, who provided valuable editorial service in the final stage of manuscript preparation. In this regard, my special thanks go to Julidta C. Tarver for her enthusiasm for my manuscript and to Pamela J. Bruton for her precious editorial advice and comments.

Thanks are also due to my *lao pengyou* (old friend) Laura Newby of St. Hilda's College at Oxford, who has always been patient and helpful in answering my queries about the English translation of Chinese documents.

Last but not least, I would like to express my gratitude to my family. I thank my brother, Yat-chee Kwan, and my cousin, Kwok-ying Kwan, for their generosity in sending me to study overseas. My heartfelt appreciation goes to my wife, Lai-mei, and my daughter, Shui-kei, for making my life fuller and more meaningful.

Although many teachers, colleagues, and friends have helped me in preparing this work for publication, any error found in this book is my own responsibility.

Marxist Intellectuals and the Chinese Labor Movement

Introduction

O N *15 MAY 1933*, the International Settlement's Shanghai Municipal Police raided an underground Chinese Communist cell located in the French Concession and arrested several labor agitators. About three months later, the Nationalist government requested the Shanghai Municipal Police to extradite one of their captives to the Chinese authorities immediately. The request was granted; and the Nationalist government was soon delighted by the confirmation that this recently arrested political criminal was the most influential Communist labor movement leader of the mid-1920s. His name was Deng Zhongxia.

Deng was well known by the leaders of the Nationalist government because he had been an active supporter of the First United Front policy, which was a joint political venture between the Chinese Communist Party (CCP) and the Guomindang (the Nationalist Party) in the years 1924–27. When the news of Deng's arrest reached Jiang Jieshi, the latter instructed his subordinates to persuade Deng to defect from the CCP. But his attempt met with failure. Jiang then ordered that Deng be executed without delay. The order was carried out secretly on 21 September on the outskirts of Nanjing, where the capital of the Nationalist government was located. Like his ideological mentor Li Dazhao at Beijing University, Deng also sacrificed his life at the age of thirty-nine for the Communist movement, which he considered the only solution to China's problems.

In spite of Deng's significant role in leading the Chinese labor movement during the first decade after the CCP was founded, scholars outside China have somewhat neglected his contribution to the Chinese Communist movement. This is part of a general neglect of labor in the Chinese revolution. A major peasant movement leader of the same period, Peng Pai, has received considerable attention in the scholarly world. At least three books on Peng and a translation of his major political work have been published in English.[1] By contrast, all that exists on Deng is one short article in an academic journal published in the former Soviet Union.[2]

The disregard of Deng Zhongxia outside China in the past is largely due to insufficient documentation; only in recent years have his writings been edited and published by scholars in China.[3] But the problem is perhaps also related to the fact that the Chinese Communist movement before 1949 has generally been interpreted by many historians in the West as a peasant revolution. Thus, the non-Chinese scholarship of the Chinese Communist movement tends to emphasize the interplay between the peasantry and CCP policy.

The state of research on Chinese labor history, however, has made considerable progress since the publication of *The Chinese Labor Movement, 1919–1927,* by the preeminent French Sinologist Jean Chesneaux, who has in one way or another stimulated the growth of scholarship in this field.[4] In the past decade, a small group of American scholars has also made significant contributions to our understanding of Chinese labor history, helping us to place the role of the Chinese working class in proper historical con-

1. The list of publications includes Roy Hofheinz Jr., *The Broken Wave: The Chinese Communist Peasant Movement, 1922–1928* (Cambridge: Harvard University Press, 1977); Robert Marks, *Rural Revolution in South China: Peasants and the Making of History in Haifeng County, 1570–1930* (Madison: University of Wisconsin Press, 1984); Fernando Galbiati, *Peng Pai and the Hailufeng Soviet* (Stanford: Stanford University Press, 1985); and Peng Pai, *Seeds of Revolution: Report on the Haifeng Peasant Movement,* trans. D. Holoch, Cornell East Asia Paper (Ithaca, 1973).

2. T. Akatova, "Deng Zhongxia: A Leading Figure in the Chinese Labor Movement," *Far Eastern Affairs* 4 (1982).

3. The most important one is certainly *Deng Zhongxia wenji* [Collected Works of Deng Zhongxia] (Beijing: Renmin chubanshe, 1983).

4. His monumental study of Chinese labor history focuses on the 1920s and was first published in French in 1962. The English translation was published in 1968. See Jean Chesneaux, *The Chinese Labor Movement, 1919–1927,* trans. H. M. Wright (Stanford: Stanford University Press, 1968).

text.[5] Our knowledge of this subject, important as it is in the history of the Chinese revolution, is still incomplete; we know very little about the political language and overall culture of the Chinese working class. We understand fully neither their political consciousness nor their relationships with the other social classes.

This book, however, does not address the sociological or cultural dimensions of Chinese labor history.[6] It focuses instead on what I take to be another crucial issue in the Chinese revolution: the relationship between workers and Marxist intellectuals during the early period of the Chinese Communist movement. It traces the process of ideological conversion of a young intellectual during the May Fourth period to a Communist labor leader and assesses the relationship of his ideological commitment to his organizational ability and mobilizational achievements in leading the Chinese working class, especially in south China during the mid-1920s. The study's premises can be stated briefly. Ideas alone do not create history. The process of historical change, especially in a revolutionary society, is a product of dialectic between theory and practice, which is manifested as a relationship between Party leadership and mass participation. It would be meaningless to study the thought of Mao Zedong in the light of Marxist-Leninist ideological tradition without referring to the driving force of his ideas in shaping the historical reality of China, which in turn requires attention to the native forces that shaped or contributed to Mao's Marxism, or vice versa. By the same token, we cannot fully understand the dynamic of the working-class movement without considering the concepts of labor organization and strike strategy as formulated by its leaders, which may have been inspired by theory but, to be effective, also required taking into account local circumstances.

5. See Ming K. Chan, *Historiography of the Chinese Labor Movement, 1895–1949: A Critical Survey and Bibliography* (Stanford: Hoover Institution Press, 1981); Lynda Shaffer, *Mao and the Workers: The Hunan Labor Movement, 1920–1923* (New York: Armonk, 1982); Emily Honig, *Sisters and Strangers: Women in the Shanghai Cotton Mill, 1919–1949* (Stanford: Stanford University Press, 1986); Gail Hershatter, *The Workers of Tianjin, 1900–1949* (Stanford: Stanford University Press, 1986); and the recent publication by Elizabeth J. Perry, *Shanghai on Strike: The Politics of Chinese Labor* (Stanford: Stanford University Press, 1993).

6. Two studies have touched on the social and cultural dimensions of the working class in early-twentieth-century Guangdong. See Ming K. Chan, "Labor and Empire: The Chinese Labor Movement in the Canton Delta, 1895–1927" (Ph.D. diss., Stanford University, 1975); and Michael Tsang-woon Tsin, "The Cradle of Revolution: Politics and Society in Canton, 1900–1927" (Ph.D. diss., Princeton University, 1990). But much work remains to be done in this regard.

One of the characteristics of the labor movement during the mid-1920s in south China was that its leaders were normally men of intellectual background. The emergence of labor movement leaders from a working-class origin, such as Su Zhaozheng and Lin Weimin, both of whom were seamen by profession, was quite exceptional. To be sure, we also need to understand the phenomenon of the conversion of ordinary workers like Su and Lin, who had received little schooling, to Communist labor movement leaders. Their history refutes Lenin's elitist conception of Party leadership wherein the guiding of the working class toward socialism had to be led by revolutionary intellectuals; and their political experience exemplifies Gramsci's ideal that revolutionary intellectuals can emerge from the working-class community. Except perhaps for a few historians in China who enjoy the privilege of access to local records and unclassified archival documents relating to certain early Chinese Communists, the task of undertaking a systematic and thorough study of these leaders of working-class background is difficult in view of the few documents they left behind. Thus, notwithstanding these working-class leaders' significant contribution to the Chinese labor movement, we have, for the time being, to address those leaders who left behind a written corpus during the course of their political lives.

The study of Deng Zhongxia is essential not merely because he was a proficient political writer and a skilful Party editor but because his ideological conversion during the May Fourth period represents the general trend toward social and political radicalism among a small group of young intellectuals who were in search of a solution for China's crisis. Besides, his writings provide us with much reliable information on Chinese labor history even though they were written from the Marxist perspective. But most important, his political experience also reveals the fundamental dilemma caused by the conflicting interests of workers and Marxist intellectuals in the revolutionary process under the CCP leadership.

My purpose is therefore to elucidate the development of Deng's political ideas and to assess the relationship between his labor movement strategy and the Chinese revolution, and in so doing to shed light on the worker-intellectual dilemma of the Chinese Communist movement during his lifetime. A large portion of this study is devoted to the analysis and interpretation of his strategy and leadership in, and the related ideological, political, and diplomatic complexities arising from, the Shenggang (Guangzhou–Hong Kong) General Strike of 1925–26. The reason for my attention to south China is not only because Deng reached the peak of his political career through his leadership in this massive and protracted general strike and boycott in the mid-1920s but also because a thorough examination of this monumental labor movement reveals, *inter alia,* the differences between workers and Marxist intellectuals on the one hand and the unique interrelationship between local interests and national problems in the process of Chinese revolution on the other.

South China in the mid-1920s was not a fully modernized society by any standard, and therefore, an investigation into the role of local forces in a national revolutionary movement is essential because, as Eric Hobsbawm observes, "class consciousness in pre-modern society may be entirely localized."[7] After all, it was in Guangzhou during the mid-1920s that the local Communist leaders, many of whom had been student radicals involved in the May Fourth Movement in 1919, acquired their first experience in urban mass mobilization through the implementation of the Leninist concept of democratic centralism. Furthermore, it was also in this treaty port that the Chinese Communists obtained a signal opportunity to exercise their techniques of manipulating the workers' antiforeign sentiment, which had developed mainly as a result of local and national foreign influence, to further the course of the anti-imperialist movement. Yet the phenomenon of Guangzhou as a revolutionary center for Communist urban mobilization has generally been ignored by scholars outside China because they tend to interpret the political movement in this southern Chinese city in the mid-1920s mainly from the perspective of the power struggle between the Guomindang and the CCP.[8] The study of Guangzhou as a center of labor radicalism can therefore help us to identify certain fundamental but crucial problems between local working-class movements and national revolutionary struggles, a subject of vital importance for our understanding of the predicament of the Chinese Communist movement.

The book is divided into seven chapters. The first chapter deals with the process of Deng's ideological conversion from a May Fourth student radical to a Communist labor leader. Chapter 2 discusses the importance of local identity and traditional attitudes among the workers in south China in germinating their class consciousness and in molding their political experiences. The assessment of the strengths and weaknesses of the alliance between intellectuals and workers in the Chinese Communist movement during the mid-1920s is the dominant theme in chapters 3 and 4. The prob-

7. E. J. Hobsbawm, "Class Consciousness in History," in István Mészáros, ed., *Aspects of History and Class Consciousness* (London: Routledge & Kegan Paul, 1971), p. 9.

8. See, e.g., the excellent study by C. Martin Wilbur, *The Nationalist Revolution in China, 1923–1928* (Cambridge: Cambridge University Press, 1983), esp. pp. 1–55.

lems created by party politics and gunboat diplomacy during the heyday of the labor movement in south China are examined in chapter 5. The last two chapters trace the tragedy of Deng Zhongxia, which reflects the larger tragic dissonance between workers and Marxist intellectuals within the CCP leadership and the changing course of the Chinese Communist movement after 1928.

1

The Emergence of a Labor Leader

DENG ZHONGXIA, whose original name was Deng Longbo and who was usually known as Deng Kang or Deng Zhongxie during his student days, was born into a gentry official family in Yizhang, Hunan Province, on 5 October 1894.[1] His father, Deng Dianmo, who earned the official title of *juren* after he had successfully attempted the provincial-level Imperial Civil Service Examinations (a recruitment system for bureaucrats), held various senior positions in Hunan during the late Qing period. Deng Dianmo remained a civil servant even after the collapse of the Qing dynasty (1644–1912); he was appointed a representative in the Hunan Provincial Assembly and an advisor to the Hunan provincial government during the early Republican period.[2]

But before Deng Zhongxia was one year old, China was defeated by

1. Feng Zirong, "Deng Zhongxia de chusheng riqi ji qi mingzi" [The Names and Date of Birth of Deng Zhongxia], in *Dangshi yanjiu ziliao* [Sources of Party History], vol. 6, pp. 130–31.

2. Wei Wei and Qian Xiaohui, *Deng Zhongxia zhuan* [Biography of Deng Zhongxia] (Beijing: Renmin chubanshe, 1981), p. 2. Deng's classmate at Beijing University, Luo Zhanglong, who later became a major labor movement organizer, claims that Deng's father studied for a while in Japan. See Luo Zhanglong, *Chunyuan daiji* [Reminiscences in Garden Chun] (Beijing: Sanlian chubanshe, 1984), p. 63.

Japan. Like most of the Chinese who were born in the last decade of the nineteenth century, Deng grew up in a society in which the government had for decades been unable to handle various domestic problems as a result of rapid demographic change and declining bureaucratic administrative efficiency. The socioeconomic pressure stemming from these problems had led to the outbreak of peasant rebellions, which had a profound impact on the treasury of the Qing dynasty. For instance, the state had to spend about 120 million taels of silver to suppress a major rebellion known as the White Lotus in five far western provinces between 1796 and 1804. But the movement did not die out completely; it broke out anew in the Henan-Anhui border region during the 1820s and 1830s.[3] The government could not fully recover from this huge financial loss while China's economy continued to deteriorate during the 1830s owing to the illegal opium trade, which resulted in an enormous outflow of silver. While facing a heavily unfavorable trade balance, the Qing dynasty encountered an unprecedented challenge from the south during the Taiping Rebellion (1851–64). The rebel leaders practiced an antidynastic and anti-Confucian ideology, and from their own capital in Nanjing, they attempted to implement, with very limited success, many radical social reforms in the areas under their control. Although they were eventually suppressed after they had occupied Nanjing for eleven years, the cost of this final victory for the Qing government was high; political and military decentralization began, and the seeds of national disintegration were sown.

While the Qing government was exhausting itself trying to keep peace and order at home, its problems were further complicated by the establishment of the treaty port system after China's defeat in the two opium wars during the mid–nineteenth century. The treaty ports undoubtedly facilitated the development of China's modern economic sector through the introduction of foreign capital and modern industrial facilities. But this was not the foreigners' initial intention. The Chinese saw the treaty ports, where foreigners enjoyed special privileges and were protected by extraterritoriality agreements, mainly as a national humiliation.

Although various reform measures had been introduced by Chinese officials since the end of the Second Opium War (1856–60), China remained weak and powerless to halt further foreign encroachment throughout the last decades of the nineteenth century. One of the major reasons for its

3. Susan Mann Jones and Philip A. Kuhn, "Dynastic Decline and the Roots of Rebellion," in John K. Fairbank, ed., *The Cambridge History of China*, vol. 10 (Cambridge: Cambridge University Press, 1978), p. 144.

failure to strengthen its economic power and military capacity during this period was the persistence of conservatism in China. Neither the officials nor the intellectuals could see, or were willing to claim, that the Confucian ideology and its institutions had to be modified in order to cope with the decline in state power resulting from domestic turmoil and foreign penetration. After China was defeated by Japan in 1895, a small group of patriotic intellectuals, headed by Kang Youwei and Liang Qichao, proposed to launch a more radical institutional reform to deal with the crisis. But the force of conservatism remained strong and powerful within the Qing government even during this period. With opposition from all sides, the so-called Hundred Days Reform was doomed to failure as soon as Emperor Guangxu endorsed the Kang-Liang reform proposals. While ignoring the need for change, some conservative-minded Chinese officials turned their attention to utilizing the phenomenon of the popular movement as a means to prevent further foreign penetration in China. By the last few years of the nineteenth century, a major peasant movement, known as the Boxer Uprising, developed in north China. This antiforeign movement was later sanctioned by some senior Qing officials.

When Deng Zhongxia was about six years old, the Boxers, who were originally mobilized by secret societies and influenced by religious sects, attacked the foreign legations in Beijing, which resulted in a joint military operation by the major powers in China's capital. As a young boy, Deng may have been confused by these events; he might not have known whether the Boxers should be hailed as national heroes for their anti-imperialist activities or should be condemned as uncivilized xenophobes for their superstitious beliefs and irrational acts. But he certainly could see, even as a young boy, that China was in chaos.

Like most young boys from well-to-do traditional Chinese families, Deng was trained in major Confucian classics. But the value of classical learning became less important by the 1900s because of the abolition of the Imperial Civil Service Examinations in 1905. Through this radical reform measure, the Qing government attempted to modernize China's educational system. Instead of saving the dynasty from further decline, however, this reform in certain ways hastened its destruction. In the modern schools, Chinese youth were no longer educated only by memorizing the classical texts but were enlightened by new ideas and concepts, some of which differed from the traditional Confucian ideology. A new vocabulary containing "modern" words like "liberty" and "democracy" began to appear frequently, especially in the urban Chinese media. The rapid development in the publication of popular novels and newspapers in this period also changed the conservative worldviews of many Chinese, who began to see, as Lee and Nathan aptly describe, "their region as part of a nation, their nation as a fragile entity in a threatening world, their civilization as only one among many, and not self-evidently the best."[4] Furthermore, their sense of national unity was magnified at the new schools also by the introduction of a uniform national language (*guoyu*).[5] To be sure, at the turn of the twentieth century it might have been too early for these young students to understand fully the meaning of modernity and its social and political implications. But they were prepared to search for their own visions of a new world based on their own observations of the conditions in their country and to raise critical questions about the value of tradition in a changing society and disintegrating nation. Like many Chinese youth of his generation, Deng's future political course was profoundly affected by his experiences at school during the 1910s.

Patriotic Student

In spite of the prosperity of his family, Deng Zhongxia did not have a happy childhood; his mother died when he was only seven years old, and his stepmother treated him cruelly. However, his biographer in China suggests that while he was in his early teens, Deng was able to make the acquaintance of the laboring people because his stepmother did not allow him to have his own bedroom and he had to share a room with a domestic worker. This experience offered him a rare opportunity to cultivate friendly relations with people from a different class background. He was also influenced by his grandmother, who was kind and gentle, as well as sympathetic and helpful to the poor.[6] By the time his parents arranged for him to be married at the age of fifteen, he was no longer content to live in a traditional family, and he left his wife after two years of marriage.[7]

4. Leo Ou-fan Lee and Andrew J. Nathan, "The Beginnings of Mass Culture: Journalism and Fiction in the Late Ching and Beyond," in David Johnson et al., eds., *Popular Culture in Late Imperial China* (Berkeley and Los Angeles: University of California Press, 1985), p. 393.

5. Mary Wright, "Introduction: The Rising Tide of Change," in Mary Wright, ed., *Revolution in China: The First Phase, 1900–1913* (New Haven: Yale University Press, 1968), p. 26.

6. Jiang Ping, *Deng Zhongxia de yisheng* [The Life of Deng Zhongxia] (Nanjing: Nanjing daxue chubanshe, 1985), pp. 2–3.

7. In spite of his unhappy arranged marriage, Deng continued to provide support to his first wife after he left home in 1915. He married again in August 1926. His second wife, Li

In 1911, the year of the Republican Revolution, Deng enrolled at the Yizhang School. Probably due to his upbringing, Deng had a special interest in Chinese classical literature and history. He was a student with great analytical power and argumentative ability and always produced excellent essays. After studying at the Yizhang School for four years, he was admitted to a prestigious school in Hunan Province, the Changsha Normal College, in 1915. Shortly before his departure for Changsha, Deng, like many young Chinese students of the same generation, organized an alumni society at the Yizhang School to keep those students with common interests in touch with each other.[8] Alumni societies and other types of student societies of the period later proved to be an important linkage for the politicization of Chinese youth.

The year 1915 perhaps can be considered a turning point in modern Chinese history. Politically, it was marked by the Japanese presentation of the aggressive Twenty-one Demands to the Chinese government. This event provoked an outcry of nationalistic sentiment among many Chinese. Intellectually, the year saw the publication of the first issue of what was later known as *Xin qingnian* (New Youth), which represented the beginning of a long struggle against Chinese cultural tradition by many Chinese intellectuals. These two events paved the way for the birth of a new group of radical intelligentsia who were committed to saving and rebuilding their country according to their new visions.

It was at this juncture that Deng began his studies at Changsha Normal College. The college supplied a liberal academic environment and good library facilities. Deng encountered his first modern political ideas here, which profoundly influenced his thinking. At the college, he also met other young people who shared his concerns and thinking. Among them were Mao Zedong and Cai Hesen.[9] One of his teachers was Yang Changji, who was well known for his liberal philosophy and deep patriotic sentiment. Under his influence, Deng, whose learning experience was similar to Mao Zedong's, became more concerned with current political affairs.[10] When Yuan Shikai, the first president of Republican China, contemplated restor-

---

Huixin, was a Communist Party member. See ibid., pp. 20, 156–57. Li later called herself Xia Ming. Deng and Xia Ming stayed in Moscow from 1928 to 1930, and they had one son, born in 1929.

8. Ibid., pp. 6–9.

9. Ibid., pp. 8–10.

10. Stuart Schram, *The Thought of Mao Tse-tung* (Cambridge: Cambridge University Press, 1989), p. 17.

ing the monarchy, Deng wrote to a local newspaper and criticized him. At that moment, Deng considered Republicanism to be the best form of government for China.[11]

In 1917, Deng entered Beida (Beijing University), where he read Chinese classics. He was an active student who participated in many academic societies, such as the Philosophical Society (Zhexue yanjiuhui), which was led by the liberal-minded university chancellor, Cai Yuanpei.[12] But his intellectual endeavors were soon disturbed by the intensification of foreign encroachment in China. In May 1918, he began his lifelong commitment to political action.

As with many other progressive youths in China at the time, it was anti-Japanese sentiment that motivated Deng to participate in the patriotic student movement. The movement opposed the threat of increasing Japanese military influence and control in China as a result of the signing of the Sino-Japanese Military Mutual Assistance Convention.[13] The overseas Chinese students in Japan protested against this agreement by returning to China en masse. Upon arrival in Beijing in mid-May, they were received by Deng Zhongxia and other students from Beida. They then held a meeting with students from other colleges in Beijing. The meeting resolved to hold a student demonstration on 21 May to press the Beijing government to annul the convention.[14] Although the demonstration failed in its mission, it sparked a wave of student movements in Shanghai, Tianjin, and Fuzhou.[15] Shortly after the 21 May demonstration, Deng, together with other Beida representatives, went to Shanghai to organize the Patriotic Society of Students (Xuesheng aiguohui), which was later renamed the Students' Society for National Salvation (Xuesheng jiuguohui). In October, this society established a printing branch, The Citizens' Press (Guomin zazhishe), to propagate the patriotic movement. They believed that it was vitally important to spread a national-awakening movement to strengthen China's ability to resist foreign aggression. Deng soon became one of the moving spirits of this publishing activity; he was elected to its General Executive Council and to

11. He Qin, "Wusi Shiqi de Deng Zhongxia" [Deng Zhongxia during the May Fourth Period], in *Wusi shiqi de lishi renwu* [Historical Figures of the May Fourth Period] (Beijing: Zhongguo qingnian chubanshe, 1979), pp. 122–23.

12. Jiang Ping, *Deng Zhongxia de yisheng*, p. 14.

13. Chow Tse-tsung, *The May Fourth Movement: Intellectual Revolution in Modern China* (Cambridge: Harvard University Press, 1960), pp. 78–80.

14. He Qin, "Wusi Shiqi de Deng Zhongxia," p. 126.

15. Chow Tse-tsung, *The May Fourth Movement,* p. 81.

the Editorial Committee of its journal, *Guomin zazhi* (Citizens' Magazine).[16] It was through his participation in this journal that Deng underwent his apprenticeship in political propaganda. Most important, like many first-generation Chinese Communists, he met some of his future comrades while taking part in this student movement and was politicized through his participation in these student organizations.[17]

Transition to Labor Activist

For centuries, Chinese intellectuals have converted their literary societies (*wenshe*) into political groups when their country was in crisis.[18] The young intellectuals during the May Fourth era were no exception. The *Guomin zazhi* was originally intended to be a student journal with a very low political profile. With the intensification of anti-Japanese sentiment and the spread of the New Culture Movement, however, it became more political, reporting on domestic sociopolitical issues as well as international affairs. Deng's contributions primarily concerned the progress of the Paris Peace Conference between January and April 1919. Judging by the titles of his articles, Deng remained a patriot and a supporter of the Republican system; he was not yet an antigovernment radical.[19] Like many Chinese patriotic intellectuals of his age-group, he believed that it was the responsibility of the edu-

16. Zhang Yunhou et al., eds., *Wusi shiqi de shetuan* [Societies of the May Fourth Period] (Beijing: Sanlian chubanshe, 1979), vol. 2, p. 38. See also Vera Schwarcz, *The Chinese Enlightenment: Intellectuals and the Legacy of the May Fourth Movement of 1919* (Berkeley and Los Angeles: University of California Press, 1986), p. 87.

17. For a detailed study of the relationship between student societies and the founding of the Chinese Communist Party, see Hans J. van de Ven, *From Friend to Comrade: The Founding of the Chinese Communist Party, 1920–1927* (Berkeley and Los Angeles: University of California Press, 1991).

18. See, e.g., William S. Atwell, "From Education to Politics: The Fu She," in William Theodore de Bary, ed., *The Unfolding of Neo-Confucianism* (New York: Columbia University Press, 1975), pp. 334–35.

19. Zhonggong zhongyang Malie zhuzho bianyiju, ed., *Wusi shiqi qikan jieshao* [Introduction to the Periodicals of the May Fourth Period] (Beijing: Renmin chubanshe, 1958), vol. 1, pp. 63–74. Deng Zhongxia's contributions included "The Problem of Peace," "The Establishment of National Defense," "The Problem of the Cabinet," and "Our Government's Representative to the Peace Conference in Europe" on 1 Feb. 1919; "New Negotiations between China and Japan" and "National Defense and Japan" on 1 Mar. 1919; and "The Progress of the Peace Conference" and "The Question of [Nationalization] of Railways" on 1 Apr. 1919. See ibid., p. 466.

cated people to help the country by enlightening the people during an age of darkness.

The editors of the *Guomin zazhi* generally shared his view, and they realized the considerable difficulties involved in promoting their propaganda in a society where illiteracy was very high. In an attempt to solve this problem, liberal and radical intellectuals at Beida encouraged their students to educate the ordinary people by the direct approach of street-corner lectures. The idea of popular education was not completely new in early-twentieth-century China; a small group of Chinese anarchists had already established their influence among the laboring people, especially in Guangdong, in the mid-1910s through their Work-Study Movement.[20] The anarchists' social and political activities perhaps helped to convince the patriotic students of the May Fourth era that it was their responsibility to serve the laboring people instead of the state.

As a result of modern economic growth in certain major Chinese cities during and after World War I, some Chinese intellectuals did become more aware of the labor problem. For instance, both Li Dazhao and Chen Duxiu (both of whom later became founders of the Chinese Communist Party) wrote at length about the miserable life of the laboring people in late 1918 and early 1919.[21] However, their writings were mainly concerned with the labor issue as a social problem rather than with labor as a political force. Influenced by the ideas of egalitarianism and social justice as expressed by many writers in the leading journals of the period, Deng Zhongxia was fully aware of the labor problem in China. However, his approach to the labor issue was to spread popular education among them.

In the early spring of 1919, Xiong Guangchu, a fellow Hunanese, proposed to Deng that popular education was one of the best means to improve the social and economic conditions of the underprivileged. Xiong also advised Deng that enlightenment through popular education of the oppressed laboring people would help them liberate themselves from oppression. He then suggested to Deng that he should encourage the teachers and students at Beida to establish libraries and reading rooms in the temples of their native villages. Deng was deeply impressed by his friend's ideas.[22]

On 15 February 1919, Deng wrote an open letter to the university chancellor, Cai Yuanpei, calling on Cai to support a program of popular educa-

20. Arif Dirlik, *The Origins of Chinese Communism* (New York: Oxford University Press, 1989), p. 86.

21. Ibid., p. 65.

22. Jiang Ping, *Deng Zhongxia de yisheng*, p. 23.

tion.[23] The chancellor as well as some progressive faculty members, notably Li Dazhao, responded to Deng's request in a positive and encouraging manner. On 7 March, Deng and several other Beida students issued an announcement in the *Beijing daxue rikan* (Beijing University Daily) calling for the formation of a society to spread education among the ordinary people. The announcement rapidly led to the establishment of what was known as the Beijing University Commoners' Education Lecture Corps (Beijing Daxue pingmin jiaoyu jiangyantuan) on 23 March 1919. Deng was responsible for drafting its manifesto; he was also elected a member of its Executive Committee and participated in its Editorial Committee.[24]

The manifesto of the Beijing University Commoners' Education Lecture Corps had a nonanarchist but liberal tone and emphasized the importance of popular education in attaining social equality and in consolidating the Republican system in China:

There are two kinds of education: academic education and education that reaches out to the people. The latter happens through open-air speeches and through publications issued for this purpose. The foundation of a republic must be the education of the common people. . . . If, however, only the offspring of the rich are able to enjoy academic education, while poor children have no chance to go to school at all the foundation of our republic will be shaken.[25]

Like his writings in the *Guomin zazhi*, Deng's speeches for the Beijing University Commoners' Education Lecture Corps also mainly related to current affairs.[26] Probably influenced by the trend of anarchist thinking of the time, his lectures also included topics with which the anarchists were concerned, namely the problems of family and mutual aid.

While he was actively involved in the *Guomin zazhi* and the Beijing University Commoners' Education Lecture Corps, the May Fourth Incident took place. The students reacted radically to the decision of the Paris Peace Conference to cede Shandong Peninsula to the Japanese, which would in-

---

23. Ibid., p. 24.

24. Zhang Yunhou et al., eds., *Wusi shiqi de shetuan*, vol. 2, pp. 137, 155, and 160.

25. Quoted from Schwarcz, *Chinese Enlightenment*, p. 90. See also Zhang Yunhou et al., eds., *Wusi shiqi de shetuan*, vol. 2, p. 135.

26. Deng delivered the following speeches between April 1919 and May 1920: "The Family System" on 4 Apr. 1919; "The Pathetic Emperor of Today" on 5 Apr. 1919; "History of the Qingdao Negotiations" on 18 May 1919; "Shouldn't We Discuss National Affairs?" on 6 Nov. 1919; and "Mutual Aid" on 16 May 1920. See Zhang Yunhou et al., eds., *Wusi shiqi qikan jieshao*, vol. 1, p. 466.

crease Japanese control in China. Deng actively participated in the 4 May demonstration. He was one of the student radicals responsible for burning the residence of the pro-Japanese Chinese official Cao Rulin, minister of communications and managing director of the Bank of Communications on 4 May.[27] Two days later, Deng was elected general secretary of the Students' Federation of the Colleges and Universities of Beijing and assumed responsibility for its propaganda department.[28] On 18 May, he was assigned by the Students' Federation to travel to other provinces to mobilize support for the May Fourth Movement. He first went back to Hunan, where, it is said, he discussed the problems of China with Mao Zedong.[29] In early June, he arrived in Shanghai, where he took part in the workers' sympathy strike to support the students.[30]

Deng's involvement in the strike might have been his first direct contact with the labor movement. However, the experience was profound; for the first time in his life, he witnessed the political power and anti-imperialist sentiment of the Chinese laboring class. He recalled the significance of this event some ten years later in Moscow:

The gentlemen of the upper stratum had so far not bothered to take note of laborers. With this movement, laborers demonstrated their power to bourgeois intellectuals, who could not but be impressed with its magnitude, and the bourgeois intellectuals began to make efforts to influence the laborers to secure their support. . . .

Certainly, there was also a group of petty bourgeois students, or perhaps they could be called radical liberal students, feeling lonely in the course of anti-imperialist struggle. They needed to search for an ally. Through their [participation in the strike], they discovered the working class as their ally. To be sure, some student leaders of the May Fourth Movement henceforth launched their "down to the people" movement and organized laborers' schools and trade unions. This group of petty bourgeois students was naturally close to the proletariat; they gradually became Communists and joined the Communist Party.[31]

27. Wei Wei and Qian Xiaohui, *Deng Zhongxia zhuan,* pp. 14–16.

28. He Qin, "Wusi Shiqi de Deng Zhongxia," p. 130.

29. Jiang Ping and Li Liangyu, "Deng Zhongxia tongzhi guanghui de yisheng" [The Glorious Life of Comrade Deng Zhongxia], in *Jinian wusi yundong liushi zhounian xueshu taolunhui lunwenxuan* [Selected Essays from the Seminar Held on the Sixtieth Anniversary of the May Fourth Movement] (Beijing: Zhongguo shehui kexueyuan, 1980), p. 195.

30. Wei Wei and Qian Xiaohui, *Deng Zhongxia zhuan,* p. 21.

31. Deng Zhongxia, *Zhongguo zhigong yundong jianshi* [A Brief History of the Chinese Labor Movement] (hereafter cited as *Jianshi*) (Beijing: Renmin chubanshe, 1951), p. 9. The first paragraph of this quotation is cited from Dirlik, *Origins of Chinese Communism,* p. 63.

Certainly, Deng himself was a petty bourgeois student leader during the May Fourth Movement and only became a Communist after a period of soul-searching. In the aftermath of the May Fourth Incident, he began to lose faith in republicanism. But he did not accept Marxism immediately. Ideologically, he was at a crossroads, not knowing which way to go. However, he was strongly influenced by anarchism for a while. He regarded self-reliance and mutual aid as the fundamental steps toward the reconstruction of China.

Three months after the 4 May demonstration, Deng organized a student cooperative residence called Xiyuan (Garden of Morning Light), which housed about thirty students from Beida. One of the participants, Zhang Guotao, later recalled that Xiyuan was colored by anarchism and that Deng was the most active member, attempting to convince the others of the need for social reform.[32] Another participant, Luo Zhanglong, said that the members of Xiyuan had a common interest in laborism and mutual aid. All the members of Xiyuan believed that an intellectual should be judged not only on his wide learning but also on his participation in labor. They also promoted new social and cultural values that were very similar to anarchist values, such as antimaterialism and a cooperative approach to socialism. Most important, they advocated a movement to investigate the living and working conditions of the laboring classes.[33] Deng was profoundly influenced by his experience in Xiyuan because of its emphasis on the close link between intellectuals and the laboring people. Although by that time he was aware of the harmful effects of industrialism and imperialism on the Chinese laboring people, he was still unsure how to mobilize this social class as a political force in the transformation of China. Like many other progressive young Chinese, Deng was well aware that Chinese society was afflicted with a serious illness but was uncertain about the cure.

Without doubt, it was his participation in the Shanghai patriotic labor movement of June 1919 that made him aware of the political potential of the Chinese working class. His involvement in Xiyuan and the Beijing University Commoners' Education Lecture Corps further convinced him of the significance of the labor movement. Soon after Deng organized the communal residence of Xiyuan, he took time off to visit his fellow Hunanese living in Changxindian, a Beijing-Hankou railway junction forty miles

32. Zhang Guotao, *Wo de huiyi* [My Memoirs] (Hong Kong: Mingbao yuekan chubanshe, 1971), p. 65.
33. Luo Zhanglong, *Chunyuan daiji*, p. 50.

from the capital and the home of about three thousand railway workers, as well as workers in other enterprises. At that time, a small group of students, many from Hunan, were studying French in a house in Changxindian. These students did not have any contact with the workers in that area because they were busy preparing themselves for further studies in France through the Work-Study Movement.[34]

Perhaps Deng's participation in the Shanghai labor movement in June had prepared him for his encounter with the Changxindian workers; he immediately showed interest in the laborers upon arrival in this railway junction.[35] More important, he also immediately saw the need not just to enlighten but to organize them. A few months later, he took his fellow students from Beida to Changxindian to spread the program of popular education beyond the city of Beijing. However, the Beijing University Commoners' Education Lecture Corps's first visit to Changxindian was a failure because it was a holiday and the workers had gone to the nearby towns for entertainment or other personal pursuits.[36] But the failure did not discourage Deng. His interest in the working class is shown in the following poem, written in early 1920 while he was still staying in Xiyuan:

In Beijing, two strange things occurred at the same time:
that is, the sun rose and I too arose.
The sun comes out and is performing its selfless task in shining
    on everything and bringing forth new life.
And me?
With my friends, I visit the workers' dwellings. . . .[37]

In May 1920, Deng took part in organizing the May Day celebration activities. It was the first time in Chinese history that May Day was jointly celebrated by intellectuals and workers, even though most of the gatherings were dominated by the former group.[38] Many journals, such as *Xin qingnian* and *Beijing daxue xuesheng zhoukan* (Beijing University Students' Weekly),

34. For the development and significance of this movement, see Marilyn A. Levine, *The Found Generation: Chinese Communists in Europe during the Twenties* (Seattle: University of Washington Press, 1993).

35. I am indebted to Mr. Wu Dabai, director of the Changxindian February Seventh Memorial Hall in Beijing, China, for this information.

36. Zhang Yunhou et al., eds., *Wusi shiqi de shetuan*, vol. 2, pp. 167–68.

37. Quoted from Wei Wei and Qian Xiaohui, *Deng Zhongxia zhuan*, p. 27.

38. Dirlik, *Origins of Chinese Communism*, p. 186.

published special issues to commemorate the event. On that day, Li Dazhao officiated as keynote speaker at Beida in front of about 500 students and workers. After Li's speech, Deng led the Beijing University Commoners' Education Lecture Corps to Changxindian.[39]

Two months after this May Day celebration, the Xiyuan was dissolved because of increasing ideological conflict among its members.[40] Some members, including Deng Zhongxia, had come to the conclusion that the utopian anarchist ideas of Xiyuan could not save China. Meanwhile, radical intellectuals' increasing concern with labor issues beginning in the spring of 1920 had somewhat modified their daily political language. The terms "class" and "class struggle" became more popular among many radical intellectuals even though their understanding of such terms, especially from the Marxist perspective, remained superficial.[41]

The June strike in Shanghai had shifted the attention of some of the radical intellectuals toward Marxism. Although some Chinese anarchists and guild socialists in 1920 discussed at length the problem of China's oppressed people under industrialism, it was the early Marxists, men like Li Dazhao and Chen Duxiu, who saw the need to mobilize the working class as a political force in the transformation of China. By 1920, both Li and Chen believed that China had already become a "proletarian country" because of the foreign, especially Western, capitalistic penetration into Chinese society and economy.[42] The mobilization of the working class thus became not just a political slogan but a call for immediate and concrete political action. In this they differed from the anarchists and the guild socialists.

In March 1920 Deng Zhongxia became an active member of the newly founded Marxist Research Society (Makesi xueshuo yanjiuhui) at Beida.[43]

39. Wu Jialin and Xie Yinming, *Beijing dang zuzhi de chuangjian huodong* [The Activities and Establishment of the Beijing Party Organization] (Beijing: Renmin daxue chubanshe, 1991), pp. 100–102.

40. Luo Zhanglong, *Chunyuan daiji*, p. 57.

41. For a critical interpretation of how Chinese Marxists understood the term "class" in 1920, see Dirlik, *Origins of Chinese Communism*, pp. 95–120.

42. Chen Duxiu argued that all Chinese held the position of laborers vis-à-vis foreign capital; see ibid., pp. 232–33. On Li Dazhao's analysis of Chinese society as a "proletarian nation," see Maurice Meisner, *Li Ta-chao and the Origins of Chinese Marxism* (Cambridge: Harvard University Press, 1967), p. 188. For an interpretation of other early Chinese Marxists' views on Chinese society in 1920, see Michael Y. L. Luk, *The Origins of Chinese Bolshevism: An Ideology in the Making, 1920–1928* (Hong Kong: Oxford University Press, 1990), pp. 47–48.

43. Jiang Ping, *Deng Zhongxia de yisheng*, p. 36. Although the founding members of this society began studying Marxism in March 1920, the society was not officially established until November 1921. See Zhang Yunhou et al., eds., *Wusi shiqi de shetuan*, vol. 2, pp. 270–73.

Ignorant of any foreign language, he could improve his knowledge of Marxism only from the writings of the leading Chinese radical intellectuals, such as Chen and Li, and from Chinese translations. Later in the year, a worker member of the Marxist Research Society from Changxindian appealed to the Beijing University Commoners' Education Lecture Corps to establish a workers' school there.[44] Together with Zhang Tailei and Zhang Guotao, Deng took part in the founding of this school, which marked the beginning of his lifelong commitment to labor organization.

Although the students wanted to bridge the gap between intellectuals and workers, Deng and his fellow students encountered serious problems in winning the trust and friendship of the Changxindian workers, due to differences in social and cultural backgrounds. They soon discovered that the only effective way to narrow these difference was to learn to speak the workers' language. To overcome this problem, a member of the Beijing University Commoners' Education Lecture Corps compiled a small dictionary of colloquial Beijing dialect.[45] The students also modified their way of life to more closely match that of the workers. In Changxindian Deng adopted a new name because he felt that the poorly educated workers would remember Zhongxia more easily than his original name, Zhongxie.

Deng played an active role in the founding of the Changxindian workers' school. Because of his inclination to talkativeness, he earned the nickname Deng Dapao (Deng the Cannon) from the workers.[46] In the workers' school, he stressed the consciousness-raising technique of drawing examples from daily life rather than quoting dogmatic doctrine. He helped produce a textbook aimed at teaching a basic vocabulary through exercises closely related to the workers' lives; for instance, the characters for "hammer," "pliers," "railway lines," and "workers" were included in the textbook.[47] Deng and his comrades lectured on the subject of imperialism by drawing an analogy with the workers' daily experience:

When we were learning the characters for "railway lines," the teacher said: "The railway lines that we are serving are just like a python. Every other country tries

44. Luo Zhanglong, "Huiyi Beijing daxue Makesi xueshuo yanjiuhui" [Memories of the Marxist Research Society at Beijing University], in *Wusi yundong huiyilu* [Memoirs of the May Fourth Movement] (Beijing: Renmin chubanshe, 1979), p. 413. See also Zhang Yunhou et al., eds., *Wusi shiqi de shetuan*, vol. 2, p. 187.

45. Luo Zhanglong, *Chunyuan daiji*, p. 111.

46. Ibid., p. 113.

47. Changxindian jiche cheliang gongchang changshi bianwenhui, ed., *Beifang de hongxing* [Red Star over the North] (Beijing: Zuojia chubanshe, 1960), p. 65.

to get a piece of meat from it. Those big guys governing our country always borrow money from other countries by offering the railway as collateral. Mortgage this, mortgage that, then all railway lines and mines will soon belong to others, and we will be finished." He then made another analogy: "This situation is just like a family in which the head of the family does not manage the house and keep its books properly and puts its property up for mortgage. Then the house will be managed by others; wouldn't the other members of the family feel miserable? This is called imperialist penetration!"[48]

This type of vivid analogy and the friendly approach of Deng and his comrades made this workers' school successful.

In November 1920, Deng and his comrades from the Beijing Communist Group published a labor journal in Changxindian entitled *Laodong yin* (The Voices of Workers).[49] The journal was partially influenced by the anarchist idea of laborism. However, Deng Zhongxia, in the editorial of its first issue, spelled out that the objective of the journal was to raise worker consciousness so that they would be able to engage in "class struggle . . . for the betterment of social organization."[50] Although it ceased publication within a few months and its circulation was about 2,000 copies per issue, the *Laodong yin* was influential among workers in Changxindian because it was written in simple language which the semiliterate workers could understand. On May Day 1921, a Workers' Club (Gongren julebu) was established by the students of the school.[51]

It is certain that the success at Changxindian was closely connected with the work of the Beijing Communist Group, which was established in the summer of 1920 under the leadership of Li Dazhao and the influence of G. Vointinsky, a representative of the Communist International (Comintern). Contrary to the usual belief in China, however, Deng was not one of its founding members[52] but became an active member after its foundation.

Although he graduated from Beida in the spring of 1920,[53] he continued

48. Ibid., p. 66.

49. Zhonggong zhongyang Malie zhuzho bianyiju, ed., *Wusi shiqi qikan jieshao*, vol. 2, pt. 1, pp. 71–74.

50. Xin Mei [Deng Zhongxia], "Women weishenme chuban zhege *Laodong yin* ne" [Why Should We Publish the *Voices of Workers?*], in *Deng Zhongxia wenji*, p. 2.

51. Deng Zhongxia, *Jianshi*, pp. 15–16. See also Ma Jianqun, "Deng Zhongxia tongzhi zai Changxindian" [Comrade Deng Zhongxia in Changxindian], *Beijing ribao* [Beijing Daily], 7 Feb. 1959.

52. See, e.g., He Qin, "Wusi Shiqi de Deng Zhongxia," p. 135; Zhu Wushan, "Huiyi Beijing gongchan zhuyi xianzu," in *Wusi yundong huiyilu*, p. 401.

53. Jiang Ping, *Deng Zhongxia de yisheng*, p. 39.

his activities with the radical students in Beijing. In late September, he became involved with the Socialist Youth Corps (Shehui zhuyi qingnian tuan). Influenced by his activity in the Marxist Research Society and by his participation in the Changxindian workers' school, Deng was by that time fully committed to the Communist movement, and he expressed his feelings by composing the following poem:

> The boundless Dong Ting Lake,
> five days crossed twice in haste.
> Snow-white waves beat against the vast sky;
> the shady forest suspects the spirits are angry.
> What of the world today?
> Evil beasts fill the road.
> Like a hunter I will slay them;
> I go in search of my aspiration.
>
> The boundless Dong Ting Lake,
> five days crossed twice in haste.
> The autumn waters hold the falling sunlight,
> red clouds like burning torches.
> What of the world tomorrow?
> Communism brings equality.
> With painstaking effort I persevere;
> I go in search of my aspiration.[54]

Apart from his involvement in the Beijing Communist Group and in Changxindian, Deng also helped spread radical ideology among senior high school students. In early 1921, he lectured on modern literary thought at Baoding Normal College in Zhili. In the summer of the same year, he taught a similar subject at Chuannan Normal College in Sichuan Province.[55] Although it is difficult to ascertain whether he was successful in interesting these youngsters in modern literature,[56] his success in politicizing his students was significant. One of his opponents later recalled:

54. Deng Zhongxia, "Gongxian yu sinshiren zhiqian" [A Contribution to the Modern Poets], *Zhongguo qingnian* [Chinese Youth] 10 (22 Dec. 1923), p. 9.

55. He Qin, "Wusi Shiqi de Deng Zhongxia," p. 138; Jiang Ping and Li Liangyu, "Deng Zhongxia tongzhi guanghui de yisheng," pp. 196–97.

56. Deng Zhongxia's lecture notes from the Baoding Normal College are deposited at the Archives of Revolutionary Martyrs in Nanjing. They are not presently accessible to foreign researchers.

In summer [1921], Deng Zhongxia and Yun Daiying went to Chuannan Normal College in Sichuan as lecturers in Chinese literature, while other members [of the Young China Society], like Yu Jiaju, Chen Qitian, and Shu Xincheng, became teachers at the Hunan First Normal College, where Mao Zedong was teaching at its affiliated primary school. . . . Regardless of whether they were primary or secondary teachers, these members launched their propaganda for the introduction of new thought and criticism of the old society among their students. . . . At the least, they were able to whip up the ambition of many youngsters of the lower Changjiang region and to pave the way [in recruiting new blood] for the Nationalist Revolution. [This phenomenon] was due to the fact that these students, after being influenced by their teachers, were no longer prepared to tolerate traditional family life; subsequently, many of them enrolled in the Huangpu Military Academy.[57]

Also during this summer Deng participated in a major debate within the Young China Society (Shaonian Zhongguo xuehui), one of the most important societies of the May Fourth period. Deng had been a leading organizer of the society since its founding in July 1919. The society was characterized by political pluralism; members like Deng Zhongxia and Mao Zedong promoted Li Dazhao's approach to reconstructing China, but conservative members like Li Huang regarded Hu Shi's liberalism and pragmatism as the solution to China's problems.[58] For the first year after the founding of the society, their common feelings of patriotism and humanitarianism overcame their ideological differences. With the increasing involvement of the radical members in the political movement, however, conservative members began to worry about preserving the "noble" ideas of its manifesto, which emphasized self-cultivation by eliminating evil traditional customs and by pursuing knowledge.[59] They became even more anxious when Deng Zhongxia, in his capacity as the society's general secretary, pressed the society to adopt a political doctrine (*zhuyi*) as its ideology in early 1921.[60] The conservative members demanded a convention to discuss this issue.[61]

The convention was held in Nanjing in July 1921. It did not adopt any resolution on the above issue but rather contributed to the ideological fragmentation of its membership. This convention, nevertheless, revealed Deng's political commitment. He remarked during the convention:

57. Li Huang, "Wusi yundong yu shaonian Zhongguo xuehui" [The May Fourth Movement and the Young China Society], *Mingbao yuekan* [Mingbao Monthly] 6 (1969), p. 42.

58. Meisner, *Li Ta-chao*, pp. 105–14; Chow Tse-tsung, *The May Fourth Movement*, pp. 218–22.

59. Zhang Yunhou et al., eds., *Wusi shiqi de shetuan*, vol. 1, pp. 225–30.

60. He Qin, "Wusi Shiqi de Deng Zhongxia," p. 137.

61. Zhang Yunhou et al., eds., *Wusi shiqi de shetuan*, vol. 1, p. 353.

The Society should pay equal attention to learning and practice; but in determining which one should come first, the Society [can decide only] if it can formulate a common goal. Therefore, [we] must adopt a doctrine [*zhuyi*] as the Society's common goal. . . . The reason that the Society has not made any contribution to the [nation] is the lack of a common doctrine. . . . As regards the threat of breaking up if the Society adopts a doctrine, I consider that only by adopting a doctrine can we help the [development of] the Society. I therefore do not care if the Society breaks up if it adopts a doctrine.[62]

His speech certainly represented his commitment to the radical political movement. In mid-October 1921, he was assigned by the Chinese Communist Party (CCP) to work at the newly formed Chinese Labor Organization Secretariat (Zhongguo laodong zuhe shujibu), commonly known as the Labor Secretariat. Henceforth, he never abandoned his work with the labor movement. Simultaneously, he continued to maintain close contact with some liberal patriotic intellectuals. For the next two years, he continued trying to persuade his former liberal fellow students to support the Communists. Although not many of them were persuaded, his dedication to the liberation of the laboring people was appreciated by some liberal scholars. In 1924, Zhu Ziqing, one of the most outstanding modern poets of the May Fourth generation, dedicated the following poem to his close friend Deng Zhongxia:

> Your hands are like torches
> your eyes like waves
> your words like stones.
> What could have made me forget? . . .
>
> You want to build a red heaven on earth
> on an earth full of thorns
> on an earth full of sly foxes
> on an earth full of the walking dead.
>
> You would make yourself into a sharp knife,
> a sword able to cut down thorns.
> You would be a roaring lion
> to set the foxes running scared.

62. Ibid., pp. 354–55.

CHAPTER 1

You would be a spring thunder
to startle into awakening the walking dead.

I love to see you ride. . . .
I imagine you as a sand and rock stirring tornado
that aims to blow down entrenched palaces of gold.
Blow on. . . .

Last year, I saw you on a summer day.
Why did you look so drained?
Your eyes were parched,
your hair too long.
But your blood was burning.

I, who had been wallowing in mud,
was baked by your fire.
You have the fragrance of a strong cigar
You have the power of hard brandy
You burn like red pepper
How can I ever forget you?[63]

In retrospect, his transformation from a patriotic student radical to a committed Communist labor activist during the May Fourth period represented the general trend of the growth of radicalism among many progressive Chinese youths. There is no doubt that, for at least half a year after the 4 May demonstration, he was influenced by the utopian ideas of anarchism. It was through his participation in the Marxist Research Society and the Beijing Communist Group that he began to comprehend the theoretical meaning of Marxism. But his experience in the Shanghai labor movement in June 1919 and later on his direct personal contact with the Changxindian workers were the decisive factors in his commitment to implementing the Marxist concept of class struggle. The workers in Shanghai and Changxindian helped Deng to "proletarianize" himself before he fully understood the theoretical meaning of Marxism and its practical relevance to China as a revolutionary ideology. The workers also led him to realize that Marxism was more practical than anarchism because it offered operational guide-

63. Quoted from Schwarcz, *Chinese Enlightenment,* p. 144. I am grateful to Professor Schwarcz for her kind permission to reprint her translation here.

lines. He said: "The ultimate goals of Communism and anarchism are not so different. The merits of anarchism are all included in Communism. But anarchism does not have the merits of Communism. Communism contains objective, operational strategy and method."[64] By late 1920, his commitment to the Communist revolution was evident, though he still did not have a clear vision of what a Communist society would be. When he became a member of the CCP, his understanding of Marxism was limited and mainly concerned its political aspect, especially relating to the basic theory of class struggle. Like many contemporary Chinese revolutionaries, he participated in the Communist movement before he had fully grasped its theoretical meaning. However, his political participation in the May Fourth period laid a solid foundation for his later activities of disseminating propaganda and organizing mass movements. And without his early labor movement experience, perhaps Deng would not have realized so rapidly the importance of uniting workers and Marxist intellectuals in the Chinese revolution during the mid-1920s.

Early Communist Labor Leader, 1921–23

When the CCP was founded in July 1921, the number of Chinese workers in the modern sector of the economy was small. Three years later, the Party's labor movement leader, Deng Zhongxia, estimated that only 1,859,423 Chinese could be described as industrial workers.[65] Yet the early Chinese Communists, even prior to the founding of their Party, had already realized the urgent need to implement the Marxist theory of class struggle in their economically premodern country. In 1920, many of them thought that Chinese society had already been "proletarianized" under foreign, especially Western, capitalist encroachment. Thus, China was mature enough to begin the transformation toward socialism through class struggle between the proletariat and the bourgeoisie, even if the criterion for their class analysis had not been clearly defined. Nevertheless, the CCP First Congress adopted a resolution in which the Chinese Communists were instructed to established a special bureau, the Labor Secretariat.[66] Its objective was to promote the

64. Zhongyuan [Deng Zhongxia], "Gongchan zhuyi yu wuzhengfu zhuyi" [Communism and Anarchism], *Xianqu* [The Pioneers] 1 (15 Jan. 1922), p. 2.

65. Deng Zhongxia, "Women de liliang" [Our Strength], *Zhongguo gongren* 2 (Nov. 1924), p. 20.

66. Luo Zhanglong, *Chunyuan daiji*, p. 99.

development of modern trade unions. Its manifesto was announced in the Party's organ, *Gongchandang* (The Communists).[67] Initially, Zhang Guotao was the general secretary of the Labor Secretariat, but Deng replaced him when Zhang left China for Moscow in mid-October 1921.[68] At the CCP Second Congress in July 1922, Deng was officially appointed to head the Labor Secretariat, a post that he retained until the organization gradually ceased functioning after the February 1923 murder of striking railway workers in north China.[69]

In July 1921, when the CCP First Congress was held, Chinese Communists resolved that their major policy was to mobilize the working class as a political force. Yet they did not specify how to implement such a policy. It was not until three months later during a CCP enlarged meeting that details on how to mobilize the working class were spelled out.[70] Because Beijing did not have many industrial workers, the Communists believed that, for the time being, they should focus on the mobilization of railway workers through their contact with the workers in Changxindian.[71] As for the labor movement in other parts of China, the Communists thought that the Labor Secretariat should play a leading role in mobilizing the workers, especially those employed in the transportation industry.[72]

Because the early CCP labor movement gave priority to the mobilization of transportation workers, Deng worked mainly among the railway workers of north China from late 1921 to early 1923.[73] His activities were supported by three favorable conditions. First, his contribution to the workers in Changxindian had been publicized by many railway workers of north China. Second, he worked as a railway inspector to establish close contact with other railway workers.[74] Third, his activity in promoting the

67. *Gongchangdang* [The Communist Party] 6 (7 July 1921), pp. 21–22.

68. Zhang Guotao, *Wo de huiyi*, p. 171.

69. Wei Wei and Qian Xiaohui, *Deng Zhongxia zhuan*, p. 67.

70. Luo Zhanglong, *Chunyuan daiji*, p. 100.

71. "Beijing Gongchang zhuyi zuzhi de baogao [1921]" [Beijing Communist Group's Report], in *Zhonggong zhongyang wenjian xuanji* [Selected Documents of the CCP Party Central] (Beijing: Zhonggong zhongyang danxiao chubanshe, 1989), vol. 1, pp. 14–15.

72. "Zhonggong zhongyang zhixing wenyuanhui shuji Chan Duxiu gei gongchan guoji de baogao (30 June 1922)" [CCP Party Central Executive Secretary Chan Duxiu's Report to the Comintern (30 June 1922)], in ibid., pp. 50–55.

73. There were five major regional secretaries appointed by the Labor Secretariat. Deng Zhongxia and Luo Zhanglong were jointly responsible for the north China region, Lin Yunan and Xiang Ying for Wuhan, Mao Zedong for Hunan, Li Qihan for Shanghai, and Tan Pingshan for Guangzhou. See Zhang Guotao, *Wo de huiyi*, pp. 167–68; and Deng Zhongxia, *Jianshi*, p. 38.

74. Li Qiu, "Deng Zhongxia zhi gongdang shenghou shi" [History of the Social Activities

labor movement was semiofficially approved by the warlord Wu Peifu as a result of an arrangement with Wu made by Li Dazhao. Wu promised "protection for the labor program" in the spring of 1922 purely for self-interest. In mid-1921, a political faction known as the Communication Clique (Jiaotong xi) had launched a series of programs among the railway workers in north China to counteract the growing influence of the Labor Secretariat. The Communication Clique supported Wu's chief enemy, Zhang Zuolin. To challenge his enemy's power, Wu therefore announced a liberal labor policy by permitting the Labor Secretariat to promote the labor movement in the areas under his control.

Deng Zhongxia and the Labor Secretariat had considerable success in mobilizing the workers in the areas under Wu's control. Within a year after the formation of the Labor Secretariat, Deng and his comrades were able to establish sixteen worker organizations in the Jinghan railway network alone and to make contact with workers of the other six major railway lines in north China. The Communists also decided that the influence of the Labor Secretariat should be extended to all major cities, with close cooperation within the cities. While they were toying with this idea, the Hong Kong Seamen's Strike took place, and its success convinced the Communists that Guangzhou, the capital of Guangdong Province, would be the ideal city in which to hold a national labor conference. In fact, after he had witnessed the victory of the Hong Kong Seamen's Strike, H. Maring, a Comintern agent of Dutch nationality in China in 1921–22, informed his Chinese comrades that the center of the Chinese revolution would be Guangzhou, not the industrialized city Shanghai.[75]

The Communists' decision to promote the labor movement in Guangzhou was also based on their understanding that they were too weak to act alone in the struggle for national liberation. Most important, the Comintern had instructed the Chinese Communists in January 1922 to seek a party alliance at the present stage of bourgeois democratic revolution.[76] Under this policy, the Chinese Communists were instructed by the Comin-

---

of Deng Zhongxia in the Communist Party], in *Xiandai shiliao* [Sources of Modern History], vol. 3, p. 396.

75. Yokoyama Hiroaki, "Ma Lin, Sun Zhongshan, guogong hezuo: yi Ma Lin dangan wei zhongxin" [Maring, Sun Yatsen, and Guomindang-CCP Cooperation, based on the Maring Archives], paper delivered at the International Conference on Sun Yatsen and Asia, Guangdong, China, 1990, p. 5.

76. Xenia J. Eudin and Robert C. North, eds., *Soviet Russia and the East, 1920–1927: A Documentary Survey* (Stanford: Stanford University Press, 1957), p. 145.

tern to treat the Guomindang as their potential ally and considered that the time was ripe to use the political umbrella provided by the Guomindang in Guangzhou to advance their activities among workers in south China. This led the CCP Central Committee in April 1922 to instruct the Labor Secretariat to organize a nationwide labor congress in Guangzhou. Soon after this instruction was released, Deng and other leading Communists were sent to Guangzhou to organize the congress.[77]

The First National Labor Congress was convened on May Day 1922, but its objectives were not radical. Apparently, the Labor Secretariat sought to avoid presenting itself as too leftist in a city where Guomindang influence was dominant. Basically, its major aim was to convince the trade unionists, regardless of their political beliefs and commitments, of the need for class unity and solidarity.[78] In spite of this moderate approach, the Communists still encountered many difficulties in expanding their influence. This was largely the result of the conservative nature of the workers in south China and the strong Guomindang and anarchist influences. Many leaders of the Labor Secretariat also faced language problems, which were overcome by a Communist from Guangdong Province, Tan Pingshan, who served as an interpreter. At the congress, the Communists were in a position to narrow the gap between the labor organizers from the north and the labor unionists in the south.[79]

The congress was attended by seventy-five labor unionists, of whom forty-nine came from Guangdong Province.[80] At the congress, Deng suggested that existing trade unions should be organized on a trade or industrial, rather than regional or ethnic, basis. He also suggested that a national labor federation (*quanguo zong gonghui*) should be established to promote the labor movement throughout the country.[81] His suggestions were a breakthrough in the development of modern labor organization in China because he was one of the earliest Chinese labor movement leaders to realize the need to combat working-class disunity resulting from localism. How-

77. Zhang Guotao, *Wo de huiyi*, p. 224.

78. Deng Zhongxia, *Jianshi*, pp. 68–69.

79. Zhang Guotao, *Wo de huiyi*, pp. 225–26.

80. *Zhongguo laogong tongmenghui yuekan* 2 (1 June 1922), pp. 17–18. The much-quoted information from Deng Zhongxia's writing claiming that "the Congress was attended by 163 trade unionists representing more than one hundred unions from twelve cities" is incorrect. See Deng Zhongxia, *Jianshi*, p. 69.

81. Deng Zhongxia, "Quanguo zong gonghui zuzhi yuanze juejian" [Resolution of the Organizational Principle of the All China Labor Union], in *Deng Zhongxia wenji*, pp. 11–12.

ever, his second suggestion, that of forming a national labor federation, was not immediately accepted by the congress, because the trade unionists in south China were afraid of losing their dominant position if such a national labor organization was formed. In fact, the pro-Guomindang labor union-ists were able to persuade the congress to adopt a resolution which called on all members of the congress to recognize the Guangdong authorities as China's legitimate government.[82] Nevertheless, the success of the Commu-nists in the congress was by no means insignificant. The congress produced a compromise resolution in which the Labor Secretariat was instructed to act as a coordinating body until such time as a proper national labor federa-tion was formed.[83] Deng was appointed executive secretary for this task.[84] The congress was adjourned with the Communist-dominated Labor Secre-tariat's reputation in the Chinese labor movement much enhanced.

In July 1922, Deng joined other leading Communists in Shanghai to attend the CCP Second Congress. This congress showed that the Chinese Communists had "a good understanding of Leninist tactics."[85] In brief, the Communists acknowledged that it was necessary to form a United Front with the Guomindang in the current stage of bourgeois democratic struggle against imperialism and warlordism. With regard to the labor movement, the CCP Second Congress resolved that it was important to improve the social and economic conditions of the working class by promoting a labor legislation movement.[86] Under this policy, Deng, in his role as the general secretary of the Labor Secretariat, immediately submitted a petition to the Beijing government asking the government to improve the working and living conditions of the laboring class. The petition made no reference to political demands[87] and, therefore, reveals Deng's moderate political stance at the time. He believed that, for the time being, it would be harmful for the working class to engage only in political struggle without taking care of their economic interests. He was one of the first CCP members to sup-

82. *Zhongguo laogong tongmenghui yuekan* 2 (1 June 1922), pp. 22–23.

83. Deng Zhongxia, *Jianshi*, pp. 73–75.

84. Akatova, "Deng Zhongxia," p. 80.

85. Hélèn Carrère d'Encausse and Stuart R. Schram, eds., *Marxism in Asia: An Introduc-tion with Readings* (London: Allen Lane, Penguin Press, 1969), p. 52.

86. Zhonggong zhongyang shuji chu, ed., *Liuda yiqian dang de lishi cailiao* [Party His-torical Materials before the Sixth Congress] (hereafter cited as *Liuda yiqian*) (Beijing: Xinhua chubanshe, 1980), pp. 10–11.

87. Deng Zhongxia, "Zhongguo laodaong zuhe shujibu zongbu Deng Zhongxia deng de qingyuanshu" [A Petition by Deng Zhongxia and Others of the Chinese Labor Secretariat], in *Deng Zhongxia wenji*, pp. 11–15.

port Lenin's theory of bourgeois democratic revolution in the semicolonial countries. In late 1923, he remarked: "The slogans used by the extreme faction are 'Overthrow the Capitalist System' and 'Political Dictatorship of Workers and Peasants.' But slogans such as 'Overthrow the Warlords' and 'Overthrow Imperialism' are adopted by the faithful supporters of the Nationalist Revolution." [88]

Demonstrating his belief in the need for economic struggle, Deng organized the Changxindian workers in an economic strike shortly after he had submitted the petition for labor legislation. The demand for a wage increase was met by success after a week of industrial action. However, he met with failure when he later led the miners of Kailuan in a similar strike.[89] The failure was largely due to organizational problems caused by the Labor Secretariat's lack of manpower.[90] But the defeat was also related to the fact that the success of the Changxindian workers and the Chinese seamen in south China had alarmed the factory owners, who improved their strike-breaking techniques. For instance, foreign factory owners in Shanghai began to maintain close contact with the police in the International Settlement, with a view to securing information regarding the activities of labor movement organizers.[91] In some cases, such as that of the Kailuan strike, factory owners even called in foreign soldiers to suppress the strike.[92]

In spite of these suppressive measures, Deng and his comrades were able to gain the support of railway workers in north China. On 5 January 1923, at the Zhengzhou railway station, he began preparations for a general union of railway workers in this region,[93] a policy initially suggested by Chen Duxiu in December 1921.[94] The United Union of Jinghan Railway Workers was formed and its inaugural congress was scheduled for 1 Febru-

88. Deng Zhongxia, "Jiehuo" [Enlightenment], *Zhongguo qingnian* 3 (3 Nov. 1923), p. 5. It is said that in late 1922 and early 1923, the Beijing Communist Group was split into "gradualist" and "radical" factions. The former was led by Deng Zhongxia, who believed that conditions were not ripe for launching a proletarian-class-led revolution in China, and that collaboration with other democratic parties in the struggle against imperialism and warlordism was essential. The latter faction was headed by Zhang Guotao, whose view on this issue was completely different from that of Deng. See Meisner, *Li Ta-chao,* p. 219.

89. Deng Zhongxia, *Jianshi,* pp. 79–83.

90. Ibid., p. 84.

91. "Enclosure, Company Correspondence, 8 Sept. 1922," Papers of John Swire and Sons Ltd., Box 37.

92. Chesneaux, *Chinese Labor Movement,* pp. 207–8.

93. Akatova, "Deng Zhongxia," p. 81.

94. "Zhongguo gongchandang zhongyang tonggao (Dec. 1921)" [Circular of the CCP Central Bureau], in *Zhonggong zhongyang wenjian xuanji,* vol. 1, p. 26.

ary.[95] However, Wu Peifu, who had earlier supported a liberal labor policy from self-interest, was now alarmed by the growth of workers' political consciousness and unity and by the financial losses due to the success of the strikers in Changxindian.[96] He therefore ordered that the inaugural congress be disbanded. When his order was ignored by the Labor Secretariat and the workers went on strike as a protest, Wu instructed his soldiers to open fire on the strikers on 7 February. This resulted in the bloody defeat of the strikers and a temporary retreat of the labor movement organized by Deng Zhongxia and the Labor Secretariat.

In reviewing Deng's involvement in the labor movement from late 1921 to early 1923, it is essential to emphasize that he was not a dogmatic revolutionary. He firmly believed that a United Front policy with the Guomindang was necessary in the struggle for national liberation. Because of his realistic and quite moderate political views, he strongly supported the policy that the main task for the current stage of struggle among the Chinese working class was to reorganize on a modern industrial basis. More important, he regarded the formation of a general trade union (*zong gonghui*) as essential in the promotion of class unity and solidarity. Furthermore, he also realized that it was urgent for the Communists to help the workers in their struggle for immediate socioeconomic improvement. He therefore believed that moderate economic struggle would promote the transformation of the workers' political consciousness. However, the Party leader, Chen Duxiu, did not completely concur. At the time, Chen considered that it was a strategic error to place too much emphasis on the economic struggle of workers.[97] Chinese historians in the Yanan period (1937–45) also strongly criticized Deng's view on this issue, claiming that, in an orthodox Marxist-Leninist approach, the economic struggles of workers are meaningless unless these struggles are integrated into a general political revolutionary movement.[98] But, in retrospect, it was justifiable for Deng to have regarded economic

95. Deng Zhongxia, *Jianshi*, p. 86.

96. According to Deng Zhongxia, the strike in Changxindian in August 1922 had caused Wu Peifu to pay, in addition to the regular wage, about 800,000 dollars annually to the workers of the Jinghan railway. See ibid., p. 91.

97. *Zhongguo laogong tongmenghui yuekan* 3 (1 July 1922), p. 5.

98. The editorial preface of Deng's major work, *Zhongguo zhigong yundong jianshi*, which was originally published in Yanan in 1942 as reading material for cadres during the Party Rectification Campaign, contains four pages of discussion and criticism of Deng's writing. This preface, apparently written by the leading Party historians of the time, no longer appears in the post-1951 edition. See the preface of *Jianshi*, p. 3.

struggle as one of the early steps toward political participation, in view of the conservative nature of many Chinese workers and the oppressive political environment.

The Years in Shanghai, 1923–25

After the 7 February attack on the strikers, Deng Zhongxia took refuge in Shanghai, and the Labor Secretariat ceased to operate in public.[99] Shanghai was a political crucible for both the Guomindang and the Communists. Both had experienced recent political defeats of different kinds, and both used Shanghai as a temporary refuge to reorganize their parties. More important, it was in this treaty port that they continued their negotiations for a United Front. In early 1923, Deng was assigned by Li Dazhao to discuss with Sun Yatsen the possibility of the Communists being admitted into the Guomindang. In March 1923, he was appointed, through the recommendation of Li Dazhao, the dean of academic affairs at Shanghai University, which was under the chancellorship of a senior Guomindang member, Yu Youren.[100] His appointment was due to his experience in leading the socialist youth movement since the Party had been founded. Shortly after the CCP First Congress, Deng had been assigned to promote the socialist youth movement in the Beijing region.[101] In January 1922, he had founded a small study group within the Young China Society to promote Marxism.[102] At the same time, he had also become a leading member of the editorial committee of *Xianqu* (The Pioneers), which was the first organ of the Socialist Youth Corps. In 1922, he attended the Socialist Youth Corps First Congress but was not appointed to its Executive Committee due to his full commitment to the Labor Secretariat.[103] However, when its Second Congress was held in August 1923, Deng was invited to become a member of its Executive Committee. He was therefore instructed by the Party to take part, for the time being, in leading the youth movement. At Shanghai University,

99. Jiang Peinan and Chen Weimin, "Zhongguo laodong zuhe shujibu shimo kao" [History of the Chinese Labor Secretariat], *Dangshi ziliao congkan* [Collected Materials on Party History] 3 (1980), pp. 113–15.

100. "Yu Youren yu Shanghai daxue" [Yu Youren and Shanghai University], in *Xiandai shiliao*, vol. 1, pp. 285–94.

101. Luo Zhanglong, *Chunyuan daiji*, p. 117.

102. Zhang Yunhou et al., eds., *Wusi shiqi de shetuan*, vol. 1, pp. 390–91.

103. Jiang Ping, *Deng Zhongxia de yisheng*, pp. 60–61.

he was mainly responsible for administrative affairs, although he offered a summer course on "The Problems of Chinese Labor."[104]

Shanghai University was not an academic institute for higher learning in the ordinary sense. Although it offered courses on social sciences and humanities, it was a center used by both the Guomindang and the Communists to recruit progressive youth. But with the appointment of Deng and other young Communists like Qu Qiubai, Zhang Tailei, Peng Shuzhi, and Cai Hesen, the influence of the Guomindang declined sharply.[105] By early 1924, Shanghai University was dominated by the Communists.

The United Front policy also enabled Deng Zhongxia to reactivate the mobilization of the working class in the Shanghai industrial area known as Xiaoshadu. As soon as the CCP-Guomindang joint venture was established, he was appointed to the Shanghai Executive Branch of the Guomindang, taking part in its Department for Workers and Peasants.[106] But he also understood that the oppressive political environment and the domination of the yellow unionists in Shanghai made conditions unfavorable. In line with the CCP Central Committee's newly adopted labor strategy, which emphasized union-cell activities, he also suggested that "the current trade union movement should be carried out secretly. Small [political] pamphlets should be distributed to the [workers] constantly to maintain and stir up their feelings of indignation and to coordinate their strength, so that they can respond to a [revolutionary] event as soon as it occurs."[107] The Party completely concurred with his suggestion and it instructed him and other Communists, including Li Lisan, to organize secretly a workers' school in Xiaoshadu. On the basis of his experience in Changxindian, Deng helped the students, many of whom were textile workers, to establish workers' clubs, which later played an influential role in the labor movement in February and May 1925.[108]

It was also during his years in Shanghai that Deng Zhongxia enhanced

104. *Zhongguo gongren yundong de xianqu* [The Pioneers of the Chinese Labor Movement] (Beijing: Gongren chubanshe, 1983), vol. 2, p. 55.

105. Jane L. Price, *Cadres, Commanders, and Commissars: The Training of the Chinese Communist Leadership, 1920–1945* (Colorado: Westview Press, 1976), pp. 38–40.

106. Van de Ven, *From Friend to Comrade*, p. 150.

107. Deng Zhongxia, "Zhongguo gongren zhuangkuang ji women yundong zhi fangzhen" [The Conditions of Chinese Workers and the Direction of Our Movement], *Zhongguo qingnian* 10 (22 Dec. 1923), pp. 5–6.

108. It is claimed that the Communists were able to recruit about 1,000 members for the Huxi Workers' Club in late 1924. See Zhang Quan, "Guangyu Huxi gongyou julebu," *Dangshi ziliao congkan* 3 (1980), pp. 116–24.

his experience in propaganda work by participating on the editorial committees of three major Communist journals. These were *Zhongguo qingnian* (The Chinese Youth), *Zhongguo gongren* (The Chinese Workers), and *Qingnian gongren yuekan* (The Young Workers' Monthly), all of which were designated by the Party Central Committee as important organs for political training among the public as well as among the cadres.[109]

Zhongguo qingnian was the official journal of the Chinese Socialist Youth Corps and replaced its predecessor, *Xianqu,* which had been suppressed by the Beijing government on 15 August 1923. Unlike *Xin qingnian* and *Xiangdao zhoubao* (The Guide Weekly), *Zhongguo qingnian* published short articles written in plain language that could be easily understood by youngsters with an elementary knowledge of political theory. More significant, *Zhongguo qingnian* published many how-to articles instructing its readers on the techniques of mass mobilization.[110] This journal seems to have become the most popular literature at Shanghai University.[111]

Zhongguo gongren, however, addressed a different kind of reader: the working class and the labor movement activists. It was edited by Deng Zhongxia and Zhang Guotao, and its first issue was published in October 1924. This labor journal also emphasized the organization and mobilization of labor movements rather than theoretical discussion.[112]

Qingnian gongren yuekan tried to attract readers from among young workers.[113] It was written in a colloquial style and its message was a call for

109. "Jiaoyu xuanchuan wenti jijuean (Nov. 1923)" [Resolution on Political Propaganda] and "Duiyu xuanchuan gongzuo zhi yijuean (Feb. 1925)" [Resolution on Propaganda Works], in *Zhonggong zhongyang wenjian xuanji,* vol. 1, pp. 207, 377.

110. To name only a few, these included Shi Ji, "Zenyang guancha shehui xianxiang" [How to Observe the Social Phenomenon], in vol. 11; Daiying, "Zenyang zuo xiaoxue jianshi" [How to Become an Elementary School Teacher], in vol. 20; Daiying, "Zenyang jinxing geming yundong" [How to Carry Out a Revolutionary Movement], in vol. 55; and Daiying, "Zenyang zuo yige xuanchuan jia" [How to Become a Propagandist], in vol. 85.

111. This may be coincidental; when the International Settlement's Shanghai Municipal Police raided Shanghai University on 9 December 1924, they seized 281 copies of *Zhongguo qingnian;* the total number of copies of Communist literature in the Chinese language seized was 522. See "Books seized by the Shanghai Municipal Police . . ." enclosed in Pratt to Macleay, 19 Jan. 1925, F.O. 228/3140.

112. *Zhongguo gongren* was initially published under the name *Zhongguo laodong zuhe shujibu* in Oct. 1924. But with the formation of the All China Labor Federation (Zhonghua quanguo zong gonghui) in early 1925, it became its organ. It ceased publication after May 1925 because of the reorganization of the All China Labor Federation as a response to the upsurge in the labor movement after the May Thirtieth Incident.

113. The first issue of this journal was published on 31 October 1923. Chinese historians so far are able to trace only three issues of this journal. The last one was published on 15 March

class unity among the workers, who were living under the yoke of capitalist and imperialist oppression. This journal drew examples from the daily life of the working people to illustrate social and political injustices. This style of political propaganda no doubt was a carryover from Deng's experiences in politicizing the workers of Changxindian.

Through his work on these three journals Deng improved his propaganda and mobilizing skills. It was also during his Shanghai years that his reputation within the Party leadership increased considerably. In the CCP Third Congress, held June 1923, he was appointed an alternate member of the Central Committee. A month later, he became the commissioner of the CCP Shanghai Regional Executive Committee, taking charge of the Party affairs of that city as well as areas covering Jiangsu and Zhejiang.[114] After the United Front policy was established, he was instructed by the Party to join the Guomindang Executive Committee in Shanghai.[115] But also during this period, he began a major ideological argument with Chen Duxiu. Perhaps due to his seniority within the Party, Deng felt confident enough to challenge Chen's pessimistic view regarding the role of the working class in the Nationalist Revolution.

Class Analysis and Labor Movement Strategy

After the 7 February bloody strikebreaking, the "liquidation faction," which consisted of a small group of right-wing Communists headed by Chen Duxiu, had concluded that the working class was not ready to lead the revolution. Although Deng Zhongxia was not an original Marxist theoretician, his criticism of this faction has been regarded by Chinese historians as a major contribution to the CCP during the Nationalist Revolution. The conventional Chinese interpretation is that Deng, after reading Chen's articles on "Zhongguo guomin geming yu shehui ge jieji" (The Chinese Nationalist Revolution and the Various Social Classes), correctly criticized Chen's pessimistic view of the role of the working class, rightly arguing that the bourgeoisie was unable to lead the Nationalist Revolution, which necessi-

---

1924. According to their findings, there is every reason to believe that this journal was edited by Deng Zhongxia while he was dean at Shanghai University. See Yu Fuyuan, "*Qingnian gongren yuekan*" [Young Workers Monthly], *Dangshi ziliao congkan* 4 (1982), pp. 141–45.

114. Jiang Ping, *Deng Zhongxia de yisheng*, p. 97.

115. Luo Zhanglong, *Chunyuan daiji*, pp. 296–97.

tated proletarian hegemony.[116] Without doubt, this interpretation contains elements of truth, but it fails to take into account some of the major mistakes Deng committed.

The Chen-Deng class analysis controversy in late 1923 was due to the ideological and political confusion arising from the United Front policy, which was a strategy initially proposed by Lenin during the Second Congress of the Comintern. The strategy was to form a revolutionary United Front between the bourgeoisie and the other oppressed social classes in the colonial and semicolonial countries for the struggle of national liberation and socialist transformation.[117] But there had long been a controversial and rather contradictory question regarding which class should become the leader in this revolutionary alliance; and this crucial and fundamental issue was never satisfactorily resolved by the Comintern, at least not during Lenin's lifetime. Even in 1920, many of the Comintern leaders, including the Indian representative, M. N. Roy, did not agree with Lenin's view that "temporarily the Communists should allow the bourgeoisie to retain the hegemony over the revolutionary movement."[118] Two years later, two leading Comintern members, G. Zinoviev and G. Safarov, expressed their disagreement with Lenin's proposal that the Chinese bourgeoisie should lead the Nationalist Revolution.

The tragic defeat of the labor movement in north China as a result of the 7 February incident no doubt lowered the morale of the Communist labor organizers and hastened contacts between the CCP and the Guomindang for closer political collaboration. Maring, a Comintern agent in China, also advocated a policy of cooperation with the Guomindang.[119] His proposal was endorsed by Chen Duxiu after the latter's visit to Moscow, where Chen attended the Fourth Congress of the Comintern. By mid-June 1923, when the CCP Third Congress was held, Maring sided with Chen that a United Front policy should be established with the Guomindang. In

116. See, e.g., Wei Wei and Qian Xiaohui, *Deng Zhongxia zhuan*, pp. 92–93; Jiang Ping and Li Liangyu, "Deng Zhongxia tongzhi guanghui de yisheng," pp. 199–200; and Jiang Ping, "Deng Zhongxia zai da geming shiqi dui Zhongguo shehui ge jieji de fenxi" [Deng Zhongxia's Analysis of the Role of the Various Chinese Social Classes in the Period of the Great Revolution], *Jindaishi yanjiu* [Modern Historical Research] 2 (1982), pp. 82–83.

117. For an excerpt from Lenin's Theses on the National and Colonial Questions, see Eudin and North, eds., *Soviet Russia and the East*, pp. 63–65.

118. Ibid., p. 26.

119. Lyman Van Slyke, *Enemies and Friends: The United Front in Chinese Communist History* (Stanford: Stanford University Press, 1967), pp. 15–16.

defense of Chen's policy, Maring claimed that the idea of an independent working class was an illusion, derived from an overestimation of the Chinese working class's revolutionary potential.[120] In such circumstances, Chen Duxiu became pessimistic about the ability of the Chinese working class to retain revolutionary leadership, and he began to argue that the bourgeoisie would lead the Nationalist Revolution. His opinion, however, met with severe criticism from Deng Zhongxia.

Because all class analysis undertaken by the Chinese Communists for the period 1923–27 is closely related to the theoretical problem of the Nationalist Revolution, it is essential to begin the discussion of the Chen-Deng ideological debate by seeking an understanding of Deng's view on the United Front policy. Basically, as has been noted above, Deng was an enthusiastic supporter of the United Front from its inception. Indeed, he was not an extreme die-hard radical or a complete iconoclast. While he was still a student at Beida, he had appealed to his fellow students to give up their personal subjective views and support the formation of a revolutionary United Front to fight for the realization of democracy.[121] To him, the concept of a United Front was not limited only to its political meaning. It also embodied ideas from intellectuals whose political commitments might not necessarily be the same as those of the Communists. For instance, he praised the scholarship of Hu Shi and appealed to the youth to follow Hu's approach to scholarship as a model for learning.[122] However, his open-minded attitude toward liberal intellectuals did not imply that he also tolerated conservative scholars like Liang Qichao and Liang Shuming. On the contrary, he strongly opposed their ideas and regarded their writings as harmful to a modern society.[123] In sum, he suggested that in the process of building a new society, the Communists should work with those intellectuals who promoted new thought. It is therefore clear that he was a person of some flexibility and was ready to join a United Front with other progressives, Communist or not.

Chen Duxiu's interpretation of the role of the bourgeoisie and prole-

120. C. Martin Wilbur and Julie How, eds., *Missionaries of Revolution: Soviet Advisers and Nationalist China, 1920–1927* (Cambridge: Harvard University Press, 1989), pp. 82–85.

121. Zhang Yunhou et al., eds., *Wusi shiqi de shetuan,* vol. 1, pp. 453–54.

122. Deng Zhongxia, "Xinshiren de banghe" [A Criticism of the Modern Poets], *Zhongguo qingnian* 7 (1 Dec. 1923), p. 5. It is interesting to note that Hu Shi also lectured at Shanghai University as a guest speaker in late 1923. See Deng Zhongxia, "Zhongguo xianzai de sixiangjie" [The Current Chinese Intellectuals], *Zhongguo qingnian* 6 (24 Nov. 1923), p. 4.

123. Deng Zhongxia, "Zhongguo xianzai de sixiangjie," pp. 3–4.

tariat in the Chinese Nationalist Revolution was closely in line with Lenin's thesis of 1920 on the colonial and semicolonial question. One of Chen's major arguments was that because of "the industrial backwardness of China, the working class is not only minimal in quantity but also poor in quality." He therefore regarded the Chinese working class as incapable of leading the revolution against imperialism and warlordism. Furthermore, it was their immaturity and underdeveloped class consciousness which left them unable to lead the revolution. In analyzing this weakness, he classified the Chinese working class into three major groups. The first group, which comprised the majority of this class, was still "sleeping in patriarchal society, [and] clanship and regional mentality remain very strong," as a result of China's limited economic development. The second group consisted of a small number of politically progressive seamen and railway workers, who had already demonstrated their nationalist sentiment and political awareness by their recent strikes. The last group, smallest in number, comprised those workers who had participated in the political movement and realized the need to form their own party. But their number was so small that "they could not develop as an independent revolutionary force." He also complained that most of the struggles organized by the workers were related only to economic issues and were without a class character or identity. Because of their weakness, Chen recommended that the workers should immediately participate in the Nationalist Revolution, and that it was too early to decide when the working class would be able to seize revolutionary leadership. He therefore concluded that "the current task [for the working class] is to join the Nationalist Revolution wholeheartedly."[124]

In contrast with his pessimistic view of the Chinese proletariat, Chen Duxiu regarded the bourgeoisie as the leading force in the current revolutionary movement. He stated that it was natural that because of their cowardly mentality, the bourgeoisie would not easily participate in any political movement. However, this class would become politicized if their economic interests were threatened and disrupted by imperialism and warlordism. To support his argument, Chen cited the example of the rise of the Chinese bourgeoisie in the 1911 Revolution. However, he also believed that the Chinese bourgeoisie was still too weak to act alone and, therefore, had to draw support from other classes in the Nationalist Revolution. He concluded:

124. Chen Duxiu, "Zhongguo guomin geming yu shehui ge jieji" [The Chinese Nationalist Revolution and the Various Social Classes], *Qianfeng* [The Vanguard] 1:2 (1 Dec. 1923), pp. 6–7, 9.

"Certainly, all social classes in the colonial and semicolonial countries are immature, but the power of the bourgeoisie is nevertheless more concentrated than that of peasants, and stronger than that of workers."[125]

Chen's pessimistic view of the proletariat was soon countered by Deng Zhongxia's passionate glorification of the revolutionary potential of this class. Deng launched his argument by saying that, on the basis of his experience in leading the labor movement, he believed the political commitment of the Chinese working class to be firmer and braver than that of any other social class. The reason for this, according to Deng, was that their daily suffering was the deepest in comparison with other classes. In view of this, Deng concluded that the working class was the most important force even though it had to join other classes in the current stage of revolutionary struggle.[126]

He also disagreed with Chen's view that the Chinese working class was too small to lead the revolution. Although the extent of industrialization and the size of the working class in China could not compare with the situation in Western countries, he argued that the strength of the Chinese working class would grow because of foreign investment in China. But how long could China wait for the maturing of such a strong proletarian force? Deng did not address himself to this question. Perhaps it was the Communists' interpretation of Chinese society as a "proletarian country" in early 1920 that had convinced Deng to support class warfare in China despite its economic backwardness. To counter Chen's argument about the numerical weakness of the Chinese working class, he noted that the importance of the Chinese proletariat lay not in its size but in the crucial role it played in the modern economy. He explained that the Chinese workers could paralyze the modern capitalist system by strike action among railway workers, seamen, and other transportation workers.[127] He even said that the proletariat's size was not as small as Chen Duxiu had claimed. In fact, according to his own survey, the strength of the Chinese working class was increasing and had reached a point where the workers were capable of forming their own powerful unions; indeed, they had successfully challenged the capitalist system before the 7 February disaster.[128] In short, he intended to prove: "Although the number of workers is minimal, their status in the society is

125. Ibid., pp. 2–4.
126. Deng Zhongxia, "Lun gongren yundong" [On the Labor Movement], *Zhongguo qingnian* 9 (15 Dec. 1923), p. 6.
127. Ibid.
128. Deng Zhongxia, "Women de liliang," pp. 21–25.

in fact more important than that of any other group."[129] Therefore, he insisted that the working class possessed the power and ability to lead the Nationalist Revolution.

Regarding the problem of politicization of the Chinese working class, he concurred with Chen Duxiu. Deng admitted that the workers had not yet been completely politicized. He therefore appealed to progressive youth to launch political propaganda campaigns and to organize the workers.[130] Although he also agreed with Chen regarding the persistence of a traditional mentality among the workers, he maintained that this problem would be solved when the workers engaged in the daily struggle for socioeconomic improvement.[131]

To a certain extent, one may say that Deng's faith in the Chinese working class embodied a strong element of voluntarism. In contrast with Chen's materialistic emphasis in determining political consciousness, he strongly emphasized the human factor. Apart from his belief that class consciousness would emerge by means of self-realization through struggle, his voluntarist approach was further supported by his faith in the power of will. He once remarked:

> Where are the thistles and thorns which can't be broken?
> Where are the wolves and tigers which can't be slain?
> Where are the hills and mountains which can't be overturned?
> You need only struggle, struggle courageously,
>   on and on,
>   forever.
> Victory will be yours!
> Victory will be yours![132]

It is certainly justifiable for any revolutionary to write a passage such as this one to encourage and consolidate the commitment among his comrades. However, Deng did not realize, at least in 1923–24, that proletarian consciousness would not emerge just through political participation and personal commitment. He completely ignored the importance of Party leadership, which Lenin had emphasized. For instance, when he was introducing

129. Deng Zhongxia, "Lun gongren yundong," p. 6.
130. Deng Zhongxia, "Geming zhuli de sange qunzhong" [The Three Social Classes as the Main Revolutionary Force], *Zhongguo qingnian* 8 (8 Dec. 1923), p. 1.
131. Deng Zhongxia, "Women de liliang," pp. 27–28.
132. Deng Zhongxia, "Shengli" [Victory], *Zhongguo qingnian* 3 (3 Nov. 1923), p. 9.

Lenin's work *What Is to Be Done?* to the readers of *Zhongguo qingnian,* he described it merely as a piece of political writing in which Lenin critically challenged the "economists," who, according to Deng's interpretation, only emphasized economic struggle and neglected the political struggle of the Russian labor movement. In the same article, he even stated that "as soon as the revolutionary high tide [in 1915] arrived, the Russian working class consciousness was awakened."[133]

It was probably also due to his passionate faith in the power of the working class that Deng Zhongxia ignored the significant role of Party leadership in politicizing the proletariat. This problem was closely related to his perception that the movement of "go to the masses" (*wang minjian qu*) and the formation of a general trade union (*zong gonghui*) were the basic conditions needed for the germination of the political consciousness of the working class. Perhaps Deng was influenced by the syndicalism that had prevailed before mid-1924, when the CCP had yet to fully develop its organization for leading the labor movement. Furthermore, he was not the only early Chinese Communist who failed to pay sufficient attention to Lenin's theory of Party leadership and organization. Even Li Dazhao must be included in this group. It was not until after the arrival of the Soviet advisors in Guangzhou that the Chinese Communists realized the significance of Party leadership.

Since Deng regarded the working class as the leading force in the Chinese revolution, he disagreed with Chen Duxiu's view of the bourgeoisie. To Deng, the bourgeoisie could hardly develop a revolutionary consciousness, because they selfishly protected personal property and interests. He also cited the examples of the Indian and Chinese bourgeoisies in his argument. The Indian bourgeoisie, he said, always compromised with the colonial government. As for the Chinese bourgeoisie, he divided this class into two groups. He said that the petty bourgeoisie tended to develop a romantic revolutionary mentality because of their economic problems resulting from market competition. The big bourgeoisie, however, was less politicized than the petty bourgeoisie because of their rich financial resources. However, he thought that even the force of the petty bourgeoisie was limited, due to their small number and scattered organization.[134] He therefore concluded that the commitment of this class to the revolutionary movement was unreliable.

As for the role of the intellectuals, Deng's view was rather contradictory.

133. Ibid., p. 18.
134. Deng Zhongxia, "Women de liliang," pp. 28–29.

To a certain extent, his analysis of this problem was similar to that of Chen: "since the intellectuals do not have any economic base, they can only attach themselves to the various classes which have stronger economic power in order to achieve their political goal. Also, due to their economic limitations, they are associated with romanticism, liberalism, and anarchism."[135] Therefore, in his discussion about the intellectuals, Deng concurred with Chen's Marxist interpretation that material well-being determined one's consciousness, and he considered the revolutionary potential of the intellectuals to be limited. However, as a Marxist intellectual, Deng did not mention that a revolutionary movement had to rely on the support of the progressive intellectuals, who were the agents for transmitting political idealism to the masses.

If Deng's understanding of the role of progressive intellectuals in building Party leadership was negligible, his knowledge of the revolutionary potential of the peasantry was superficial and lacked originality. His problem was the result of his lack of direct personal involvement in the peasant movement. Although as early as October 1923, he had appealed to the Chinese Socialist Youth Corps to mobilize the peasantry by setting up a Peasant Movement Committee within the corps,[136] his political activities since 1919 had been confined mainly to urban-based student or labor movements. Therefore, his writing on the peasantry was mainly based on the work of others. In fact, he admitted that his authority came from the writing of Chen Duxiu![137] Basically, Deng was in complete agreement with Chen's rural analysis. Without differentiating between the rural classes, he overgeneralized by asserting that two-thirds of the country's population were peasants, and that such a situation was so obvious that it did not require statistical analysis. He shared Chen's view that rural society had powerful revolutionary potential because of the miserable socioeconomic conditions.[138] He therefore encouraged progressive youth to go to the villages and organize this force. Although he praised the peasant movement in Guangdong and

135. Ibid., p. 29.

136. Deng Zhongxia, "Ben tuan ying zhuyi nongmin yundong (31 Oct. 1923)" [This Corps Should Pay Attention to the Peasant Movement], in *Deng Zhongxia wenji*, pp. 32–35.

137. Deng was referring here to Chen's "Zhongguo nongmin wenti," *Qianfeng* 1:1 (July 1923). For Deng's comment on Chen's article, see Deng Zhongxia, "Zhongguo nongmin zhuangkuang ji women yundong de fangzhen" [The Conditions of Chinese Peasants and the Direction of Our Movement], *Zhongguo qingnian* 13 (5 Jan. 1924), p. 5.

138. Deng Zhongxia, "Lun nongmin yundong" [On the Peasant Movement], *Zhongguo qingnian* 11 (29 Dec. 1923), p. 2.

Hunan, he regarded its development as only embryonic and felt that it had no parallel with the labor movement. What the peasants had achieved so far was the defense of their economic interests, and thus, their consciousness had only reached the "peasants' association level" (*nonghui de chengdu*).[139] By emphasizing that the peasant movement was only in its embryonic stage and speaking of its "peasants' association" mentality, Deng clearly implied that the working class remained the most powerful revolutionary force, and it should therefore lead the rather backward and conservative peasantry.[140] However, he was convinced that the peasants' local militia units (*mintuan*) would become an important political institution, and that the peasants would become a revolutionary army when the time of revolution arrived.[141]

His criticism of Chen Duxiu ended in January 1924, when the Guomindang was reorganized and accepted Communists as members. In view of this development, Communist leaders had to set aside their personal ideological differences and formulate a new revolutionary policy to deal with the United Front. It seems highly possible that by 1924 Chen had also realized that his pessimistic view could only damage the morale of the Party. Therefore, in March of that year, Chen modified his view by saying that there were several indications of the revival of the labor movement.[142] Two months later, while speaking to a group of students in Guangzhou, he emphasized that the working class was the leading force in the Nationalist Revolution.[143] In fact, by the time of the CCP enlarged meeting, held in May 1924, Chen had corrected his "liquidationism."[144] At the beginning of the enlarged meeting, the CCP spelled out clearly that the mobilization of the industrial working class would constitute the Party's fundamental policy,

139. Ibid., p. 9.
140. Many Chinese Marxist historians believed that Chen Duxiu's discussion on class analysis in 1923–24 was completely wrong. They therefore tended to suppress accounts written by other early Chinese Communists whose viewpoints might have been similar to those of Chen. Jiang Ping, Deng's biographer, is a case in point. Jiang Ping quotes Deng as follows: "some people say that peasants are conservative." The original text, however, reads: "Without doubt, peasants are conservative." See Jiang Ping, "Deng Zhongxia zai da geming shiqi dui Zhongguo shehui de jieji de fenxi," p. 86, and Deng Zhongxia, "Lun nongmin yundong," p. 2.
141. Deng Zhongxia, "Zhongguo nongming zhuangkuang ji women yundong de fang-zhen," p. 10.
142. Chen Duxiu, "Zhongguo gongren yundong zhi zhuanji" [The Revival of the Chinese Labor Movement], *Xiangdao zhoubao* [The Guide Weekly] 58 (26 Mar. 1924), p. 461.
143. Chen Duxiu, "Chen Duxiu guanyu shehuizhuyi wenti de jiangji" [Speech by Chen Duxiu Regarding the Problems of Socialism], in *Liuda yiqian*, p. 136.
144. Deng Zhongxia, *Jianshi*, p. 113.

which had recently been neglected.[145] The enlarged meeting also produced a lengthy resolution on the labor movement, in which it emphasized: "All these [industrial] workers are the basis of our Party. Only through unity between them and our Party can [we] develop into a political power."[146] By February 1925, during a series of economic strikes in Shanghai, Chen even said that "the working class is the most revolutionized—in fact, the only revolutionized—class."[147] In retrospect, Deng's class analysis, as expressed in this period, had successfully convinced his comrades that the power of the Chinese working class was not as negligible as Chen had suggested. More significant, his class analysis became the theoretical basis for a new labor movement strategy during the forthcoming Nationalist Revolution.

Although the CCP had emphasized the political significance of working-class mobilization under Party leadership ever since its foundation, it did not have a well-planned labor movement strategy until perhaps early 1925. The CCP labor policy prior to the establishment of the United Front was loosely defined and stressed the politicization of the working class, especially the transportation workers and miners.[148] Without doubt, the Communists should be credited for leading several major labor movements in late 1922 and early 1923 among the railway workers and miners in north China. In May 1924, the CCP Central Committee adopted a policy calling for the launching of union-cell activities.[149] Such a new labor strategy was intended to mobilize workers even under unfavorable political conditions. But in none of these movements or strategies did they regard the Chinese working class as being capable of competing with the bourgeoisie in the seizure of political power. CCP policy during these three years was also characterized by a failure to promote working-class unity on a national level; with the exception of their contribution to the First National Labor Congress, all the labor movements organized by the Communists

145. "Cici kangda zhixing wenyuanhui zhi yiyi (May 1924)" [The Meaning of This Enlarged Executive Meeting], in *Zhonggong zhongyang wenjian xuanji*, vol. 1, p. 229.

146. "Gonghui yundong wenti yijuean (May 1924)" [Resolution of the Trade Union Movement], in ibid., p. 234.

147. Chen Duxiu, "Zhongguo guomin geming yundong zhong gongren de liliang" [The Strength of the Workers in the Chinese Nationalist Revolution], *Xiangdao zhoubao* 101 (7 Feb. 1925), p. 845.

148. "Laodong yundong jinxing fanzheng yijuean (Dec. 1923)" [Resolution on the Direction of the Labor Movement], *Zhonggong zhongyang wenjian xuanji*, vol. 1, pp. 202–3.

149. Van de Ven, *From Friend to Comrade*, p. 142.

were locally based. Most important, Party leaders held conflicting views regarding the labor movement. Chen Duxiu did not fully appreciate the importance of the Labor Secretariat in the current stage of political struggle; and some members, including Zhang Guotao and Deng Zhongxia, overestimated the results of their efforts to organize the working class. During this period, Chen also underestimated the political value of economic strikes while Deng was actively leading the workers in the struggle for better wages. Because of their differences, Deng was severely criticized by Chen Duxiu in mid-1923 for neglecting the Central Committee's labor policy.[150]

In sum, shortly after the CCP was founded, personal and ideological conflicts had already become a major problem within the Party leadership. Due to their disagreements, Communists, especially those in the Central Committee, failed to seize the opportunity to expand the Party's influence among the working class. Furthermore, the Party during this period did not fully trust the organizational ability and political commitment of labor movement leaders of working-class origins.[151] The Communists insisted that the working class should be organized under Party leadership, which consisted mainly of Marxist intellectuals. For instance, the Party rejected the application of Su Zhaozheng, the leader of the Hong Kong Seamen's Strike in 1922, for Party membership several times. He later complained bitterly to his comrades that "I looked everywhere for the Communist Party but could not find it."[152] He became a Communist member only in the spring of 1925 upon the strong recommendation of Li Dazhao.[153] Thus, during the first four years after the founding of the Party, the CCP Central Committee unintentionally built a wall separating them from the workers even though they claimed that they were fighting for the interests of the working class. It was not until the CCP Fourth Congress, held in January 1925, that the Communists, then under the strong influence of the Comintern and in direct competition with the Guomindang, fully admitted the significance of the

150. "Chen Duxiu zai Zhongguo gongchandang desanci quanguo daibiao dahui de baogao" [Chen Duxiu's Report at the CCP Third Congress], in *Zhonggong zhongyang wenjian xuanji*, vol. 1, p. 172.

151. Li Lisan, "Dangshi baogao (Feb. 1930)" [Report of Party History], in *Zhonggong dang baogao xuanpian* [Selected CCP Reports] (Beijing: Zhonggong zhongyang danxiao chubanshe, 1982), pp. 214–16.

152. Deng Zhongxia, "Su Zhaozheng tongzhi chuan" [Biography of Comrade Su Zhaozheng], in *Deng Zhongxia wenji*, p. 395.

153. Lu Quan and Zhe Qianhong, *Su Zhaozheng zhuan* [Biography of Su Zhaozheng] (Shanghai: Shanghai renmin chubanshe, 1986), p. 62.

Chinese working class in the current political struggle. But it took another half a year for a detailed labor strategy to be released.

The new labor movement strategy, which served as a guideline in organizing the Chinese working class in the following years, was spelled out by Deng Zhongxia on the eve of the Second National Labor Congress, in May 1925, in his major article "Laodong yundong fuxingqi de jige zhuyao wenti" (Several Important Issues during the Period of Labor Movement Revival) in *Zhongguo gongren*. The article was a product of his personal experience in the labor movement, as well as of Comintern directives, and contained his class analysis.[154] In brief, he emphasized the reorganization of trade unions on a trade and industrial basis, with a view to solving the problem of localism and promoting class unity. He also encouraged workers to promote economic struggle and to demand freedom for the trade union movement. Above all, he warned the workers that they should not neglect the political struggle, because only with victory over capitalism and imperialism could they be truly liberated.[155]

In Deng's view, it was essential for the working class to participate in the Nationalist Revolution if the workers expected to create a socialist society after the success of the current stage of political struggle. But he reminded workers that they must seize the revolutionary leadership and form an alliance with the peasantry. As for the bourgeoisie, he warned workers that this class was unreliable as a revolutionary ally. Because of this, the working class must compete with the bourgeoisie in seizing political power. He summed up the major tasks of the working class in the Nationalist Revolution as follows:

154. By early 1925, Deng, with his extensive experience in the labor movement, had already emerged as a leading strike movement strategist. Simultaneously, the Red International (a labor organization under the Comintern) also introduced the Chinese labor leaders to strike techniques. The first issue of *Zhongguo gongren* (Oct. 1924) published a translated article on this subject. There is every reason to believe that Deng benefited from such information. This speculation is supported by the fact that he also published an article on the techniques of organizing a strike after he had led the workers in the Shanghai Japanese cotton mills in February 1925. From close examination of these two articles, one can easily conclude that he absorbed many ideas from the Red International and put these ideas into practice. See "Bagong de zhanshu" [Labor Movement Strategy], *Zhongguo gongren* 1 (Oct. 1924), pp. 20–30, and Deng Zhongxia, "Shanghai Riben shachang bagong suo delai de jingyan" [Experience from the Strike in the Shanghai Japanese Textile Factories], *Zhongguo gongren* 4 (Apr. 1925), pp. 50–57.

155. Deng Zhongxia, "Laodong yundong fuxingqi zhong de jige zhuyao wenti" [Several Important Issues on the Labor Movement during Its Revival Period], *Zhongguo gongren* 5 (May 1925), pp. 39–51.

The proletarian participation in the Nationalist Revolution will, in the first place, enable our present economic struggle and related organization to obtain a certain degree of freedom and opportunity, while, in addition, giving rise to considerable development and stability. In the second place, [it] will enable us to develop and consolidate our political position and power. Indirectly, [the proletarian participation] will enable us to prevent the bourgeoisie from becoming soft-hearted and compromising [in their attitude] toward the revolution. Directly, it will create a firm political base to prepare for the setting up of a workers' government or proletarian dictatorship in the future. . . . If we do not seize political power [in the Nationalist Revolution], the bourgeoisie will take it. Therefore, our attitude toward the Nationalist Revolution is to take part in it in order to seize political power.[156]

In Deng's view, the ultimate goal of the workers' participation in the Nationalist Revolution was to create a socialist state. Whether the Chinese workers in the mid-1920s shared his vision of the revolution is a subject of importance which will be analyzed in the following chapters.

The process of the ideological conversion of a patriotic student to a Communist labor leader, as discussed in the previous pages, reveals that during the May Fourth period the workers directly helped to politicize young radical intellectuals before the youths had fully grasped the meaning of Marxism. The students' participation in the labor movement during this period also convinced them that Marxist political practice was the only solution to China's crisis. In view of the significance of the workers in the development of Chinese Communism during this period, it is no exaggeration to claim that the early Chinese Communists, most of whom were intellectuals, owe their gratitude to the workers.

But soon after the CCP was founded, the Communists adopted a closed-door policy, setting many harsh rules to discourage workers from joining the Party. Conflicts also emerged among the Party leaders because of their different appreciations of the role of the workers in the Chinese revolution. Because of his passionate faith in the power of the working class, Deng Zhongxia was able to challenge Chen Duxiu's pessimistic view of the revolutionary potential of the Chinese workers even though he was far less qualified than Chen in terms of his theoretical understanding of Marxism. The Chen-Deng debate on the revolutionary potential of the Chinese workers in early 1924 in fact helped Deng to become the most influential and outspoken Communist labor movement leader in the mid-1920s. Although

156. Ibid., p. 58.

Deng had made considerable theoretical contributions to the formation of a new Communist labor strategy by early 1925, he remained basically a man of action. With the development of labor radicalism in Guangzhou, he was charged by the CCP to lead and organize the Shenggang General Strike during a crucial period of the Nationalist Revolution.

2

Guangdong and Hong Kong

I*F HUNAN*, the province where Deng Zhongxia was born, can be regarded as the intellectual center that shaped the minds of Chinese reformers and revolutionaries in the late Qing period,[1] then Guangdong Province can be considered the source of xenophobia and anti-imperialism and also the seedbed of revolution in modern China, at least until 1927. Guangzhou, the provincial capital of Guangdong and the administrative center of Guangdong and Guangxi Provinces during the Qing period, had been a center of conflict between China and the West ever since the early nineteenth century. It was there that foreign trade, including the illegal opium smuggling, was conducted up to the beginning of the First Opium War between China and Britain in 1839. The result of this war was the beginning of the treaty port system and the surrender of Hong Kong Island to Britain. To the Chinese, this war brought only humiliation and sowed the seeds of an antiforeign movement. From then on, Guangzhou was a cradle of intrigue and revolution.

In spite of popular xenophobia as well as anti-imperialism during the

---

1. Charlton M. Lewis, *Prologue to the Chinese Revolution: The Transformation of Ideas and Institutions in Hunan Province, 1891–1907* (Cambridge: Harvard University Press, 1976), pp. 197–98.

1840s and 1850s, which forced foreign traders to conduct their business with China through other treaty ports, especially Shanghai,[2] new social ideas did emerge in Guangzhou after the mid–nineteenth century as a result of the "treaty port culture." Western sciences and languages were taught in the missionary schools, some of which also admitted female students.

Simultaneously, Hong Kong, situated one hundred miles south of Guangzhou, was developing gradually under the control of the British Colonial Office. Hong Kong became a cultural bridge between China and the West. The colony was an ideal place for the Chinese to learn the English language and Western social values under British rule and missionary influence. For the Western missionaries and diplomats, Hong Kong provided an environment where they could study Chinese language and culture. In fact, the first translation of the complete central corpus of the Confucian classics into English was accomplished in Hong Kong by a Scottish missionary, James Legge, who was assisted by some local Chinese intellectuals. Among them was a late Qing reform thinker, Wang Tao.[3] By the last decade of the nineteenth century, Hong Kong had been an inspiration to a new group of reformers and revolutionaries in south China, men like Kang Youwei and Sun Yatsen.[4] Kang's determination to reform China was due in part to his visit to Hong Kong in 1879, when he was impressed by the economic achievement of the colony even though it was accomplished under Western civilization.[5] Sun, in his later years, admitted that the roots of his revolutionary ideas were grounded in Hong Kong; the economic prosperity of the colony inspired his commitment to build a modern China.[6]

Administratively speaking, Guangzhou and Hong Kong were two entirely different cities. But even though Hong Kong was under British colonial rule, it was, as admitted by the British Foreign Office, "to all intents and purposes a part of China,"[7] due to its geographical connection with

2. John K. Fairbank, "The Creation of the Treaty System," in John K. Fairbank, *Cambridge History of China,* vol. 10 (Cambridge: Cambridge University Press, 1979), pp. 237–43.

3. K. C. Fok, *Lectures on Hong Kong History: Hong Kong's Role in Modern Chinese History* (Hong Kong: Commercial Press, 1990), p. 7.

4. Teng Ssu-yu and John K. Fairbank, eds., *China's Response to the West: A Documentary Survey, 1839–1923* (Cambridge: Harvard University Press, 1954), p. 147.

5. Edward Rhoades, *China's Republican Revolution: The Case of Kwangtung, 1895–1913* (Cambridge: Harvard University Press, 1975), p. 19.

6. C. Martin Wilbur, *Sun Yat-sen: The Frustrated Patriot* (New York: Columbia University Press, 1976), p. 144.

7. "Memorandum on the Governorship of Hong Kong, 25 June 1924," F.O.371/10266 [F2086/169/10].

south China and its huge Chinese population. Other British officials even claimed that "in origins and in reality Hong Kong is part of the mainland of China."[8] In actual life, there was obviously a close social and economic connection between Hong Kong and south China.

Social and Economic Connections

Hong Kong Island and the southern part of Kowloon Peninsula were ceded to Britain after the two opium wars in the mid–nineteenth century. But during the heyday of international rivalry in China in the last few years of the nineteenth century, Britain obtained a ninety-nine-year lease from China for the northern part of Kowloon and extended its rule to the New Territories, located in Baoan, the southernmost county of Guangdong. After acquiring the New Territories and with a view to resisting the growing French influence in southeastern China in the years of the so-called Scramble for Concessions (1897–99), Britain hoped to launch a major railway construction project to link Kowloon with Guangzhou. This Guangzhou-Kowloon railway line scheme was in fact a major imperial project expected to connect Hong Kong with Beijing via Hankou.[9] Although it was the French capitalists who eventually secured the right to construct the Beijing-Hankou railway line, the British investment in building the Guangzhou-Kowloon railway facilitated migration from south China to Hong Kong.

In the early part of the twentieth century, there was no restriction on movement between south China and Hong Kong; Chinese people could travel freely to the colony by paying a modest railway fare. Chinese from the seacoast of Guangdong could travel to Hong Kong by steamer. Most of the new immigrants from south China were from the cities of Guangzhou or Chaozhou. Between 1922 and 1925, the majority of the new Chinese immigrants to Hong Kong, as indicated in table 1, spoke either Chaozhou or Guangzhou dialect.

The majority of the population in Hong Kong was Chinese, and 92 percent, in 1921, were natives of Guangdong.[10] During the 1920s, these Chinese,

8. Alston to Tyrell, 22 June 1922, F.O.371/8040 [F2805/2805/10].

9. L. K. Young, *British Policy in China, 1895–1902* (Oxford: Clarendon Press, 1970), pp. 79–81.

10. Hong Kong Government, *Report on the Census of the Colony in 1921*, Government Sessional Paper (Hong Kong, 1921), pp. 203–5.

Table 1. Dialects Spoken by Immigrants to Hong Kong (1922–25)

DIALECT	NUMBER OF IMMIGRANTS (%)
Chaozhou	23,490 (41.8%)
Guangzhou	20,671 (36.8%)
Kejia	8,964 (15.9%)
Total	56,099

Source: Hong Kong Government, *Hong Kong Administrative Report,* 1922–25 inclusive: 1922, p. c-22; 1923, p. c-24; 1924, p. c-23; 1925, p. c-26.

however, did not have a sense of belonging to the colony. To many of the ordinary local Chinese, the colony was only a city where they could earn a living and support their families in their native villages by regularly sending home their savings. To the wealthy Chinese, Hong Kong was a city for investment under a stable political environment. In fact, the newly arrived Chinese investors in the colony played a crucial role in the development of Hong Kong as a major entrepôt trade center. For instance, these newly arrived wealthy Chinese in Hong Kong increased their import-export establishments from 215 to 395 during the period 1876–81, and they were mainly responsible for extending Hong Kong's role as an entrepôt between China and North America as well as Southeast Asia.[11] Nevertheless, Hong Kong, in the minds of its Chinese residents, was not their permanent home. Therefore, the term *qiaogang* (residing in Hong Kong) came into common use among the Hong Kong Chinese people, who maintained close ties with their families in south China. For example, the successful Hong Kong Chinese businessmen kept in close contact with their families and compatriots back home by donating to charity organizations in their native provinces.[12] Whether they were wealthy or humble, these Hong Kong Chinese visited their native villages or towns in south China very frequently; 435,933 passengers went to China by train from Hong Kong in 1921, and 462,379 came to the colony by the same route in the same year.[13]

11. Fok, *Lectures on Hong Kong History,* pp. 104–5.

12. Ibid., pp. 111–14.

13. Though the above statistic includes those passengers who might proceed to other provinces after arriving in Guangzhou, it nevertheless reflects the high frequency of visits made by Hong Kong Chinese to their native provinces. See *Hong Kong Daily Press,* 23 June 1922.

Although Hong Kong's population was mainly Chinese, it was a major commercial center for the British to advance their economic activities in the Far East; the headquarters of the major British firms and banks in China were located in the colony. By the early twentieth century, Hong Kong had emerged as a major seaport in the Far East. For example, total imports to Hong Kong in 1920, exclusive of those from south China, were valued at £130 million. Though the goods imported to Hong Kong from the United Kingdom in the same year only made up 14.5 percent of the total value,[14] the actual value of the Chinese market was not as significant to British manufacturers and traders as China's market potential, as proclaimed by British diplomats and merchants.[15] Therefore, Hong Kong was an important gateway to the Chinese market for British merchants.

The most important economic connection between Hong Kong and China perhaps lay in the former's function as an entrepôt. In 1920, total exports from the colony were valued at £108 million, of which £53 million worth of goods, or 49 percent, went to China.[16] To be sure, Shanghai competed with Hong Kong, often quite successfully, for this entrepôt trade. But Hong Kong enjoyed the advantage of trading with south China, especially with Guangdong. To take the year 1881 as an example, Hong Kong supplied 99.73 percent of Guangzhou's total imports.[17] It was commonly known that because of geographical reasons, Guangdong could conduct its foreign trade efficiently only with Hong Kong's entrepôt facilities. The Hong Kong–Guangzhou economic interdependence can therefore be aptly summarized by the following observation of the British Foreign Office in the mid-1920s:

Hong Kong and Canton, as ports, are not competitive but complementary. Hong Kong is a sea port which can accommodate ocean-going steamers. Canton is a shallow river port, accessible only to small coastal craft and vessels of shallow draught. If Canton is to conduct foreign trade on a large scale, it can only do so through Hong Kong where the cargoes of ocean steamers are transhipped to the small craft which can penetrate to Canton. Hong Kong is an entrepôt and can only live by acting as middlemen for the mainland, that is to say, broadly speaking, Canton. Hong

14. Hong Kong Government, *Handbook on Conditions and Cost of Living in Hong Kong* (Hong Kong, 1921), p. 9.

15. In terms of the actual value of British overseas exports in the early 1920s, the Chinese market was ranked 15 on an annual average between 1923 and 1929. See Peter Clark, "Britain and the Chinese Revolution, 1925–27" (Ph.D. diss., University of California, Berkeley, 1973), p. xv.

16. Hong Kong Government, *Handbook on Conditions and Cost of Living*, p. 10.

17. Fok, *Lectures on Hong Kong History*, p. 105.

Kong is the port of Canton just as Liverpool may have been in the early days the port of Manchester.[18]

Another aspect of the close economic connection between Hong Kong and south China was the role of the Hong Kong and Shanghai Banking Corporation in offering loans to the Chinese government. This bank, incorporated in 1866 in Hong Kong, was the first foreign bank to offer a loan to a Chinese provincial government. The loan, amounting to £540,000, was offered to the local government of Fuzhou in 1875.[19] Henceforth, this bank was involved in almost all the major government and railway loans in China.[20] In 1905, a loan of £1.1 million was jointly offered by this bank and the Hong Kong government to the provincial governments of Hunan and Hubei for the purpose of redeeming the Guangzhou-Hankou railway concession.[21] By 1926, about £43 million remained to be repaid by the Chinese government to the British, either to public or to private financial establishments.[22]

The actual British investment in Guangzhou was insignificant in comparison with Britain's economic activities in other treaty ports. The reason was that Guangzhou was neither an ideal seaport nor, even by contemporary Chinese standards, a modern industrial center. Most of the direct British investment was in Shanghai and Hong Kong, as shown in table 2.

Although direct British investment in Guangdong was very limited, and this province was not, economically, a key element in British economic expansion in the Far East, nonetheless, Hong Kong had to maintain cordial relations with Guangdong because of its socioeconomic links with the rest of China in order to defend the overall British interest in China. Thus, Sir Victor Wellesley, the deputy assistant under-secretary of state for foreign affairs, recognized that Hong Kong "had assumed a political significance which no other Crown Colony possesses."[23]

18. "Memorandum on Political and Economic Relations between China and Hong Kong, 26 Oct. 1925," F.O.371/10957 [F5210/5210/10].

19. C. F. Remer, Foreign Investment in China (reprint, New York: Howard Press, 1968), p. 341.

20. G. B. Endacott, A History of Hong Kong (Oxford: Oxford University Press, 1958), pp. 272–73.

21. "Memorandum on British Interests in China and Our Competitors, 10 Oct. 1921," F.O.371/6666 [F3498/3498/10].

22. "Memorandum Respecting British Interests in China, 7 Feb. 1927," F.O.371/12471 [F1170/1170/10].

23. "Minutes by Wellesley, 2 July 1924," F.O.371/10266 [F2086/169/10].

Table 2. Direct British Investment in 1921

	SHANGHAI	GUANGZHOU	HONG KONG
Number of British-owned industrial concerns	37	1	28
Number of British-owned mercantile companies	69	9	24
Number of British-owned newspapers	10	0	4

Source: "Memorandum on British Interest . . . 10 Oct. 1921," F.O.371/6666 [F3498/3498/10].

Industry

Although mechanization of the silk-reeling industry in Guangdong was first introduced in the early 1870s by Chen Qiyuan, a returned overseas Chinese merchant from Annam, Guangzhou lagged behind other cities, such as Shanghai and Tianjin, in industrial development by the mid-1920s.[24] Large factories employing hundreds of workers and using modern machinery were rare.[25] Many of the factories in Guangzhou were poorly equipped, and some of their labor force was supplied by the owners' family members. Even in the early 1930s, only 31 out of 205 sampled factories employed more than a hundred workers.[26] The slow pace of modern industrial development in Guangzhou was partly due to a long period of social and political instability in south China.

But the problem of industrialization in Guangzhou, or in Guangdong,

24. Chen Qiyuan's descendants recalled that Chen stayed in Annam between 1854 and 1872, where he learned the Western technique of silk-reeling, which he later applied in his factory established in his native village, Jiancun. See Chen Tianjie and Chen Quitong, "Guandong de yi jian zhingqi saosi chang Xu Chang Long ji qi chuangbanren Chen Qiyuan" [The First Steam-Engine Silk-Reeling Factory in Guangzhou, Xu Chang Long, and Its Founder, Chen Qiyuan], in *Guangzhou wenshi ziliao* [Historical Materials on Guangzhou Culture and History], vol. 8 (1963), pp. 59–60. See also Gong Jun, *Zhongguo dushi gongyehua cheng du zhi tongji fenxi* [Statistical Analysis of the Extent of Chinese Urban Industrialization] (Shanghai: Yinshuguan, 1934), p. 128.

25. *Canton: Its Port, Industries, and Trade* (Canton, 1931), pp. 149–51.

26. Michael Tsang-woon Tsin, "The Cradle of Revolution: Politics and Society in Canton: 1900–1927" (Ph.D. diss., Princeton University, 1990), p. 100.

was also related to the small extent of foreign and native capital investment. Some of the former industrialists of the early Republican period have admitted that the extortion demanded by local officials and secret societies discouraged them from establishing factories in Guangzhou.[27] It was also common for the rich in Guangdong to invest their capital in the nearby British colony for the sake of security. As for those few returned overseas Chinese investors in Guangzhou, they normally did not have sufficient technical expertise in the production of more sophisticated goods.[28] Thus, many of them tended to invest in commerce rather than in industry.

Although there was some foreign industrial investment in Guangdong during the late nineteenth century, the amount was insignificant. In fact, many foreign investors transferred their capital to other treaty ports after a short period of investment in Guangdong. A case in point is the French merchant who had invested in the silk-reeling industry in Nanhai in 1878 but decided to close his factory after several years of operation because of the strong local competition.[29] By the early 1920s, there appear to have been only a British-owned aerated-water company, a Danish woolen factory, and about five factories owned jointly by local Chinese and Japanese investors.[30]

Partly because of the lack of incentive capital investment, industrialization in Guangdong was not focused on textile manufacturing, shipbuilding, mining, or chemical industries, where large amounts of capital and modern technology were necessary. The development of heavy industry was basically weak. For instance, the local government in the early 1930s recognized that the mining industry generally suffered from lack of capital and modern technological support.[31] The major heavy industry in Guangdong during the early 1920s was perhaps no more than a few poorly equipped mining fields, three cement factories, and about sixteen electric power plants.[32] The "modern" sector of Guangdong's economy was dominated by light industry and import-export commercial activities.

Guangdong's light industry was fairly well developed in the produc-

27. Chen Tianjie and Chen Quitong, "Guandong de yi jian zhingqi saosi chang Xu Chang Long ji qi chuangbanren Chen Qiyuan," p. 60.

28. Tsin, "The Cradle of Revolution," p. 102.

29. Chen Zhen, ed., *Zhongguo jindai gongye shi ziliao* [Historical Materials on Modern Chinese Industries] (Beijing: Sanlian shudian, 1961), vol. 2, p. 402.

30. Guangdongsheng zhengfu, *Wunian de jianshe* [Five-Year Development] (Guangzhou, 1933), vol. 2, p. 35. See also Chen Zhen, ed., *Zhongguo jindai gongye shi ziliao*, vol. 2, p. 402.

31. Guangdongsheng zhengfu, *Wunian de jianshe*, vol. 2, p. 32.

32. Gong Jun, *Zhongguo xin gongye shi* [History of China's New Industries] (Shanghai, 1933), pp. 218, 236–37.

tion of household commodities, which mainly consisted of chinaware, pottery, matting, and cane furniture. Other local light industry included mechanics workshops, rubber-manufacturing factories, papermaking factories, match-manufacturing factories, and peanut-oil-processing factories. In all these industries, the owners of the factories would normally mobilize their family members as labor forces.[33] Two local agricultural products, silk and tea, were refined as export commodities. Silk, in fact, was the most important export item, earning an annual average of 59.81 percent of the province's total export value between 1919 and 1927.[34] Most of the silk-reeling factories were established on the outskirts of Guangzhou, especially in the counties of Nanhai and Shunde.[35] In fact, many factories of other light industries equipped with modern machines were established in the Guangzhou delta. For instance, the pottery industry was well developed in Shiwan,[36] and paper manufacturing in Beijiang.[37]

As a British colony, Hong Kong's modern economic development was, in contrast to that of Guangdong, strongly influenced by foreign capital. By the end of the Second Opium War (1856–60), sixty-two British mercantile firms and banks had already been established in Hong Kong.[38] British capitalists in the Far East were mainly interested in commerce, but because of their privileged sociopolitical status, they began to invest in modern industry in the colony. By the turn of this century, the British capitalists enjoyed what amounted to a monopoly in public utilities, docks, cement, sugar, rope, and shipbuilding. Without doubt, British industrial investment exceeded local Chinese investment. In 1920, the British had H.K.$50 million invested in Hong Kong's modern industry, whereas industrial investment by Chinese capitalists amounted to only H.K.$17.5 million.[39]

The huge British capital investment was accompanied by modern technology and management, which facilitated the development of certain industries. Among them, the shipbuilding and ship-repairing industries were

33. Tsin, "The Cradle of Revolution," pp. 99–107.

34. Chen Zhen, ed., Zhongguo jindai gongye shi ziliao, vol. 4, p. 191.

35. Ibid., p. 185.

36. Guangdong jingji yanjiusuo, ed., Guangdong jingji gaiguan [An Overview of Economic Conditions in Guangdong] (Guangzhou, 1935), p. 7.

37. Yang Dajin, Xiandai Zhongguo sheyi zhi [History of Modern Chinese Industries], (Zhangsha, 1938), p. 301.

38. W. V. Pennell, History of the Hong Kong Chamber of Commerce, 1861–1961 (Hong Kong: Hong Kong Chamber of Commerce, 1961), pp. 7–8.

39. Hong Kong Government, Causes and Effects of the Present Trade Depression, Government Sessional Paper (Hong Kong, 1931), p. 87.

well developed owing to geographical advantage and commercial need. One of the major companies in this industry, the Hong Kong and Whampoa Dock Company Limited, founded in 1865 with British capital, had expanded to take the lead in this field along the China seacoast by 1925, with 7,000 Chinese workers and 100 European overseers. Other major British investors involved in the Hong Kong sea-transport industry were the Kowloon Wharf and Godown Company Limited, founded in 1868, with a work force of 800 Chinese, supervised by European staff,[40] and the Butterfield and Swire Company, which had interests not only in the sea-transport industry but also in sugar refining. By the turn of this century, Hong Kong had earned a good reputation in the sea-transport industry in the Far East. Even during the post–World War I recession period, Hong Kong remained a major center of shipbuilding along the China seacoast. The colony produced twenty-two vessels with a total tonnage of 23,309 in 1922, and seventeen vessels with a total tonnage of 15,118 in 1923.[41]

The British also had the lion's share of investment in local utilities. The electric supply was monopolized by the China Light and Power Company and the Hong Kong Electric Company in Kowloon and Victoria Island respectively. Local public transport was also monopolized by British investors, who owned the Hong Kong Tramway Company and the Peak Tramway Company.[42] The Dairy Farm Company, financed by the leading British firm Jardine and Matheson, was the most important company in food manufacturing and storage in the Far East.[43] In sum, the most modern and the heaviest industries in the colony were dominated by British investment.

Chinese investment in the colony was concentrated in domestic and light industries. Wealthy Chinese, mostly southerners, invested their capital in Hong Kong from the early colonial days because of the sociopolitical instability in China. Since the years of peasant rebellions in the early 1850s, Hong Kong had become a shelter for many southern Chinese who wanted to simply earn a living or to enrich themselves. By the late 1870s, the Hong

40. Allister Macmillan, *Seaports of the Far East: Historical and Descriptive, Commercial and Industrial Facts, Figures and Resources* (London: W. H. & L. Collinbridge, 1925), pp. 234–35, 242.

41. "The Customs Tariff Conference 1925 in Relation to the Industries of Hong Kong: Memorandum by the Hong Kong General Chamber of Commerce, 9 Oct. 1925," Butterfield & Swire Company Archives, box 40.

42. "Memorandum on British Interest in China," F.O.371/6666 [F3498/3498/10].

43. Arnold Wright, ed., *Twentieth Century Impression of Hong Kong, Shanghai, and Other Treaty Ports* (London: Lloyd's Greater Britain Publishing Co., 1908), p. 240.

Kong governor, Sir John P. Hennessy, had to report to his home government about the threatening commercial situation caused by the increase in rich Chinese merchants settling down in Hong Kong and competing with the local British merchants.[44] In spite of this, Chinese investors were not in a position, financially or politically, to challenge the dominate role played by their British counterparts in modern and heavy industries, as has been noted. Of the H.K.$17.5 million Chinese industrial investment in Hong Kong in 1920, H.K.$15 million was invested by the Nanyang Brothers Tobacco Company, and the remaining H.K.$2.5 million was distributed among the rattan furniture, biscuit, preserved ginger, vermilion, and other domestic industries.[45] Other major enterprises under Chinese capitalization and management were firecracker factories and knitting factories for underwear.[46] However, these industries were still quite weak during the first half of the 1920s.

Labor

Due to the nature of the economy in Guangdong and Hong Kong, which was dominated by small-scale light industries and entrepôt trade respectively, the number of workers in these two places engaged in modern industrial production like mining and textile manufacturing was not significant. Except for those workers engaged in the modern transport industry, either as seamen or as workers in the dockyards, the bulk of the working population in both places was employed in light or service industries. In Hong Kong, there were only 213,837 employed people, including those in service industries, out of the total population of 625,166 in 1921.[47] The size of the working population in Guangdong Province as a whole is difficult to determine,[48] but in 1915 a labor force of 54,181 was estimated to be working in

44. United Kingdom, *Memorandum by Governor Sir John P. Hennessy on Chinese Merchants in Hong Kong* (London, 27 Sept. 1877).

45. Hong Kong Government, *Causes and Effects of the Present Trade Depression,* p. 87.

46. *Commercial and Industrial Hong Kong: A Record of 94 Years of Progress in the Colony, 1841–1935* (Hong Kong: Bedikton Co., 1935), p. 46.

47. Hong Kong Government, *Report on the Census of the Colony in 1921,* Government Sessional Paper (Hong Kong, 1931), pp. 151, 193–200, 206–18, 222–23, and 226–27. See also table 4.

48. A pioneer study in this field also admits that, especially in Guangdong, it is very difficult to estimate the exact size of the working class because of the lack of reliable documents. See Ming K. Chan, "Labor and Empire," p. 81.

Table 3. Number of Workers in Guangzhou in 1926

INDUSTRY OR TRADE	NUMBER
Industrial workers	17,000
Handicraft industry workers	145,000
Dockyard coolies	13,000
Inland seamen	13,000
Shopkeepers	12,000
Total	200,000

Source: Deng Zhongxia, *1926 nian zhi Guangzhou gongchao,* pp. 55–56.

various workshops and factories in Guangzhou.[49] By the mid-1920s, there were about 263,380 workers in Guangzhou, engaged in various industries and trades, out of a total city population of 729,616.[50] For another estimate of the Guangzhou work force, see table 3. (For the number of workers in Hong Kong, see table 4.) The Guangzhou municipal government claimed that there were 298,615 unionized workers in Guangzhou in 1926.[51] To be sure, the numbers of industrial workers, in the usual sense, would have been smaller than the above figures if seamen, transportation workers, and laborers employed in personal services, handicrafts, and home-based industries had been excluded.

Because of the decentralization of industrial establishments in Guangdong, workers in south China were mainly recruited locally. Most of the workers in the Guangzhou delta were from urban areas.[52] Thus, many of them were not first-generation working class, and few workers were recruited from distant villages and cities. The Xu Chang Long Company, a major silk-reeling factory in Guangdong, illustrates this situation; of its 300 female workers, about 120–30 came from Jiancun, where the factory was

49. Chen Zhen, ed., *Zhongguo jindai gongye shi ziliao,* vol. 1, p. 16.

50. The estimation of the size of the Guangzhou working class is based on Ming K. Chan, "Labor and Empire," p. 88, and the city's population is drawn from Guangzhoushi shizhengting, *Shehui diaocha baogao: renkou wenti* [Report of Social Investigation: Population Problem] (Guangzhou, 1927), p. 2. For a conservative but reliable estimation compiled by Deng Zhongxia, see table 3.

51. Guangzhoushi shizhengting, *Tongji nianjian* [Annual Handbook of Statistics] (Guangzhou, 1929), pp. 285–330.

52. Ming K. Chan, "Labor and Empire," p. 94.

Table 4. Number of Workers in Hong Kong in 1921

INDUSTRY OR TRADE	MALE	FEMALE
Mining and quarrying	1,392	47
Manufacturing	53,203	21,771
Construction and interior design	8,507	1,752
Public transportation (including dockers and godown coolies)	65,176	12,756
Public utilities	1,390	0
Personal services (domestic servants and restaurant workers, etc.)	28,089	19,754
Total	157,757	56,080

Source: Hong Kong Government, *Report on the Census of the Colony in 1921,* pp. 193–200, 206–18, 222–23, and 226–27.

located, and the rest were from villages no more than three miles distant.[53] In other cases, factories recruited local peasants during the off-season.[54] A survey completed in 1934 of 311 workers employed in Guangzhou indicated that only two of them came from Guangxi.[55]

But the labor force in Hong Kong was mainly drawn from the newly arrived immigrants from south China. Even in 1931, of the total urban Chinese population living on Victoria Island and the Kowloon Peninsula, only 38.5 percent had lived in the colony for over ten years, and fewer than 16 percent had a record of twenty or more years of residence. Those who had lived in Hong Kong for over thirty years made up only 6.4 percent of the total.[56]

No matter what industry or trade they entered, working people in south China had to suffer the social evils brought about by early industrialization just as had been the case in Western society half a century previously. They lived at subsistence level; many had to share a small flat with other families. Some of those who were better paid could perhaps afford, but

53. Chen Tianjie and Chen Quitong, "Guandong de yi jian zhingqi saosi chang Xu Chang Long ji qi chuangbanren Chen Qiyuan," p. 62.

54. Feng He, ed., *Zhongguo nongcun jingji ziliao xupian* [Selected Materials on the Chinese Rural Economy] (Shanghai: Liming shuju, 1935), pp. 711–14.

55. Yu Qizhong, ed., *Guangzhou gongren jiating zhi yanjiu* [A Study of Workers' Families in Guangzhou] (Guangzhou: Guoli zhongshan daxue, 1934), p. 12.

56. Hong Kong Government, *Report on the Census of the Colony in 1931,* p. 134.

not frequently, an evening at the local Chinese opera or at a brothel. Many workers spent their free time smoking or chatting with their friends in the teahouses; but gambling was one of their major problems. Newspapers and novels were not commonly read by the working people because of the high rate of illiteracy; even in the mid-1930s, only about 20 percent of those Guangzhou workers who had completed a survey were able to read and write simple letters.[57] In sum, the social life of the majority of the Guangzhou and Hong Kong workers in the 1920s was uncolorful.[58]

As for their working conditions, the problem was basically one of long working hours and low wages. In Guangzhou, for instance, manufacturers in the candy and noodle industry required their employees to work twenty hours a day during the busy season. The Guangzhou-Hankou Railway, whose management agreed to limit working hours to an eight-hour day in 1926, was quite exceptional; of the 138 trade unions registered by the Guangzhou municipal government in 1926, only 20 were able to press their employers to follow this example.[59] In Hong Kong, working hours in all industries and trades were equally long. Even women and child laborers commonly spent ten hours a day in the factory, excluding mealtimes, seven days a week.[60] Adult male workers often had to work even longer hours.

In spite of the long working hours, workers in Guangzhou and Hong Kong normally received a wage that failed to meet the basic cost of living. In fact, ever since 1913, the annual index of the Guangzhou workers' wage fell below that of wholesale prices for basic items (see table 5). In general, it was very difficult for a worker to maintain his family without mobilizing some of his family members to participate in wage-earning. For instance, to support a family of six living in Guangzhou in 1926 would cost at least Ch.$47.80 monthly, but the monthly income for a printing worker there was only Ch.$10-16 (see also table 6).[61] In Hong Kong, numerous reports on this subject were published by contemporary writers, either left-wing or liberal, after World War I. They all emphasized one simple fact, that workers, either

57. Yu Qizhong, ed., *Guangzhou gongren jiating zhi yanjiu*, pp. 24, 74-75.

58. It is still very difficult to locate written documents on Chinese working-class culture. When I asked my colleagues in China about this important question, they said that they also encountered similar problems. My interpretation here is based on my conversations with some elders living in Guangzhou.

59. Guangzhoushi shizhengting, *Shehui diaocha baogao: laogong wenti* [Report of Social Investigation: Labor Problem] (Guangzhou, 1926), pp. 2-3.

60. *South China Morning Post*, 16 Feb. 1921.

61. Deng Zhongxia, *1926 nian zhi Guangzhou gongchao* [Labor Disputes in Guangzhou in 1926] (Guangzhou, 1926), pp. 14-16. See also table 6 for wage rates of Guangzhou workers.

Table 5. Wage and Wholesale Price Indexes in Guangzhou (1913–25)

YEAR	WAGES	WHOLESALE PRICES
1913	100.0	100.0
1914	102.9	103.6
1915	105.0	111.8
1916	109.3	118.7
1917	114.4	123.2
1918	117.4	129.4
1919	121.8	132.9
1920	126.7	132.4
1921	133.5	140.5
1922	146.1	146.6
1923	151.4	153.1
1924	156.1	162.0
1925	159.8	172.0

Source: Fang Fu-an, Chinese Labour: An Economic and Statistical Survey of the Labour Conditions and Labour Movement in China (Shanghai: Kelly & Welsh Ltd., 1931), p. 54; Diyici Zhongguo laodong nianjian, vol. 1, p. 146.
Note: The wholesale price index includes the following items: rice, basic food items, clothing, utilities, and construction materials.

skilled or unskilled, had great difficulty in making ends meet, even at a minimum living standard.[62] Because of poor earnings, high unemployment, and strong competition, workers in both places faced hard times during the first half of the 1920s. It was for this reason that a commission member assigned by the Hong Kong government to investigate the problem of child employment in the colony commented that children should be permitted, under certain regulated conditions, to work because "[their] earnings are essential to the 'scheme of thing' in the daily life of the poor, and without them it would mean so much less income to feed the family."[63]

62. For a leftist interpretation, see "Xianggang bagong jin" [Account of the Hong Kong Strike], Xin qingnian [New Youth], 1 May 1920, pp. 1–2; and for a liberal account, see Hong Kong Daily Press, 19 Apr. 1920.
63. Hong Kong Government, Report of the Commission Appointed to Enquire into the Conditions of the Industrial Employment of Children in Hong Kong, Government Sessional Paper (Hong Kong, 1921), p. 141.

Table 6. Average Wage Rate for Workers in Guangzhou in 1925

INDUSTRY OR TRADE	DAILY INCOME (IN DOLLARS)
Skilled workers	
Highest	1.60
Lowest	1.20
Clothing	
Western style	1.20
Chinese style	1.00
Coolie (average)	1.20
Rickshaw coolie	0.80
Match manufacturing	
Men	0.65
Women	0.35
Silk manufacturing	
Highest	1.30
Lowest	0.90
Domestic servant	
Men	0.60
Women	0.53
Rubber manufacturing	
Men	0.90
Women	0.50

Source: *Diyici Zhongguo laodong nianjian,* vol. 1, p. 45.

Women and child laborers were employed in both Guangzhou and Hong Kong. But the extent of this problem was not as serious as in Shanghai. In 1915, it was estimated that female workers in Guangdong made up 13.2 percent of its industrial force.[64] By the early 1930s, a large portion of women and children in Guangzhou were employed in the match-manufacturing factories.[65] But in Hong Kong, figures show a female working population of some 56,800 and a relatively small group of child laborers, some 13,600, in 1921. Unlike in Shanghai, female and child workers in the

64. Chesneaux, *Chinese Labor Movement,* p. 147. See also *Diyici Zhongguo laodong nianjian* [The First Annual Report of the Chinese Workers] (Beijing, 1928), vol. 1, p. 549.
65. Tsin, "Cradle of Revolution," pp. 110–11.

colony were mainly employed in Chinese-owned factories.[66] Light industry, as mentioned previously, was dominated by local Chinese investment in Hong Kong. Most of the foreign investment was either in commercial trades, sea-transport industries, or public utilities, where a certain level of technical skill and strong physical labor were required. Therefore, the employment of women and children in Hong Kong was much less common in foreign-owned enterprises. Nevertheless, the employment of female and child labor in the Chinese-owned factories caused much concern among a small group of missionary organizations and liberal-minded local British residents after World War I.[67] The colonial government's response to critics was to commission its own inquiry, but it adopted no practical measures to solve the problem.[68] In fact, as one scholar has rightly pointed out, the employment of children remained a major social problem in Hong Kong fifty years after the first inquiry was commissioned.[69]

As in any other society in transition from an agrarian to an industrial base, workers in Guangzhou and Hong Kong found they were exploited by the traditional employment system. For instance, many workers in both places, especially those engaged in handicraft and machine industries, had to undergo a long period of apprenticeship. This system, though it offered professional training to new workers, in fact served the interest of the trades' masters and skilled laborers.[70] The subcontracting system was another means of exploiting workers in many industries and trades. A typical case in Guangzhou can be found among rickshaw coolies, who were under subcontract to three major local guilds, which paid the municipal government an annual license fee of Ch.$100 for each rickshaw. The guilds then sublet their rickshaws to local coolies, charging an average daily rent of Ch.$0.60 for each. Most of the rickshaw coolies lived in the lodge pro-

66. According to a 1921 government investigation, all factories employing children were Chinese owned. See Hong Kong Government, *Report of the Commission to Enquire into the Industrial Employment of Children in Hong Kong.*

67. Carl T. Smith, "The Chinese Church, Labor, and Elites, and the Mui Tsai Question in the 1920's," *Journal of the Hong Kong Branch of the Royal Asiatic Society* 21 (1981), pp. 93–100.

68. A Chinese member of the commission stated that it would be impractical to try to solve the problem of child employment by introducing compulsory education because of the financial burden it would impose on the government and its tendency to encourage the immigration of children from China. See Hong Kong Government, *Report of the Commission to Enquire into the Industrial Employment of Children in Hong Kong,* p. 137.

69. Robin Porter, "Child Labor in Hong Kong," *International Labor Review* 5 (May 1975).

70. Chen Da, *Zhongguo laogong wenti* [Problems of Chinese Labor] (Shanghai: Shangwu yinshuguan, 1928), pp. 84–88; Chesneaux, *Chinese Labor Movement,* pp. 54–56.

vided by the guild at a monthly rent for a bed of Ch.$1.50. Many of the coolies earned only Ch.$1.10 a day, and after paying all the necessary bills to the guild and after extortion by the chief coolies or local police, they did not have much left for themselves.[71]

In Hong Kong, a typical case of this type of labor exploitation can be found among inexperienced seamen or nonunionized dockworkers. Chinese seamen in the colony sought employment by registering in a "Master's Lodge" (*junzhu guan*), which in name was a private employment agency for seamen but in practice was a means to extract money from inexperienced and nonunionized seamen. The Master's Lodge was said to have close connections with the leading shipping firms and the seamen's "Fraternal Lodges" (*xiongdi guan*). The Fraternal Lodges were supposed to be democratically run by seamen, but in fact they were controlled by a small group of the wealthier members and leaders of local secret societies. Any seaman expecting to obtain a job through this channel had to pay a fee to both lodges and was given accommodation until his sailing. Once engaged, however, he became a completely free wage earner.[72] This system, together with other social and economic hardships facing the Hong Kong seamen after World War I, sowed the seeds of discontent which subsequently led to the outbreak of a seamen's strike in 1922.

What were industrial relations like between Chinese workers and foreign overseers in south China, particularly in Hong Kong, where modern and heavy industries were monopolized by British investors? In general, there was little tension between them. With the exception of the Hong Kong Seamen's Strike in 1922 and the strike organized by Chinese workers in Shamian, where the foreign consulates in Guangzhou were located, in 1924, there is no evidence to support the contention that industrial action taking place between 1919 and 1925 originated with maltreatment of Chinese workers by foreign overseers.

Hong Kong, though a colony, was not Shanghai, where there was strong international competition, weak local Chinese government, and the incentive to pay very low wages. Even though the colony did not have a policy for regulating industrial relations, a small group of liberal-minded local Europeans had successfully pressured the government to pay some attention to industrial problems. For instance, the local branch of the YMCA was able

71. *Hong Kong Daily Press*, 25 Nov. 1922. Another study, conducted in 1925, shows that the daily wage of a rickshaw coolie in Guangzhou was only $0.80 (see table 6).

72. Ming K. Chen, "Labor and Empire," p. 109.

to press the colonial government to regulate certain conditions of domestic servants in 1921.[73] Furthermore, direct personal contact between foreign overseers and the vast Chinese labor force was not common, because there was always a small group of senior, skilled Chinese workers serving as the middlemen between the two. The secretary for Chinese affairs of the Hong Kong government, with the assistance and advice of the local Chinese elite, also was responsible for mediating major industrial disputes.

Hong Kong Chinese workers employed in foreign firms received higher wages than those employed by native Chinese employers. Unskilled laborers employed by foreign firms in 1925 were paid from H.K.$180 to H.K.$312 annually, but those employed in Chinese firms received only from H.K.$60 to H.K.$312 annually; gardeners employed by foreigners received H.K.$144–312 a year, but Chinese employers tended to pay their gardeners H.K.$120–288 annually.[74] Without doubt, a small working-class aristocracy did exist in Hong Kong. Therefore, if Chinese workers in Hong Kong were satisfied with their socioeconomic condition, especially those employed in foreign firms, they were likely to be less politically conscious than workers in Guangzhou because of their different economic status.

Because of the difference in the standard of living between Hong Kong and south China, Chinese workers in the colony were generally better paid than their counterparts in Guangzhou. The different economic status between workers employed in foreign and Chinese firms in the colony on the one hand and between workers in Hong Kong and those in Guangdong on the other certainly must have posed a problem for class solidarity and unity in this region. Nevertheless, the social origins of Hong Kong Chinese workers and their family ties with their counterparts in Guangdong somehow went a long way in overcoming this weakness.

Many Chinese workers in Hong Kong not only came from the same province or county and spoke the same dialect but also shared another common social characteristic: their experience of Hong Kong was relatively new. As mentioned previously, only 38.5 percent of Chinese in Hong Kong in 1931 had been living in the colony for more than ten years. Besides, it was a common practice among Hong Kong workers to find jobs in the factories where they were employed for their relatives and friends from Guangdong.[75]

73. Smith, "Chinese Church, Labor, and Elites," p. 100.
74. Hong Kong Government, *Hong Kong Blue Book* (Hong Kong, 1925), p. 279.
75. Hong Kong Government, *Report of the Commission to Enquire into the Industrial Employment of Children in Hong Kong,* p. 125.

Furthermore, their social contact was maintained through family ties. Many Hong Kong Chinese workers sent their newborn babies to be brought up in their native villages by their grandparents.[76] Because of this close contact, some early labor organizations in Guangzhou and Hong Kong were formed on the basis of clan relations, and their contact with labor organizers in Guangdong remained very close. By the early 1920s, half of the unionized Hong Kong Chinese workers were originally from Guangdong.[77]

In sum, although Hong Kong was under British colonial rule, it was basically a Chinese society because of its close social and economic connection with south China. However, due to the extensive British investment in the colony, the society of Hong Kong was more modern than that of Guangzhou, where the economy was dominated by import-export commercial activities rather than by highly sophisticated industrial production. But the different level of economic development between these two cities did not sever the Hong Kong Chinese workers' emotional attachment to China, owing to their social bonds and family ties with Guangdong. Thus, if south China experienced unfair treatment imposed by foreign powers, this type of local sentiment among the Hong Kong Chinese working people would promote collective action with their colleagues in Guangzhou.

Unionization

As in other parts of China, early forms of labor organization in south China were derived from the traditional guild system, which had its roots in the Han dynasty but developed rapidly only in the Ming dynasty due to the flourishing economy of the time.[78] The guild system, as has been pointed out by many scholars, was originally established by merchants whose objective was either to protect their own trade or to offer protection and shelter to their fellow merchants of common geographic origins while they conducted business in cities outside their home province. Skilled laborers in certain handicraft industries were permitted to join the guild formed by merchants in that trade. The major reason for the membership of workers

76. Hong Kong Government, *Report on Labor and Labor Conditions in Hong Kong,* Government Sessional Paper (Hong Kong, 1939), p. 124.

77. Chen Da, *Zhongguo laogong wenti,* p. 183.

78. Ma Chao-chun, *History of the Labor Movement in China* (Taibei: China Culture Service, 1955), p. 73; Peter J. Goals, "Early Ching Guilds," in G. William Skinner, ed., *The City in Late Imperial China* (Stanford: Stanford University Press, 1977), p. 555.

was to enable a guild to maintain its monopoly by limiting certain special craft skills to its own members. Examples are the chinaware and ivory-ball industries in Guangzhou. New workers in these industries were obliged to serve an apprenticeship with a guild member. After they had completed the apprenticeship, the new workers were introduced by their masters and joined the guild as members.[79] Nevertheless, merchants and employers were the pillars of this guild system for centuries.

One of the responsibilities of the traditional guild was to reduce conflict and, whenever possible, solve disputes between employers and employees. However, it could also serve as a system of social control, keeping workers in line. It has been said that cases of labor-capital conflict in traditional China were rare partly because of the willingness of local officials to form de facto coalitions with employers against workers.[80] Such coalitions were often brought about by bribery, but they certainly also reflected the rising social reputation of merchants.

It is unclear exactly when guilds began to develop that were composed solely of workers. One scholar suggests that it was sometime in the late eighteenth century or early nineteenth century as a result of the increasing economic differential between producers and traders.[81] This type of guild, however, was not widely developed, and it mainly attracted those craftsmen who were working in a city away from their native village or town. For instance, the Guangdong carpenters established a guild in Shanghai called Gongsheng Tang, which only accepted members from Guangdong.[82]

In the early years of the twentieth century, partly due to the increase in mechanization in certain industries in Guangdong, workers began to establish their own organizations on a trade or industrial basis. For instance, a labor union (*gonghui*) composed only of workers had already been established in Guangzhou by 1906.[83] The development of labor unions was no doubt related to modern economic growth. But the introduction of new social ideas of labor collectivism by some returned overseas Chinese was equally important. At least four Chinese who returned from abroad, all of

79. Chen Da, *Zhongguo laogong wenti,* pp. 84–87.

80. Goals, "Early Ching Guilds," p. 573.

81. Ibid., p. 558.

82. Peng Zeyin, "Shijiu shiji houqi Zhongguo chengshi shougongye shangye hanghui de chongjian he zuoyong" [The Reestablishment and Function of the Guilds for Urban Handicraft Industry and Commerce in the Late Nineteenth Century], *Lishi yanjiu* [Historical Research] 1 (1965), p. 76.

83. Li Baiyuan, *Guangdong jiqi gongren fendou shi* [History of the Guangdong Mechanics' Struggle] (Taibei: Zhongguo laogong fulibu chubanshe, 1955), pp. 28–29.

them natives of Guangdong, deserve particular attention because of their contribution to the development of modern labor unions in Guangzhou and Hong Kong. These men were Ma Chaojun, Chen Bingsheng, Xie Yingbai, and Liu Shifu.

Ma Chaojun came from a poor family.[84] After completing his apprenticeship in mechanics with excellent results in Hong Kong, he was sent to receive further training in San Francisco, where he met Sun Yatsen in 1905. Ma was attracted by Sun's political ideas and later supported the Republican revolutionary movement in China. On his return to Hong Kong in 1908, he began to organize a number of workers' clubs among the local mechanics. In order to disguise his activities, because trade unions were illegal in the colony, Ma registered his organization as the China Institute for the Study of Mechanics (Zhongguo yanji shushu); its declared purpose was to cultivate friendship among fellow workers. This institute did not have any employers among its membership. However, when Ma organized a similar club among the local mechanics in Guangzhou in 1909, he had to extend its membership to local employers and mechanics workshop owners. The reason, as Ma himself explained, was simply that local factory owners and gentry were more conservative than those in Hong Kong; they were not yet willing to accept the establishment of any major social organization without their participation. Largely due to its connection with local employers, the mechanics' union in Guangzhou became conservative. In fact, Ma was responsible for the founding of the leading "yellow union" for the mechanics in Guangzhou, the Guangdong Mechanics' Union (Guangdong jiqi gonghui), which was well known for its close connection with the Guomindang's right-wing faction during the mid-1920s.

Chen Bingsheng, from a family background similar to that of Ma, worked in Hong Kong during his teenage years.[85] He was employed in a foreign-owned factory, first as an unskilled laborer and later, after having completed a basic English course, as a junior clerk. His true career, however, started when he was assigned by his firm to work on an oceangoing vessel in Yokohama. This career gave him the opportunity to see the world. After having seen the material achievements of other countries and after having come to the realization of the unfairness of the relationship between China and the West, Chen, like many other oceangoing Chinese seamen of his time, began to feel sympathy for the Republican revolutionaries and to

84. Ma Chaojun, *Zhongguo laogong yundong shi* [History of the Chinese Labor Movement] (Taibei: Zhongguo laogong fulibu chubanshe, 1958), pp. 48–52.
85. Ibid., pp. 86–87, 92–93, 97–98.

participate in the propagation of revolutionary ideas among his colleagues and among overseas Chinese. He joined the Chinese Revolutionary Party (Zhonghua gemingdang) and became one of the founding members of the Overseas Communication Department of the Lianyi Society at Yokohama. The membership of this society was composed not only of seamen but also of overseas Chinese in Japan. However, a society offering Chinese herbal medication exclusively to seaman members was founded by Chen in 1915 on a vessel on which he was serving. With his experience in propaganda and his personal contacts through the Lianyi Society, Chen was able to establish other similar Chinese herbal medication societies on many oceangoing vessels employing Chinese seamen and to found a headquarters in Yokohama in 1915. In 1916, Chen moved this headquarters to Hong Kong, and in early 1917, he registered it legally under the name Chinese Seamen's Philanthropic Society. This was the forerunner of the well-organized south Chinese labor union exclusively for seamen: the Hong Kong Seamen's Union (Xianggang haiyuan gonghui).

Although both Ma and Chen had close contact with the Republican revolutionaries while organizing their early labor organizations, it was Xie Yingbai, who came from a rich Guangdong family and had been educated at the Rand School in New York,[86] who was responsible for the politicization of labor organizations in Guangzhou several years before the founding of the CCP and the reorganization of the Guomindang. It was reported that Xie maintained a long relationship with Sun Yatsen: he took part personally in the 1911 revolutionary events; he was appointed Sun's representative in America between 1912 and 1914; and he became the Guangdong delegate in the National Assembly in Beijing in 1915 and followed Sun, as his personal secretary, to Guangzhou when the assembly was dissolved in 1917.[87] In the same year, Xie acquired experience in mobilizing local workers to resist the military control imposed by the Guangxi faction.[88] His belief in the political value of the labor movement was further reinforced by his visit to Moscow in 1919 and his witnessing of the success of strikes in Shanghai and Hong Kong in late 1919 and early 1920. Upon arrival in Guangzhou in 1920, he immediately began to organize a labor union with strong party influence. The General Mutual Aid Society (Huji zonghui), as it was called, was different from other early labor organizations in Guangzhou because it

86. I am indebted to Dr. Ming K. Chan for this information.
87. "Biographical note of Che Ying Pak," enclosed in Giles to Alston, 8 July 1922, F.O.228/3140.
88. Ma Chaojun, *Zhongguo laodong yundong shi*, p. 134.

completely excluded non-Guomindang members and its membership extended to workers from various trades. It also emphasized the unity between intellectuals and workers. Most important, this society, in contrast to others, was only interested in directing workers' political lives and did not interfere in economic matters.[89] Thus it could be said to presage the Guomindang's bureaucratic control over labor unions.

Liu Shifu, a conventionally educated intellectual from a well-to-do family in Guangdong, made the acquaintance of the Republican revolutionaries while he was studying in Japan between 1904 and 1906. He returned to China in 1906[90] and worked on the staff of a Hong Kong Chinese newspaper. But he became more radical and participated in the political assassination movement organized by some revolutionaries. In June 1907, he was arrested for terrorist action in Guangzhou. After he was released from prison in 1909, Liu went to Hong Kong, where he reestablished his contact with the revolutionaries. His political commitment also began to change as he became more influenced by anarchism. In 1911, Liu went to Shanghai and Hankou, where he worked out a detailed plan for an anarchist movement in China. About one year later, upon arriving in Guangzhou, he immediately organized his first anarchist group, the Cock-crow Society (Huiming xueshe), and in the following year published the influential local anarchist journal *Minsheng* (People's Voice). Probably influenced by Tolstoy, Liu disliked urban materialistic life and planned to retire to a rural area, with a group of friends, in the northern part of the New Territories of the colony. His plan did not materialize, and instead he founded the Commitment Club (Jueran julebu) in 1913 and began to organize workers. Because of his social ideas, the labor movement under his leadership appealed, not to those workers associated with modern industrial production or transportation, but to nonindustrial workers like masons, shoemakers, barbers, and restaurant employees.[91] In spite of his ideological commitment to anarchism, Liu was a capable organizer; the barbers' union in Guangzhou under his leadership had an endowment fund of Ch.$100,000.[92] His influence was not limited to Guangzhou but extended to Hong Kong and Shantou.[93] Although Liu died in 1915, his followers, headed by Liang Bingxuan, were

89. Barton to Macleay, 6 July 1923, F.O.228/3140.

90. Howard L. Boorman and Richard C. Howard, eds., *Biographical Dictionary of Republican China* (New York: Columbia University Press, 1968), vol. 2, pp. 413–16.

91. Barton to Macleay, 6 July 1923, F.O.228/3140.

92. Deng Zhongxia, *Jianshi*, p. 5.

93. Barton to Macleay, 6 July 1923, F.O.228/3140.

able to form the Workers Mutual Aid Society (Gongren hezuoshe) in 1921, which comprised at least forty handicraft labor unions in Guangzhou.[94]

These brief biographical sketches of four early labor organizers in south China indicate that the transition from a guild system based on mixed membership to labor unions with their membership drawn exclusively from workers took place in Guangdong in the early years of this century. But the development of modern labor unions in south China was problematic because of social and political reasons. Many of the "modern" labor unions in the early 1920s maintained traditional elements in their membership and organizational structure. For instance, one of the founders of the Guangdong Mechanics' Union in 1920, Huang Huanting, was a mechanic by profession but was also owner of a mechanics workshop. Many small labor unions in Guangzhou during this period were founded by labor contractors.[95] Some traditional clan organizations also played a dominate role in the formation of certain "modern" labor unions. For instance, in the Shunde branch of the Guangdong Provincial Inland Shipping Union, 78 union members out of a total of 166 had the same surname, Pan, which was also the surname of its seven chief executive members; another 21 members shared the surname of Feng.[96] Although there is a lack of comprehensive statistical information regarding the number of labor organizations in south China formed on the basis of clan relations, it is generally believed that coolies, dockers, and inland seamen had a strong tendency to form their unions on this basis.

The traditional elements of "modern" labor unions in south China during the early twentieth century were also related to the unions' association with local secret societies. The Triad was active among the dockers; and it was well known that many local opera singers were intimidated and coerced into joining certain "unions" which were headed by secret societies.[97] Another major problem of the so-called modern labor unions in the early 1920s was caused by factional struggles over conflicting economic interests or regional differences. Armed conflict among the rickshaw coolies or the dockers was common in Guangzhou during the early 1920s.

94. Huang Yibo, "Wuzhengfu zhuyi zhe zai Guangzhou gao gonghui huodong huiyi" [Memories of the Anarchists' Labor Activities in Guangzhou], *Guangzhou wenshi ziliao* 5 (1962), pp. 1–4.

95. Tsin, "Cradle of Revolution," pp. 114–15.

96. Ming K. Chan, "Labor and Empire," p. 94.

97. Zhang Hong, *Xianggang haiyuan da bagong* [Hong Kong Seamen's Strike] (Guangzhou: Guangdong renmin chubanshe, 1979), pp. 38, 54.

The question of labor unity was further complicated by politics; some early labor leaders were "seasoned politicians" and some became bureaucrats. Ma Chaojun, for example, was condemned by the pro-Communist labor activists in 1925 as a traitor to the workers because of his alleged collaboration with the capitalists and with the right-wing Guomindang leaders. Xie Yingbai, after the reorganization of the Guomindang in early 1924, moved to its right wing and opposed labor radicalism. Liu Shifu's anarchist group was on the verge of breakdown by 1922 because of factionalism and the departure of forty capable young leaders to study in France.[98] Apart from political issues, personal factors also contributed to the weakening of labor union management. Chen Bingsheng, who had helped to organize the Hong Kong seamen, was arrested after he gunned down his wife in February 1922 over a family dispute.[99]

In spite of these weaknesses, it is not possible to deny the contributions these men made in the formation of early modern labor unions in south China. But their contributions were facilitated by a local government that sought to use the labor movement for political purposes. For instance, whereas the Shanghai workers went on strike in June 1919 as a response to Japan's aggressive policy in China, the Guangzhou workers took industrial action in July 1919 to show their support for their local political leaders, who were then engaged in a struggle with the Guangxi faction over the governorship of Guangdong.[100] In late 1920, the Guangxi faction was eliminated and Guangdong was administered by a local military leader, Chen Jiongming. The local government immediately launched a series of liberal policies in favor of the development of modern labor unions.[101] Thus, of the 179 different social organizations registered by the Guangzhou municipal government in 1921, 88 had registered as labor unions (gonghui).[102] By 1922, the Guangdong Mechanics' Union, founded by Ma, was reported to have about thirty branches and over 30,000 members; and the General Mutual Aid Society, founded by Xie, was claimed to have about sixty branches with

98. In the absence of concrete documentary sources on the relation between secret societies and labor unions in Guangdong, a confidential report compiled by the Hong Kong Police in the early 1920s nevertheless provides some interesting information. See "The Crime Wave in Hong Kong, 1922," enclosed in Jamieson to Alston, 9 Oct. 1922, F.O.228/3140.

99. "Anarchism and Communism in Canton and Its Connection with the Labour Movement," enclosed in Denham to Alston, 25 July 1922, F.O.228/3140.

100. Chesneaux, Chinese Labor Movement, p. 165.

101. Tsin, "Cradle of Revolution," pp. 113-14.

102. Guangzhoushi shizhengting, Guangzhoushi shizheng gaiyao 1921 [Outline of Guangzhou Municipal Administration] (Guangzhou, 1921), pp. 37-59.

100,000 members.[103] The Hong Kong Seamen's Union, under Chen Bing-sheng's leadership, was reported to be able to mobilize nearly 30,000 men to go on strike during the early phase of the Hong Kong Seamen's Strike in early 1922.[104] It was only Liu's anarchist labor organization that failed to establish a powerful labor union. Nevertheless, despite their weak organizational ability, the anarchists, especially during the years 1921–25, were regarded by the Communists as the latters' major rivals in appealing to the working class in Guangdong.[105]

Thus, Guangzhou had successfully transformed itself into an important base for China's modern labor movement by the early 1920s. But localism, a traditional guild mentality, and the lack of class solidarity remained major problems for these newly founded unions, many of which were craft-based unions and some of which were based on common geographic origins regardless of the members' type of employment.[106] Although some industry-based unions were founded in Guangzhou during this period, there was a strong sense of disunity among the members. For example, the Guangdong Railway Workers' General Union in the years 1920–24 was characterized by the formation of different small "unions" on the basis of job titles; the locomotive drivers and mechanics formed a self-defense corps, and the workers in the dining cars created their own workers' club.[107] In September 1921, the pro-Guomindang labor leaders Ma Chaojun and Huang Huanting established a Guangdong General Union (Guangdong zong gonghui), which, in its early years, attracted fewer than 100 small unions in Guangzhou.[108] This union achieved its real provincial status only starting in 1925, when it was able to recruit union members from the surrounding regions of Guangdong.[109] Therefore, labor organization in Guangzhou, in terms of quantity, was fairly impressive by the mid-1920s, but its quality was weak because of the lack of class unity and political autonomy.

The development of labor unions on a modern basis in Hong Kong was,

103. "Anarchism and Communism in Canton and Its Connection with the Labour Movement."

104. Chesneaux, *Chinese Labor Movement,* p. 181.

105. Huang Yibo, "Wuzhengfu zhuyi zhe zai Guangzhou gao gonghui huodong huiyi," pp. 1–4.

106. Ming K. Chan, "Labor and Empire," p. 182.

107. "Guangdong gonghui yundong de baogao (1926)" [Report on the Trade Union Movement in Guangdong], in *Guangdong geming lishi wenjian huiji, 1921–1926* [Collected Documents on the History of the Guangdong Revolution] (Guangzhou, 1982), pt. 1, vol. 6, p. 336.

108. "Anarchism and Communism in Canton and Its Connection with the Labour Movement."

109. Ming K. Chan, "Labor and Empire," p. 191.

as has been generally recognized, dependent on the achievements of the labor movement in Guangzhou. In fact, of the previously mentioned four early Guangdong labor leaders, at least three, Ma, Chen, and Xie, maintained close contact with Chinese workers in the colony. Ma was responsible for the founding of a powerful labor union among the Hong Kong Chinese mechanics working in the dockyards and other major mechanical industries, and Chen should be credited for his contribution to the development of the Hong Kong Seamen's Union. But because Hong Kong was a British colony, Chinese workers there had to observe the laws of the colonial government in establishing legally recognized societies.[110]

As early as 1845 an ordinance was discussed by the newly established Hong Kong government to eliminate unlawful secret societies. However, it was not until 1887 that the Triad and Unlawful Societies Ordinance was passed. In 1911, another ordinance was passed to control the political activities of all local associations. But some merchant and master guilds were permitted to be legally registered because of their nonpolitical nature. These included the two Chinese general merchant associations, thirty-four Chinese master trade guilds and societies (three of which included workers in their membership), and only seven guilds with membership exclusively for workers. However, by about 1919, the number of guilds with membership limited to workers had increased to thirty-five; this indicates that there was a transitional period for guilds, from mixed membership to membership exclusively for workers, in the early years of this century. In spite of this achievement, the social and political control exerted by the colonial government hindered any further development in labor organization. For example, because of successful press censorship and social control imposed by the Hong Kong government, the Hong Kong workers failed to seize the opportunity during the May Fourth Movement of 1919 to promote the organization of their unions and to increase their political participation.[111]

The social consequences of the postwar economic recession, however, led to the outbreak of various strikes in Hong Kong, even though most of these industrial actions were apolitical in nature and loosely organized.[112]

110. Unless otherwise specified, the following discussion of the development of legal trade unions is based on Hong Kong Government, *Report on Labor and Labor Conditions in Hong Kong*, pp. 116–17. For an excellent scholarly study on the development of the labor movement in early colonial Hong Kong, see Jung-fang Tsai, *Hong Kong in Chinese History: Community and Social Unrest in the British Colony, 1842–1913* (New York: Columbia University Press, 1993).

111. Brett to Jordan, 23 May 1919, F.O.228/3526.

112. A sympathetic British reader informed a local newspaper, after gathering information from low-paid workers and coolies, that "during the past six years, rents have advanced on

One study shows that there were forty-two strikes between 1920 and 1922, all of which were directly related to the demand for better wages.[113] In 1923, there were about twenty strikes for a similar reason.[114] In the following year, there were only about eight industrial actions in the colony.[115] Although the number of industrial actions declined into the mid-1920s, the postwar economic strikes led to the development of labor organizations in the colony. In 1920, the Hong Kong Chinese mechanics staged an economic strike which lasted for twenty-five days. After their success, many local labor activists saw the need to organize their members, and they consulted with the leaders of the Hong Kong Chinese Mechanics' Union (Xianggang Huaren jiqi hui) about the forming of their own labor organizations.[116] By the mid-1920s, there were more than a hundred labor unions in Hong Kong. But they were loosely organized and many were still dominated by local secret societies. For instance, it was commonly known by the local Chinese that the secret societies had a strong influence over many labor organizers, some of whom were in fact members of the most powerful secret society in south China, the Triad.[117]

In the early 1920s, there was also a movement toward the formation of labor federations in Hong Kong. This development, however, was not derived from the workers' commitment to consolidating their class unity.

---

an average of 33.5%, rice 100%, provisions 25%, clothing 10% on their normal prices, which equals 25%, 50%, 20%, and 9% on their present value." See *Hong Kong Daily Press,* 19 Apr. 1919.

113. Ming K. Chan, "Labor and Empire," p. 46. In fact, at least one industrial action during this period was not economic. On 24 June 1921, Chinese fitters employed in the Hong Kong Electric Company went on strike because some of their members had been assaulted and dismissed. See *South China Morning Post,* 27 June 1921.

114. *Hong Kong Daily Press,* 20 Sept. 1924.

115. Hong Kong Government, *Hong Kong Administrative Report* (1924), pp. c-15–16.

116. "Shenggang da bagong lishi ziliao huibian" (Guangzhou, May 1962, unpublished manuscript prepared by the Guangdong Provincial Academy of Philosophy and Social Sciences), p. 3. This restricted and internally circulated oral history material is a collection of memoirs provided by labor activists who had taken part in the general strike. There are eight volumes under three different titles in this collection. The titles will be abridged as follows in my citations: "Shenggang da bagong lishi ziliao huibian" [Collected Historical Sources of the Guangzhou-Hong Kong General Strike], 2 vols. (May 1962), will be cited as "Lishi ziliao huibian"; "Shenggang da bagong huiyiliu" [Memoirs of the Guangzhou-Hong Kong General Strike], 4 vols. (Mar. 1962), will be cited as "Huiyiliu"; and "Shenggang da bagong huiyiliu ziliao" [Memoir Sources of the Guangzhou-Hong Kong General Strike], 2 vols. (Dec. 1962), will be cited as "Huiyiliu ziliao."

117. For instance, two labor activists who also participated in the Guangzhou-Hong Kong General Strike in 1925–26, Huang Jinyuan and Liang Zhiguang, were members of the Triad. See ibid., p. 4

Instead, their motivation was based on factional struggle among workers. In 1921, the General Association of Labor Syndicates (Gongtuan zonghui) was founded and was able to attract about seventy unions as members. Its early members came mainly from the craft industries. But labor unions of the service industries and the hawkers, which were then dominated by the local secret societies, also joined this association. Because of the association's support of the Seamen's Strike in early 1922, the Hong Kong Seamen's Union also became a member in that year; and the seamen gradually captured the leadership of the association prior to the outbreak of the general strike in mid-1925.[118]

In May 1925, another Hong Kong labor federation, the General Union of Chinese Workers (Huagong zonghui), was founded during the Communist-dominated Second National Labor Congress, which proposed the development of a general labor union in China. But one of the powerful participants of the congress, the Hong Kong Chinese Mechanics' Union, strongly opposed this proposal for fear of losing their influence over their members. The Mechanics' Union also worried that if the proposed general labor union was founded, they would lose their leading position among the Hong Kong unions to their major rival, the Hong Kong Seamen's Union. However, without the support of the Mechanics' Union, the Communist labor activists mobilized some Hong Kong leftist unionists to form the General Union of Chinese Workers in the colony. Among the approximately thirty early members of this labor federation were the unions of tramway workers, dockyard coolies, printers, and office clerks.[119] Thus, a pro-Communist labor federation, although relatively small, was founded in Hong Kong on the eve of the Shenggang General Strike.

The labor organizations in Hong Kong during the early 1920s, as in Guangzhou, still suffered from the problems of a traditional guild mentality, factional struggle between unions, and the influence of secret societies. The political environment in the colony also hindered the politicization of the Hong Kong labor movement. However, the Hong Kong Chinese workers were by no means completely apolitical; they participated in various types of antiforeign activity in the pre-1911 period, and they were prepared to do so again if they felt British policy toward China, particularly toward their native province, Guangdong, was far from acceptable. Thus, although localism was usually an obstacle to creating a national move-

118. "Huiyiliu," vol. 4, pp. 4–5.
119. "Lishi ziliao huibian," p. 7.

ment, the Hong Kong Chinese workers demonstrated that their regional ties with Guangdong in fact facilitated their development of national sentiment, especially when south China was penetrated by foreign powers.

Labor and Politics

Basically, it was the change in the political environment, not in economic conditions, that provided the driving force for the rapid development of a labor movement in south China during the first half of the 1920s. Prior to the consolidation of Guangzhou as a Guomindang revolutionary base in 1924, the unionized workers in Guangdong were dominated by traditional guild organizations or by the anarchists. Nevertheless, under the liberal labor policy first introduced by Chen Jiongming and then by Sun Yatsen starting in 1920, Guomindang influence grew among the workers in this southern city. Besides, due to the work of the early labor organizers, as previously discussed, the anarchist influence in the labor movement was gradually replaced by Guomindang and, to a certain extent, by CCP influence.

Workers in south China had an extensive record of political participation since the mid-nineteenth century. One of the earliest collective actions organized by the Hong Kong workers was a protest against a personal tax on recently arrived Chinese, imposed by the newly established Hong Kong British government in 1844. The workers won a victory after a three-month strike, and the Hong Kong government made a concession to workers by "delaying" the application of the personal tax. Eleven years later, the first instance of Chinese workers in Hong Kong returning to Guangzhou en masse to boycott the British government took place. About 20,000 Hong Kong Chinese returned to Guangzhou or to their native villages to protest British military aggression during the Second Opium War. The Franco-Chinese military conflicts over their disputes in Indochina in 1884 provoked another major strike among Hong Kong dockyard workers.[120]

Besides supporting the antiforeign movement, Chinese workers in the colony also offered assistance to the Republican revolutionaries at the turn of this century. Some 600 coolies were involved in the abortive revolt organized by the Chinese Restoration Society (Xingzhong hui) in 1895.[121] In 1911, a "suicide squad" was organized by returning Hong Kong workers and was

120. Cai Luo and Lu Quan, *Shenggang da bagong* [The Guangzhou-Hong Kong General Strike] (Guangzhou: Guangdong renmin chubanshe, 1980), pp. 7–9.
121. Ming K. Chan, "Labor and Empire," p. 31.

led by Ma Chaojun during the revolutionary events in Hankou.[122] In 1915, a small group of local workers protesting the Twenty-one Demands contemplated the assassination of the Guangdong military governor, Long Guang; but they did not execute the plot.[123] The Guangzhou workers were even more radical than those of Hong Kong. In 1919–20, workers in Guangzhou were mobilized by Xie Yingbai to resist the penetration of the Guangxi militarist faction into Guangdong. This matter was settled only after the local leader, Chen Jiongming, expelled the Guangxi military faction in October 1920.[124]

The climax of this long record of political participation by workers in south China was certainly the Hong Kong Seamen's Strike in early 1922. This strike, begun for economic reasons, turned into a massive anti-British movement after the Hong Kong Police killed some strikers who were on their way back to Guangzhou. As several scholars have observed, the Seamen's Strike was the most successful labor movement ever organized by Chinese workers against unfairness and exploitation imposed by capitalists and foreign government.[125] A large number of Chinese Hong Kong workers were politicized by the Seamen's Strike; they began to use terms such as "capital" and "labor" more frequently even though, as the colonial administration observed, they did not fully understand their meanings.[126] The strike demonstrated the unity and solidarity between Hong Kong and Guangdong workers. Most important, the strike also enhanced the Guomindang's reputation among the workers in south China due to its financial support; the Hong Kong strikers paraded through the streets of Guangzhou en masse on 20 January to the government office proclaiming their loyalty to the Guangdong government,[127] and some 12,000 seamen from south China joined the Guomindang as party members by the end of the strike.[128] The strike also produced a small group of highly capable labor movement

---

122. Ma Chaojun, *Zhongguo laogong yundong shi*, pp. 62–64.

123. Ibid., pp. 91–92.

124. Chesneaux, *Chinese Labor Movement*, pp. 184–85; and Zhang Hong, *Xianggang haiyuan da bagong*, p. 76.

125. For a detailed description of this event, see Zhang Hong, *Xianggang haiyuan da bagong*, pp. 146–49; and Chesneaux, *Chinese Labor Movement*, pp. 165–66.

126. Chan Wai Kwan, *The Making of Hong Kong Society: Three Studies of Class Formation in Early Hong Kong* (Oxford: Clarendon Press, 1991), p. 183.

127. *Hong Kong Daily Press*, 21 Jan. 1922.

128. Lin Jiayou and Zhou Xingliang, *Sun Zhongshan yu guogong deyici hezuo* [Sun Yatsen and the First Guomindang-Communist Cooperation] (Chengdu: Sichuan renmin chubanshe, 1988), p. 210.

leaders of working-class origin, men like Su Zhaozheng and Lin Weimin, who later joined the CCP as members.

It is certain that the workers' nationalistic sentiment was a key element binding them together in the course of the antiforeign movement. However, the solidarity between Hong Kong and Guangdong workers was also due to their social and family ties. Therefore, there was also a strong feeling of mutual obligation and collectivism between the workers of these two cities. For instance, in 1915 the Hong Kong Postmen's Labor Club donated generously to help victims of flooding in Guangzhou.[129] Five years later, the mechanics in Guangzhou helped their counterparts in Hong Kong to find employment after the latter had gone on strike and returned to their native province.[130] During the Hong Kong Seamen's Strike in 1922, class solidarity between workers from these two cities was increased. For example, seamen in Guangdong helped some of the returned Hong Kong seamen find temporary employment.

However, one should not romanticize the revolutionary potential of these workers; many of them were passive politically, and some of them were in fact reactionaries. This situation was related to the fact that some workers were almost certainly still under the control of the traditional guild system, even though statistics to prove this are difficult to obtain. As has been mentioned, merchant guilds in Guangzhou were more influential, both socially and politically, than the modern labor unions. They refused to support any political movement that threatened their economic interests. For instance, in an attempt to resist new taxation imposed by the local government to raise funds for the revolutionary movement, the cargo guilds in Guangzhou mobilized their workers to go on strike in 1923.[131] One year later, a similar strike occurred among all inland seamen and coolies working on the launches and junks sailing along the Guangzhou delta.[132] The attempted merchants' coup in the summer of 1924, to be discussed later, clearly reflected the reactionary mentality of merchants when their economic interests were threatened by a revolutionary movement. Therefore,

129. "Xianggang gongtuan zhi dalue diaocha" [A Rough Survey of the Hong Kong Labor Unions], in *Xianggang daguangbao gengshen zhengkan* [Supplementary Issue of Hong Kong Daguangbao] (1920).

130. *Hong Kong Daily Press,* 16 Apr. 1920.

131. Company Correspondence, Canton to Hong Kong, 27 Sept. 1923, Papers of John Swire and Sons Ltd., box 38.

132. "Canton Intelligence Report: Apr. to Sept. 1924," enclosed in Giles to Macleay, 30 Sept. 1924, F.O.228/3276.

the major task facing any revolutionary leader, either of the Guomindang or of the CCP, was not only finding a way to transform the antiforeign sentiment shared by workers and the other social classes in Guangdong and Hong Kong into political action but also dealing with the problems arising from some conservative-minded merchants and workers.

Before mid-1925, the Communists were far less successful than the Guomindang in mobilizing the workers in south China. Besides the obvious reason that they were newcomers to the political scene in China, there were other important factors. First, Sun Yatsen, the founder of the Guomindang, was highly regarded in south China because he was a native of Guangdong Province. British observers even said that "the Chinese people in [Guangdong] and Hong Kong regarded Sun in much the same way as Gandhi was regarded in India."[133] A Russian journalist reported in mid-1923 that the workers in Guangzhou were prepared to support Sun.[134] Second, many of the first generation of labor movement leaders in south China, as previously mentioned, were supporters of the 1911 Revolution. Finally, the liberal labor policy as implemented by Sun Yatsen and his associate Liao Zhongkai in the early 1920s strongly encouraged the workers to support the Nationalist Revolution even though many of them did not understand the Guomindang ideology.[135] Therefore, the Communists encountered serious difficulty in gaining support from the working class in south China. But did the Communists ever try to establish a stronghold among the workers in Guangzhou and Hong Kong once their party was founded in 1921? Indeed, they did, but the result was not as impressive as Chinese Marxist historians have usually claimed.

It is true, as many Chinese Marxist historians have pointed out, that the early Communists, headed by Chen Duxiu and his students from Beida (Beijing University), namely Chen Gongbo, Tan Pingshan, and Tan Zhitang, began to organize evening schools for laborers, publish labor journals,

---

133. Jamieson to Alston, 11 Mar. 1922, F.O.371/8030.

134. "Translation of Extractions from Russian Newspapers (June 1923)," *Shanghai Municipal Police Archives*, I.O.5167, box 104.

135. When Sun told a group of workers in Guangzhou in 1921 that he wanted to become "the president of the workers and to accomplish, [by working] together with the workers, the Nationalist Revolution," many of them did not understand his political meaning or his plans for implementation. Luo Daming et al., "Da geming shiqi Guangdong gongren yundong qingkuang de huiyi" [Memoirs of the Guangdong Labor Movement during the Period of Great Revolution], in *Guangzhou da geming shiqi huiyi lu xuanpian* [Selected Memoirs of the Great Revolution in Guangzhou] (Guangzhou: Guangdong renmin chubanshe, 1986), p. 206.

and take part in industrial action after Chen was appointed head of the Guangdong Provincial Education Commission organized by the local military governor, Chen Jiongming, in December 1920.[136] However, apart from this limited achievement, there is no evidence to prove the extent of their claimed success in organizing the labor movement in this treaty port. From a careful examination of Party documents and the contemporary political environment in Guangzhou, it is possible to determine that they have exaggerated the achievement of the early Communists in Guangzhou before the Shenggang General Strike. According to Chen Duxiu, there were only thirty-two Communists in Guangdong in 1921–22, and their role in the labor movement was limited to participating in one strike organized by local building workers and in a union reform movement organized by local mechanics. Apart from this, Chen claimed that they established three workers' schools, but he did not report the numbers enrolled. The Communists' limited participation in the Guangdong labor movement is further revealed in the same report, which states that during the Hong Kong Seamen's Strike, the Communists could only launch a street-corner speech corps movement and distribute 3,000 copies of Communist handbills in a city that had a population of about 800,000. The situation did not improve in the following years: in 1923, the CCP Guangdong Regional Committee admitted that they had great difficulty in mobilizing workers to form pro-Communist labor unions.[137]

But the year 1924 can be considered a turning point in the Communist labor movement in south China because the Communists could openly mobilize the working class under the umbrella of the United Front. The idea of the United Front originated from Lenin's thesis which he had presented to the Second Congress of the Comintern in 1920. He suggested that, due to the economic backwardness in the colonial and semicolonial countries, the bourgeoisie and the proletariat in these countries should be united in

136. See, e.g., Cai Luo and Yuan Bangjian, "Guanyu diyici guonei geming zhanzheng shiqi zhonggong Guangdong quwei de jige wenti" [On Several Issues Relating to the CCP Guangdong Regional Committee during the First Revolutionary Civil War], *Xueshu yanjiu* [Academic Studies] 4 (1981), pp. 5–14; and Chen Zhiwen, "Zhongguo gongchandang zai Guangdong diqu jiandang chuqi de yixie shiliao" [Certain Historical Materials on the CCP Guangdong Regional Committee during Its Founding Period], *Guangzhou wenshi ziliao* 17 (1979), pp. 1–19.

137. Zhonggong zhongyang danganguan, ed., *Zhonggong zhongyang zhengzhi baogao xuanji, 1922–1926* [Selected Political Reports of the CCP Central Committee] (Beijing: Zhonggong zhongyang dangxiao chubanshe, 1981), pp. 1, 6, 21.

their struggle against imperialism and colonialism.[138] When Maring met Sun Yatsen in Guangxi in December 1921, the latter was still hesitant to accept the Comintern's proposal. But in mid-1922 Sun faced serious problems because of the betrayal of Chen Jiongming, from whom Sun had sought support since 1917.

The Sun-Chen alliance was unstable from its inception because of the strong competition between the two men. Chen was backed by his army, and Sun enjoyed considerable prestige as leader of the Guomindang but lacked military strength loyal to him. Sun considered his primary objective to be the unification of China. But Chen believed priority should be given to the economic reconstruction of Guangdong.[139] Sun also had to face the military threat posed by the local warlords. The seesaw political struggles between Sun and the local warlords in south China contributed to the former's political exile both in 1918 and in 1922. It was during his exile in Shanghai in late 1922, which was the result of a coup staged by his former ally Chen Jiongming, that two important decisions were made regarding his revolutionary strategy. These were that a United Front with the CCP should be formed, and that Guangzhou should be recaptured as the base for the Nationalist Revolution.[140]

Without doubt, Guangzhou was strategically valuable to Sun's revolutionary movement; and it was the home base of the 1911 Revolution. Geographically speaking, Guangzhou was far enough from Beijing that any military attack on it, as might be launched by any powerful Beiyang warlord, would be unlikely to succeed. As for the local warlords in Guangdong, they were not strong enough to pose any serious and long-term challenge to the Guomindang. Many of these local warlords were the product of the military disbandment in 1913; they were poorly equipped and organized, and some were even being threatened by the local secret societies.[141] Thus, even the powerful local military leader Chen Jiongming, who had staged a coup d'état against Sun in June 1922, was abandoned by Sun's supporters in February 1923.

While facing unstable internal conditions resulting from various political challenges by the local warlords, Sun's revolutionary career was further threatened by his diplomatic setbacks. None of the Western powers was

138. D'Encausse and Schram, eds., *Marxism and Asia,* pp. 26–47.
139. Wilbur, *Sun Yat-sen,* pp. 29–32.
140. Wilbur and How, eds., *Missionaries of the Revolution,* pp. 60–63.
141. Chen Zhirang [Jerome Ch'en], *Junshen zhengquan* [The Military-Gentry Coalition] (Hong Kong: Sanlian chubanshe, 1979), pp. 18–21.

willing to offer financial aid or goodwill to Sun during the early 1920s. Because of these frustrations he eventually, in January 1923, accepted Comintern aid and took steps to form a United Front with the CCP.

It was also in Guangzhou that the CCP finalized their prolonged debate about the formation of a United Front with the Guomindang. Prior to the CCP Third Congress, which was held in June 1923 in Guangzhou, some leading Communists, notably Zhang Guotao and Cai Hesen, worried about the future status of the Party if its members were admitted to the Guomindang. In fact, Zhang believed that the Party's influence in the labor movement would be ceded to the Guomindang if the United Front policy was adopted. But, as analyzed in the previous chapter, the CCP in early 1923 received a major defeat because of the bloody suppression of the Communist labor movement by a warlord in north China. They then began to realize that they were too weak to fight independently. Thus, Maring seized the opportunity to convince the Chinese Communists to accept the United Front policy; he even claimed that "the idea of an independent labor policy was an illusion . . . , and [it was] derived from an overestimation of the Chinese proletariat's potential."[142] Consequently, the Communists accepted his proposal in the CCP Third Congress. With a view to strengthening the Communists' confidence in the forthcoming CCP-Guomindang joint venture, the labor movement leader Deng Zhongxia reminded his comrades: "no one objects to us working together with the Guomindang. But we are not working *for* them. From now on, we have to modify our strategy in our cooperation [with the Guomindang]."[143]

By mid-1923, Guangzhou had emerged as a new center of revolutionary ferment because of the impending United Front. In October of that year, a team of Soviet political and military advisors, head by Michael Borodin, arrived in Guangzhou. The formal adoption of the United Front policy in early 1924 had a dramtic impact on the political fortunes of both the Guomindang and the CCP. Under Comintern influence and endorsed by Sun Yatsen, the Guomindang now changed its party ideology to emphasize a policy of anti-imperialism and to stress the mobilization of the urban masses and rural peasantry for political purposes.

There can be no doubt that the policy of anti-imperialism had a powerful emotional appeal for many contemporary Chinese. To many of them, the ideology and policy of anti-imperialism were neither radical nor im-

142. Wilbur and How, eds., *Missionaries of the Revolution,* p. 84.
143. Hiroaki, "Ma Lin, Sun Zhongshan, guogong hezuo," p. 10.

practical. It was a basic policy that would help China regain its full sovereignty and achieve equal standing within the international community. Unlike that of the Communists, Sun Yatsen's anti-imperialism did not embody a determination to eliminate foreign capital from Chinese soil. Rather, he considered foreign investment in China, without the attachment of unequal trading terms, a necessity in China's modernization.[144] But anti-imperialism was also a policy that would provoke foreign military intervention. Sun, in fact, fully understood this danger. Hence, in late 1923, he regarded an anti-imperialist alliance between the Soviet Union and the Guomindang, as suggested by Michael Borodin, as strategically inappropriate for fear that it might bring joint military intervention by Britain and other major Western powers.[145] Nevertheless, the newly adopted anti-imperialist policy in the Guomindang ideology had a profound effect on the labor movement in south China.

The Guomindang's decision to implement the Bolshevik concept of mass mobilization was derived from its leaders' frustration at repeated military challenges from local warlords. A Russian military advisor, General Alexander I. Cherepanov, has recalled that, during a party meeting with the Guomindang leaders after Chen Jiongming had captured a town near Guangzhou in November 1923, Borodin criticized the Guomindang for not having the support of any particular social class.[146] The Guomindang leaders accepted this criticism. Subsequently, the Huangpu Military Academy was established in early 1924 to meet the need of strengthening the Guomindang military force, and separate departments responsible for politicizing workers and peasants were also established. The Peasant Movement Training Institute was set up under these circumstances. Though the Guomindang did not organize a similar institute for Guangzhou workers, the trade union movement under its influence was strong at that time. Apparently influenced by the Comintern advisors, the Guomindang established a labor department, headed by a prominent left-wing Guomindang leader, Liao Zhongkai, and a local Communist, Feng Jupo, during its First

144. Hung-ting Ku, "The Emergence of the Kuomintang's Anti-imperialism," *Journal of Oriental Studies* 16 (1978), p. 92; see also Patrick Cavendish, "Anti-imperialism in the Kuomintang, 1923–28," in Jerome Che'n and Nicholas Tarling, eds., *Studies in the Social History of China and South East Asia* (Cambridge: Cambridge University Press, 1970), p. 28.

145. Chiang Yung-ching, "Borodin and the Re-organization of the Chinese National Party," in *Symposium on the History of Republican China* (Taibei, 1981), vol. 3, p. 77.

146. Borodin is reported to have said: "despite its objective revolutionary nature, the Guomindang is still indecisive and does not rely on any particular class or classes." See Alexander I. Cherepanov, *As Military Advisor in China* (Moscow: Progress Publishers, 1982), p. 34.

Congress in early 1924 to direct the labor movement.[147] Most important, all these ideological and institutional changes within the Guomindang also created a favorable environment for the Communists, under the auspices of the United Front policy, to openly and actively transform their ideas on the labor movement into practical political action.

Thus, the Communists seized this opportunity to extend their influence among the workers in south China. In July 1924, the CCP witnessed the Comintern's attempt to radicalize the working class in Guangzhou; the Conference of the Transport Workers of the Pacific, sponsored by the Profintern (Communist Trade Union International), was held in this southern city. The conference advised the transport workers of the Pacific region to get organized and prepare themselves for anti-imperialist activity.[148] In October of the same year, Deng Zhongxia published an abstract, in Chinese translation, of the resolution that had just been adopted by the Profintern Third Congress, which called for an intensification of political participation by the workers due to the growing differences between capital and labor. At the end of his short article, Deng drew his readers' attention to the following issues that had been raised by the Profintern: "(1) [China] is now attacked jointly by foreign and native capital; (2) the proletariat in the East should participate in the struggle for class and national liberation; (3) the new [labor] strategy should be organized with the cooperation of peasants and handicraft workers; and (4) [we] need a solid revolutionary organization."[149]

To strengthen the Communist organization under the United Front policy, the CCP not only dispatched many able young Party leaders to Guangzhou[150] but also recruited progressive labor activists locally. Therefore, when the Guomindang launched a movement to establish local party offices in Guangzhou to increase its influence at the grass-roots level in late 1923, the Communists grasped this opportunity to expand their influence by sending their members to work side-by-side with the Guomindang. Out of a total of thirteen local party offices, the Communists were able to

147. Lin Jiayou and Zhou Xingliang, *Sun Zhongshan*, p. 212. See also Lydia Holubnychy, *Michael Borodin and the Chinese Revolution, 1923–1925* (New York: East Asian Institute, Columbia University, 1979), pp. 390–91.

148. Eudin and North, eds., *Soviet Russia and the East*, p. 268.

149. Deng Zhongxia, "Chise zhigong guoji zhi dongfang celue" [The Profintern's Labor Strategy in the East], *Zhongguo gongren* 1 (Oct. 1924), p. 8.

150. At the very beginning of the United Front policy, about 300 Communists were working in the CCP Guangdong Regional Committee. See Zhang Guotao, *Wo de huiyi*, p. 448.

occupy seats in eight; there were thirty Communist members in the first local office, seven in the tenth, three in the second, and one in each of the third, fourth, fifth, sixth, and eleventh local party offices.[151]

Furthermore, although the CCP still maintained a closed-door policy regarding the selection of its members, it began to accept the basic fact starting in 1924 that the Party could hardly survive without new members coming from the working-class community. Thus, the seamen's movement leader, Lin Weimin, was admitted to the Party in late 1924, and his close comrade Su Zhaozheng, whose early application to join the Party had been repeatedly denied, became a Communist a few months later. Simultaneously, the CCP Guangdong Regional Committee also recruited members from the local labor activists. For instance, Luo Dengxian, a Hong Kong mechanic whose father was a poor seaman, was encouraged by Yang Yin, a Guomindang member who also joined the CCP in early 1923, to disseminate political propaganda among the workers in Guangzhou in 1924. Luo then joined the CCP in 1925 and became an active labor organizer during the Shenggang General Strike.[152] Another example was Deng Fa, a Hong Kong seaman who came from a poor peasant family in Guangdong and was recruited by the CCP as a Party member after his participation in the Hong Kong Seamen's Strike of 1922. He later became a leading member in the Communist labor movement in south China in 1925–27.[153] In fact, many rank-and-file labor activists in Guangzhou during this period were locally recruited. Without them, the CCP would never have been able to organize such a massive urban movement so efficiently in south China during the mid-1920s, an important subject that will be analyzed in the next chapter.

In sum, the Communists made considerable achievements in appealing to the workers in Guangzhou soon after the United Front policy was formalized. By late 1924, they were influential in many industrial sectors in Guangzhou, ranging from arsenal and railway line workers to postal service workers and rickshaw coolies.[154] Their achievements were associated also

151. Cherepanov, *As Military Advisor in China*, p. 39.

152. Li Hongnuan and He Jinzhou, "Luo Dengxian," in *Zhongguo gongren yundong de xianqu* [The Pioneers of the Chinese Labor Movement] (Beijing: Gongren chubanshe, 1985), vol. 4, pp. 77–86.

153. *Nanyue yinlie chuan* [Biographies of Martyrs in South Guangdong] (Guangzhou: Guangdong renmin chubanshe, 1983), vol. 1, pp. 439–40.

154. "Zhonggong Guangdong quwei guanyu gongren yundong de baogao (Oct. 1925)" [Report on the Labor Movement by the CCP Guangdong Regional Committee], in *Guangdong geming lishi wenjian huiji*, pt. 1, vol. 6, pp. 45–80.

with their attempt to create a labor federation in Guangzhou as well as with the growth of antiforeign sentiment among the laboring people in that year.

On 6 May 1924, the Guangzhou Workers' Delegates Congress (Guangzhou gongren daibiao dahui) was held under the auspices of the local Communists, who intended to challenge the leading position of the conservative labor unions, headed by the Guangdong Mechanics' Union, by forming a pro-Communist labor federation. But the congress was disrupted by the Mechanics' Union and ended with fighting between the two labor factions. However, an able locally recruited Communist, Liu Ersong, was appointed chairman of its Executive Committee.[155] Under his leadership, the local Communists established contact with the Guangdong railway workers, who, in early 1925, played an influential role in the defense of the Guangdong government when it was attacked by the local anti-Sun warlords.[156] By the summer of 1926, the congress had 150,000 members. However, the success of the congress was due to the Communists' taking advantage of the United Front; many of them were leaders in the Guomindang's Departments of Workers and Peasants and intimidated every new union into joining the Workers' Delegates Congress.[157]

The politicization of the workers in Guangzhou was also stimulated by two major political events which occurred in the summer of 1924. The first one was the assassination of the governor-general of French Indochina, Martial Merlin, who was visiting Shamian, where the foreign consulates in Guangzhou were located, by a Vietnamese nationalist. After the assassin had sacrificed his life soon after the event, the Guangdong government staged a massive memorial service in his honor. Liao Zhongkai, the left-wing Guomindang leader, spoke emotionally at the memorial service about the harmful effects of foreign encroachment in China and praised the Vietnamese assassin as a revolutionary martyr. The body of the Vietnamese

155. *Nanyue yinlie chuan,* vol. 1, p. 30. Liu was a student studying in a local technical school when the May Fourth Incident took place. Like most of the Chinese students in 1919, he joined the anti-Japanese demonstration and later became a member of the Socialist Youth Corps in 1922. Afterward, he was associated with the Guangdong branch of the Communist organization and the Labor Secretariat and became a major leader during the heyday of the Communist labor movement in south China. For further details, see Luo Hequn and He Jinzho, *Liu Ersong* (Guangzhou: Guangdong renmin chubanshe, 1986).

156. Luo Daming et al., "Da geming shiqi Guangdong gongren yundong qingkuang de huiyi," pp. 226–27.

157. "Guangzhou gonghui yundong de baogao (summer 1926)" [Report on the Labor Movement in Guangzhou], in *Guangdong geming lishi wenjian huiji,* pt. 1, vol. 6, p. 345.

nationalist was then buried in Huanghua gang, which was the cemetery for the martyrs of the 1911 Revolution. The Chinese workers in Shamian were deeply touched and began to question some simple political realities such as the special privileges enjoyed by foreigners in China under the treaty port system.[158]

After the assassination, the French and British consuls in Guangzhou tightened their security. They imposed many restrictions and regulations with a view to controlling all Chinese entering or leaving Shamian. Most of these measures were in fact discriminatory against the local Chinese, who reacted with anger. The local Communist labor activists, with the support of the Guangdong government, immediately seized this opportunity by inducing the workers in Shamian to go on strike until the foreign consuls had withdrawn the newly imposed regulations. Influenced by the recent Vietnamese anticolonial event, the workers in Shamian collectively participated in the strike, which was successful.[159]

The second incident promoting the political consciousness of the Guangzhou workers was the coup staged by the local merchants in August 1924 to overthrow the local government, which they deemed radical and pro-Communist.[160] In response, the CCP Guangdong Regional Committee organized a Worker-Soldier Corps to help defend the local government.[161] The members of the corps, about 300 of them, were recruited from the supporters of the Guangzhou Workers' Delegates Congress, with the local Communist Liu Ersong as their leader. They took part in the actual fighting to suppress the merchants' coup in October.[162]

Consequently, by late 1924, the workers in Guangzhou were not only more politicized under the Guomindang-Communist anti-imperialist policy but also more militant. However, they remained basically pro-Guomindang. The Communists still encountered a serious problem in winning the support of the pro-Guomindang workers in Guangzhou. Further-

158. Liang Guozhi, "Guangzhou Shamian yangwu gongren de zuzhi ji bagong jingguo" [The Organization and Experience of the Workers Employed in Foreign Firms in Shamian, Guangzhou], in *Guangzhou da geming shiqi huiyilu xuanpian* [Selected Memoirs of the Great Revolutionary Period in Guangzhou] (Guangzhou: Guangdong renmin chubanshe, 1986), pp. 255–56.

159. Ibid., pp. 258–61.

160. Wilbur and How, eds., *Missionaries of the Revolution*, pp. 115–16.

161. Luo Hequn and He Jinzho, *Liu Ersong*, pp. 52–54.

162. Luo Daming et al., "Da geming shiqi Guangdong gongren yundong qingkuang de huiyi," pp. 222–25.

more, as admitted by the Communist labor activists, they also had to handle the problems arising from traditional guild mentality, conflicts between unions, and unrealistic demands from the workers.[163]

As for the situation in Hong Kong, both the Guomindang and the Communist Parties admitted that they faced great difficulty in recruiting members because the colonial government suppressed party activity. Nevertheless, unlike the Communists, the Guomindang had at least established some contact with workers in Hong Kong thanks to the efforts of early labor leaders like Ma Chaojun, Xie Yingbai, and Chen Bingsheng; about 16,000 Guomindang members were living in the colony by 1925.[164] The Communist influence was very weak. In fact, there were fewer than forty pro-Communist activists engaged in the labor movement among the mechanics, dockyard workers, and carpenters in 1924.[165]

But starting in 1924, the CCP Guangdong Regional Committee sent some of their recently recruited members to Hong Kong; some of whom were in fact dual-party members under the United Front. The work of Yang Yin can perhaps serve as the best illustration of the success of the Communist tactics in taking full advantage of the United Front. Yang had been a supporter of the 1911 Revolution and had remained loyal to Sun Yatsen ever since. But influenced by the socialist doctrine during the May Fourth period, he joined the CCP in early 1923. After the United Front policy was adopted, Yang continued his activities in the labor movement as a Guomindang member, but secretly he implemented the Communist policy.[166] In fact, a small group of Guangdong Communists promoted political propaganda among the Hong Kong workers during this period by identifying themselves as Guomindang members. Both Huang Ping, a Russian-language student who turned Communist and became a major leader in the labor movement in south China during the years 1924–27, and Liang Furan, a Hong Kong seaman who joined the CCP in late 1923, belonged in this category.[167] Thus, the Communists were able, through the United Front policy, to maintain a certain level of contact with the Hong Kong Chinese workers even though the political environment in the colony was

163. "Guangzhou gonghui yundong de baogao (summer 1926)," pp. 321–46.

164. *Zhongguo Guomindang dierci quanguo daibiao dahui huiyi jilu* [Minutes of the Second National Congress of the Guomindang] (Guangzhou, 1926), p. 49.

165. "Zhonggong Guangdong quwei guanyu gongren yundong de baogao (Oct. 1926)," p. 78.

166. *Nanyue yinlie chuan,* vol. 1, pp. 258–60.

167. "Huiyiliu," vol. 4, pp. 15–16.

unfavorable. They also enjoyed the benefit of the close social link between the workers in Hong Kong and those in south China. Therefore, although the number of Communists working in the labor movement in Hong Kong was small, their potential to mobilize the workers was by no means weak.

Seeds of Discontent

Beijing had been the main center of Chinese politics ever since the Qing dynasty was founded. But when the Qing Empire entered its last decade, south China, especially Guangzhou and Hong Kong, was used by the reformers and revolutionaries as the base from which to prepare their political activities. For instance, Kang Youwei established a school in 1891 in Guangzhou which later became an intellectual center promoting the abortive Hundred-Day Reform. Sun Yatsen's early revolutionary movement also started in Guangzhou, with the founding of the Chinese Restoration Society in 1894. Because of the close social and economic ties between Guangdong and Hong Kong, the governor of the colony, from the early twentieth century, was obliged to extend the scope of his responsibility to include the handling of affairs related to Chinese politics, even though such duties were normally managed by the British consul general in Guangzhou.[168] For this reason, a new department under a secretary for Chinese affairs was created within the Hong Kong colonial administration in 1913.[169]

Though the task of this department was to administer affairs relating to the local Chinese population, it also had the responsibility of reporting and advising on affairs in China, particularly concerning the southern provinces, to the Hong Kong governor, who would in turn consult either the British consul general in Guangzhou or the British minister in Beijing before taking any action.[170] From the turn of this century, the Hong Kong governor's management of Chinese affairs had generally been well received by Whitehall. For instance, British senior officials in London did not criticize Governor Blake's request that Li Hongzhang retain his post as governor-general of Guangdong and Guangxi, instead of assuming the post of viceroyalty of Zhili Province, in order to prevent Hong Kong from being

168. Before March 1857, the Hong Kong governor had dual duties: he was the chief official administrator of the colony as well as the chief British diplomatic representative in China.

169. Endacott, *History of Hong Kong,* pp. 270–71.

170. "Confidential Memorandum on Relations between Hong Kong and Canton, 26 Sept. 1922," enclosed in Jamieson to Alston, 28 Sept. 1922, F.O.228/3484.

attacked by Chinese rebels during the Boxer Uprising. A few years later, his policy in curbing Sun Yatsen's revolutionary activities in the colony also received general approval from the Foreign Office.[171] The major reason for the Foreign Office's approval of the Hong Kong government's handling of affairs relating to China was the close cooperation between the colonial government and the British consul general in Guangzhou.

However, the Hong Kong government became increasingly concerned with political developments in south China after the collapse of the Qing Empire. In the aftermath of the 1911 Revolution, the colonial administration was deeply worried about Guangdong's social and financial stability as a result of the growth of militia (*mintuan*) in south China, which could easily affect Hong Kong.[172] But during the first decade after the 1911 Revolution, local politics in south China were further complicated by a series of power struggles among the local warlords and by the establishment of Sun Yatsen's de facto government in Guangzhou in 1917 as a response to the dissolution of Parliament by the premier, Duan Qirui. Such complicated problems persisted in south China even after the First World War. In mid-1919, a new governor, Sir Reginald Edward Stubbs, arrived in Hong Kong. Largely due to his mishandling of the complicated political issues in south China, the seeds of confrontation between the Hong Kong Chinese community and the colonial administration were sown.

A graduate of Oxford University, Sir R. E. Stubbs entered the Colonial Office in 1900. Thirteen years later, he was appointed the colonial secretary in Ceylon, where he stayed until he was promoted to the governorship of Hong Kong in mid-1919.[173] But the British colony under his administration was basically a Chinese society, with more than 90 percent of its population originally from Guangdong. More important, they did not have much of an emotional attachment to the colony. In fact, they were generally more interested in Guangdong affairs than in events occurring in the colony. The Chinese secretary at the British legation recognized this and sent the following report to his senior:

We British in Hong Kong appear to have built a Great Wall between ourselves and the Chinese. We and they live in different worlds, mentally, politically and socially. For us, Hong Kong is a little bit of England; and for them, it is one of the gates of

171. Endacott, *History of Hong Kong,* pp. 271–73.

172. Chan Lau Kit-ching, *China, Britain, and Hong Kong, 1895–1945* (Hong Kong: Chinese University Press, 1990), p. 108.

173. *The Dominions Office and Colonial Office List: 1939* (London, 1939), p. 827.

China. Our newspapers discuss the Irish Question, the Genoa Conference, or mosquitoes at the Peak, and all but ignore the existence of China; during five days of April [in 1922], momentous for China, the only news from parts of the country other than Canton which appeared in our English press was a telegram saying that there was great congestion of passengers and mail at Shanghai owing to the railway line being interrupted between two stations which do not exist. The Chinese press of Hong Kong, on the other hand, writes of Chinese politics and affairs in the same manner as if its organs were published in China; almost as if the government of Hong Kong was just a temporary accident and as if its acts and decisions were too trivial to be mentioned in the same breath as those of a provincial satrap in China. The result of the chasm which thus separates the two races is that neither understand[s] the other; the result of this lack of understanding is a mutual dislike.[174]

But the reason for the discontented feeling among many local Chinese was also related to the governor's handling of Chinese affairs both locally and in Guangdong. Basically, Sir R. E. Stubbs was hostile toward the Guangdong government, which he considered to be a menace to British interests in south China. Such an attitude originated from the fact that China was a divided country in 1919.

After the death of Yuan Shikai, the first appointed president in China, in 1916, warlordism and provincialism were the dominant political problems threatening peace and stability in China. Beijing, the city recognized by the foreign powers as China's capital and legitimate authority, became the center of a power struggle among the Beiyang military leaders. However, Sun Yatsen and the members of the Chinese Revolutionary Party, later renamed the Nationalist Party (Guomindang), established their de facto government in Guangzhou in 1917. But Sun's government, which was formed with the support of a powerful local military leader, Chen Jiongming, was not recognized by any major power as China's legitimate authority. Thus, when Sun Yatsen was appointed the "Extraordinary President" of China in May 1921, the Hong Kong government prohibited any inauguration ceremonies in the colony to celebrate the event.[175] Besides, the Guangdong government was stigmatized by the British officials as a rebel government whose intention was to upset China's political stability. In early 1922, Governor Stubbs even referred to Sun Yatsen as the "head of a gang of thieves" during the Seamen's Strike, which was initiated for economic reasons; the Hong Kong Chinese seamen demanded a wage increase to meet the increase in the cost

174. Enclosure in Alston to Tyrell, 22 June 1922, F.O.371/8040 [F2805/2805/10].
175. Jamieson to Alston, 11 Mar. 1922, F.O.371/8030 [F1496/927/10].

of living in the postwar recession period.[176] The Hong Kong government also complained that the strike was a result of "pressure and intimidation" from the Guangdong government.[177] In fact, Sun Yatsen was not in Guangzhou when the seamen went on strike; he was in Guilin, setting plans to launch a military expedition to the north to reunify China. The handling of the strike by the Hong Kong government led to the growth of anti-British sentiment among the local Chinese.

The Hong Kong governor's failure to understand Chinese politics in Guangdong and his prejudice toward Sun Yatsen even met with criticism from James Jamieson, the British consul general in Guangzhou. Jamieson had thirty-five years of experience in China, including thirteen years, up to 1922, serving as consul general in Guangzhou, and was considered an "old China hand" by his senior colleagues in Beijing and London. He was critical of the governor's handling of Chinese affairs and referred to his ignorance of Chinese politics as "abysmal."[178] After the Seamen's Strike, it seemed that the consul general ran out of patience with the governor; he submitted a report to the British legation and complained:

In Hong Kong, there existed a large body of trained and efficient government servants, but these in the higher and more responsible positions were trained in China under the [Qing] Empire, and have little opportunity of absorbing the atmosphere of the Republic—more especially that of [south China]. . . . the Governor and the Colonial Secretary are entirely non-conversant with Chinese and thus entirely relied on their advisors.[179]

Consequently, tension between the Hong Kong government and the local Chinese community was mounting by the early 1920s because of mutual dislike and misunderstanding. Without doubt, the Hong Kong government was also increasingly concerned with Guangdong's political radicalization under the United Front policy since early 1924 because of the Guomindang leaders' emphasis on anti-imperialist ideology, which would certainly threaten British interests in China.

176. "Canton Intelligence Report: December Quarter 1922," enclosed in Jamieson to Clive, 26 Feb. 1923, F.O.228/3276.

177. "Report on the Seamen's Strike by Fletcher, 14 Mar. 1922," enclosed in Stubbs to Churchill, 18 Mar. 1922, F.O.405/236.

178. Jamieson to Alston, 13 Mar. 1922, F.O.228/3527.

179. Ibid.

Certain remarks may be made in concluding this chapter. In the first place, the development of modern labor unions in south China was not a direct product of rapid industrial change. Rather, it was closely connected with local politics. Thus, labor unions were not generally social organizations used by the working class to improve its economic condition or achieve political autonomy. Instead, labor unions were manipulated by politicians or revolutionaries for their own political purposes.

Second, although the trade union movement in south China was deeply influenced by local politics, the political consciousness of the majority of unionized workers was relatively backward. Traditional guild mentality, localism, and union factionalism remained major problems mediating against working-class unity. Nevertheless, the close social and economic ties between the Hong Kong Chinese workers and the people in Guangdong helped, to a certain extent, to overcome these obstacles. In this regard, the "politics of place," a concept used by Elizabeth J. Perry to analyze the politicization of Shanghai workers,[180] was relevant to the Chinese workers in Hong Kong and Guangdong. It is safe to say that the major reason the Hong Kong Chinese working people became involved in the momentous political event of 1925–26 was their emotional attachment to, and social relations with, Guangdong. Most of the Chinese in the colony did not fully understand the ideology of the Nationalist Revolution. However, the news of the killing of Chinese in Shamian on 21 June 1925 during a major anti-British demonstration (to be discussed in the next chapter) dramatically aroused Hong Kong workers to declare their support for the people in Guangzhou. To be sure, for the CCP to seize leadership from the Guomindang in the labor movement in south China and maintain collaboration between the Guangzhou and Hong Kong workers, the Communists had to manipulate this sentiment and transform it into political action. But how long could the workers' practical support continue when their personal economic interests were being sacrificed during a long strike? This was, in fact, one of the major problems confronting the Communists.

Third, due to the mishandling of Chinese politics in Guangdong by the Hong Kong colonial government in the early 1920s, a major political confrontation between the revolutionary forces in Guangzhou and British colonial policy in Hong Kong seemed inevitable. The revolutionaries, whether Guomindang or Communist, intended to demonstrate their commitment

180. Perry, *Shanghai on Strike*, p. 12.

to the anti-imperialist policy, while the hypercritical attitude of the Hong Kong governor toward the newly established Guangdong government dramatically increased tension between the local Chinese community and the colonial administration. Deng Zhongxia was quick to recognize the situation in late 1924; he even declared that the Communists would support Sun Yatsen wholeheartedly if Sun intended to settle all disputes with the British imperialists in Guangdong by military action.[181] Thus, the mutual dislike between the local Chinese and British in the colony later became a major reason for the outbreak of a massive anti-British strike and boycott by the Hong Kong workers.

Finally, although the Communists were latecomers to the task of mobilizing workers in south China, they were remarkably successful in appealing to them and organizing them during the general strike, to be discussed below. The main source of their success lay in their ability to build a new form of revolutionary alliance by unifying intellectuals and workers. The chief architect and executor of this leadership was a May Fourth student radical who had evolved into a Marxist labor movement organizer: Deng Zhongxia.

181. Deng Zhongxia, "Gongnongjun yu beifa" [Workers, Peasants, Soldiers, and the Northern Expedition], *Zhongguo gongren* 1 (1924), p. 3.

3

The Triumph of the Alliance between Workers and Marxist Intellectuals

T*HE OUTBREAK* of the Shenggang (Guangzhou–Hong Kong) General Strike on 19 June 1925 was not simply a spontaneous response to the May Thirtieth Incident in Shanghai. Rather, the strike was the result of a new labor strategy formulated by the Communists in early 1925 and took place because political conditions for launching a mass movement in south China were favorable.

Prelude to the Shenggang General Strike

In January 1925, the CCP Fourth Congress was held in Shanghai. Its main objective was to review the resolutions of the Comintern Fifth Congress, which called for, *inter alia*, the proletariat to seize leadership of the Chinese Nationalist Revolution.[1] On the basis of the Comintern resolutions, the Chinese Communists adopted a new policy which emphasized the independence of the labor movement under CCP leadership in the current stage of political struggle. Although the workers were engaged in a joint

1. Xiang Qing, *Gongchan guoji he Zhongguo geming quanxi de lishi gaishu* [General History of the Relations between the Comintern and the Chinese Revolution] (Guangzhou: Guangdong renmin chubanshe, 1983), pp. 49–50.

venture with the bourgeoisie in the anti-imperialist and anti-feudal political struggle, the Party reminded the workers that they should never forget their own class identity and their mission as proletarians.[2] With a view to coordinating the labor movement throughout the country, a new Labor Movement Committee (Zhigong yundong weiyuanhui) was established within the CCP central Party leadership; Zhang Guotao was appointed its committee commissioner and Deng Zhongxia became its secretary general.[3] Most important, the Party, for the first time since its foundation, formulated a policy to expand the recruitment of Party members from the progressive-minded workers and peasants. This recruitment policy was certainly due to the fact that the Communists had realized that they were too weak in terms of numbers to compete with the Guomindang in seizing the revolutionary leadership. Thus, the CCP admitted that the expansion of Party membership had become its "most important task."[4]

After the formation of the Labor Movement Committee in the CCP Fourth Congress, Deng Zhongxia was instructed by the Party to organize the Second National Labor Congress. According to a resolution adopted in the First National Labor Congress, the congress was to be convened by the Labor Secretariat. But the Communist-dominated Labor Secretariat had been criticized by many non-Communist unionists as being too radical. In order to rally support from all sides, the Communists decided to convene the Second National Labor Congress in the home base of the Nationalist Revolution, Guangzhou, under the auspices of four pro-Communist labor unions: the Chinese Seamen's Union, the All China Railway Union, the Hanyeping General Union, and the Guangzhou Workers' Delegates Congress.[5]

In spite of the large number of participants (about 281 delegates, representing a trade union membership of 540,000) attending the congress, which was held on May Day, the Communists were unable to enhance their influence among certain conservative-minded trade unions. For example, the Shanghai Federation, a conservative labor organization, denounced the congress as a "Bolshevik enterprise," and two powerful unions in south

2. "Duiyu zhigong yundong zhi jueyian" [Resolution on the Labor Movement], in *Zhonggong zhongyang wenjian xuanji*, vol. 1, pp. 342–49.

3. Ibid., p. 356; Jiang Ping, *Deng Zhongxia de yisheng*, p. 114.

4. "Duiyu zuzhi wenti zhi yijuean" [Resolution on the Question of Organization], in *Zhonggong zhongyang wenjian xuanji*, vol. 1, pp. 379–80.

5. *Zhongguo gonghui lici daibiao dahui wenxian* [Documents of the Various Chinese Labor Congresses] (Beijing: Gongren chubanshe, 1984), vol. 1, pp. 13–14.

China, the Guangdong Mechanics' Union and the Hong Kong Federation of Labor, refused to become members of the congress.[6] This weakness sowed the seeds of further conflicts between the two major union factions in the following months, an issue of significance to the history of the labor movement that will be analyzed in the next chapter.

Nevertheless, the Communists, through this congress, launched a very successful movement by establishing the All China Labor Federation (ACLF; Zhonghua quanguo zong gonghui) under their leadership. Soon after its formation, the ACLF voted for affiliation with the Red International. Among the twenty-five executive members of the ACLF were the well-known Seamen's Union leaders Deng Pei, Su Zhaozheng, and Lin Weimin; the labor leader of the Anyuan miners, Liu Shaoqi, was also elected.[7] However, it was Deng Zhongxia who became the driving force of the ACLF; he was appointed its secretary and took charge of the Propaganda Department. He was also appointed as the CCP Central Committee's designated secretary to the ACLF.[8] The Second National Labor Congress adjourned with the adoption of several resolutions which clearly revealed the powerful Communist influence in the labor movement.

As discussed in the previous chapter, the new Communist strategy regarding the role of workers in the Nationalist Revolution was first spelled out by Deng Zhongxia on the eve of the Second National Labor Congress. A close examination of his writings of the time and the congress's resolutions reveals that the congress agreed with him on all key issues. In brief, both Deng and the congress concluded that the most important task, in terms of trade union development, was the establishment of modern industrial- and trade-based labor unions with a view to eliminating localism and the traditional guild system, and that these unions should be developed on the principle of democratic centralism. They also believed that the economic issues in the labor movement could not be separated from the political ones and, therefore, urged workers to launch economic and political struggles concurrently. As for the role of the working class in the Nationalist Revolution, both shared the view that the working class should maintain its class identity in the course of revolutionary struggle. Deng observed that "the proletariat's participation in the Nationalist Revolution is for the interest of its own class; its participation should not be affiliated with that of the bourgeoisie," while the congress resolved that "as various social classes par-

6. Chesneaux, *Chinese Labor Movement*, pp. 258–59.
7. *Zhongguo gonghui lici daibiao dahui wenxian*, vol. 1, p. 37.
8. Jiang Ping, *Deng Zhongxia de yisheng*, pp. 119–20.

ticipate in the Nationalist Revolution, the proletariat . . . should not mix with other classes [during its participation]; any commingling would lead to the danger of negating its own class interest and being betrayed by the bourgeoisie."[9] The bourgeoisie, both agreed, was unreliable as a revolutionary partner. The success of the Nationalist Revolution could only rest on a revolutionary alliance between peasants and workers under the banner of proletarian hegemony. In keeping with the Comintern line, the significance of internationalism was also spelled out in both documents.[10] The congress therefore gave a mandate to Communist labor activists to intensify the mobilization of the labor movement as a means of achieving their political goals. In fact, a member of the British consulate staff in Shanghai, John Pratt, observed this development as early as two months before the congress was held. Pratt predicted that the Communists would soon use the general strike as a political weapon.[11]

Deng Zhongxia should be credited with shaping a new labor movement strategy in early 1925 with his theoretical writings, which no doubt reflected his political experience in leading the workers. To be sure, his ideas were also partially influenced by Comintern directives. However, the growth of antiforeign sentiment, germinated in Guangzhou under the influence of the Guomindang's anti-imperialist ideology, prepared the ground for the outbreak of a general strike.

The death of Sun Yatsen on 12 March 1925 in Beijing provided an occasion for the Guomindang and CCP members to implement a successful anti-imperialist propaganda campaign. In Guangzhou and Hong Kong, numerous memorial services were held by various social organizations. In fact, the CCP Central Committee, although located in Shanghai, was quick to see the profound emotional impact of Sun's death on the southerners. It issued a special circular in which it instructed the Communists to lead this propaganda campaign in every memorial service. The Central Committee expected the Communists to strengthen the Guomindang leftists and recruit more CCP members through this campaign.[12] Although it is unclear

9. Deng Zhongxia, "Laodong yundong fuxingqi zhong de jige zhuyao wenti," p. 51; "Dierci quanguo laodong dahui jueyian" [Resolutions of the Second National Labor Congress], in *Liuda yiqian,* p. 276.

10. The comparison is based on Deng Zhongxia, "Laodong yundong fuxingqi zhong de jige zhuyao wenti," pp. 38–57; and "Dierci quanguo laodong dahui jueyian," pp. 275–81. For a general interpretation of this congress, see Chesneaux, *Chinese Labor Movement,* pp. 258–61.

11. Pratt to Macleay, 4 Mar. 1925, F.O.228/3529.

12. "Zhongyang tonggao de shijiu hao" [Central Circular no. 19], *Zhonggong zhongyang wenjian xuanji,* vol. 1, p. 404.

whether the Communists were able to increase Party membership during this period, the movement created a major wave of anti-British sentiment among Chinese working people in Hong Kong.

The Hong Kong trade unionists had a tradition of being pro-Guomindang; many were also admirers of Sun Yatsen. To them, Sun's death meant the loss of the founder of Republican China. Soon after the news of his death arrived in the colony, many trade unions organized memorial services to pay tribute to their national hero. The proposal by the pro-Communist labor activists to read out Sun's political bequest, which emphasized the need to accomplish the Nationalist Revolution, in every memorial service was widely accepted. But the services were prohibited because the Hong Kong Police claimed that such events were in fact political gatherings; they disbanded the memorial services that convened and arrested three Communist agitators. This suppression immediately led to a major outcry from the Chinese community. Seeing the strong reaction from the local Chinese, the Hong Kong authorities released the three in their custody and withdrew their previous decision of forbidding the memorial services after they had reached an agreement with the workers' representative, the seamen leader Su Zhaozheng.[13] Although the problem was solved, anti-British sentiment among the Hong Kong Chinese was much enhanced by these events.

Though the Communists still found it difficult to appeal to workers in Guangzhou owing to the pro-Guomindang political traditions of that city, the Second National Labor Congress held in Guangzhou in May 1925 somewhat enhanced Communist influence among workers. In fact, because of the mass demonstration held on May Day and the radical resolutions adopted by the congress, Guangzhou had become, according to the local Communists, the "Second Moscow."[14] In this atmosphere a massive political movement might be triggered at any moment. In the event, the May Thirtieth Incident offered a golden opportunity to the revolutionaries in Guangzhou.

Preparation and Outburst

On 30 May 1925, the British-commanded police in the Shanghai International Settlement opened fire on a group of demonstrators protesting the

13. "Huiyiliu," vol. 4, no. 6, p. 16.
14. Yi Long, "Jin nian wuyi Guangzhou zhi liang dai chengju" [The Two Outstanding Events in Guangzhou during This Year's May Day], *Xiangdao zhoubao,* 10 May 1925.

killing of a Chinese worker employed in a Japanese-owned cotton mill. Because of this incident, the general antiforeign sentiment among many Chinese shifted to focus on the British alone. Both in Guangzhou and in Hong Kong, the May Thirtieth Incident intensified anti-British feeling among the Chinese, which was in any case deep-rooted among many southerners owing to the Hong Kong government's hostile policies toward Sun Yatsen. The Chinese revolutionaries in south China therefore decided to utilize this incident in promoting their political cause.

Because of his responsibilities in the ACLF, Deng Zhongxia was staying in Guangzhou when the May Thirtieth Incident occurred.[15] Due to the favorable political conditions for launching a labor movement in Guangzhou, the ACLF had decided to base its headquarters, not in Shanghai, which was the most industrialized city and where the CCP Central Committee was located, but in this southern city. In May 1925, the ACLF had a plan to intensify its propaganda under Deng's leadership. One part of its program was to publish a workers newspaper, *Gongren zhi lu* (The Road of Workers), under his editorship. Even as he was working on the publication of its first issue, Deng was instructed by the Central Committee to prepare for a major general strike in Guangzhou and Hong Kong in support of the anti-British movement in the wake of the May Thirtieth Incident in Shanghai.[16]

The news of the May Thirtieth Incident was certainly ill received by the Chinese community in Hong Kong. But in view of the political suppression in the colony, there was no indication among the Hong Kong Chinese that a general strike would soon be launched.[17] In fact, a Hong Kong school inspector who was also a Chinese Socialist Youth Corps member, Lin Changzhi, was deported from the colony and lost his job after he published an article denouncing the Shanghai incident in a local Chinese newspaper.[18]

15. Jiang Ping and Li Liangyu, "Deng Zhongxia tongzhi guanghui de yisheng," p. 200.

16. *Gongren zhi lu,* 1 July 1925. Before Deng abandoned the publication of *Gongren zhi lu* temporarily, he had already written two articles for its first issue. These short articles have been unearthed by Chinese scholars, and they can be found in *Deng Zhongxia wenji,* pp. 140–48. In brief, he reemphasized the need for the working class to participate in the Nationalist Revolution.

17. Huang Ping, "Guanyu Shenggang da bagong de huiyi ziliao" [Memoirs of the Guangzhou-Hong Kong General Strike] (Guangzhou, 1963), p. 49. Huang was a CCP delegate to Hong Kong in early 1925. He was a major leader throughout the general strike. This oral history material was based on a series of interviews with Huang in 1957 and was circulated internally.

18. To be sure, Lin carried out his Communist activities secretly in Hong Kong. After he

In Guangzhou, the local Communists also did not expect that they would be able to organize a massive general strike, because Guangzhou was then under the threat of attack from the Yunnan military faction.

The CCP Guangdong Regional Committee received a telegram from the Central Committee on 1 June that instructed them to stage a massive demonstration as a response to the Shanghai incident. Only about 2,000 people participated in this Communist-organized demonstration on the next day.[19] On 6 June, the Yunnan army launched its attack on Guangzhou; many local Communists joined in the defense of the city. Also on this date the CCP Central Committee issued its protest against the killing that took place on 30 May in its organ *Xiangdao zhoubao* (The Guide Weekly).[20] It was impossible at this stage, however, to organize any popular protest movement in Guangzhou because of the outbreak of the local war. Deng Zhongxia left Guangzhou for Hong Kong on 8 June. Before his arrival in Hong Kong, he was not optimistic about winning the support of the Hong Kong workers for a general strike in the colony.[21]

When Deng went to Hong Kong on 8 June, he was accompanied by Yang Baoan, a Guangdong Communist who also occupied a post in the Guomindang. In Hong Kong, Deng and Yang were received by other Guangdong Communists who had been able to infiltrate the Hong Kong working-class community. Among them were Su Zhaozheng, Yang Yin, and Huang Ping.[22]

---

was deported, he went back to Guangzhou and played a leading part in the political propaganda movement among the strikers. See "Lishi ziliao huibian," vol. 1, no. 1, p. 25.

19. "Zhonggang Guangdong quwei guanyu Shenggang da bagong de baogao (July 1925)" [CCP Guangdong Regional Committee's Report on the Guangzhou-Hong Kong General Strike], in *Guangdong geming lishi wenjian huiji*, pt. 1, vol. 6, p. 25.

20. On 5 June, the Guomindang sent a telegram addressed to the whole nation urging people to participate in the anti-imperialist movement; see "Canton Events and Rumours, 5 June 1925" (unpublished documents of the Canton Customs Services); Chinese translation in Guangdong zhexue shehui kexueyuan, ed., *Shenggang da bagong ziliao* [Historical Materials on the Guangzhou-Hong Kong General Strike] (Guangzhou: Guangdong renmin chubanshe, 1980), p. 822.

21. "Zhonggang Guangdong quwei guanyu Shenggang da bagong de baogao (July 1925)," p. 26. Correspondence from company archival material also reveals that Deng and his colleagues arrived in Hong Kong on 8 June; see Company Correspondence, Hong Kong to London, 9 June 1925, Papers of John Swire and Sons Ltd., box 40.

22. Lu Qi, "Ji zai Shenggang da bagong zhong de Deng Zhongxia tongzhi" [Memories of Comrade Deng Zhongxia in the Guangzhou-Hong Kong General Strike], *Guangdong wenshi ziliao* 29 (1980), p. 63. Lu's writing is very informative because he has based his work on the personal papers and account given by Guo Shouzhen, who worked in Deng Zhongxia's office throughout the course of the strike.

Perhaps with the exception of Huang Ping, who was relatively inexperienced, these Communists were highly respected by the Hong Kong workers.

Hong Kong trade unionists were impressed by Deng Zhongxia's role in leading the two National Labor Congresses in Guangzhou in 1922 and 1925. His official title as the secretary of ACLF further enhanced his reputation among many workers even though some conservative Hong Kong unions had not joined the ACLF. Su was known by many Hong Kong workers, particularly seamen and dockyard coolies, for the part he had played in the Seamen's Strike in 1922. The two Yangs were active labor organizers in Guangzhou. Most important, although they had joined the CCP, they identified themselves, while working in Hong Kong, as Guomindang members and faithful followers of Sun Yatsen.[23] Su and the two Yangs also came from the county in Guangdong where Sun Yatsen was born, Xiangshan. Their connection to Sun and their regional tie with the majority of Hong Kong Chinese workers, who were born in Guangdong, had helped them win the trust of the workers in the colony. The Guangdong Communists were quick to manipulate the workers' fidelity, especially of those born in Guangdong. For instance, Chen Richang, a native of Baoan, was instructed by the CCP Guangdong Regional Committee to work exclusively among the Hong Kong seamen and fish-market workers because many of these people were also natives of Baoan.[24] Another example was Liu Ersong, whose successful agitation among the workers of the peanut-oil-refining industry in mid-1924 owed much to the origins of many of these workers in the same county, Dongjiang, where Liu was born.[25] Deng now looked to use these regional ties of the Guangdong organizers to overcome any perception that they were outsiders.

According to Deng's personal account, there were two meetings between the representatives of the ACLF, which he headed, and the Hong Kong labor union leaders to discuss detailed plans for a general strike in the colony.[26] The first meeting took place on the evening of Deng's arrival in Hong Kong. About seventy labor unions were represented at the meet-

23. Ibid., pp. 62–63; see also Chen Zhiwen, "Da geming shiqi de Guangzhou gongren yundong" [The Guangzhou Labor Movement during the Period of Great Revolution], *Guangzhou wenshi ziliao* 21 (1980), p. 12. Chen was an active member in the strike and served as an interpreter for those strike leaders who could speak only northern dialect.

24. "Huiyiliu ziliao," vol. 1, p. 87.

25. Ibid., vol. 2, p. 12.

26. Deng Zhongxia, *Shenggang bagong gaiguan* [A General Account of the Guangzhou-Hong Kong Strike] (Guangzhou, 1926), p. 5.

ing, which resolved that if the Shanghai trouble was not settled within a week, Guangzhou and Hong Kong would go on strike.[27] The meeting also resolved to draft a manifesto and to establish a Provisional Strike Committee.[28] Some representatives from Hong Kong labor unions, however, were afraid that there would be inadequate material support during the course of a general strike. Deng therefore returned to Guangzhou on about 11 June to seek advice from the CCP Guangdong Regional Committee, which was headed by Chen Yannian, the eldest son of Chen Duxiu.[29]

When Deng returned to Guangzhou, the political situation had become more stable because the Guomindang was confident that it could defeat the Yunnan military faction within a few days. The CCP Provisional Guangdong Regional Executive Committee, composed of Chen Yannian, Zhou Enlai, Tan Pingshan, Luo Yinong, and Michael Borodin,[30] after receiving Deng's report on the situation in Hong Kong, decided that a general strike should be staged as soon as the local warfare was over. It then instructed Deng Zhongxia, Su Zhaozheng, Huang Ping, Yang Yin, and Yang Baoan to head the preparations for and lead the general strike. Meanwhile, Borodin approached Liao Zhongkai for financial assistance in anticipation of the strike.[31] Liao, as a left-wing Guomindang leader and a supporter of the labor movement, granted Borodin's request without any hesitation.[32]

27. Company Correspondence, Hong Kong to London, 9 June 1925, Papers of John Swire and Sons Ltd., box 40.

28. Deng Zhongxia, *Shenggang bagong gaiguan*, p. 5.

29. Chen Yannian was two years younger than Deng Zhongxia. Like many of the radical intellectuals of the May Fourth period, Chen converted to Marxism after he had been influenced by anarchism. He joined the CCP while studying in France in 1922. In March 1923 he was sent to study in Moscow by the Party and returned to China about one and a half years later. In October 1924, he was assigned to lead the newly established CCP Guangdong Regional Committee. He played a major role in leading the Guangdong Communists during the First United Front period. But his revolutionary career was brief due to his arrest by the Guomindang in Shanghai in June 1927. One month later, he was executed. See Zhonggong Guangzhou shiwei dangshi yanjiushi, ed., *Guangzhou yinlie chuan* [Biographies of Martyrs in Guangzhou] (Guangzhou: Guangdong renmin chubanshe, 1991), pp. 120–25.

30. This provisional executive committee was formed in early May 1925 as a result of the upsurge of the political movement in south China. Its members were appointed by the CCP Central Committee, which also authorized it to make important and urgent decisions on behalf of the central leadership. See Li Zhiye and Ye Wenyi, "Guangdong dangtuan huodong jiyao, 1920–1927" [Chronology of the Guangdong Regional Committee's Activities], in *Guangdong dangshi ziliao*, vol. 6, p. 206.

31. "Zhonggong Guangdong quwei guanyu Shenggang da bagong de baogao (July 1925)," pp. 26–29.

32. Lu Qi, "Ji zai Shenggang da bagong zhong de Deng Zhongxia tongzhi," p. 66. The

Armed with the mandate from the Provisional Guangdong Regional Executive Committee and the Guomindang's financial support, Deng returned to Hong Kong on 13 June. Also on this day, the Guomindang defeated the Yunnan military faction, and the CCP Guangdong Regional Committee and the ACLF simultaneously published their statements: the Guangdong Communists called for an intensification of the revolutionary movement in Guangdong, and the ACLF announced its decision to form a committee to organize a general strike in Hong Kong and Guangzhou.[33] Soon after his arrival in the colony, Deng entered into the second round of negotiations with the Hong Kong labor unions' representatives.

The negotiations were not without difficulty, because some labor leaders in the colony were conservative. Thanks to the work of Su Zhaozheng, Yang Yin, and Yang Baoan, these conservative labor leaders finally agreed to support the strike on the condition that they would be appointed leading members of the Strike Committee.[34] Su Zhaozheng was able to rally the support of the seamen, transportation workers, and dockyard coolies. Yang Baoan appealed to the mechanics because of his association with their counterparts in Guangzhou. Yang Yin perhaps played the most influential role in winning the support of the Hong Kong Chinese workers. He appealed to the patriotism of the unions that had close connections with local secret societies, claiming that even members of secret societies had an important role in the defense of their nation at a time of political crisis. His appeal was so successful that many leading participants of the strike later recalled that, without Yang Yin, it would have been impossible for Deng Zhongxia and his close comrades to launch the general strike.[35]

Stirring up the nationalistic sentiments of the Hong Kong workers was

British Naval Intelligence Service informed the British government that the Guomindang, as soon as their battle with the Yunnan faction was over on 13 June, utilized the news of the May Thirtieth Incident as propaganda to win popularity for themselves; see "Memorandum Respecting Canton, 3 Feb. 1926," F.O.228/3153.

33. "Zhongguo gongchandang Guangdong zhixing weiyuanhui duiyu Guangdong shihu xuanyan (13 June 1925)" [The CCP Guangdong Executive Committee's Declaration on the Guangdong Situation]; and "Zhonghua quanguo zonggonghui zuzhi Shenggang bagong weiyuanhui qushi, 13 June 1925" [The All China Labor Federation's Announcement for the Organizing of the Guangzhou-Hong Kong Strike Committee], in Zhonggong zhongyang dangxiao dangshi jiaoyanshi, ed., Zhonggong dangshi cankao ziliao [Reference Materials on CCP Party History] (Beijing: Renmin chubanshe, 1979), vol. 2, pp. 153–57.

34. Lu Qi, "Ji zai Shenggang da bagong zhong de Deng Zhongxia tongzhi," p. 67; and Deng Zhongxia, Jianshi, pp. 223–24.

35. "Lishi ziliao huibian," vol. 1, no. 1, p. 22; see also "Huiyiliu ziliao," vol. 1, pp. 6–7.

the most effective way to mobilize them, and this is what Deng Zhong-xia and his comrades did. All political handbills distributed to the Chinese population in the colony were issued under the name of "A Patriot" (*aiguo renshi*).[36] On 18 June, the ACLF issued an open letter to the Hong Kong labor unions appealing to them to go on strike immediately.[37] At noon on the same day, the local pro-Communist labor activists swiftly distributed their handbills to the Hong Kong Chinese. Although the labor activists were under threat of arrest for distributing political messages, many local Chinese on that day received handbills calling for a general strike in support of the Shanghai victims.[38]

In Guangzhou, the CCP Guangdong Regional Committee formed an ad hoc committee to make the final preparations. With the exception of Chen Yannian, who was the secretary of the CCP Guangdong Regional Committee and a native of Anhui, all the members of this ad hoc committee were active labor leaders and Guangdong natives; they were Liu Ersong, Feng Jupo, Li Sen, Lin Weimin, and Shi Bu.[39] With the approval of the Guomindang, they mobilized local workers and confiscated many gambling houses, brothels, temples, and clan association meeting places in the heart of Guangzhou. They converted these premises into hostels and dining halls for the Hong Kong workers who would be returning to Guangzhou after the outbreak of the general strike in the colony.[40] By 18 June, arrangements for the general strike had been completed.

It was also on 18 June that the students of a Hong Kong government school took the first step in reacting to the Communists' appeal for a general strike. On that day, about 80 percent of the students studying

36. Guangdong renmin chubanshe, ed., *Nutao: Shenggang da bagong huiyi lu* [Furious Billows: Memoirs of the Guangzhou-Hong Kong General Strike] (Guangzhou: Guangdong renmin chubanshe, 1960), pp. 4–5. Inducing workers to go on strike by issuing handbills under the name of "A Patriot" or under the name of certain patriotic associations was a tactic of both the Communists and the Guomindang. In Xianmen, handbills issued under the name of "The Branch of the Chinese Patriots Association" were circulated among the Chinese workers of John Swire and Sons; see enclosure, Company Correspondence, Shanghai to London, 23 June 1925, Papers of John Swire and Sons Ltd., box 40.

37. "Zhonghua quanguo zonggonghui wei 'wusa' canan zhi Xianggang ge gongtuan de xin, 18 June 1925" [Letter from the All China Labor Federation to the Hong Kong Trade Unions on the May Thirtieth Tragic Case], in *Zhonggong dangshi cankao ziliao*, vol. 2, p. 15.

38. "Lishi ziliao huibian," vol. 1, no. l, p. 18.

39. "Zhonggong Guangdong quwei guanyu Shenggang da bagong de baogao (July 1925)," p. 30.

40. "Lishi ziliao huibian," vol. 1, no. 3, p. 2.

at Queen's College, a prestigious government secondary school, went on strike.[41] They were followed the next day by coolie cargo carriers. One after another, members of pro-Communist unions — the Hong Kong Tramway Company's drivers and conductors, seamen, typesetters — went on strike. When the news of the Hong Kong strike reached Guangzhou on the morning of 20 June, all the Chinese workers in Shamian (a district of the city), a total of 2,000, immediately walked out and joined the Hong Kong strikers.[42]

The general strike in Hong Kong was not widespread in its early stages, because some conservative trade unionists delayed their action.[43] The Hong Kong governor, Sir R. E. Stubbs, claimed confidently that "there is at present no sign of any anti-foreign sentiment" and that he could control any situation in the colony that might be caused by the strike.[44] The Shaji Incident was to change this situation, leading to a major outburst of anti-foreign sentiment in the colony.

A resolution had been adopted by the ACLF Executive Committee on 22 June calling for a protest march in support of the Hong Kong strike on the following day. As the march was in progress along Shaji, the embankment opposite Shamian, with members of various labor unions, merchant guilds and student unions and student-cadets of the Huangpu Military Academy participating, the British and French soldiers opened fire from Shamian: 52 demonstrators were killed and 117 wounded.[45] It is still unclear who opened fire first; each side accused the other.[46] But official publications reveal that the British were well prepared for such an event and had strengthened their fortifications by putting in place two Lewis gun detachments prior to the march.[47]

The British action in strengthening their armed forces may be justified by the fact that the consul general, James Jamieson, had received an intel-

41. *Times* (London), 19 June 1925.

42. "Extract from the Hong Kong Monthly Intelligence Summary, no. 7, 1925," enclosed in "Memorandum Respecting Canton, 3 Feb. 1926," F.O.228/3153. See also "Zhonggong Guangdong quwei guanyu Shenngang da bagong de baogao (July 1925)," pp. 27–28, 30–31.

43. Deng Zhongxia, *Jianshi*, p. 224.

44. Stubbs to Amery, 26 June 1925, enclosed in C.O. to F.O., 5 Aug. 1925, F.O.405/248 [F2668/194/10].

45. Qian Yizhang, *Shaji tongshi* [Painful History of Shaji] (Guangzhou, 1925), pp. 22, 25.

46. Jean Chesneaux's research, however, shows that it was "the British and French sentries in Shameen that opened fire [first]"; see Chesneaux, *Chinese Labor Movement*, p. 291.

47. Commander Scott to Commodore, Hong Kong, 24 June 1925, in United Kingdom, Parliament, *Papers Respecting the First Firing in the Shameen Affair of June 23, 1925,* Cmd.2636 (1926), p. 4 (hereafter cited as *First Firing*, Cmd.2636).

ligence report on 22 June stating that "the student element intend to make martyrs of themselves by attacking the bridge leading to Shameen [Shamian]."[48] Having received this report, Jamieson informed Wu Chaoshu, the foreign minister of the Guangdong government, and warned that "any attempt to penetrate to the British concession on Shameen will be resisted by force of arms."[49] However, it is very difficult to defend the British action in the incident because of the high number of casualties, and the assertion by the British that "very little firing really took place on our side"[50] can hardly be accepted. Furthermore, the British should be criticized for overreacting to the protest: the British commander in the field, writing a week after the event, admitted that he was not sure if "[the Chinese] attack was meant seriously or merely to create an incident."[51] This incident, whether or not intentionally precipitated by the Chinese revolutionaries, brought forth a wave of sympathetic strikes in Hong Kong.

Having heard the news of the killing in Shaji, many Chinese started leaving the colony for Guangzhou or for their native villages. By the middle of July, some 250,000 Chinese, about 45 percent of the Chinese population in the colony, had left for Guangdong. About 50,000 workers returned to the colony for financial or personal reasons after about four months,[52] and the numbers increased as the strikers encountered financial difficulties as the course of this political action was prolonged. However, at least 50,000–60,000 workers remained in Guangzhou, and an unknown number of strikers stayed with their families in their native villages, throughout the sixteen months of strike and boycott.[53] In Guangzhou, some Hong Kong strikers stayed with their friends or families, and others, about 30,000 of them, stayed in the reception centers organized by the Strike Committee.[54] The large number of strikers who came to Guangzhou offered a golden opportunity to the Communists to test their ability to transform the patriotic workers into revolutionaries by means of mobilization and propaganda techniques.

48. Sir J. Jamieson to Mr. Wu, 22 June 1925, in ibid., p. 2.

49. Ibid.

50. Commander Scott to Commodore, Hong Kong, 24 June 1925, in ibid., p. 5.

51. Ibid., p. 7.

52. Enclosure, Stubbs to Amery, 24 Oct. 1925, C.O.882/11.

53. Deng Zhongxia, *Shenggang bagong gaiguan*, p. 78.

54. *Gongren zhi lu*, 23 Oct. 1925. Apart from the articles written by Deng Zhongxia, information cited from *Gongren zhi lu* will be identified only by its date of publication.

Leadership

Prior to a discussion of the strike organization and labor mobilization during the Shenggang General Strike, it is essential to clarify several important issues: Who were the leaders in the preparation for the outbreak of the strike? What was the relationship between the Strike Committee and the CCP leadership? Who was the chief architect of this massive movement?

The strike was prepared by Communist labor movement leaders who held dual Guomindang-CCP memberships and who had obtained official recognition for their activities in the labor movement during the period of Guomindang Party reorganization. All the members (except Chen Yannian) of the ad hoc committee in Guangzhou formed on the eve of the strike by the CCP Guangdong Regional Committee belonged to this category. The Communists responsible for agitating the Hong Kong workers to declare a general strike were also dual-party members. Deng Zhongxia was a member of the Guomindang Executive Committee in Shanghai, in charge of the labor movement in that city from early 1924 to April 1925, when he was sent by the CCP Central Committee to Guangzhou.[55] Two of his companions and close comrades during his two visits to Hong Kong for negotiations with the local trade unionists in mid-June, Yang Baoan and Yang Yin, were appointed members of the Guomindang Regional Committee in late 1923.[56] Of the other important strike planners, Tan Pingshan was appointed head of the Party Organizational Department of the Guomindang in January 1925, and Lin Weimin was a veteran Guomindang member before joining the CCP in late 1924.[57]

Of the five-man planning team designated by the CCP Guangdong Regional Committee and the ad hoc committee in Guangzhou, only two were not natives of Guangdong. Five out of these ten planners were intellectuals in class origin and the other five were workers. At least seven were Guomindang members prior to joining the CCP. Most important, all but one had experience in leading the labor movement in south China. Thus, many of the members of these two planning teams could make full use of their Guomindang connections and regional ties to induce workers to support their

55. Jiang Ping, *Deng Zhongxia de yisheng,* p. 98.

56. Zhonggong dangshi renwu yangjiuhui, ed., *Zhonggong dangshi renwu chuan* [Biographies of the Chinese Communists] (Xian: Shaanxi renmin chubanshe, 1982), vol. 4, p. 214, and vol. 8, p. 177.

57. Cai Luo and Yuan Bangjian, "Guanyu diyici guonei geming zhanzheng shiqi zhonggong Guangdong quwei de jige wenti," p. 6.

appeal. The five of working-class origin played a vital role in helping their comrades of intellectual background to overcome the workers' suspicion. For instance, without the help of Su Zhaozheng, it would not have been easy for Deng Zhongxia to win the trust of the Hong Kong workers, especially because Deng was referred to by some Hong Kong and Guangdong conservative trade unionists as a "buddy from the other province" (*waijiang lao*).[58]

It is generally recognized that the strike, from its planning stage to its end, was approved by the Guomindang and was materially supported by it. As soon as the workers went on strike on 19 June in Hong Kong, the ACLF, through a financial source from the CCP, immediately contributed $20,000 to the provisional strike organization, the Guomindang donated $10,000, and the Guangdong merchants contributed $20,000. Xu Chongzhi, a local military leader and supporter of the Nationalist Revolution, contributed $5,000 to the strikers.[59] Although the Guomindang continued to provide financial support to the strike, it did not take an active part in leading the movement. In fact, some of its party leaders opposed labor radicalism during the strike.

Although the strike was led by the Communists, the CCP Central Committee seemed to have little direct responsibility, perhaps due to the political developments in Shanghai after the May Thirtieth Incident. Few directives relating to strike policy were issued by the CCP Central Committee to the Guangdong Regional Committee. The center of gravity of the Communist leadership during the strike was the Provisional Guangdong Regional Executive Committee, headed by Chen Yannian. It was through him and Borodin that they worked closely with Deng Zhongxia and Su Zhaozheng in formulating different tactics throughout the course of the strike.

Although Deng was neither a member of the Guangdong Regional Committee nor a member of its Provisional Executive Committee, he was the most influential person within the group of strike leaders. Deng was the CCP's designated secretary to the ACLF and could fully represent the CCP Central Committee on issues relating to the labor movement. However, as recalled by the strikers, he did not identify himself as a person coming from the Central Committee either in public or in secret meetings. Instead, he was known by the workers and strikers as a leader of the ACLF.

The headquarters of the ACLF was located, until October 1925, in

58. "Lishi ziliao huibian," vol. 1, no. 27, p. 1.
59. "Zhonggong Guangdong quwei guanyu Shenggang da bagong de baogao (July 1925), pp. 33–34.

the building of the Guomindang's Central Executive Committee office.[60] Though the ACLF was Communist oriented, its location in Guangzhou during the period of revolutionary upheaval created a major problem of communication with the CCP Central Committee in Shanghai. During the course of the strike, the Central Committee had great difficulty in obtaining firsthand and reliable information from their comrades in Guangzhou and had to rely on the news released by the foreign press, mostly hostile to the political developments in Guangzhou, to keep themselves informed about the situation in south China.[61] In short, there was a lack of communication between the CCP Central Committee and its Guangdong Regional Committee. Most important, it is highly possible that the Guangdong Communists were running a revolution without the full approval of their Central Committee and that the Central Committee gave little attention to what was going on in south China.[62]

Partly because of this problem, but also because the Soviet advisors regarded Guangzhou as a revolutionary base, Borodin suggested, in early 1925, moving the Central Committee from Shanghai to Guangzhou.[63] Though his suggestion was rejected by the Chinese Communist leaders, the influence of Borodin and other Soviet advisors on the Guangdong Communists was profound. Some historians even claim that the Guangdong Regional Committee "unfailingly followed [Borodin's] instructions, which were often at variance with those received from party Central Committee headquarters in Shanghai."[64] A Chinese Communist leader who later defected from the Party complained that Borodin ruled over the CCP Guangdong Regional Committee.[65] However, such an interpretation of the relationship between Borodin and the Guangdong Communists is incorrect. Most of the policies and strategies, analyzed below, for dealing with the strike were initially proposed by Deng Zhongxia, whose ideas were generally well received by Borodin and Chen Yannian.[66] Soviet accounts repeat-

60. Chen Zhiwen, "Da geming shiqi de Guangzhou gongren yundong," p. 11.

61. Zhang Guotao, Wo de huiyi, p. 459.

62. In 1957, Huang Ping repeatedly talked about the lack of CCP Central Committee influence during the strike. He was an interpreter for Deng Zhongxia and Su Zhaozheng during most of their meetings with Chen Yannian and Borodin. See Huang Ping, "Guanyu Shenggang da bagong de huiyi ziliao," pp. 3–4, 53–54, 65.

63. Zhang Guotao, Wo de huiyi, p. 452.

64. Dan N. Jacobs, Borodin: Stalin's Man in China (Cambridge: Harvard University Press, 1981), p. 177.

65. Zhang Guotao, Wo de huiyi, p. 453.

66. Huang Ping, "Guanyu Shenggang da bagong de huiyi ziliao," pp. 3–4, 10, 19–20, 53–54.

edly emphasize the cordial relations between Borodin and the Guangdong Communists, especially Zhang Tailei, and note that strike leaders, such as Deng Zhongxia and Su Zhaozheng, frequently called at Borodin's office for discussion.[67] However, even though their relationship was friendly, the Guangdong Communists enjoyed a high degree of autonomy in implementing their policy, and their policy may have diverged from that of the Central Committee, a subject that will be analyzed in the next chapter.

Because the leadership of the Strike Committee was dominated by the Communists, its relationship with the ACLF and with the CCP Guangdong Regional Committee was close. In fact, during the course of the strike, the buildings of the Strike Committee headquarters, Dongyuan (the Eastern Garden), and of the ACLF office were connected by a wooden bridge, constructed shortly after the outbreak of the strike.[68] The office of the CCP Guangdong Regional Committee was located within walking distance of the Dongyuan and the ACLF office.[69] The office of the Soviet advisors, however, was situated in the outskirts of Guangzhou, near the Huangpu Military Academy. The office of the Guangdong Regional Committee was the major meeting place for the strike leaders and other revolutionary activists.[70] But who was the chief architect of the strike?

Though the Strike Committee was presided over by Su Zhaozheng, policymaking was under the guidance of the Strike Advisory Committee.[71] The original members of this committee were Huang Ping, Wang Jingwei, and Deng Zhongxia,[72] but Liao Zhongkai and Yang Baoan were invited to join shortly after the outbreak of the strike.[73] Both Liao Zhongkai and Wang Jingwei, the major leftist Guomindang leaders, were merely nominal members; Liao was assassinated two months after the start of the strike. Deng took the leading role in the strike movement not merely because of his seniority over Huang and Yang in the ACLF but also because of his extensive experience in the labor movement. Most important, Deng was the Party's

---

67. Cherepanov, *As Military Advisor in China*, pp. 45–46; and Vera V. Vishnyakova-Akimova, *Two Years in Revolutionary China, 1925–1927*, Harvard East Asian Monographs (Cambridge, 1971), p. 231.

68. Chen Zhiwen, "Da geming shiqi de Guangzhou gongren yundong," p. 29.

69. Site observation during my first research trip to Guangzhou in December 1980.

70. Zhang Guotao, *Wo de huiyi*, p. 448.

71. Deng Zhongxia, "Shenggang bagong gongren de zuzhi" [Workers' Organization in the Guangzhou-Hong Kong Strike], *Gongren zhi lu*, 17 July 1925.

72. Zhonghua quanguo zonggonghui, *Shenggang bagong weiyuanhui: zhiyuan yilanbiao* [Staff List of the Guangzhou-Hong Kong Strike Committee] (Guangzhou, n.d.), p. 1.

73. Guangdong zhexue shehui kexueyuan, ed., *Shenggang da bagong ziliao*, p. 158.

designated secretary of the ACLF; he represented the Central Committee in this very powerful Communist labor organization. A leading participant of the strike organization later recalled the significant role played by Deng and his relationship with other Communist leaders as follows:

The leadership and overall organization of the Shenggang General Strike were certainly centered on Deng Zhongxia, Su Zhaozheng, and Li Sen [head of the Strike Organizational Department]. But decisions regarding strike strategy, detailed organization, the boycott against Hong Kong, struggle in dealing with internal and external problems, the problems of [strikers'] livelihood, and worker education and training were initially proposed and formulated by Comrade Deng Zhongxia. [He] would finalize his plans after his discussion with Comrades Chen Yannian and Zhou Enlai. Because problems in dealing with returned workers' food and lodging and the diplomatic negotiations [for strike settlement] had ramifications for the Guangdong revolutionary government, [policies relating to these problems] frequently had to be argued among the leaders of the Guomindang and its government, especially with the leader of its leftist faction, Mr. Liao Zhongkai, and approved by the Soviet political advisor, Borodin, who was invited by Mr. Sun Yatsen. On such problems, Borodin sometimes also presented his own view.[74]

In the early 1960s, when the Guangdong Provincial Academy of Philosophy and Social Sciences launched a major oral history project on the Guangzhou–Hong Kong General Strike, many of the former strikers repeatedly emphasized that Deng was the most important leader in this massive movement. Certainly any revolutionary leader, no matter how brilliant, needs the support of close comrades. In this respect, Deng Zhongxia was no exception. He needed the full support of other outstanding local labor leaders, men like Su Zhaozheng, Lin Weimin, Yang Baoan, Liu Ersong, Yang Yin, and many others. They helped him not only to narrow the gap between Marxist intellectuals and workers but also to break down regional and linguistic barriers.

Organization and Strategy

During the first few days after the Shaji Incident, the Guomindang military leaders and Soviet advisors discussed the possibility of attacking the Inter-

74. Lu Qi, "Ji zai Shenggang da bagong zhong de Deng Zhongxia tongzhi," p. 61.

national Settlement of Shamian.[75] In fact, the young and ambitious military officer Jiang Jieshi drew up a detailed plan for attacking Shamian and submitted it to the Soviet military advisor, General Galen, for approval.[76] There were pros and cons to such a military operation. Some advisors thought that an open declaration of war against the foreign consulate would precipitate a nationwide anti-imperialist revolutionary movement. But others thought such an operation was risky and feared it would bring about direct British military action in Guangzhou, which, according to their estimate, could hold out only for one or two months if a direct British military attack was launched.[77] The majority of the Soviet advisors, including Borodin, believed that the relative geographic isolation of Guangzhou would mean that an independent military operation against the British would fail to create a nationwide anti-imperialist movement.[78] Thus, the idea of launching a direct attack on Shamian was shelved, and the anti-imperialist strategy was focused on boycott and strike. At the beginning, the strategy emphasized an economic boycott of all foreign goods entering Guangzhou. But to protect local economic interests, the boycott policy was modified after two months of action. Thereafter, only British goods and vessels were prohibited.

To mobilize hundreds of thousands of strikers in a prolonged political struggle required a well-disciplined and highly efficient organization and leadership. During this period in south China, Deng Zhongxia was the best qualified to take on this responsibility because of his seniority in the ACLF, his personal experience in the labor movement, and his firm belief in the importance of trade unions and workers' collective power in the current stage of political struggle.

Deng always believed that a labor federation of industry- and trade-based unions was the best means to maintain worker unity and solidarity. He suggested that the federation, like the ACLF, should be based on the principle of democratic centralism; each trade union would send elected representatives to the federation, the number of representatives from each union to be determined according to the size of its membership. Only through the collective power of workers and trade unions, Deng emphasized, would the working class be able to overthrow the capitalist system.[79]

75. "Conditions at Canton after the Event at Shameen on 23 June 1925: Extract from a Report of General Galen, 20 Sept. 1925," Jay Huston Collection, pack II.

76. Wilbur and How, eds., Missionaries of Revolution, pp. 502–5.

77. "Conditions at Canton after the Event at Shameen on 23 June 1925."

78. Ibid.; see also Jacobs, Borodin, pp. 180–81.

79. Deng Zhongxia, "Gonghui lun" [On Trade Unions], in Deng Zhongxia wenji, p. 183.

If workers went on strike, either for economic or for political reasons, Deng deemed that the chance of their success would be based on whether they had established a well-disciplined and efficient Strike Committee. His recent experience in leading a series of economic strikes among the Shanghai workers employed in the Japanese-owned cotton mills in February 1925 served as the basis for the tactics he devised.[80] He felt that a Provisional Strike Committee should be established while plans for a strike were formulated, and that a Central Strike Committee, composed of various departments responsible for different duties, should be formed as soon as a strike materialized. He also believed that the problem of worker commitment during a prolonged period of struggle could be overcome by a carefully planned strike strategy and by a well-disciplined strike organization.[81] Therefore, soon after the workers in Hong Kong declared their general strike, Deng emphasized to the striking workers the importance of forming a well-disciplined strike organization:

This nationalistic general strike [organized by] our working class is not an economic struggle aiming either at wage increase or at reduction of working hours; it is a political struggle for [the promotion of] anti-imperialism and for the demand of national liberation. . . . [Any] political movement can only achieve its goal after an enduring struggle. . . . As we have already seen that this struggle will be a protracted one, our indignation and determination should be supported by a well-organized system so as to maintain its [revolutionary spirit] for a long time to come.[82]

But the process leading to the formation of a strike organization was problematic. Soon after the Hong Kong strikers had gone back to Guangzhou, some conservative members of the Hong Kong General Association of Labor Syndicates suggested that Hong Kong workers should form their own Strike Committee. If their proposal had been adopted, it would have led to a serious problem of disunity among the strikers. Deng Zhongxia and Su Zhaozheng were both uncomfortable about this proposal. Lin Weimin

80. Deng claimed that about 40,000–50,000 workers from twenty-two factories participated in this economic strike, which lasted for eighteen days. See Deng Zhongxia, "Shanghai Riben shachang bagong suo delai de jingyan" [Experience from the Strike in the Shanghai Japanese Textile Factories], *Zhongguo gongren* 4 (Apr. 1925), p. 50. For a recent Western interpretation of the Shanghai labor movement in early 1925, see Perry, *Shanghai on Strike*, pp. 78–81. In retrospect, Deng regarded this strike as the "blasting fuse" of the May Thirtieth Incident. See also Deng Zhongxia, *Jianshi*, pp. 142–43.

81. Deng Zhongxia, "Shanghai Riben shachang bagong suo delai de jingyan," pp. 52–53.

82. Deng Zhongxia, "Shenggang bagong gongren de zuzhi," 16 July 1925.

found a solution by suggesting that the membership of the Strike Committee be based on a ratio of 7:4:2. According to this formula, Hong Kong trade unions would send seven representatives to the Strike Committee, whereas the number of representatives from the Shamian unions and the ACLF would be four and two respectively. Meanwhile, Deng did his best to convince all the participating strikers that it was important for the ACLF to lead the Strike Committee. He claimed that the current labor movement, though taking place in south China, had a national character because it was a response to foreign encroachment in China. His appeal to the strikers' patriotism was successful. He also gained strong support from an influential Hong Kong conservative labor unionist, Huang Jinyuan, who admired Deng. To rally Huang's support, Deng told Huang secretly that he would appoint Huang the chief of the Picketing Corps. Huang accepted Deng's offer and also helped Deng to persuade the other Hong Kong conservative trade unions to accept Lin's formula for forming the Strike Committee and to accept the ACLF's leadership in the strike organization.[83] The policy of buying off some conservative labor unionists later proved vital in maintaining, although with great difficulty, ACLF leadership throughout the prolonged struggle.

About four weeks after the outbreak of the strike, Deng was able to finalize the formation of a detailed strike organization. On 17 July 1925, he published a chart of the organization (see table 7). The Strikers' Delegates Congress was the supreme governing organ of the strike movement. Under the guidance of the Advisory Committee, headed by Deng, the congress formulated and passed resolutions relating to strike policy during its meetings. There were about eight hundred delegates, each representing one hundred workers. If the membership of a union fell below one hundred, that union was still eligible to send one delegate.[84] From their first meeting on 15 July 1925, the strikers' delegates met once every two days; the minutes and the resolutions adopted were published in the newspaper edited by the Strike Committee, *Gongren zhi lu*, on the day after each meeting. One study shows that 283 resolutions dealing with the strike and with other related political movements were passed by the congress by the end of March 1926,

83. "Lishi ziliao huibian," vol. 1, no. 3, pp. 16–17, 34.

84. The original official document on this subject states that each delegate represented 100 workers, but for some unknown reason, Deng mistakenly stated that each delegate represented 50 workers. See *Gongren zhi lu*, 23 July 1925; and Deng Zhongxia, *Shenggang bagong gaiguan*, p. 7.

Table 7. Strike Organization

Strikers' Delegates Congress ——— Advisory Committee

Shenggang Strike Committee

(Composed of union members of Hong Kong General
Association of Labor Syndicates, United Trade Union of
Guangzhou, Union of Workers Employed in Foreign Firms,
and All China Labor Federation)

Special Organizations	*Executive Council*
Picketing Dept.	Transport and Communications Dept.
Financial Dept. (Accounting Div.)	Public Relations Dept.
(Business Dept.)	Reception Dept.
Stores and Auction Dept.	Propaganda Dept.
Joint Hearing Committee	Recreation Dept.
Workers' Hospital (Public Hygiene Div.)	
Workers' Propaganda Training School	

Source: Gongren zhi lu, 17 July 1925.

when the one-hundredth congress was held.[85] Once policy was adopted, it was implemented under the leadership of the Strike Committee.

Although Deng Zhongxia interpreted the Strikers' Delegates Congress as a triumph of the theory and practice of democratic centralism,[86] its existence and its function were in fact based on the concept of checks and balances. Since there were many conservative labor unionists from Hong Kong and Guangzhou who participated in the general strike, the Communists had to find a way to ensure that all the Communist proposals and policies would be respected and adopted by the strike organization. Thus, Deng suggested the formation of the Strikers' Delegates Congress and mobilization of the pro-Communist delegates to make motions and adopt policy in favor of the Communists.[87] His suggestion turned out to be a success. One former striker recalled how the Communists made use of this congress to achieve their influence:

85. Cai Luo and Lu Quan, *Shenggang da bagong,* p. 41.
86. Deng Zhongxia, "Gongren jieji de yishou gongke" [A Lesson of the Working Class], *Gongren zhi lu,* 31 Mar. 1926.
87. "Lishi ziliao huibian," vol. 1, no. 3, p. 21.

Prior to the congress meeting, a Communist member would prepare for making a motion, which was based on the CCP's idea and instruction. He would also prevail upon the other delegates to support his motion and to make sure that his motion would be adopted by the Congress. . . . He was also responsible for planning a detailed strategy for the meeting's procedure, such as designating certain pro-Communist delegates to speak in favor of his motion.[88]

Soon after the formation of the Strikers' Delegates Congress, the local CCP Regional Committee confidently predicted that, by providing the delegates with more political experience, the congress would gradually be transformed into a workers' soviet.[89]

The Strike Committee was composed of leading and experienced labor organizers. Its main responsibility was to supervise the implementation of various policies that had been adopted by the Strikers' Delegates Congress. Of the thirteen members on the Strike Committee, at least four had already joined the CCP; these were Su Zhaozheng, Lin Weimin, Li Sen, and Zeng Ziyan. The four representatives from Shamian and the two from the ACLF were certainly pro-Communist. Among the seven Hong Kong representatives, two were Communists, two were neutral, and only three were pro-Guomindang.[90] Thus, there was a strong Communist influence within the Strike Committee. As for their professional background, the Union of Workers Employed in Foreign Firms (Yangwu gonghui) was the largest group, with five members on the council.[91] Only one member, Su Zhaozheng, represented seamen on the council.[92] Other members were two dock cargo coolies, one tramway transport worker from Hong Kong who was a Communist, one each from rattan furniture and sewing (clothing) trade unions, and two official representatives from the ACLF, namely Li Sen and Lin Weimin.[93] Analysis of their professional backgrounds reveals that those trade unionists who had been working in foreign firms were the majority in the Strike Committee. Excluding the two official representatives from

88. Ibid., p. 25.

89. "Zhonggong Guangdong quwei guanyu Shenggang da bagong de baogao (July 1925)," pp. 31–32.

90. "Lishi ziliao huibian," vol. 1, no. 3, p. 18.

91. Zhonghua quanguo zonggonghui, *Shenggang bagong wenyuanhui: zhuyuan yilanbiao*, p. 1. Of the five members from the Union of Workers Employed in Foreign Firms, one came from Hong Kong and the rest came from Shamian.

92. According to the staff list issued by the Strike Committee, Lin Weimin, though a seaman by profession, was classified as an ACLF representative. See ibid.

93. Ibid., p. 1.

the ACLF, only two members on the council were workers in light industries, rattan furniture and sewing, and seemed to have no direct connection with foreign capital investment. This breakdown attests to the success of the revolutionaries in inducing workers, particularly those employed by foreigners, to participate in this movement by stirring up antiforeign sentiment.

Whereas the Strike Committee served mainly as a planning and supervisory body, the Executive Council, which was headed by a Communist labor activist, Li Sen, and was subordinate to the Strike Committee, had the responsibility of implementing important policies concerning the organization and mobilization of the strikers. The departmental structure as designed by Deng Zhongxia in the early stages of the strike was not immutable; new departments were created during the strike to meet new demands raised by a changing political environment. For instance, a Special Court, legally recognized by the Guomindang Nationalist government, was set up on 30 September to handle all illegal smuggling cases after the Strike Committee had declared a new strike strategy of boycotting only goods imported from Hong Kong or carried by British vessels. Another example is the Special Transport Committee, formed in June 1926 to mobilize some of the strikers to provide their labor to the Northern Expedition.[94]

In general, the responsibilities of the various departments can be classified into four major groups: (1) strikers and labor problems, (2) financial matters, (3) picketing, and (4) political propaganda and worker mobilization. Four major departments were responsible for helping returned strikers settle down in Guangzhou.[95] All returned strikers, whether workers from Hong Kong or seamen from abroad, registered in the Reception Department, which found lodgings for them in one of the eleven reception centers.[96] The Business Department, incorporated into the Financial Department, handled the supply of food, clothing, and other basic needs for the strikers. The services of the Business Department were quite well organized. For instance, a "food token" was issued to each striker as an identity

94. *Gongren zhi lu,* 1 Oct. 1925, 30 June 1926; see also Deng Zhongxia, *Shenggang bagong gaiguan,* p. 80.

95. Unless otherwise specified, information relating to the duties of various departments is based on *Gongren zhi lu,* 23 July 1925, and on a detailed report published in ibid., 11 Mar. 1926, by the Strike Committee on the daily routine work of the various departments.

96. As of 22 August 1925, there were 1,286 Chinese seamen who gave up their employment while sailing to foreign countries. All of them returned to Guangzhou from ports in Japan; see ibid., 22 Aug. 1925.

card for admission to the dining hall organized by the Strike Committee.[97] During the early winter, additional cotton blankets and jackets were distributed to strikers.[98] In order to ensure that the basic needs of the strikers were met, and to understand the problems and conflicts among workers, the Transport and Communication Department was created for conducting social and political surveys among strikers. By early August 1925, two surveys had been completed by this department on the types of union to which the strikers belonged.[99] The Transport and Communication Department also issued all permits, governing the right to cross the border from Guangdong to Hong Kong, to people living in areas close to the colony.[100] To boost the spirits of the strikers, the Recreation Department organized entertainment such as local opera, plays, and concerts. This entertainment, together with other social events organized by the Recreation Department, also helped raise funds to support the strike and carry out political propaganda.[101] With the support of the Recreation Department, some strikers organized their own drama companies to propagandize and to entertain their fellow strikers.[102]

All financial matters relating to the strike were handled by the Financial Department, which had its own Accounting Division. The Stores and Auction Department worked closely with the Financial Department; the former transmitted to the latter all the income it earned from the auctioning of smuggled goods confiscated by the strike pickets. But the major financial resource was the Guomindang, which contributed $300,000 monthly to the Strike Committee throughout the course of the strike.[103] In the traditional manner, the revolutionary Guomindang also supported the strike by granting special official honors to financial donors among the wealthy class.[104]

97. Ibid., 7 June 1926.

98. Due to financial problems, the Strike Committee could only provide one cotton blanket to every two strikers lodging in the reception centers in the early winter; see ibid., 23 Oct. 1925.

99. See ibid., 6 July 1925 and 10 Aug. 1925.

100. Ibid., 11 Mar. 1926.

101. Ibid., 20, 26, 28 July 1925.

102. Chen Zhiwen, "Da geming shiqi de Guangzhou gongren yundong," pp. 17–18.

103. Guangdongsheng danganguan and Zhonggong Guangdong shengwei yanjiu weiyuanhui bagongshi, eds., *Guangdongqu dang tuan yanjiu shiliao, 1921–1926* [Historical Materials on the Guangdong Regional and Corps Committees, 1921–26] (Guangzhou: Guangdong renmin chubanshe, 1983), p. 240.

104. Guangdongsheng zhengfu, *Guangdongsheng zhengfu gongbao: faze* [Guangdong Provincial Government Bulletin: Legislation] (Guangzhou, 1926), pp. 86–88.

Another common practice of the Guomindang to raise additional funds for the strike was the imposition of a surcharge on land tax in the territories under its control.[105] Such measures, however, created a negative feeling among the rich, who regarded the strike as economically unsound. In spite of this, the financial support extended by the Guomindang was crucial in maintaining the protracted strike, a fact recognized by Deng Zhongxia.[106]

The overseas Chinese were the second-largest financial supporters of the strike; their donations made up 22.6 percent of the total revenue of the Strike Committee. Other financial support came from native Chinese and from foreign labor unions.[107] Table 8 shows the major sources of revenue for the Strike Committee until June 1926. It was said that the amount of revenue was sufficient to meet the cost of maintaining the strike.[108] All income and expenses were accurately recorded by the Accounting Division. Though there were rumors after the strike headquarters was destroyed by fire on 6 November 1926 that the strike leaders had been corrupt, there was no evidence to prove this, as all account books were saved from the fire.[109]

The duties of maintaining order among strikers and enforcing a boycott against Hong Kong were carried out by the Picketing Department, which had a force of 2,000 men but was armed with only 200 guns.[110] The idea of forming the Picketing Department originated with Deng Zhongxia. He saw the urgent need to establish an armed picket line to maintain the effectiveness of the boycott.[111] Basic military training for the pickets was supplied by student-cadets from the Huangpu Military Academy.[112] A large number of pickets were deployed along the picket line between Shantou and Beihai. Because many smugglers trying to penetrate the picket line were armed, and some were even supported by gang leaders, the number of casualties

105. *Gongren zhi lu,* 2 July 1925.

106. Deng Zhongxia, *Jianshi,* pp. 239–41.

107. The largest contribution made by foreign workers came from the Russians, who donated 10,000 rubles; see *Gongren zhi lu,* 3 July 1925. A British trade union, without disclosing its name to the public, contributed £130 to the strikers; see ibid., 23 Sept. 1925. By the end of August 1925, it was reported that 100,000 German marks had been donated by various foreign trade unions; see ibid., 2 Sept. 1925.

108. Cai Luo and Lu Quan, *Shenggang da bagong,* p. 43. A defected leading strike member informed the Hong Kong government that the Strike Committee spent 12,000 dollars daily; see Enclosure, Clementi to Amery, 8 Oct. 1926, F.O.228/3156.

109. Guangdong zhexue shehui kexueyuan, ed., *Shenggang da bagong ziliao,* pp. 411–30.

110. Deng Zhongxia, *Shenggang bagong gaiguan,* p. 29.

111. Huang Ping, "Guanyu Shenggang da bagong de huiyi ziliao," p. 6.

112. *Gongren zhi lu,* 6 July and 21 Sept. 1925.

Table 8. Major Sources of Revenue of the Strike Committee up to June 1926

SOURCE	AMOUNT (%)
Nationalist government	$2,800,000 (56%)
Overseas Chinese	$1,130,000 (22.6%)
Auction of confiscated goods	$400,000 (8%)
Native Chinese	$250,000 (5%)
Penalties[a]	$200,000 (4%)
Guangdong wealthy class	$20,000 (0.4%)
Other sources	$200,000 (4%)
Total	$5,000,000

Source: Deng Zhongxia, Shenggang bagong gaiguan, pp. 64–65.
[a]The penalties were imposed by the Special Court of the Strike Committee on merchants arrested by the pickets for smuggling goods to Hong Kong.

among pickets was quite high. In fact, numerous reports were drawn up by the Strike Committee and were submitted to the Nationalist government on the killing of pickets along the border region between Guangdong and Hong Kong, particularly in areas like Yangjiang, Baoan, and Danshui, where smuggling occurred along the small streams leading to Hong Kong.[113] Smugglers caught by the pickets faced trial in the Special Court. Any smuggled goods confiscated by the pickets were sold in auctions by the Stores and Auction Department. Only three months after the start of the strike, the Stores and Auction Department had made $26,450 from selling confiscated goods.[114] It is true, as one historian has revealed, that some of the popular organizations established in the areas under the Guomindang's control during this revolutionary era wielded considerable political and judicial power, even to a degree that would not normally be accepted in a conventional legal system.[115] But the power of the Special Court was not completely unchecked. In fact, the Strike Committee frequently complained about the interference of some conservative Guomindang leaders

113. For smuggling in Baoan County, see Gongren zhi lu, 9 Sept. and 23 Nov. 1925; in Danshui, see ibid., 18, 30 July and 19 Aug. 1926; in Yangjiang, see ibid., 18, 19 Aug. 1926. For a Hong Kong British account of similar events, see Clementi to Amery, 18 Feb. 1926, C.O.882/11.

114. Gongren zhi lu, 1 Oct. and 15 Sept. 1925.

115. Patrick Cavendish, "The New China of the Kuomintang," in Jack Gray, ed., Modern China's Search for a Political Form (Oxford: Oxford University Press, 1969), p. 142.

in the Special Court.[116] However, there were also cases in which smugglers were executed by the pickets right on the spot.[117] There is no doubt that violence was common. By the end of the strike, it was said that about 120 pickets had sacrificed their lives.[118]

Though the pickets were regarded as "lawless elements" by the Hong Kong government,[119] many of them were fairly well educated. In a survey conducted among 1,055 pickets, only 147, or 14 percent, were illiterate, and 628, or 60 percent, could even read the major Communist Party publications like *Renmin zhoukan* (People's Weekly), *Xiangdao zhoubao,* and *Gongren zhi lu*.[120] However, some of the pickets, as later admitted by the Strike Committee, abused their power and were corrupt.[121] To solve this problem, Deng Zhongxia was appointed to supervise the conduct of the pickets and be responsible for "politicizing" them. Indeed, Deng is praised by Chinese historians as an outstanding labor leader of the period for his direct contribution in politicizing pickets and strikers.[122]

Politicization and Mobilization

Deng Zhongxia, in his capacity as the head of the Propaganda Department of the ACLF, took the major responsibility for politicizing workers in south China throughout the course of the general strike. The general principle of propaganda among workers was defined during the Second National Labor Congress, in which it was resolved that the two major tasks of worker education were the development of class consciousness and training in the technique of revolutionary struggle.[123] Prior to this period, Deng had felt that Chinese workers possessed an innate power of "self-realization" of their

116. *Gongren zhi lu,* 25, 30 July 1925; 2 Aug. 1925; 11, 25, 30 July 1926; 11 Aug. 1926.

117. "Testimony by Lam Wo, 15 Dec. 1927," enclosed in Clementi to Amery, 22 Dec. 1927, F.O. 371/13199 [F928/84/10].

118. Cai Luo and Lu Quan, *Shenggang da bagong,* p. 45. The official figure on the death of strikers, including pickets, until the end of July 1926 was 881; see *Gongren zhi lu,* 30 July 1926.

119. Clementi to Amery, 18 Feb. 1926, C.O.882/11.

120. *Gongren zhi lu,* 20 Oct. 1926.

121. Ibid., 7 Nov. 1925.

122. See, e.g., Jiang Ping and Li Liangyu, "Deng Zhongxia tongzhi guanghui de yisheng," p. 202; Wu Jianlin and Xie Yinming, *Beijing dang zuzhi de chuangjian huodong,* pp. 5–6; and Lu Qi, "Ji zai Shenggang da bagong zhong de Deng Zhongxia tongzhi," pp. 76–77.

123. *Zhongguo dierci quanguo laodong dahui: Gongren jiaoyu de yijuean* [The Second Chinese Labor Congress: Resolution on Workers' Education] (Guangzhou, 1925).

own class interest and identity as a result of their daily struggles against the capitalists. But his voluntarist approach to the development of class consciousness among the Chinese workers changed considerably while he was organizing the massive group of strikers in Guangzhou between 1925 and 1926. Because many of them were politically backward, Deng modified his view on the development of class consciousness in early 1926 to emphasize the importance of political education and training among workers.[124] His direct contribution to propaganda work in this period was enormous.

Apart from editing the major daily newspaper published by the Strike Committee, *Gongren zhi lu,* Deng also joined the editorial committee of the CCP Guangdong Regional Committee organ, *Renmin zhoukan,* which was under the chief editorship of Zhang Tailei. Deng was also the major organizer of several workers' schools and cadre training centers.

Of all the major publications issued by the Strike Committee, *Gongren zhi lu* was the most popular and influential. Initially it was designed as a national workers' daily newspaper published by the ACLF as a substitute for *Zhongguo gongren,* a journal issued by the Labor Secretariat between October 1924 and May 1925.[125] However, owing to the intensification of the labor movement in south China as a result of the May Thirtieth Incident, the ACLF decided to publish *Gongren zhi lu* as the Strike Committee's official organ. Unlike other Party publications, articles appearing in *Gongren zhi lu* were not focused on revolutionary theory. In fact, its primary purpose was to keep strikers informed about the strike situation and other related political affairs. It also published all official announcements from the Strike Committee or from the Nationalist government. Because of its importance, all divisional heads of pickets had to read the leading articles of *Gongren zhi lu* to their fellow pickets every morning as their first duty.[126] Some local merchants also found *Gongren zhi lu* useful because of its information on the conditions of the boycott and regulations governing imports and exports in Guangzhou.[127] In view of this popular demand, the circulation of *Gongren zhi lu* reached over ten thousand copies daily.[128] In terms

124. Deng Zhongxia, "Gonghui de zuoyong" [The Functions of Labor Unions], *Gongren zhi lu,* 13–15 Dec. 1925.

125. Ibid., 1 July 1925.

126. Lu Qi, "Ji zai Shenggang da bagong zhong de Deng Zhongxia tongzhi," p. 81; see also *Gongren zhi lu,* 15 Aug. 1925, which published a report on the routine daily duties of the pickets.

127. Lu Qi, "Ji zai Shenggang da bagong zhong de Deng Zhongxia tongzhi," p. 81.

128. *Gongren zhi lu,* 11 Mar. 1926.

of its written style, it was characterized by plain language and colloquial expression. Probably remembering his experience in Changxindian, Deng Zhongxia, as suggested by many Chinese historians, was responsible for formulating this style with a view to increasing its appeal to local workers.[129]

Apart from publishing *Gongren zhi lu*, the Propaganda Department was also very active in publishing many pamphlets and monographs on subjects related to the strike; some of these publications were written by Deng.[130] Besides using printed materials, the Propaganda Department also dispatched speech corps, composed of student and labor activists, to the various union offices and striker reception centers and dining halls.[131] The major content of this propaganda, whether written or oral, was directly related to the issue of anti-imperialism. Though some writings or speeches demanded that the Nationalist government improve socioeconomic conditions among workers and peasants, none of them argued the need for an immediate implementation of a radical revolutionary socialist program. In brief, the strike leaders agreed with Deng's view that the fundamental problem confronting China was the evil of foreign penetration, that the Nationalist government should launch a movement to eliminate the unequal treaties and to improve the livelihood of the working and peasant classes, and that the strikers should in the present stage of struggle support the Guomindang in promoting the Nationalist Revolution under the United Front policy.[132] As the next chapter will show, Deng's moderate political views and the content of strike propaganda became increasingly radical about half a year into the strike after he had witnessed the rapid spread of the mass urban and rural movements and the growth of counterrevolutionary forces led by a group of conservative Guomindang leaders. Throughout the course of the strike, however, anti-imperialism was the most important subject in all the propaganda.

Deng was also the first labor leader to call for the spread of propaganda into the countryside, especially to those areas located near the border with

129. See, e.g., Lu Qi, "Ji zai Shenggang da bagong zhong de Deng Zhongxia tongzhi," p. 80; and Xue Haozhou and Li Xiangjun, "Deng Zhongxia yu *Gongren zhi lu*" [Deng Zhongxia and *The Road of Workers*], *Xinwen yanjiu ziliao* [Research Materials on Journalism] 2 (1980), p. 8.

130. These included *Shenggang bagong gaiguan, Shenggang bagong zhong zhi zhongying tanpan* [Sino-British Negotiations in the Period of the Guangzhou-Hong Kong General Strike] (Guangzhou, 1926), and *1926 nian zhi Guangzhou gongchao*.

131. *Gongren zhi lu*, 24 July 1925.

132. Deng Zhongxia, "Xu Guomin zhengfu" [To Remind the Nationalist Government], *Gongren zhi lu*, 2 July 1925; see also *Gongren zhi lu*, 27 July 1925.

Hong Kong. A few days after the start of the strike, he discussed the need to maintain close contact with the peasantry:

The peasants are our assistants. We must unite closely [with them] in order to defeat all the [privileged] classes which are oppressing us. Unfortunately, some of our peasant brothers, for geographical reasons, still do not fully understand our anti-imperialist movement. A small number of them even smuggle food [to Hong Kong] for a minimal profit. We therefore must send people to the villages to propagandize and correct their mistakes. By doing so, we can also consolidate the foundation of unity between the working and peasant classes. Therefore it is necessary to form a Rural Public Speech Corps [*nongcun xuanjiang dui*].[133]

His appeal was supported by the Peasant Movement Training Institute, which announced its decision to organize special classes for prospective Rural Public Speech Corps members.[134] Having received two weeks of training in the institute, the approximately fifty members of the first graduating class were dispatched to the rural areas on 2 September 1925. To overcome suspicion and misunderstanding on the part of the peasants, each group of speech corps members was accompanied by two representatives from local peasant associations.[135] Because the speech corps lacked sufficient personnel to cover the vast rural area, pickets deployed along the border region were also mobilized to spread propaganda by forming their own speech corps in early August.[136] The result of this speech corps movement in the rural areas was mixed; there was success in one area, but failure in another. This complex result will be examined in the next chapter.

The strike propaganda campaign in Guangzhou was more extensive than that in the countryside because the Strike Committee, besides having its own Propaganda Department, was assisted by other popular organizations in launching a political appeal among the people of that city. About one hundred returned Hong Kong students organized their own students' society, and a women workers' union was formed in Shamian to support the strike and other related political movements by launching their own propaganda campaign.[137] Other labor unions, like the General Transport

133. Deng Zhongxia, "Zenyang shixing gongnong lianhe" [How to Implement Worker-Peasant Unity], *Gongren zhi lu,* 28 July 1925.
134. *Gongren zhi lu,* 28 July 1925.
135. Ibid., 31 Aug. 1925.
136. Ibid., 8 Aug. 1925.
137. *Zhongguo qingnian* 98 (28 Sept. 1925), pp. 723–25.

Union, also had their own propaganda programs in support of the strike.[138] The various entertainments organized by the Strike Committee were also frequently used as a means to politicize workers.[139]

In spite of this massive propaganda work, the Strike Committee still needed more people, particularly low-level cadres, to organize and lead the strikers. Therefore, the Strike Committee established a Workers' Propaganda Training School, which conducted its first class on 1 July 1925. By the middle of July, about 300 strikers were registered in this school.[140]

The Workers' Propaganda Training School offered a short-term but intensive program. Trainees received physical training early in the morning, between 6:00 and 8:00. Class instruction was offered between 11:00 A.M. and 2:00 P.M. The curriculum of instruction included the following subjects:

1. Why a Strike Is Necessary (1 lecture)
2. History of Imperialist Aggression in China (3 lectures)
3. The Working Class and Political Struggle (1 lecture)
4. The Working Class and Economic Struggle (1 lecture)
5. Why Unity among Labor Unions Is Necessary (2 lectures)
6. Brief History of the Red International and Its Relationship with the Labor Movement in the East (2 lectures)
7. The Conditions of Workers in Foreign Countries (3 lectures)
8. Workers and Labor Legislation in the Soviet Union (1 lecture)
9. How to Carry out Propaganda Work among Workers (1 lecture)
10. Why a Worker-Peasant Alliance Is Necessary (1 lecture)
11. The Nationalist Government and the Working Class (1 lecture)
12. History of the Chinese Labor Movement (1 lecture)
13. History of Social Development (3 lectures)
14. Brief Lecture on Capitalism (3 lectures)
15. The Current Situation in International Relations (2 lectures)
16. The Current Political Conditions in China (1 lecture)[141]

The curriculum offered a variety of ideological training. But in reality, as confirmed by Deng Zhongxia, it could only produce low-level strike pro-

138. *Gongren zhi lu,* 16 Mar. 1926.
139. Ibid., 20 July 1925.
140. Ibid., 2, 20 July 1925.
141. Ibid., 18 July 1925.

pagandists, who usually carried out their duties in the strikers' reception centers or dining halls after being briefed shortly before their assignment.[142]

It was only in late October 1925 that the ACLF organized another program to train labor activists at the local leadership level. The idea for the new training program might have originated from the CCP Central Committee in October 1925, which criticized the Guangdong Communists for ignoring the interests of the Party while working individually with the Guomindang. The CCP Central Committee also thought that the Guangdong Communists' major mistake was their failure to make use of the strike to increase Party membership.[143] In order to correct this problem, the ACLF recruited about a hundred labor movement trainees, who were nominated by their trade unions to participate in the local leadership training program that commenced on 22 October. During one month of training, classroom instruction and military training were offered. Each trainee received four hours of classroom instruction daily on the following major subjects: The International Labor Movement, The Chinese Labor Movement, The History of Imperialist Aggression, and Study of the Resolutions of the Second National Labor Congress.[144] Unlike the curriculum that was outlined by the CCP Central Committee, this one did not include any classroom training in Marxist political economy or other revolutionary theory.[145]

Meanwhile, the ACLF also extended their propaganda at the grass-roots level by regularly holding public evening meetings starting in early December. The meetings invited leading labor organizers to talk about their political ideas and experiences. Speakers included Su Zhaozheng, Li Sen, Huang Ping, and Deng Zhongxia.[146] In general, all these programs contributed to the creation of a new generation of labor activists.[147] But this impact was not strong enough to meet the increasing demand for capable labor activists at the local leadership level as a result of the rapid political development in

142. Ibid.; Deng Zhongxia, *Shenggang bagong gaiguan*, p. 58.

143. "Resolutions on the Question of Organization, Oct. 1925," in Wilbur and How, eds., *Missionaries of Revolution*, pp. 530–32.

144. *Gongren zhi lu*, 23 Oct. 1925.

145. See "An Outline of the Curriculum of the Chinese Communist Party's 'A' and 'B' Party Schools," in Wilbur and How, eds., *Missionaries of Revolution*, pp. 539–42.

146. *Gongren zhi lu*, 4 Dec. 1925.

147. The writings of Feng Zhichu, one of the workers who received training during this period, illustrate the success of the Strike Committee and the ACLF in politicizing strikers and workers. His writings, though lacking Marxist theoretical discussion, are characterized by strong anti-imperialist sentiment and an urgent desire to participate in revolutionary struggle. See *Gongren zhi lu*, 10, 11 Aug. 1925.

Guangzhou. Furthermore, the Strike Committee was completely occupied organizing the massive number of strikers and had no time to implement a large-scale training program.[148] Nevertheless, the Strike Committee reorganized its Workers' Propaganda Training School in March 1926, appointing Deng Zhongxia its honorary director.[149]

In April 1926, the Strike Committee established a special department to deal with the political education of strikers and the children of the local working class. Two months after the implementation of this new policy, twenty-one workers' schools had been established.[150] In spite of the increase in tension and suspicion between the Guangdong Communists and the Guomindang members after the March Twentieth Coup (an important issue that will be analyzed in the next chapter), the strike leaders continued to regard the subjects of anti-imperialism and the Nationalist Revolution as basic, as revealed by several schools' curricula.[151] Meanwhile, in order to overcome the problem of insufficient qualified personnel for local leadership, further cadre training was implemented by Deng Zhongxia in early June 1926, a month before the issuing of a document by the Central Committee calling for an immediate expansion of the cadre training program.[152] Deng was responsible for the supervision of a labor movement cadre training center, the School of Labor Movement Studies (Gongren yundong yanjiu xuexiao), which attracted about 300 candidates to its entrance examination, which took place on 19 June.[153]

The entrance examination was quite demanding. It consisted of one written paper on the candidate's experience in the labor movement and one on his or her understanding of the meaning of the current strike and of the Northern Expedition. In addition, an oral examination was required to test the candidate's ability in reading reports and in answering general political questions. The 193 candidates who passed (another 29 were put on a waiting list) underwent a two-month training program under major labor movement leaders like Xiao Chunu, Huang Ping, Tan Zhitang, Feng Jupo, Li Sen,

148. Deng Zhongxia, *Shenggang bagong gaiguan*, p. 58.

149. *Gongren zhi lu*, 13 Mar. 1926.

150. Deng Zhongxia, *Shenggang bagong gaiguan*, pp. 58–59; see also Cai Luo and Lu Quan, *Shenggang da bagong*, p. 111.

151. See, e.g., the curriculum as recalled by a participant in Guangdong renmin chubanshe, ed., *Nutao*, p. 17.

152. "Resolutions on the Labor Movement, July 1926," in Wilbur and How, eds., *Missionaries of Revolution*, p. 743.

153. *Gongren zhi lu*, 12 June 1926.

Liu Shaoqi, and Deng Zhongxia.[154] The first class graduated on 6 October,[155] and in spite of the fact that the strike and boycott were officially terminated on 10 October, the Strike Committee and the ACLF continued to run similar training schools. In fact, on 25 October, the School of Labor Movement Studies commenced its second session with an enrollment of 221.[156] Other workers' schools continued to operate under the influence of the Strike Committee after the strike was called off. For example, the Guangsan Railway General Trade Union established a school for the children of its members, and the Labor Movement Propaganda Department of the Strike Committee operated eleven tutorial schools for workers.[157]

The role played by Deng Zhongxia in mobilizing workers in south China was significant. Under his planning and organization, the CCP was able to capture the leadership of the massive Shenggang General Strike even though the strike was endorsed and materially supported by the Guomindang. This study clearly refutes any claim that the Shenggang General Strike was led by the Guomindang, a view recently advocated even by a mainland Chinese historian.[158]

Despite Deng's contribution to organizing the strikers and workers, the CCP Central Committee was anxious to see a sharp increase in Party membership during the early months of the strike and criticized the Guangdong Communists in October 1925 for their failure to expand the Party's influence.[159] This criticism was unfair to the Guangdong Communists; the Central Committee was impatient and underestimated the Guomindang's influence among the working class in south China. And in fact, the strike and other mass movements in south China in 1925–26, especially the peasant movement organized by Peng Pai, had expanded the Party membership considerably. By the end of 1926, Guangdong was the province with the highest percentage of Communist Party members at the national level, with 27.2 percent, or 5,039, Party card holders. The Communist Party member-

154. Chen Zhiwen, "Da geming shiqi de Guangzhou gongren yundong," p. 27; *Gongren zhi lu,* 24 June 1926.

155. *Gongren zhi lu,* 9 Oct. 1926.

156. Ibid., 25 Oct. 1926.

157. Ibid., 9 Oct. and 2 Nov. 1926.

158. Li Xiaoyong, "Guomindang yu Shenggang da bagong" [The Guomindang and the Guangzhou-Hong Kong General Strike], *Jindaishi yanjiu* 4 (1987), pp. 232–342.

159. "Resolutions on the Question of Organization, Oct. 1925," in Wilbur and How, eds., *Missionaries of Revolution,* p. 532.

ship in Guangdong was fairly well distributed among three major social classes: 42.68 percent were workers; 30.14 percent were peasants; and 27.4 percent were intellectuals and others.[160]

Another major achievement of the strike was the creation of a favorable environment in Guangzhou for the Nationalist government to advance its political course. The mobilization of strikers under Deng's leadership for various political gatherings and demonstrations psychologically, and to a lesser extent physically, strengthened the Nationalist government for carrying out its tasks of suppressing local warlords and preparing for the Northern Expedition. The long picket line between the colony and Guangdong, though not powerfully armed, also contributed to the strengthening of the seacoast defense. Even the Guomindang leaders were not slow in seizing the opportunity to increase their party's revolutionary power by appealing directly to the strikers.

Wang Jingwei appealed for support to a massive meeting of strikers a few days before the Nationalist army was dispatched to Dongjiang to pacify the Guomindang's major opponent, Chen Jiongming.[161] His appeal was fully backed up by the Strike Committee, which simultaneously published a pamphlet and several leading articles in *Gongren zhi lu* on the subject of the Eastern Expedition.[162] Among the strike leaders, Deng Zhongxia was the major spokesman. In his view, the defeat of Chen Jiongming, the struggle against the aggressive policy of the British in Hong Kong, and the defense of the revolutionary base in Guangzhou were closely related. He explained that after the Hong Kong government had failed to receive direct military help from its home government, it had decided to offer material support to the anti-Guomindang warlords in south China with a view to defeating the revolutionary Nationalist government and the Strike Committee. Therefore, he urged his fellow strikers to morally and physically assist the Eastern Expedition.[163] As a result of these appeals from the Guomindang and the strike leaders, about 2,000 strikers volunteered to participate in the East-

160. "Zhongyangju baogao, 5 Dec. 1926" [Report of the Central Bureau], in Zhonggong zhongyang danganguan, ed., *Zhonggong zhongyang zhengzhi baogao xuanji, 1922–1926*, pp. 117–19. As admitted by the editors of this document, the Chinese Communists did not present an accurate calculation.

161. *Gongren zhi lu*, 20 Sept. 1925.

162. Ibid.; Shenggang bagong weiyuanhui, ed., *Bagong yu dongzheng* [Strike and Eastern Expedition] (Guangzhou, 1925).

163. Deng Zhongxia, "Women duiyu dongzheng de zeren" [Our Responsibilities toward the Eastern Expedition], in *Bagong yu dongzheng*, pp. 7–11.

ern and Southern Expeditions to defeat Chen Jiongming and his associate Deng Benyin during the winter of 1925.[164]

Though the major contribution of the striker volunteers was in the transport of army supplies, their work was deeply appreciated and highly praised by the Nationalist government. Jiang Jieshi, who was regarded by many at the time as a leftist, even showed his appreciation of the striker volunteers by seeing them off personally after the Nationalist army had captured Shantou and Chaozhou in late November 1925.[165] The chief Soviet advisor, Borodin, is said to have given credit to the strikers for their role in the consolidation of the revolutionary base in Guangzhou when he submitted his report to the Soviet commissioner in early 1926.[166]

But the strikers' achievement also increased tension and suspicion among a group of Guomindang leaders who were afraid that the color of their party would change to red. It therefore exacerbated the power struggle between the Guomindang and the Communist members over control of the revolutionary masses. Apart from this party rivalry, the strike leaders also faced an awkward situation in that their contribution to worker mobilization in Guangzhou was not completely appreciated by the CCP Central Committee. The major criticism centered on the issue of the Guangdong Communists' working individually with labor organizations, peasant associations, and the Guomindang but ignoring the interests of the Communist Party as a whole.[167] Furthermore, in spite of the success of mass propaganda and a comprehensive program for training low-level labor movement cadres, the Central Committee still complained that its Guangdong comrades had failed to offer systematic training in revolutionary theory to newly recruited Party members.[168] In retrospect, these criticisms merely show the Central Committee's impatience and lack of information about Guangzhou. These problems could only lead to confusion about strategy among the young Party leaders in Guangzhou, including Deng Zhongxia, whose decisions were also influenced by Soviet advisors. Under such cir-

164. Deng Zhongzia, *Shenggang bagong gaiguan,* pp. 80–81. On the military operations of these two expeditions, see Chen Zhiling, *Xinbian diyici guonei geming zhanzheng shigao* [Draft History of the First Revolutionary Civil War, new ed.] (Xian: Shaanxi renmin chubanshe, 1981), pp. 70–77.

165. *Gongren zhi lu,* 23 Nov. 1925.

166. Cherepanov, *As Military Advisor in China,* pp. 184–85.

167. "Resolution on the Question of Organization, Oct. 1925," in Wilbur and How, eds., *Missionaries of Revolution,* pp. 531–32.

168. "Political Report of the Central Committee, July 1926," in ibid., pp. 725–26.

cumstances, the Guangdong Communists encountered great difficulty, and sometimes were indecisive, in handling some major and urgent political situations. This confusion, as will be seen in the next chapter, proved to be the fatal flaw in Communist leadership in this period.

Deng Zhongxia as a teenager

139

Gathering of the Young China Society in Beijing in 1920: *second from left,*
Deng Zhongxia; *third from right,* Li Dazhao

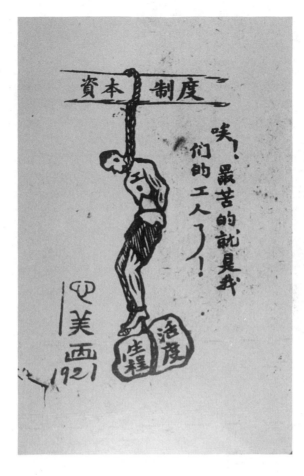

Political cartoon drawn by Deng Zhongxia (pseudonym Xinmei) in 1921
portraying the miserable life of workers under capitalism (photographed by
Daniel Y. K. Kwan in the Changxindian Memorial Hall, Beijing, China)

The Communist members of the Guomindang Shanghai Branch Executive
Committee in 1924: *front row, first from left,* Deng Zhongxia; *front row,
first from right,* Xiang Jingyu; *back row, second from left,* Mao Zedong;
back row, third from right, Yun Daiying

Deng Zhongxia, standing in the middle, with members of the strike picket in
Guangzhou in 1926

Labor demonstration in Guangzhou during the Shenggang General Strike

Demonstration led by the Strike Committee in support of the Second
Guomindang National Congress in early 1926

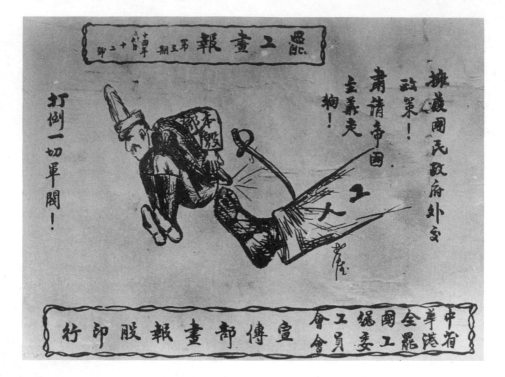

A political cartoon issued jointly by the All China Labor Federation and
the Strike Committee calling for support of the Nationalist government's
anti-imperialist foreign policy

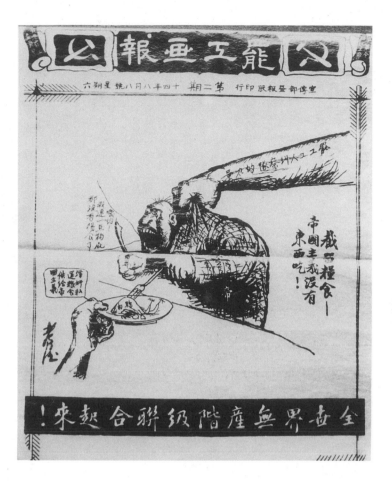

A political cartoon issued by the Strike Committee calling for the unity of the proletarians of the whole world

A meal token for strikers, with political slogans on the left-hand side

佈告

「中華全國總工會省港罷工委員會前與商務廳公安局外交部共同議決給出入口貨之特許證，原期一以便利貿易。」以保障罷工。惟查情形既有變更，此項特許證已經省港罷工工人代表大會通過在予取銷，並經罷工會等共同決議取銷特許證後之辦法特條例六條茲特公佈之。

取銷特許證後之辦法條例

（一）從香港澳門來的，任何國貨物，都不准來廣東，從廣東運主的，無論任何國貨物，都不准往香港及澳門。

（二）凡是英國船，及經過香港之任何國船隻，均不准來往廣東內地，起卸貨物。

（三）凡不是英國船，不是英國貨，及不經過香港及澳門的，均可自由起卸。

（四）廣東界內只要不是英國貨，英國船，均可自由貿易及東來。

（五）凡存在廣州之貨，只要不是英貨，而且不是英國人的，均可開會發賣。（如有干政府專賣者）

（六）此條例由四商會聯同省罷工委員會共同簽字公佈之，自公佈之日起，直接由省罷工委員會行使對鎖職權。如有違背前條例者，一律完全充公。（凡違背怠例者先須輕過工商兩界所派代表左委員會審查議後，自公佈之日起。卽發生效力。望我商界同胞幸共遵守奉行）以期共同達到打倒帝國主義之目的。有厚望焉。此佈。

中華全國總工會省港罷工委員會
廣州總商會
廣東全省商會聯合會
廣州市商會
廣州商民協會

中華民國十四年九月三日

An anti-British boycott statement issued jointly by the Strike Committee and the four leading local merchants' associations in Guangzhou

The first two pages of the 10 Dec. 1925 issue of *Gongren zhi lu,* with a lead article on the classification of Hong Kong unions by Deng Zhongxia

【九、米糧部】【米糧同德等】

【十、雜貨部】【水貨恊隆，翕窩鴻隆，超立華藥，海味什貨等。】

【二、顏業部】【出口洋庄類菓，醬料雜菓，京菓等。】

【三、西貨部】【洋貨貨部，綢漲絨作，綠窣，覆香，小販類立，洋貨聚益等。】

【五、玻璃部】【粵港玻璃，僑港玻璃，鏡器玻璃等。】

【六、銅器部】【銅器工會等】

【七、冠履部】【履業，華履，唐鞋，詠安，革履，木屐等。】

【八、被服部】【車衣，洋衣研究，西區堂等。】

【九、裝飾部】【同益首飾，洋庄金銀器等】

【十、藥業部】【公誠工務社，販藥實講頭，中藥研究，醒群工社，羣茸洋藥，意誠工社等。】

【士、酒業部】【怡誌聯恊，煙業研究，員販煙草等。】

【圭、菜業部】【藤器愛群，沙藤平樂，同義，志群，織補座纈等】

【茶行總工會等】

【酒業聯合會等】

【盂、紙業部】【公源紙務社等】

【夬、皮業部】【皮業工會等】

【七、理髮部】【方國，義安等】

【大、雜業部】【海陸理貨，卸貨，公平等】

【九、染業部】【藥聲，歡樂聯益堂等】

【廿、汽燈部】【汽燈等】

【廾、桶行部】【桶行廣聯等】

【十、印刷】

【一】西文部

【二】漢文部【漢文拣字，石印等】

【景源印務等】

【十一、織造】

【女子學傚，女子千業，進蔴女子，織造研究等】

罷工消息

中華各界開闢黃埔商埠促進會開會

昨日因公致祭紀盛

解決工潮當中之情狀

Front cover of a booklet written by Deng Zhongxia on the Sino-British
negotiations during the Shenggang General Strike

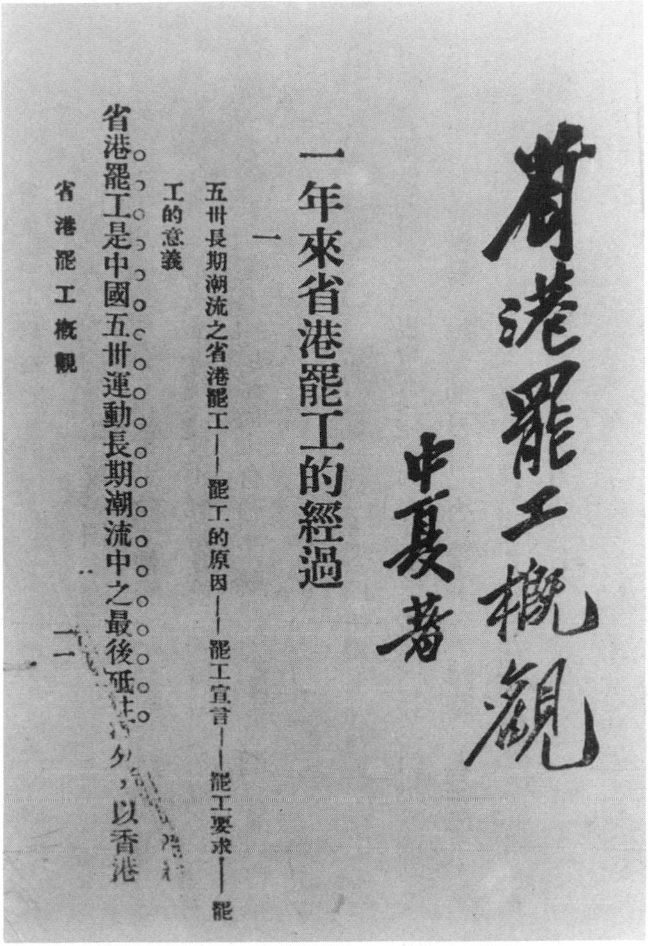

省港罷工概觀

中夏著

一年來省港罷工的經過

一

五卅長期潮流之省港罷工——罷工的原因——罷工宣言——罷工要求——罷工的意義

省港罷工概觀

省港罷工是中國五卅運動長期潮流中之最後砥柱，此外，以香港

二

Shenggang bagong gaiguan (A General Account of the Shenggang General Strike), by Deng Zhongxia

Deng Zhongxia with his wife, Xia Ming, and child in Moscow, ca. 1929

A handbill issued by the Comintern-affiliated Chinese Revolutionary Mutual
Aid Association protesting the arrest of their labor leader, Deng Zhongxia, by
the Guomindang
(Photograph courtesy of the National Archives, Washington, D.C.)

4

Revolution and Counterrevolution

O*N 1 JULY 1925*, a week after the outbreak of the Shenggang General Strike, the Nationalist government was established by the Guomindang in Guangzhou. This political development, according to the Communists, was a product of the strike.[1] Although this is something of an exaggeration, the early phase of the strike did reflect the success of a new revolutionary strategy in mass mobilization implemented jointly by the CCP and the Guomindang. However, because of ideological differences and conflicts of interest between the two parties, the maintenance of this joint political venture was by no means easy. Tension had begun to intensify after the death of Sun Yatsen in March 1925. Shortly before the outbreak of the strike, Dai Jitao, a Guomindang theoretician, had published two small booklets that presented a conservative interpretation of Sun's political thought and called for an immediate termination of the United Front in order to preserve the purity of Guomindang ideology.[2] Some other veteran Guomindang leaders, such as Zou Lu in Shanghai, openly criticized

1. Deng Zhongxia, *Jianshi*, pp. 233–35. A Soviet advisor praised the strike for "[playing] a positive part in the consolidation of the Revolutionary Government." See "The Hong Kong Strike," enclosed in Peking Chancery to Foreign Office, 16 June 1927, F.O.371/12501 [F6462/3241/10].

2. Wilbur, *Nationalist Revolution in China*, pp. 18–21, 30–33.

the United Front policy because they feared that it would turn their party Communist.

Relations with the Guomindang

At the beginning, the strike had the full support of the Guomindang because of its evident political value and also because after Sun's death the Guomindang was led by the left-wing leader Liao Zhongkai. However, none of the Guomindang leaders expected the strike to last very long. According to a Soviet advisor's report, the strike was initially intended to last for three months. While preparing for the strike, Deng Zhongxia, with the problem of food supplies in mind, had also been worried about its lasting for more than three months.[3] Indeed, about three months into the strike, some Guomindang leaders, for financial and political reasons, began to voice their opinion that the strike should be ended. Jiang Jieshi, for instance, requested the Strike Committee to consider calling off the strike in September and again in November 1925. However, his requests were turned down.[4] The Guomindang's Political Council also informed the Strike Committee on 22 September 1925 that conditions were ripe for settling the strike.[5] That the strike developed into a protracted struggle was in fact a surprise not only to the Guomindang but also to the Communists.

Right-wing Guomindang leaders viewed the strike as a breeding ground for the young Communists to expand their influence among the working class at the Guomindang's expense. Some complained that Liao Zhongkai should be criticized for the growth of Communist influence in Guangzhou. Others held the view that the strike had created an impression in Guangzhou that only the Communists were revolutionary, and was thus detrimental to the reputation of the Guomindang among the strikers and workers.[6]

3. Deng Zhongxia, "Jinlai po youxie huaiji jia" [There Are Certain Skeptics Recently], *Renmin zhoukan* 19 (20 Aug. 1926), p. 10.

4. "The Hong Kong Strike," enclosed in Peking Chancery to Foreign Office, 16 June 1927, F.O.371/12501 [F6462/3241/10]. See also *Hong Kong Daily Press,* 28 Sept. 1925.

5. The Political Council was originally established by Sun Yatsen, on the advice of Borodin, in July 1924. After the founding of the Nationalist government, it was composed of Wang Jingwei as chairman, with Liao Zhongkai, Hu Hanmin, and Xu Chongzhi as members. See Wilbur, *Nationalist Revolution in China*, pp. 19, 25, 27. See also Deng Zhongxia, *Shenggang bagong gaiguan*, p. 23.

6. Chen Gongbo, *Kuxiao lu* [Matters of Wry Smile] (Hong Kong: Xianggang daxue chubanshe, 1979), pp. 46–47.

There was widespread feeling that the labor movement should be checked and that Liao's pro-Communist policy should be halted.

Liao Zhongkai was assassinated on 20 August 1925. It is still unknown who was responsible for the assassination, though the pro-Communist literature generally accuses the right-wing Guomindang leaders of planning of the plot. But the assassination of Liao Zhongkai did not immediately create a new political environment in Guangzhou, because an alternative, right-wing Guomindang leadership had not yet emerged.

On the day of the assassination, the Guomindang's Political Council was dissolved; Borodin immediately appointed a three-man ad hoc committee, composed of Jiang Jieshi, Wang Jingwei, and Xu Chongzhi, to take over political and military leadership.[7] Xu was soon dismissed and expelled from Guangzhou because of his refusal to arrest the suspected plotters, a small group of right-wing Guomindang leaders which included Hu Hanmin. Jiang and Wang, for the time being, shared political power in the Guomindang leadership.

Although the change in the Guomindang leadership on 20 August provided favorable conditions for the rise of Jiang Jieshi, he was not yet powerful enough, at least in the last few months of 1925, to implement a reactionary policy toward the CCP. Meanwhile, the Communists continued to enjoy strong influence among the urban working class. Communist influence among the strikers and their ability to mobilize the masses, as a leading Guomindang member later commented, directly led to a situation in which a breakdown of the United Front became inevitable even without the rise of a small group of extreme-right-wing Guomindang leaders, the so-called Western Hills faction.[8]

In mid-1925, the Guomindang found itself in an awkward situation: it had fully endorsed the urban anti-imperialist mass movement but the movement was slipping out of its control. The finance minister of the Guomindang Nationalist government, Song Ziwen, admitted to the governor of Hong Kong on 19 December 1925 that "the present government of Canton would not last a single day, if it shot down the strike pickets."[9] Eight months later, Eugene Chen, the foreign minister, expressed a similar concern when he admitted to the British acting consul general in Guangzhou,

7. Duan Zhimin, "Shi lun da geming shiqi Bao luoting dui Jiang Jieshi celue de xiang-xiang fazhang" [On Borodin's Dual Strategy toward Jiang Jieshi during the Period of Great Revolution], *Guangdong shehui kexue* [Guangdong Social Sciences] 3 (1989), p. 45.

8. Chen Gongbo, *Kuxiao lu*, pp. 47–48.

9. Clementi to Amery, 24 Dec. 1925, C.O.882/11.

John F. Brenan, that "any action which looked like an attempt to suppress the Strike Committee would be regarded as a betrayal of Nationalist aspirations, and was not to be contemplated."[10] This dilemma left the Guomindang leaders no alternative but to adopt a dual policy in dealing with the strike: openly, they proclaimed their support of the strikers, but secretly, they contemplated settling the dispute as early as possible.[11]

This attempt to deceive the Communists was, to a large extent, fairly successful. Even in the final phase of the strike, the Guomindang party opinion expressed no antipathy toward the strikers. On the contrary, messages of encouragement were printed repeatedly in party publications. Some Guomindang leaders, such as Hu Hanmin and Wu Chaochu, even delivered enthusiastic speeches at the Strikers' Delegates Congress. But they were cautious in their choice of words: their speeches only emphasized the role played by the strikers in the current stage of the anti-imperialist movement, avoiding any reference to the social and economic problems of the workers.[12] Wu remarked in the Guomindang's official daily press that "the Shenggang General Strike is a political strike, not an economic strike. An economic strike is related to the personal interest of workers, but a political strike concerns the interest of the whole nation."[13] To the Guomindang, support of the strike symbolized their commitment to the policy of anti-imperialism. Therefore, Guomindang leaders regarded their continuing support as a political obligation which had to be maintained in spite of financial difficulty and the risk of providing an opportunity for the Communists to expand their influence.[14] The profound impact of this policy to

10. Brenan to Clementi, 29 Aug. 1926, enclosed in Brenan to Macleay, 29 Aug. 1926, F.O.228/3155.

11. My interpretation of this issue differs sharply from that of Jean Chesneaux, who argues that relations between the Strike Committee and the Guomindang were cordial because of the effects of the strike on the Guangdong economy. See Chesneaux, *Chinese Labor Movement*, pp. 308–9.

12. *Gongren zhi lu*, 29 July and 17 Aug. 1925.

13. Chinese newspaper cuttings, 13 July 1925, Guomindang Party History Archives, 447/39.28. Although the Communists similarly regarded the strike as basically an anti-imperialist political movement, the Strike Committee, however, also demanded social and economic improvement on behalf of the Hong Kong strikers and workers. See the terms for the resumption of work by strikers in Hong Kong presented by the Strike Committee to the Hong Kong government on 2 October 1925; documents printed in C.O.882/11, pp. 128–29.

14. In early December 1925, Wang Jingwei reported that the Nationalist government had lately encountered financial difficulties due to the cost of the military operation to capture Shantou and the cost of the strike. See Wang Jingwei, "Zhengzhi baogao" [Political Report], *Zhengzhi zhoubao* [Political Weekly] 2 (13 Dec. 1925), p. 2.

delude the Communists was twofold. First, it misled many Chinese Communist leaders, including Deng Zhongxia, into believing that the majority of the Guomindang leaders remained faithful to the revolution. Second, it led to further deterioration of the relations between the two parties because it increased the suspicion of conservative Guomindang leaders of the radicalization of the labor movement under increasing Communist influence.

As a strong supporter of the United Front from the early stages of its development, Deng Zhongxia regarded cooperation with the Guomindang in the current stage of political struggle as strategically important. He also insisted, however, that the Chinese working class must maintain its own class identity and cultivate the ability to seize revolutionary leadership. However, political reality was to transform this theoretical appreciation of the situation.

By the time of Inauguration Day, celebrating the founding of the Nationalist government, many leaders of the Strike Committee had come to believe that the Guomindang had established a government for the working class. Deng Zhongxia considered his comrades' enthusiasm premature.[15] On the following day, he expressed his congratulations to the Nationalist government on its founding in the *Gongren zhi lu*. Despite his cordial greetings, he reminded the strikers that this new government was not a government for the working class and peasantry. Nevertheless, owing to its commitment to anti-imperialism and anti-warlordism, the new government should be supported. In the same article, he also appealed to the leaders of the Nationalist government to take immediate steps to eliminate the "unequal treaties" and to improve the conditions of the masses.[16] Deng was therefore wary of the Guomindang and did not completely trust its revolutionary commitment because of its conservatism where the socialist movement was concerned. But his view of the Guomindang remained fairly moderate and favorable; he considered it a revolutionary party because of its contribution to the policy of anti-imperialism.

To Deng Zhongxia, the Guomindang was revolutionary because it believed that the Chinese revolution was part of the world revolution, that the local gang leaders and compradors were counterrevolutionaries, and that the workers and peasants were the leading force of the current political struggle. However, he realized that the Guomindang as a political party was not homogeneous, because of ideological divergence among its leaders;

15. Huang Ping, "Guanyu Shenggang da bagong de huiyi ziliao," pp. 43–44.
16. Deng Zhongxia, "Xu Guomin zhengfu" [To Remind the Nationalist Government], *Gongren zhi lu*, 2 July 1925.

right-wing Guomindang leaders even contemplated betraying the revolutionary policy of the late Sun Yatsen.[17] He classified the Guomindang's leadership into three groups. The first was headed by military leaders such as Xu Chongzhi; the second consisted of bureaucrats and frustrated politicians, of whom Hu Hanmin was the leader; and the third was composed of left-wing Guomindang members under the leadership of Wang Jingwei and Jiang Jieshi. It was the third group, according to his analysis, that was truly revolutionary. He also emphasized that, during the first five months of the strike, the left-wing Guomindang leaders enhanced their strength and consolidated their leadership in Guangzhou as a result of the political mobilization of the strikers.[18] These leaders accounted for his optimism and his confidence in criticizing those Guomindang leaders who had regarded class struggle as an obstacle in the Nationalist Revolution. Speaking to a group of Guomindang delegates during a reception organized by the ACLF held in early January 1926, Deng ended his speech by declaring that "only with the revolutionary working class leading the peasantry can the Nationalist Revolution be achieved."[19] A month later, he optimistically proclaimed that the Chinese working class had seized the revolutionary leadership from other classes thanks to the development of the labor movement after the May Thirtieth Incident.[20]

Deng's optimism concerning working-class leadership was well grounded. The situation in Guangzhou, even after the assassination of Liao Zhongkai, remained favorable to the Communists — at least until mid-March 1926. During this period in Guangzhou, it was unusual if a day passed without some sort of political demonstration by strikers organized by the Communists.[21] The Guomindang seemed unwilling or unable to control this radical urban movement. After 20 August, right-wing Guomindang leaders, men like Hu Hanmin and Xu Chongzhi, had to retreat from Guangzhou temporarily. Under these circumstances, the young Communist leaders easily believed that they had captured the revolutionary leadership and that the future of the revolution lay in their hands. Their spirit was high; and they predicted that the realization of a socialist society was

---

17. Deng Zhongxia, "Zhongshan xiansheng shishi hou zhi Guomindang" [The Guomindang after the Death of Sun Yatsen], *Renmin zhoukan* 5 (12 Mar. 1926), pp. 6–8.

18. Deng Zhongxia, *Shenggang bagong gaiguan*, pp. 15–17.

19. *Gongren zhi lu*, 12 Jan. 1926.

20. Deng Zhongxia, "Wusa hou Zhongguo zhigong yundong de xin xianxiang" [The New Situation of the Chinese Labor Movement after 30 May], *Renmin zhoukan* 1 (7 Feb. 1926), p. 7.

21. Chen Gongbo, *Kuxiao lu*, p. 47.

not remote. In mid-March 1926, they launched a series of commemorative events to celebrate the Paris Commune.

On 18 March, a massive meeting was organized by the ACLF which Deng Zhongxia and two other prominent Communist leaders, Liu Shaoqi and Zhang Tailei, attended.[22] On the following day, Zhang published a leading article on the Paris Commune in the local Communist party organ, *Renmin zhoukan*. After giving a brief account of the revolutionary struggle in Paris in 1871, Zhang reminded the Chinese revolutionaries that they should learn from the experience of their French counterparts: "the bourgeoisie have a conciliatory tendency; they may be traitors; the proletariat is the leader of the Nationalist Revolution, as was proved by the Paris Commune; [we] must have confidence, understand our strength, and know how to seize political power; the proletariat is the ruling class most capable of promoting humanity and society!"[23] The very next morning, the young Guangdong Communist leaders' enthusiasm for keeping the proletarian hegemony in the Nationalist Revolution was to be proven naive, when Jiang Jieshi quietly staged a coup and arrested the captain and crew, many of whom were Communist members, of a Chinese gunboat, the SS *Zhongshan*, moored at Huangpu. This event, together with its ramifications, was to dramatically deflate Deng Zhongxia and other Guangdong Communist leaders' previous optimism regarding the power of the Chinese working class in the current stage of revolutionary struggle.

The ascent of Jiang Jieshi to power and its political implications before the coup had been disregarded by many Guangdong Communist leaders and Soviet advisors. In January 1926, Borodin confidently claimed that the joint leadership of Wang Jingwei and Jiang Jieshi would be able to maintain unity in Guangdong.[24] Although Jiang, a professional military man, was designated by Sun Yatsen as the founding director of the Huangpu Military Academy in early 1924, he had not been given much recognition in the Guomindang as a political leader. The change of party leadership after the assassination of Liao Zhongkai raised his political status dramatically. In January 1926, Jiang was able to further enhance his reputation as a

22. According to *Gongren zhi lu*, Deng delivered a speech at this commemorative gathering on the subject of the Paris Commune, but unfortunately, it was not printed in the press. See *Gongren zhi lu*, 19 Mar. 1926.

23. Zhang Tailei, "Bali gongshe jinianri" [Anniversary of the Paris Commune], *Renmin zhoukan* 6 (19 Mar. 1926), p. 11.

24. Duan Zhimin, "Shi lun da geming shiqi Bao luoting dui Jiang Jieshi celue de xiangxiang fazhang," p. 46.

political leader when the Guomindang Second National Congress was held in Guangzhou and he was elected to the Guomindang's Central Executive Committee.[25] In the same congress, the Communists' influence in the Guomindang's new central committee declined significantly; only seven of them were able to gain seats on the Central Executive Committee. Simultaneously with Jiang's rise, many right-wing Guomindang leaders who had formerly left Guangzhou for political reasons returned to the city.[26]

Thus, there was a revival of right-wing Guomindang activity in Guangzhou after January 1926. Guangdong Communists did not seem to grasp the significance of the new political development, possibly because of their overconfidence in the power of the mobilized urban working class in south China. Moreover, many of them, including Deng Zhongxia, considered Jiang Jieshi a capable left-wing Guomindang leader. But they also failed to realize that the term "left-wing Guomindang," after the death of Liao Zhongkai, had become an illusion. The March Twentieth Coup therefore came as a "lightning shock" to the Chinese Communists and their Soviet advisors.[27]

The motivation for Jiang to stage the coup was most likely his fear that he was about to be sent to Moscow by his political opponents in Guangzhou. But who wanted to send him away in early 1926? That the local Communists and their Soviet advisors wanted Jiang out of the way is unconvincing since both camps had regarded him as a major left-wing Guomindang leader after the death of Liao Zhongkai.[28] The plot was probably hatched by the right-wing Guomindang leader Wu Chaoshu, who, after inviting the Soviet advisors to a dinner party, asked Jiang on the following day if he was planning to visit Moscow. Jiang, suspecting that his fear of being sent to Moscow would become a reality, acted rapidly on the morning of 20 March.[29] The coup was certainly motivated by Jiang's commitment to defending his military leadership in Guangzhou; but it might also have been prompted by his impatience with the labor radicalism in the city.

25. Wilbur, *Nationalist Revolution in China*, p. 33.

26. Zhou Enlai, "Guanyu 1924–26 nian dang dui Guomindang de guanxi" [On the Party's Relations with the Guomindang in 1924–26], in *Zhou Enlai xuanji* [Selected Works of Zhou Enlai] (Beijing: Renmin chubanshe, 1980), vol. 1, p. 119.

27. "Stepanov's Report on the March Twentieth Incident," in Wilbur and How, eds., *Missionaries of Revolution*, p. 703.

28. Tien-wei Wu, "Chiang Kai-shek's March Twentieth *Coup d'Etat* of 1926," *Journal of Asian Studies* 27 (1967), p. 602; Duan Zhimin, "Shi lun da geming shiqi Bao luoting dui Jiang Jieshi celue de xiangxiang fazhang," pp. 44–46.

29. Chen Gongbo, *Kuxiao lu*, pp. 77–78.

It may not be coincidental that the coup took place shortly after the Guangdong Communists had celebrated the anniversary of the Paris Commune. Perhaps Jiang believed that the Communists had become too radical and that the time was ripe to halt them. He had, in fact, wanted to settle the strike in November 1925. The establishment of an *imperium in imperio* by the Strike Committee could hardly be tolerated by a military leader. While he continued publicly to denounce the right-wing Guomindang in early 1926,[30] he was possibly waiting for an opportunity to roll back the increasing Communist influence, or at least to test their strength. By mid-March, when the rumor that he was about to be sent to Moscow appeared to have some foundation, and when the local Communists, thinking that they had seized the revolutionary leadership, had repeatedly mobilized the working class with such slogans as "Proletarian Dictatorship" and "Long Live the Paris Commune," Jiang had no other alternative than to act rapidly.

The leaders of the Strike Committee were shaken by the news of the coup and the surrounding of their headquarters by Jiang's army until early afternoon of the twentieth.[31] Rumor had it that on the same day, the strike leaders, including Deng Zhongxia and Su Zhaozheng, had appealed to the British consul general in Guangzhou, James Jamieson, for an immediate strike settlement after a payment from the Hong Kong government of $16,000. Although even the Hong Kong governor doubted the truth of such a rumor,[32] the city was full of rumors and uncertainties. The garrison was reinforced and martial law was proclaimed.

The Communists were completely caught by surprise. They were also unable to react immediately because they were unable to consult the key Soviet advisor, Borodin, or the general secretary of the CCP Central Committee, Chen Duxiu; neither of whom was in Guangzhou at the time. Chen Yannian, the secretary of the CCP Guangdong Regional Committee, had

30. Speaking to the Sun Yatsenism Society, an organization formed by a group of right-wing Guomindang military cadres of the Huangpu Military Academy in December 1925, Jiang Jieshi criticized its members for attempting to betray the ideals of the late Sun Yatsen. He argued that the Communists were an important force in anti-imperialism; anyone attempting to break the United Front policy would therefore become a traitor of Sun Yatsenism. See Guangdongsheng danganguan and Zhonggong Guangdong shengwei yanjiu weiyuanhui bagongshi, eds., *Guangdongqu dang tuan yanjiu shiliao, 1921–1926* [Historical Materials on the CCP Guangdong Regional and Corps Committees] (Guangzhou: Guangdong renmin chubanshe, 1983), p. 210.

31. Ibid., p. 249.

32. Clementi to Amery, 15 Apr. 1926, C.O.882/11.

just returned to Guangzhou from Shanghai a day or two prior to the coup and was inadequately prepared, according to Zhou Enlai's account, to deal with this sudden crisis.[33]

Chinese Marxist historians have claimed that Zhou Enlai, Mao Zedong, Chen Yannian, and others contemplated military action in response to Jiang's coup, and this seems likely, because their power was not inferior to Jiang's. The CCP Guangdong Regional Committee claimed to have 600,000 peasants and 200,000 strikers under its influence and leadership.[34] Though Party membership in early 1926 was only over 300 in Guangzhou,[35] the Party also claimed about 1,400 members in the Chinese Socialist Youth Corps in the city and nearby counties.[36] Jiang Jieshi admitted that until mid-1926 about 20 percent of the graduates of the Huangpu Military Academy were Communists.[37] However, three important memoirs written by local Communist leaders make no mention of any meeting taking place between the local Party leaders and the Communist members of the Huangpu Military Academy after the coup with the intention of launching a military offensive.[38] Mao himself was not active in the CCP Guangdong Regional Committee, nor did he have a close relation with the Soviet advisors in early 1926.[39]

However, the local Communists did not sit still after the coup. Huang Ping recalled a special Party meeting at the leadership level vividly and bitterly:

[As] Jiang Jieshi's reaction became more obvious, Party members and the masses asked what was going on, and how to deal with it. Yannian called for a special meeting. I, as usual, served as an interpreter, translating his Anhui dialect into Guangzhou dialect. Now I can remember only one of his statements: "Jiang Jieshi possesses the army, we have the masses; no matter where he goes, he cannot go beyond the palm of the Buddha." This type of revolutionary optimism is certainly honor-

33. Zhou Enlai, "Guanyu 1924–26 nian dang dui Guomindang de guanxi," p. 120.

34. *Guangdongqu dang tuan yanjiu shiliao, 1921–1926*, p. 200.

35. "Guangdong gonghui yundong de baogao (summer 1926)," p. 346.

36. *Guangdongqu dang tuan yanjiu shiliao, 1921–1926*, p. 224.

37. Guangdong geming lishi bowuguan, ed., *Huangpu junxiao shiliao, 1924–27* [Historical Materials on the Huangpu Military Academy] (Guangzhou: Guangdong renmin chubanshe, 1982), p. 371.

38. See Zhou Enlai, "Guanyu 1924–26 nian dang dui Guomindang de guanxi"; Huang Ping, *Wangshi huiyi* [Memories of the Past] (Guangzhou: Guangdong renmin chubanshe, 1981); Deng Zhongxia, *Jianshi*.

39. Huang Ping, *Wangshi huiyi*, p. 21.

able and valuable. But I suppose even Yannian did not know how to deal with the situation.[40]

In short, the Communists were completely unprepared for Jiang's action on 20 March.[41] Under such circumstances, it was impossible for the Guangdong Communists to respond to Jiang's coup with any radical action. On the following day, the Communist-dominated Strike Committee issued the following announcement:

Our committee has been affected by today's military affair. In fact, our committee was not involved in it. We, the strikers, are only concerned with anti-imperialism and continuing to work with great effort to achieve a successful revolution. We must keep calm and wait quietly for its solution. We hope that all members of this committee will act accordingly and continue to carry out their normal duties. None of our members should be confused or thrown into turmoil.[42]

This announcement clearly reflected the state of mind of the major strike leaders, whose views concurred with those of many local Communists. Nine days later, the CCP Guangdong Regional Committee issued an open letter, in which the local Communists expressed their concern about the problem of disunity within the Guomindang and about the threat of imperialism, which might disrupt the CCP-Guomindang alliance. In the same letter, the Guangdong Communists emphasized the significance of the United Front policy and that Guangzhou had already been transformed into a revolutionary base with the Guomindang as the leader of the revolution. In closing, the Guangdong Communists declared that their support of the Guomindang would be maintained throughout (*shizhong*) the Nationalist Revolution.[43] Therefore, the Guangdong Communists had decided, from the very

40. Ibid., p. 39. Shortly after the coup, many Party members questioned their superiors on what type of policy they should follow. According to one participant, who was a member of the Socialist Youth Corps in Guangzhou and an active striker, the Party cadres failed to respond to this question satisfactorily. One of them said that "we should retreat." The Party and Corps members then asked, "Where to?" The reply was simply that "we should retreat to the masses." Interview with Li Peiqun, a participant of the Shenggang General Strike, in Guangzhou, 28 Dec. 1984.

41. Zhou Enlai, "Guanyu dang de liuda de yanjiu" [On the Study of the CCP Sixth Congress], in *Zhou Enlai xuanji*, vol. 1, p. 159.

42. *Gongren zhi lu,* 21 Mar. 1926.

43. Zhongguo gongchandang Guangdongqu weiyuanhui, "Gei Guomindang zhongyang guomin zhengfu guomin gemingjun ji Guangdong renmen de yifeng gongkai xin" [An Open

moment of the coup, to maintain the United Front policy regardless of the cost they would have to pay. It is certain, however, that the compromise agreement reached between Jiang and the Soviet advisors after the coup did reduce the tension in Guangzhou temporarily, and that the Soviet advisors were influential in pressing the Chinese Communists to implement a conciliatory policy.[44] But the Guangdong Communists found themselves without any other alternatives. After all, since they had not found any justification for calling for a counterattack by mass mobilization, how could they or the strike leaders tell the strikers to give priority to the struggle with the Guomindang for revolutionary leadership and not to the anti-imperialist movement? This dilemma was made clear by Chen Duxiu during the CCP Fifth Congress.[45]

Chen Duxiu in early 1926 did not appreciate what the Guangdong Communists had achieved, especially in leading the Shenggang General Strike. He believed his Guangdong comrades had executed an unrealistic and radical labor policy in south China. He was also worried that such a radical policy would undermine CCP-Guomindang relations. Although the views of the Guangdong Regional Committee and the Central Committee differed greatly concerning the strike,[46] Chen was equally disturbed by the events of 20 March and also wanted to maintain the United Front.

The initial response of the CCP Central Committee to the events of 20 March was similar to that of the Guangdong Regional Committee. On 3 April, without waiting for the arrival of a full report from the Guangdong Communists, Chen Duxiu, having read the accounts given by Shanghai newspapers, hurried to issue an open letter to clarify the position of the Central Committee concerning the coup. The main theme of this letter was similar in substance to that of the Guangdong Communists' open letter of 30 March, differing only in detail.[47] Both letters emphasized the importance

---

Letter to the Guomindang Central Nationalist Revolutionary Army and to the People of Guangdong], *Renmin zhoukan* 7 (30 Mar. 1926), p. 1.

44. Eudin and North, eds., *Soviet Russia and the East,* pp. 288–97; Xiang Qing, "Gongchan guoji Sulian he Zhongshan jian shijian" [The Comintern, the Soviet Union, and the S.S. *Zhongshan* Incident], *Dangshi zhiliao congkan* 2 (1983), pp. 94–113.

45. "Chen Duxiu zai Zhongguo gongchandang diwuci quanguo daibiao dahui shang de baogao" [Chen Duxiu's Report at the CCP Fifth Congress], in *Zhonggong dangshi ziliao* [Historical Materials on CCP Party History], vol. 3, p. 35.

46. Li Lisan, "Dangshi baogao (Feb. 1930)" [Report of Party History], in *Zhonggong dang baogao xuanpian,* p. 230.

47. Chen Duxiu, "Zhongguo geming shili tongyi zhengce yu Guangzhou shibian" [The

of keeping the United Front policy alive. The major difference was that Chen referred to Jiang Jieshi as one of the pillars of the Nationalist Revolution, whereas the Guangdong Communists praised the Guomindang as the revolutionary leader. In its analysis of the political situation in Guangdong from a distance, the Shanghai-based CCP Central Committee concluded that a policy of retreat should be implemented by the Communists after the coup, in the belief that the combined military strength of the local Communists and the left-wing Guomindang members was not enough to match that of Jiang.[48]

Only by mid-April, after a full report submitted by Chen Yannian concerning the coup and its aftermath had reached the Central Committee, did Chen Duxiu decide to formulate a new policy with a view to challenging Jiang. He proposed to arm the peasants and strikers of Guangdong, to unite with the Guomindang leftists, and to strengthen the Second and Sixth Divisions of the Nationalist army.[49] Peng Shuzhi was then assigned to Guangzhou to seek the approval of the Soviet advisors and to form a special committee there to deal with the problem of Jiang. But the Soviet advisors disapproved of this plan because they regarded Jiang as politically and militarily useful.[50] Moreover, they were also confident that, due to his lust for power and glory, Jiang would cooperate with them if they provided him with material support.[51] Thus, the Soviet advisors instructed the Guangdong Communists to strengthen their power by allying with the left-wing Guomindang.

Unity of Chinese Revolutionary Power and the Guangzhou Incident], *Zhongguo qingnian* 118 (3 Apr. 1926).

48. Chen Duxiu, "Chen Duxiu zai Zhongguo gongchandang diwuci quanguo daibiao dahui shang de baogao," p. 36.

49. Peng Shuzhi, *Ping Zhang Guotao de "Wo de huiyi"* [Critique of Zhang Guotao's *My Memoirs*] (Hong Kong: Qianwei chubanshe, 1975), pp. 5–6. In his book-length study of Chen Duxiu, Lee Feigon implies that Chen adopted this policy immediately after the coup. This is misleading. See Lee Feigon, *Chen Duxiu: Founder of the Chinese Communist Party* (Princeton: Princeton University Press, 1983), p. 188.

50. Peng Shuzhi, *Ping Zhang Guotao de "Wo de huiyi,"* pp. 6–10. According to Peng, it was Borodin who disapproved of the Central Committee's plan. But Martin Wilbur and Julie How believe that the disapproval came from Voitinsky. See Wilbur and How, eds., *Missionaries of Revolution*, p. 258. However, recent research, based on Li Lisan's political report submitted to the Comintern in 1930, reveals that indeed it was Borodin who turned down the Chinese Communists' proposal. See Xiang Qing, "Gongchan guoji Sulian he Zhongshan jian shijian," pp. 106–7.

51. "Stepanov's Report on the March Twentieth Incident," in Wilbur and How, eds., *Missionaries of Revolution*, pp. 705–7.

Soviet advisors also sought to take precautions against Jiang. At the end of April, Borodin, after a lengthy discussion with Chen Yannian and the strike leaders, decided to check Jiang by exploiting the personal conflict between him and Song Ziwen over the issue of leadership of the Guomindang. Deng Zhongxia was instructed to help form an armed picket with approval and material support from Song Ziwen, who intended to diminish Jiang's influence in the Guomindang. But these measures proved useless in challenging Jiang.[52]

The impact of the March Twentieth Coup was profound. Jiang Jieshi had detected the Communists' weaknesses; they would maintain the United Front even if it meant serving as coolies for the Guomindang.[53] Thus, in May 1926 when the Second Plenum of the Guomindang Central Executive Committee was held, he introduced a series of measures to limit the Communists' influence and activities in the Guomindang.[54] Although some Communists called for an immediate showdown with Jiang, the CCP bitterly accepted this policy. Although some Guangdong Communists planned to launch an anti-Jiang movement during the forthcoming Northern Expedition, the plans did not materialize.[55]

The political consequence of the coup among the Guangdong Communists was profound; they even admitted that their morale fell dramatically.[56] The local Communists were also confused by the policy of allying with the left-wing Guomindang faction, which, according to a Soviet advisor, did not exist after the coup.[57] Furthermore, the directive from the Comintern in mid-March, which warned against certain Chinese Communists who were trying to "skip over the revolutionary-democratic stage of the movement straight to the tasks of proletarian dictatorship and Soviet power,"[58] discouraged the Guangdong Communists, who had just celebrated the Paris

52. Huang Ping, *Wangshi huiyi*, pp. 30–31. Huang's account is supported by Qu Qiubai's report to the CCP Central Committee in September 1926. See *Guangdongqu dang tuan yanjiu shiliao, 1921–1926*, pp. 416–17.

53. Conrad Brandt, *Stalin's Failure in China* (Cambridge: Harvard University Press, 1958), p. 82.

54. Wilbur, *Nationalist Revolution in China*, pp. 48–49.

55. Duan Zhimin, "Shi lun da geming shiqi Bao luoting dui Jiang Jieshi celue de xiangxiang fazhang," p. 48.

56. *Guangdongqu dang tuan yanjiu shiliao, 1921–1926*, p. 344.

57. "Stepanov's Report on the March Twentieth Incident," in Wilbur and How, eds., *Missionaries of Revolution*, p. 712.

58. "Theses on the Chinese Revolution of the Sixth Enlarged Plenum of the ECCI, 17 Feb.–15 Mar. 1926," in Eudin and North, eds., *Soviet Russia and the East*, p. 349.

Commune with such enthusiasm. Henceforth, the Guangdong Communists withdrew their previous radical political slogans such as "Proletarian Dictatorship" and "Long Live the Paris Commune" from their publications.

The disappointment and frustration Deng Zhongxia experienced as a result of the coup were clearly perceptible. Ten days after the coup, Deng admitted that the objective and subjective conditions were not yet mature for establishing a working-class dictatorship in China.[59] And on May Day, he complained bitterly that the Chinese working class had fallen into an isolated and lonely position.[60] His analysis of revolutionary leadership also changed dramatically. Previously, he had thought that the Chinese working class had already seized the revolutionary leadership. But after the coup, he began to realize that such optimism was premature and that the Nationalist Revolution could be achieved only by maintaining the United Front policy, even at the cost of admitting the Guomindang as the true revolutionary leader. In late 1926, in an obscure passage, he stated: "There should be a distinction between revolutionary leadership [*lingdao*] and revolutionary leader [*lingxiu*]. In the Nationalist Revolution, the leader is naturally the Guomindang, who is just like the commander-in-chief [*zongsiling*]. [But] leading the various classes in the front line is the proletariat, which is just like the general commander [*zongzhihui*]."[61] Although this statement sought to salvage a significant role for the working class, Deng's writings after the coup reveal that he now believed that the Chinese working class had retreated from a leading to a supporting position in the Nationalist Revolution. In fact, with a view to keeping the United Front alive and to strengthening the power of the Guomindang leftists, he even appealed to workers and trade unionists to join the Guomindang as party members immediately![62] He, therefore, remained firm in the view that the Guomindang was still revolutionary, and that the chief counterrevolutionaries were the compradors and big bourgeoisie. He believed that there was still a chance

59. Deng Zhongxia, "Gongren jieji de yishou gongke" [A Lesson of the Working Class], *Gongren zhi lu*, 31 Mar. 1926.

60. Deng Zhongxia, "Jin nian wuji de mubiao" [The Objective of This Year's May Day], *Renmin zhoukan* 10 (30 Apr. 1926), p. 5.

61. Deng Zhongxia, *1926 nian zhi Guangzhou gongchao*, p. 91.

62. Ibid., pp. 89–92. Deng's attitude toward the Guomindang after the March Twentieth Coup was similar to that of most contemporary Communists. Conrad Brandt's comment on this issue, though written nearly thirty years ago, still merits being quoted: "for fear of losing themselves in the surrounding Kuomintang, [the Communists] had lost sight, or almost lost sight, of one of their own objectives. They had forgotten . . . that they were to guide the KMT left, not to supplant, or to become it" (*Stalin's Failure in China*, p. 85).

for the working class to capture the revolutionary leadership. The way to do this, according to his analysis, was to compete with the big bourgeoisie in gaining the support of the urban petty bourgeoisie and of the peasantry in the countryside.[63]

This strategy could not be implemented successfully, because the Communists misjudged the Guomindang. More important, labor factionalism and the lack of cooperation among workers, peasants, and petty bourgeoisie prevented the creation of a revolutionary situation favorable to the Communists.

The Attempt to Create Working-Class Solidarity

It is certain that the general strike brought about an upsurge in the Communists' influence among the working class in south China. But their success was not achieved without difficulty. Major obstacles were the traditional localism and factionalism among the working class in south China. Their problem was further complicated by the simple fact of job competition. The sudden injection of tens of thousands of job hunters from Hong Kong into Guangzhou, where the economy was weak, no doubt created tension between the returned strikers and the local workers.[64] But the main source of conflict was political rather than economic. Having witnessed the growth of conflicts within the working class during the first few months of the strike, Deng complained bitterly that this problem was directly related to the collusion between the right-wing Guomindang leaders and the conservative-minded workers, who were thus attempting to challenge the Communists' growing influence.[65]

During the early months of the strike, Deng predicted that the strike could only achieve its goal by two means: support from the Nationalist government and unity among strikers and workers.[66] It seemed unlikely that the Guomindang would act, at least openly, as a strikebreaker, because the Nationalist government regarded the support of the strike as a political obligation. But the task of promoting working-class unity and solidarity was problematic.

63. Deng Zhongxia, 1926 nian zhi Guangzhou gongchao, p. 91.
64. Tsin, "Cradle of Revolution," p. 268.
65. Deng Zhongxia, "Ping Guangzhou gonghui zhi zheng" [On the Strife of Labor Unions in Guangzhou], Renmin zhoukan 3 (24 Feb. 1926), p. 5.
66. Gongren zhi lu, 21 Nov. 1925.

In July 1925 during a local Communist Party meeting responsible for leading the strike, Deng Zhongxia spelled out explicitly the need for launching a movement to unify the various trade unions according to their industrial basis (*tongyi gongye yundong*). He observed that he was amazed by the large number, about 150, of different types of labor union in the small area of Hong Kong. The fragmentation of unions in the British colony created many obstacles to the development of working-class unity; if the CCP wanted to implement proletarian hegemony, it must help workers consolidate their unity by the formation of a general union (*zong gonghui*). Only through the centralization of the unions, he concluded, could the CCP effectively mobilize the workers for political purposes.[67]

A special committee consisting of some local Communists and ACLF representatives was formed with Li Sen as chairman to organize this movement. Deng did not sit on this committee but served as a chief advisor. It was Li Sen, a native of Hunan and representative of the ACLF, who took the leading part in organizing the movement for the formation of a Hong Kong general union.[68]

Prior to the outbreak of the strike, there were two major general trade unions in Hong Kong. These were the General Association of Labor Syndicates (Gongtuan zonghui), which had a membership of about seventy unions, and the General Union of Chinese Workers (Huagong zonghui), with a membership of about thirty unions. In both general trade unions, the majority of members were handicraft workers, although the General Union of Chinese Workers also had a fairly large membership recruited from public transport and utilities.[69] Many skilled industrial workers, such as the mechanics, did not join either of these unions, because they thought themselves superior to the other workers, in terms of both professional status and economic condition.[70] In fact, during the strike, the chairman of the Hong Kong Chinese Mechanics' Union (Xianggang Huaren jiqi hui), Han Wenhui, strongly opposed his members' participation in the strike.[71] Although the Communists' influence in the two general trade unions was relatively limited before mid-1925, they managed, after some difficult bar-

67. "Lishi ziliao huibian," vol. 2, no. 13, p. 2.
68. Ibid., pp. 3–4.
69. Ibid.; see also Ma Chaojun, *Zhongguo laogong yundong shi,* p. 490.
70. Interview with Liang Meizhi, a participant in the Shenggang General Strike, in Guangzhou, 27 Dec. 1984.
71. *Gongren zhi lu,* 10 Feb. 1926.

gaining among Deng Zhongxia, Su Zhaozheng, Yang Yin, and the union leaders, to win the unions' support during the strike.

In Guangzhou, a major labor confederation had already been established prior to the outbreak of the strike. This was the Guangdong General Union (Guangdong zong gonghui), which was reported to have a membership of 30,000 workers.[72] It was strongly influenced by the right-wing Guomindang leaders and was reluctant to participate in the strike. During the Shenggang General Strike, the workers in Guangzhou, with the exception of those working in Shamian, did not take any industrial action. Another major union, consisting of about 100,000 members, was the Guangdong Mechanics' Union (Guangdong jiqi gonghui), which was well known for its political conservatism and close connection with the right-wing Guomindang faction. Its early leader, Ma Chaojun, was condemned by the Second National Labor Congress as a leading scab (*gongzei*).[73] During the course of the strike, the Guangdong Mechanics' Union maintained close links with the Guangdong General Union in challenging the Communists and engaging in strikebreaking.[74] These two labor organizations had their own pickets, who were assigned to provoke conflicts with the strikers and left-wing labor activists. After the March Twentieth Coup, these labor organizations intensified their troublemaking because they realized that their actions would be approved, albeit not openly, by most of the Guomindang leaders, who had already secretly expressed their impatience to reach a strike settlement.[75]

The basic strategy adopted by the Communists to resist this strong conservative force within the labor movement was to strengthen the unity among those workers and trade unions that were under Communist influence, with emphasis on the development of industry-based labor unions and the formation of a general trade union. An important resolution to this effect was formulated during the Second National Labor Congress.[76]

72. Deng Zhongxia, *1926 nian zhi Guangzhou gongchao*, p. 60.

73. *Zhongguo dierci guanguo laodong dahui juejian, 1925.*

74. Chen Baqui, "Ji fandong de Guangdong jiqi gonghui shushi" [On Several Reactionary Events of the Guangdong Mechanics' Union], *Guangzhou wenshi ziliao* 12 (1964), pp. 111–12.

75. Interview with Li Peiqun in Guangzhou, 28 Dec. 1984. For documentary sources, see *Guangdongqu dang tuan yanjiu shiliao, 1921–1926*, p. 355; and Lu Qi, "Ji zai Shenggang da bagong zhong de Deng Zhongxial tongzhi," p. 85.

76. *Zhongguo dierci guanguo laodong dahui juejian, 1925.* Liu Shaoqi, in his report on the development of the Chinese labor movement to the Third National Labor Congress in 1926, regarded this resolution as the most important issue during the Second National Labor Con-

The ACLF launched a campaign for the formation of a Hong Kong general trade union four months after the start of the strike.[77]

Under the leadership of Li Sen in late July 1925, the Hong Kong mechanics started organizing their own general union as an alternative to the conservative Guangdong Mechanics' Union. Li was an able organizer and he won the trust of the Hong Kong workers, partly by delivering his speeches in the Guangzhou dialect. After about a month, a Hong Kong Mechanics' Federation (Xianggang jigong lianhe hui) was formed, with strong Communist influence. The local CCP members also expanded their activities in this newly formed labor federation and were able to recruit more than eighty new Party members within a short period of time.[78]

The second group of workers to unify their unions on an industrial basis was the Hong Kong printers, who were considered better educated than the other workers. Also under the strong influence of the Communist-dominated ACLF, they began to prepare for the formation of their labor federation by unifying the existing four major printers' unions in mid-November 1925.[79] A week later, a manifesto issued by the ACLF was printed *in extenso* on the front page of the *Gongren zhi lu* encouraging Hong Kong workers to consolidate the various existing trade unions into different labor federations (*zong gonghui*) according to industry and to establish a general trade union for all Hong Kong workers. A drafted regulation of the prospective Hong Kong General Union was attached to this manifesto which outlined its aims as follows:

1. To promote unity among various trade unions and to correct the previous mistake of individualism.
2. To restructure the trade union organizations—all modern industrial workers should join industry-based unions, and handicraft and small-factory workers should join trade-based unions—to promote the interests of workers.
3. To serve as the leader of the various unions in order to prevent the problem of individualism.

---

gress; see Liu Shaoqi, "Yi nian lai Zhongguo zhigong yundong de fazhan" [The Development of the Chinese Labor Movement over the Past Year], *Zhengzhi zhoubao* 13 (1926), p. 15.

77. *Gongren zhi lu,* 28 Nov. 1925.

78. "Lishi ziliao huibian," vol. 2, no. 13, pp. 4–6.

79. *Gongren zhi lu,* 20 Nov. 1925. See also Chen Zhiwen, "Da geming shiqi Guangzhou gongren yundong," p. 13.

4. To settle disputes among union members and to promote friendship among workers.

5. To promote the welfare of workers and to provide relief to those in need as well as to arrange for employment for those unemployed.

6. To promote education among workers and to establish schools and libraries for workers and their children.

7. To achieve the grand union [*da lianhe*] among all workers in China and to promote unity between workers in China and Hong Kong.[80]

This very moderate appeal, however, did not immediately receive a favorable response from the Hong Kong trade unions. The reason may have been the political instability of Guangzhou (the Nationalist government was engaged in a major military conflict with Chen Jiongming in Shantou), as well as persistent Guomindang influence among Hong Kong union activists.

Starting in early 1926, the Hong Kong Seamen's Union engaged in an effort to unify all the major transportation unions of the colony. On 3 January, it convened a congress, which about 2,000 seamen representatives from all over China attended. The congress managed to create an All China Seamen's Union.[81] Its most important achievement, however, was its contribution to the formation of a labor federation for all Hong Kong transportation workers. By mid-March 1926, the seventeen leading transport workers' unions, consisting of 200,000 members, were grouped into a Federation of Hong Kong Transport Workers' Unions (Xianggang yunshu gonghui lianhehui).[82]

Ironically, this federation was formed on the day before the March Twentieth Coup. Its inaugural ceremony was attended by leading Communist labor organizers. Among them were Deng Zhongxia, Su Zhaozheng, and Liu Shaoqi. Unlike the printers' general union formed in mid-November, this new federation was marked by its adoption of a political resolution, which emphasized the importance of anti-imperialism and anticolonialism, the struggle for national independence, and support of the Nationalist Revolution.[83] In its application for admission to the Red International of Transport Workers' Federation, the Federation of Hong Kong Transport Workers' Unions emphasized that their contribution to the course of anti-

80. *Gongren zhi lu,* 28 Nov. 1925.
81. "Lishi ziliao huibian," vol. 2, no. 13, pp. 14–16.
82. *Gongren zhi lu,* 20 Mar. 1926.
83. Ibid., 20, 28 Mar. 1926.

imperialism was decisive and influential: "Hong Kong is not only the base of British imperial economic penetration [in China], but also a naval bastion in the East. Yet, the reason that Hong Kong has become so important is due to us—the Hong Kong transport workers. Therefore, the control over the life or death of Hong Kong is in our hands."[84]

The politicization of this federation was certainly related to the influence of the Hong Kong Seamen's Union, whose success in 1922 made it a model par excellence in the Chinese labor movement. But equally important was the formulation of a new labor movement strategy by the local Communists to militarize and politicize the working class in early 1926. As has been noted earlier, Deng Zhongxia and the other local Communist leaders did not object to forming a "united front" with all labor unions, including the conservative labor organizations, in the present stage of political struggle.[85] But following the March coup, they concluded that the rapid expansion of Communist influence among the strikers and workers was an urgent task. It was reported that Chen Yannian, during a special Party meeting after the coup, reminded his comrades that "from now on, we must strengthen our efforts in the labor movement by the reorganization and unification of labor unions. . . . [and] bring these unions under our command."[86] The March Twentieth Coup was a turning point in Communist labor movement strategy. The old strategy of emphasizing the maintenance of a "united front" policy with all labor unions was abandoned; the new strategy stressed open rivalry with the "yellow unions."[87] The new strategy, not surprisingly, intensified conflict among rival labor unions.

In April, the Communists were able to extend their influence with the formation of two other major labor federations: the Federation of Hong Kong Workers Employed in Foreign Establishments (Xianggang yangwu zong gonghui) and the Labor Federation of Hong Kong Metallurgical In-

84. *Diyici guonei geming zhanzheng shiqi de gongren yundong* [The Labor Movement during the First Revolutionary Civil War] (Beijing: Renmin chubanshe, 1954), p. 190.

85. See, e.g., Deng's speech to the Strikers' Delegates Congress during the early stage of the strike: *Gongren zhi lu*, 27 July 1925.

86. Lai Xiansheng, "Zai Guangdong geming hongliu zhong: huiyi 1922 nian–1927 nian de douzheng" [In the Current of Guangdong Revolution: Memoirs of the Struggle during 1922–1927], *Guangdong dangshi ziliao* 1 (1983), p. 128. Lai claims that he was responsible for taking minutes during this meeting.

87. Chen Yu, "Chen Yu zizhuan" [Autobiography of Chen Yu], *Guangdong dangshi ziliao* 1 (1983), p. 199. This autobiography was in fact written by Chen in Yanan during the Party Rectification Campaign in 1941 as a piece of personal history and self-criticism.

dustries (Xianggang jinshuye zong gonghui).[88] However, the Communists'
political influence in these two labor federations was not as strong as in
the Federation of Hong Kong Transport Workers' Unions due to these
workers' traditionally close association with the Guomindang and with the
guild system in Guangzhou. It was the organizational concept of labor federation, rather than Communist ideology, that attracted members to these
two general trade unions.[89] In fact, though Feng Jupo, a major Guangdong
Communist leader, addressed the First Congress of the Labor Federation of
Hong Kong Metallurgical Industries, its resolution emphasized economic,
not political, struggle.[90] But even economic struggle was viewed by the
Guomindang as dangerous at the time.

The profound impact of the Communists on the Hong Kong working
class was evident in the establishment of the Hong Kong General Union
(Xianggang zong gonghui) on 15 April.[91] From the initial planning in late
1925 to its foundation, the ACLF played a very active role. The newly formed
Hong Kong Mechanics' Federation and the Hong Kong Seamen's Union
were the two other important organizations to promote the formation of
this union. In order to overcome the suspicion of some pro-Guomindang
unionists, the Communist-dominated ACLF deliberately arranged the first
planning meeting for the formation of the Hong Kong General Union to
be held at the Guomindang headquarters. The leading members of the
planning committee were also activists in the Strike Committee. After

88. *Gongren zhi lu*, 12, 13, 14, 15 Apr. 1926.

89. It seems natural that many Chinese historians, including those living in Taiwan, have
exaggerated the extent of the Communists' political influence in these two labor federations.
See, e.g., Cai Luo and Lu Quan, *Shenggang da bagong*, pp. 108–9; and Ma Chaojun, *Zhongguo laogong yundong shi*, pp. 529–30. The Marxist historians' interpretation may have been
based on their need to see the labor movement under Party leadership as a success; but their
writings are poorly documented. The interpretation by historians in Taiwan may be related
to their disapproval of the upsurge of Communist influence among workers in Guangdong,
including among those skilled mechanics who had long been associated with the conservative
political force. The major questionable point of Ma's book is that he quotes extensively from
"documents" without identifying their sources. He has, in fact, mistakenly assumed that it was
Liu Shaoqi who spoke at the opening ceremony of the Labor Federation of Hong Kong Metallurgical Industries. Furthermore, there is no record indicating that this federation adopted a
radical political resolution.

90. *Gongren zhi lu*, 12 Apr. 1926.

91. Ibid., 16 Apr. 1926; see also Deng Zhongxia, *Shenggang bagong gaiguan*, p. 58. Jean
Chesneaux mistakenly attributes the founding of the Hong Kong General Union to 15 May
(*Chinese Labor Movement*, p. 517).

five months of preparation, the First Congress of the Hong Kong General Union, which was attended by some 600 union representatives, was held on 15 April 1926.[92]

At its First Congress, Deng Zhongxia was invited to present a political report, which later formed the basis of the political resolution of the congress. In his report, Deng strongly condemned British imperialism in China and colonialism in Hong Kong and appealed emotionally to the delegates to unite the Hong Kong workers to resist the inequality and unfairness resulting from British exploitation. He also urged the Hong Kong workers, with the exception of the compradors, to maintain the revolutionary United Front and consolidate the revolutionary base in Guangzhou. He then concluded that they should also promote internationalism by allying with the British working class and other member unions.[93]

Although the General Union was able to recruit eighty union members, some conservative trade unions refused to be affiliated with it and formed their own labor federation, which was known as the All Hong Kong General Association of Labor Syndicates (Quangang gongtuan lianhehui).[94] It therefore constituted a major drawback to the Communist attempt to establish control over the Hong Kong trade unions.

For strategic reasons, the Communists gave priority to promoting their influence among the workers in Guangzhou. Since the founding of the United Front in early 1924, the local CCP labor activists, such as Chen Zhiwen and Yang Yin, had been able to extend their influence openly among the railway workers, who had previously been influenced by the conservative Guangdong Mechanics' Union.[95] By mid-April 1926, the five railway workers' unions in Guangdong were grouped together under the leadership of Deng Pei, a local Communist of working-class origin responsible for the railway workers' union movement, and formed a local office of

92. "Lishi ziliao huibian," vol. 2, no. 13, pp. 6, 20.

93. "Deng Zhongxia tongzhi zhengzhi baogao" [Political Report by Comrade Deng Zhongxia], Gongren zhi lu, 24, 26 Apr. 1926. For the political resolutions of this congress, see also Gongren zhi lu, 23 Apr. 1926.

94. Gongren zhi lu, 23 Apr. 1926. It is unfortunate that there is no statistical information regarding those unions that refused to join the Hong Kong General Union. For a complete list of the unions affiliated with this organization, see Diyici Zhongguo laodong nianjian, vol. 2, p. 80.

95. Chen Zhiwen, "Da geming shiqi Guangzhou gongren yundong," pp. 30–35. See also Zhongguo gongren yundong de xianqu [The Pioneers of the Chinese Labor Movement] (Beijing: Gongren chubanshe, 1983), vol. 2, pp. 202–5.

the All China Railway Union.[96] Simultaneously, Guangdong Communists launched a campaign to rally the Guangdong trade unions with a view to challenging right-wing labor organizations.

In mid-March 1926, Liu Ersong, who had been appointed secretary of the Labor Department of the Guomindang's Central Executive Committee in late 1925, was elected provisional chairman by the Preparatory Committee for the reorganization of the Guangzhou Workers' Delegates Congress,[97] which had been established in mid-1924. The success of the early Guangzhou Workers' Delegates Congress was limited due to strong opposition from pro-Guomindang unions and the conservative mentality of many local workers. Under Liu's leadership in early 1926, a labor newspaper, *Guangdong gongren zhi lu* (The Road of Guangdong Workers), was published to promote the idea of labor unity.[98] On 1 April 1926, the first meeting of a new Guangzhou Workers' Delegates Congress was held, with Liu as chairman. It was attended by about 2,000 delegates representing 138 unions and 162,876 unionists.[99] Its resolution was more or less an open declaration of its commitment to challenging the right-wing labor unions; it included strong condemnation of localism, of the traditional guild system, and of labor movement opportunists, whose motivation was based on self-interest rather than on the welfare of the working class. The resolution also called for the politicization of the labor movement by indoctrinating the working class on the following themes:

1. The theory of class struggle
2. The theory of the international labor movement
3. The relationship between the Nationalist Revolution and world revolution
4. The grand unity of the working class
5. Worker-peasant unity
6. Unity among workers of the whole world
7. The need to abolish traditional localism, the guild system, and traditional trade associations.[100]

96. *Gongren zhi lu,* 16 Apr. 1926. See also Chen Zhiwen, "Da geming shiqi Guangdong gongren yundong," p. 35; and Ma Chaojun, *Zhongguo laogong yundong shi,* pp. 543–44.

97. *Gongren zhi lu,* 19 Mar. 1926.

98. *Zhongguo gongren yundong de xianqu,* vol. 2, p. 229.

99. Deng Zhongxia, *1926 nian zhi Guangzhou gongchao,* p. 59. See also *Gongren zhi lu,* 2 Apr. 1926.

100. Jean Chesneaux interprets the resolution of this conference concisely and lucidly; see

Elsewhere, Communist labor leaders called on the congress to intensify the political struggle in the labor movement.[101] Largely due to the radical political resolution of this congress and the domination of the Communists, the two major right-wing labor organizations, the Guangdong Mechanics' Union and the Guangdong General Union, withdrew from the congress.[102] Their withdrawal signaled an increase in armed conflict between right-wing and left-wing labor unions during the last few months of the strike.

Right-wing labor unions in Guangzhou were dominated by the Guangdong General Union and by the Guangdong Mechanics' Union. The former was established in 1921 with about 100 union members, consisting largely of handicraft workers and shopkeepers. It was known to have a strong guild tradition, and its founder, Huang Huanting, was said to have collaborated with the employers. Due to its conservatism, the growth of its union membership was slow, and it consisted of about 300 unions by mid-1926. Moreover, the Nationalist government refused to register most of its members because they were regarded as major troublemakers among the Guangdong workers.[103]

The chief of police in Guangzhou, Wu Tiecheng, also attempted to organize under his control a group of conservative union activists by proposing to form a Labor Movement Committee of Municipal Guangzhou (Guangzhoushi gongren yundong weiyuanhui) in mid-March 1926.[104] His proposal met with very limited success due to the Communists' domination of the labor movement at the time. In fact, Wu later became a political victim because he was dismissed by Jiang Jieshi on 24 April as the price for regaining the Soviet advisors' support after the coup.[105] In spite of his dismissal, the unity of the labor movement in Guangzhou was greatly disrupted by the armed conflicts between the two leading union factions.

From May 1926 onward, the labor movement in Guangzhou was characterized by armed conflict between left-wing and right-wing labor unionists.

Chinese Labor Movement, p. 296. The text of this resolution can be found in *Diyici guonei geming zhanzheng shiqi de gongren yundong*, pp. 199–218.

101. *Renmin zhoukan* 8 (6 Apr. 1926), pp. 5–8.

102. *Gongren zhi lu*, 9 Apr. 1926. See also Ma Chaojun, *Zhongguo laogong yundong shi*, p. 519.

103. "Anarchism and Communism in Canton and Its Connection with the Labour Movement," enclosed in Denham to Alston, 25 July 1922, F.O.228/3140; *Zhongguo gongren yundong de xianqu*, vol. 2, p. 70; *Xiangdao zhoubao* 169 (28 Aug. 1926), p. 1715; *Renmin zhoukan* 17 (1 Aug. 1926), pp. 2–3.

104. Ma Chaojun, *Zhongguo laogong yundong shi*, pp. 513–15.

105. Clementi to Amery, 29 Apr. 1926, C.O.882/11.

In response to the Communists' new labor movement strategy, the right-wing Guomindang union activists armed their pickets. To disguise their identity, right-wing-union pickets wore uniforms similar to those of the Strike Committee's pickets. Therefore, the Strike Committee published a demand in mid-July that each union's pickets should have a different style of uniform.[106]

The increased conflict among the unions after May was an indication of the growth of a conservative force within the Nationalist government as a result of the March Twentieth Coup. Many of these confrontations were provoked by the right-wing unions, which were supported by the right-wing Guomindang leaders. The case of Chen Sen is a most revealing illustration.

Chen Sen, chairman of the Guangdong General Union and founder of several small unions for teahouses and small noodle restaurants, was claimed to have been in close collaboration with counterrevolutionaries, most notably with the Hong Kong comprador Chen Lianbai.[107] His conservative reputation was well established even before the outbreak of the strike because of his refusal to take part in the Second National Labor Congress and his reluctant participation in the anti-British boycott. Shortly after the outbreak of the strike, he was condemned for the murder of two local workers. In September 1925, he was again criticized for secretly setting up a strikebreaking movement. One month later, he was blamed for causing working-class disunity by having his followers join newly established unions so that they could disrupt the organizations from within. This strategy was fairly successful; several newly formed unions, especially in the handicraft and light industries, were badly affected. On 13 July 1926, he was accused of responsibility for the murder of two toothbrush factory workers while they were engaged in a union membership recruitment campaign.[108]

This event immediately led to the outburst of a series of armed conflicts between the Guangdong General Union and the Toothbrush Worker' Union, an affiliated member of the Guangzhou Workers' Delegates Congress. Chen was arrested by congress pickets and was sent to the Police

---

106. *Gongren zhi lu,* 19 July 1926.

107. This accusation was not groundless, because the Strike Committee discovered some personal correspondence between Chen Sen and Chen Lianbai concerning their plan to disrupt the labor movement in Guangzhou; see *Gongren zhi lu,* 11 Aug. 1926.

108. The account of the accusations against Chen Sen is based on "Chen Sen shiqing zhi zhenxiang," *Xiangdao zhoubao* 169 (28 Aug. 1926); "Chen Sen wenti zenyang jiejue," *Renmin zhoukan* 17 (1 Aug. 1926); and "Chen Sen wenti de jiaofei," *Renmin zhoukan* 18 (12 Aug. 1926).

Department pending trial.[109] However, he was soon released upon the instruction of Jiang Jieshi and even attended a public meeting where a farewell party was held for the soldiers participating in the Northern Expedition.[110] The release of Chen Sen encouraged the right-wing unions to intensify armed conflicts with their competitors. Thereafter, the Communists, extremely frustrated by Jiang's decision, launched a major campaign criticizing the Nationalist government. Both sides strengthened their forces by arming their pickets. The Guangdong General Union, by late August, possessed "several hundred" guns; four months later, its major rival, the Guangzhou Workers' Delegates Congress, had a self-defense unit consisting of more than 1,000 members.[111]

Continued armed conflicts among workers caused great disillusionment among many Communist labor leaders. It also destroyed the hopes of Deng Zhongxia, who had previously expected that any conflict among the working class could be solved through the channel of a labor federation, either by political or legal means.[112] Indeed, although armed conflict among workers in Guangzhou was basically a political issue, to him it was also evidence of their conservative and backward mentality, which were beyond his control.

The Communists in Guangzhou were of the view that such armed conflicts might serve as a means to challenge, or to defeat, the yellow unions. In fact, this was a major divergence in labor movement strategy between the CCP Central Committee and the Guangdong Regional Committee. The former emphasized a United Front policy with the yellow unions, whereas the latter insisted that open confrontation with the yellow unions was the only strategy possible to maintain the Communists' leading position in the labor movement.[113] Guangdong Communists did not realize that they had

109. *Gongren zhi lu,* 19 July 1926. The Chinese historians in Taiwan completely distort this event. They state that Chen was "kidnapped" by the Communists on 9 July and that he was beaten nearly to death. Whether or not the arrest should be interpreted as a "kidnapping," it occurred on 18 July. If he was really beaten "nearly to death," how was he able to attend a public meeting on 20 July? See Ma Chaojun, *Zhongguo laogong yundong shi,* pp. 547–50.

110. *Gongren zhi lu,* 20 July 1926; "Chen Sen shiqing zhi zhenxiang," pp. 1716–18. The Guangdong Communists commented that "the case of Chen Sen is not a personal question. It is neither a legal nor a labor movement question. In fact, it is a question directly related to the Nationalist Revolution" ("Chen Sen wenti de jiaofei," p. 3).

111. "Chen Sen wenti de jiaofei"; "Guangzhou gongren daibiao dahui yu Guangzhou gongren yundong zhi xianzhuang" [The Guangzhou Workers' Congress and the Condition of the Guangzhou Labor Movement], *Renmin zhoukan* 33 (3 Dec. 1926), p. 4.

112. *Gongren zhi lu,* 9 Mar. 1926.

113. *Guangdongqu dang tuan yanjiu shiliao 1921–1926,* p. 420.

committed a grave strategic error, which was later acknowledged by one of the leading participants, Chen Yu:

due to our inadequate understanding of the conditions of the workers in Guangzhou and also due to our one-sided analysis, we committed many mistakes in terms of [labor movement] organizational policy, especially in dealing with the Guangdong Mechanics' Union. At that time, there was a strong emphasis on the reorganization of unions according to industry; but [we] ignored the role played by the members and leaders of the Guangdong Mechanics' Union in the whole area around Guangzhou. . . . the Guangdong Mechanics' Union and the Guangdong General Union were [organizations] with mass support and basis. [During the strike], they adopted a policy of "divide and conquer," and we promoted a policy of reorganization of unions according to industry as a response to their policy. This led to the struggle against each other, and [subsequently] we were separated from the working-class masses.[114]

On the other hand, it seems unfair to criticize the Communists' labor movement strategy without referring to the actual political problems of the period. After the March Twentieth Coup, the force of conservatism in Guangzhou increased significantly. By mid-May, Jiang Jieshi's political power was fully consolidated, which enabled him to restrict Communist influence within the Guomindang. Under such circumstances, it seemed that the Communists had no alternative but to adopt a strategy of expanding their influence among the masses by an open confrontation with the yellow unions. Deng Zhongxia and his comrades in Guangzhou in mid-1926 could accept, albeit reluctantly, a conciliatory policy toward the Guomindang after the March Twentieth Coup, but a compromise policy with the yellow unions was an anathema.

The Attempt to Create a Revolutionary Alliance with the Petty Bourgeoisie and Peasantry

In the mid-1920s, with the exception of a few modern and sizable commercial establishments which were capitalized by returned overseas Chinese, the major economic activities in Guangzhou were mercantile in character and small-scale in operation.[115] Unlike Shanghai, where a class of Chinese bourgeois with its own ideology and political experience had already

114. Chen Yu, "Chen Yu zizhuan," p. 199.
115. Tsin, "Cradle of Revolution," pp. 105–6.

emerged, the entrepreneurs in Guangzhou were generally financially weak and politically passive. Within the first decade after the 1911 Revolution, their political participation was loosely organized and their commitment did not go beyond support for the local government or protection of their own economic interests,[116] though on occasion they responded with anti-foreign sentiments to national humiliation or to unfair international settlements that threatened their economic positions.

In general, Guangzhou lacked modern industrialists and financiers, who were the backbone of the bourgeoisie in Shanghai. As of the 1920s, it seemed that the bourgeoisie, in its political and in its economic sense, had yet to form in Guangzhou. But the infant modern economic structure and activities of this southern city had created a small class of what the Communists would label "petty bourgeois."

To contemporary Chinese Communists, the term "petty bourgeoisie" denoted more of a political orientation than a social origin or economic basis. It was generally used to describe a group of people whose financial position was relatively independent but not solid, and whose revolutionary commitment had not yet been firmly established. For instance, Chen Duxiu referred to small factory owners and intellectuals as members of the petty bourgeoisie.[117] Mao Zedong, due to his strong interest in rural problems, used the term to describe small landholders in the countryside.[118] Deng Zhongxia averred that handicraft workers possessed a petty bourgeois mentality because of their conservative political outlook.[119] But all of them shared the view that the small factory owners and businessmen with little capital investment should be classified as members of the petty bourgeoisie. For clarity, the term is used here to refer to the small-capital merchants (*xiao shangren*), a generalization that had been widely adopted by the Chinese Communists, including Deng Zhongxia.[120]

Before the outbreak of the strike, Deng Zhongxia regarded the petty

116. Even during the so-called Chinese bourgeois revolution in 1911, the role of the Guangzhou merchant class was insignificant. See Edward Rhoads, "Merchant Associations in Canton, 1895–1911," in Mark Elvin and G. William Skinner, eds., *The Chinese City between Two Worlds* (Stanford: Stanford University Press, 1974), pp. 108–17.

117. Chen Duxiu, "Zhongguo guomin geming yu shehui ge jieji," p. 4.

118. Mao Zedong, "Zhongguo shehui ge jieji de fenxi" [Analysis of the Various Chinese Social Classes], in Takeuchi Minoru, ed., *Mao Zedong ji* [Works of Mao Zedong] (Tokyo: Hokubosha, 1972), vol. 1, pp. 166–68.

119. Deng Zhongxia, "Ping Guangzhou gonghui zhi zheng," p. 5.

120. See, e.g., Deng Zhongxia, "Zhongshan xiansheng zhi gongnong zhengce" [The Worker-Peasant Policy of Mr. Sun Yatsen], *Renmin zhoukan* 5 (12 Mar. 1926), p. 12.

bourgeoisie, which was exploited by foreign imperialism, as an unreliable revolutionary force. However, the local merchants' enthusiastic support during the strike convinced him that they were not as untrustworthy as he had thought. In fact, during the strike, he believed that the ultimate success of proletarian hegemony in China would depend on the ability of the working class to rally the support of the urban petty bourgeoisie and the rural peasantry.[121]

The merchants' support of the strike was related more to economic than to political factors. Li Langru, a representative of the Guangzhou General Chamber of Commerce (Guangzhou zong shanghui), lucidly explained the attitude of the local merchants toward the strike in early August 1925 while attending a reception hosted by the Strike Committee:

Usually, we were the losers whenever there was a business dispute with foreign merchants. Besides, the rise and fall of prices were completely controlled by the foreign merchants; the price of foreign goods could be raised according to their own will, whereas prices of Chinese goods were forced lower. All these injustices are our merchants' painful sufferings. At the present moment, the strikers and workers are devotedly fighting against foreign imperialists. We, the merchants, should naturally offer our best support, and [our mutual support] should not be diverted by the bastards' rumors. Whether [to implement] Communism or not is an internal question of our country. We therefore should not listen to these rumors while we are jointly fighting against foreign enemies. Furthermore, transportation in Hong Kong has been cut off; our trading profit [as a result of this situation] would be increased tremendously if we also develop Huangpu as a [modern] port. But there is a problem that we would like to bring to the attention of the Strike Committee and the government. [We understand that] the application for import and export permits is a special and important arrangement during the strike. But it is very often that the issuing of the permit to the merchants takes more than a week. This problem leads to a long delay in shipment and to damage to goods. We hope that improvement regarding this matter can be arranged.[122]

Thus, the merchants' support was due to their frustration with the adverse effects of foreign capital in the Chinese market.[123] They would maintain their support as long as their economic interests were not damaged.

121. Deng Zhongxia, *1926 nian zhi Guangzhou gongchao,* pp. 92–93. See also Deng Zhongxia, "Gongnongshang lianhe zhanxian wenti" [Issues on the United Front of Workers, Peasants, and Merchants], *Gongren zhi lu,* 12 June 1926.

122. *Gongren zhi lu,* 15 Aug. 1925.

123. Foreign commercial activities in Guangzhou were generally centered on the export

To a certain extent, the merchants' economic interests had been immediately affected by the outbreak of the strike because the Nationalist government, in order to provide financial support to the strikers, had imposed a special property tax of half a month's rent and a surtax on all trading licenses.[124] Due to their antiforeign sentiment and patriotism, the merchants and other local businessmen did not, for the time being, voice their opposition. However, when the local economy was badly hurt by the prohibition against foreign ships entering Guangzhou via Hong Kong, they asked the Strike Committee, by submitting complaints directly to the Nationalist government, to modify the shipping regulations.

During the strike, the four major merchants' associations in Guangzhou worked in close consultation with each other with a view to protecting and promoting their economic interests.[125] It was due to this "pressure group" that the Strike Committee modified some of the boycott policies. During a local Party meeting which took place about two months after the outbreak of the strike, the chief Soviet advisor, Borodin, suggested that, in order to maintain normal economic activities in Guangzhou, the boycott policy should be limited to British vessels and goods. His suggestion was immediately accepted by Deng Zhongxia and Chen Yannian. But the strikers did not fully understand the rationale for the modification of the boycott policy,

---

business; exporters bought agricultural products, notably sugarcane and silk, from the producers through the Chinese merchants. Because of the foreigners' abundant capital and modern shipping facilities, the local Chinese merchants were not in a position to compete on favorable terms with them or with the Chinese compradors working for the major Hong Kong-based foreign firms such as Jardine and Matheson or Butterfield and Swire. In most cases, many local Chinese merchants served as the dealers between the producers and foreign buyers. Therefore, the merchants complained constantly that their profits had been taken by foreign businessmen, even though they themselves had profited considerably at the expense of the producers. For a Chinese account, see, e.g., Li Weishi, "Guangdongsheng cansiye de maoyi ji qi shuailuo" [The Silk Trade and Its Decline in Guangdong Province], *Guangzhou wenshi ziliao* 16 (1965), pp. 70–79. For a Western analysis and interpretation, see Marks, *Rural Revolution in South China*, pp. 100–108.

124. Guangdongshen zhengfu, *Guangdongsheng zhengfu tekan: jijuean* [Guangdong Municipal Government: Resolutions] (Guangzhou, 1926), p. 31.

125. These included the Guangzhou General Chamber of Commerce (Guangzhou zong shanghui), the Guangdong Federation of Chambers of Commerce (Guangdong quansheng shanghui lianhehui), the Guangzhou Municipal Chamber of Commerce (Guangzhoushi shanghui), and the Guangzhou Merchants' Association (Guangzhou shangmin xiehui). Some of the correspondence between these four associations and the Strike Committee concerning the associations' requests to modify the shipping regulations can be found in Guangdong zhexue shehui kexueyuan, ed., *Shenggang da bagong ziliao*, pp. 290–97.

and Deng had to explain this issue to the Strike Delegates' Committee.[126] On 28 August 1925, the Strike Committee issued the following notification:

With a view to respecting the wishes of the Political Council of the Nationalist government, the Strike Committee has resolved to abolish the use of the permit granted by this committee. From now on, all business related to import and export shall be conducted under the regulations that have been formerly laid down. This means that all non-British cargoes and non-British ships that did not come to Guangzhou via Hong Kong will be free to enter and leave this port.[127]

This policy was immediately appreciated by the local merchants because Guangzhou emerged, overnight, as the most important entrepôt in south China. On the basis of this modified boycott policy, the ACLF and the Strike Committee, supported by the four local major merchants' associations, issued a series of new commercial and shipping regulations for firms and steamers of Japan, America, and France in mid-September 1925.[128] Two months later, about eighty foreign firms had moved their offices from Hong Kong and Shamian to Guangzhou.[129] The local Chinese merchants enjoyed a business boom because of the absence of strong economic competition from the British merchants.[130] Their temporary economic success was witnessed even by Hong Kong officials, and the governor remarked in late December 1925 that "the boycott has shown that it is possible for Canton to make itself to a certain extent independent of this Colony; and the longer the boycott lasts, the greater is the probability of a permanent loss of trade to Hong Kong."[131] Half a year later, the secretary of Chinese affairs reaffirmed the governor's observation and noted that "the merchants in Canton do not seem to be very anxious for a strike settlement; at least they have not so informed the [Nationalist] Government."[132]

The economic situation in Hong Kong after the outbreak of the strike,

126. Huang Ping, "Guanyu Shenggang da bagong de huiyi ziliao," p. 23.

127. *Gongren zhi lu*, 28 Aug. 1925.

128. Guangdong zhexue shehui kexueyuan, ed., *Shenggang da bagong ziliao*, pp. 296–97.

129. *Gongren zhi lu*, 29 Dec. 1925.

130. For a concise discussion of the strike's positive economic impact on the Chinese merchants in Guangzhou, see Cai Luo and Lu Quan, *Shenggang da bagong*, pp. 53–58; and Chesneaux, *Chinese Labor Movement*, pp. 309–10.

131. Clementi to Amery, 24 Dec. 1925, C.O.882/11.

132. "Memorandum by R. H. Kotewell, 4 June 1926," enclosed in Clementi to Amery, 8 June 1926, C.O.882/11.

however, was chaotic. The shipping and cargo transport industries, which were the major sources of Hong Kong financial operations, were nearly at a standstill. The financial system was on the verge of bankruptcy. Hong Kong, as recalled by the American secretary of state Henry Stimson in the mid-1930s, seemed almost a dead city.[133] During the first few weeks of the strike, a run on the banks resulted in a temporary suspension of payment by practically all Chinese banks. This unstable financial situation subsequently caused the bankruptcy of eight major Chinese banks, and two others went into liquidation. Many small native-Chinese enterprises were badly affected. Local commercial activity fell at least 40 percent below normal. The price of food increased sharply.[134] In response to this financial crisis, the Hong Kong government implemented the following policies: (1) control over the export of currency, (2) a moratorium on Chinese banks from 22 to 29 June, (3) the offer of a government-guaranteed loan of $6,000,000 to local Chinese banks, and (4) the request of a loan of £3,000,000 from the British government.[135]

In view of the financial crisis that had been brought about by the strike, the Hong Kong Chinese merchants, whether owners of small or large firms, were hostile to the strike from the beginning. A week after the Hong Kong Chamber of Commerce had requested the British minister in Beijing, Sir James Macleay, to introduce a firm policy against the strikers by strengthening the military force in the colony in mid-July 1925, the Hong Kong Chinese merchants held a public meeting to condemn the spread of Communism and radicalism among the strikers in Guangzhou.[136] Their hostility toward the strikers caused much displeasure even among the officials

133. Henry L. Stimson, *The Far Eastern Crisis* (New York: Harper & Brothers Publishers, 1936), p. 112.

134. "Effects of the Strike and Boycott on Business in Hong Kong," enclosed in Company Correspondence, Hong Kong to London, 19 Feb. 1926, Papers of John Swire and Sons Ltd., box 41.

135. "Memorandum by R. H. Kotewell, 24 Oct. 1925," enclosed in Stubbs to Amery, 30 Oct. 1925, C.O.882/11.

136. Telegram, Hong Kong Chamber of Commerce to Macleay, 22 July 1925, F.O.228/3146. Macleay did not consider the request favorably, because, as was normal in 1920s British diplomacy, the Foreign Office did not consider seriously merchants' opinions on political issues. The officials in London believed that businessmen "are usually very superficial and for that reason [their political opinions] are more often embarrassing than of assistance. . . . It is therefore desirable to encourage them to devote their activities to the solution of the economic rather than the political parts of the problems presented by China." See, e.g., "Minutes by Newton, 10 Mar. 1925," F.O.371/10917 [F740/2/10]. On the public meeting, see *Times* (London), 5 Aug. 1925.

of the Nationalist government. While visiting Guangzhou to seek a strike settlement in late December, the representatives of the Hong Kong Chinese merchants were criticized by the Guomindang official press as the "cold-blooded foreign slaves and rebels of the Chinese Republic."[137] The major strike leaders certainly found themselves in complete agreement with the Nationalist government.

Unlike his passionate view of the Hong Kong working class, Deng Zhongxia did not believe that any member of the Hong Kong Chinese merchant class would turn out to be a reliable revolutionary partner, even though he mentioned in passing that some newly established middle and small merchants were in sympathy with the strikers. He considered that the majority of the Chinese merchants in the colony were either pro-British or apolitical.[138] Therefore, when meeting with a group of Hong Kong merchants' representatives in early October 1925, he bluntly criticized their weaknesses:

Gentlemen, the reason that you have been suffering over the past three months is your mistaken thinking and soft-hearted attitude. Why is there mistaken thinking? It is because you considered that [our strike] would not last so long; you did not take any action in assisting or cooperating with us. Some members in your merchant community even tried their best to break the strike; they wanted to become the running dogs of the imperialists. Why is your attitude so soft-hearted? The reason is that you never utilized your own power to fight against imperialism. [The imperialists] therefore always look down on you; you are gullible.[139]

Though he spoke to the representatives of the Hong Kong Chinese merchants with a less critical voice and asked for their support on the following day,[140] his earlier, severe criticism truly represented his antipathy for them. Furthermore, unlike his policy in dealing with the merchant associations in Guangzhou, he did not propose forming a revolutionary united front with the Chinese merchant class in Hong Kong. His critical view of this class in the colony was not groundless: they never offered any substantial support to the strike, and their primary concern was to settle it as soon as possible.

Although Deng Zhongxia regarded the Chinese merchants, or the petty bourgeoisie, in Guangzhou to be generally sympathetic to the strike, they

137. *Guangzhou minguo ribao,* 31 Dec. 1925.
138. Deng Zhongxia, *Shenggang bagong gaiguan,* pp. 37–38.
139. *Gongren zhi lu,* 2 Oct. 1925.
140. Ibid., 3 Oct. 1925.

were not, in reality, any more revolutionary than their counterparts in Hong Kong. Deng's early suggestion for the formation of a revolutionary alliance of the working class, the peasantry, and the petty bourgeoisie simply could not be realized. It seemed unlikely that the merchant class in Guangzhou would continue their enthusiastic support of the boycott if they had to pay the extra costs incurred in shipping their cargo via other ports instead of Hong Kong over a long period of time. Besides, they could not easily handle the various surtaxes that had been imposed by the Nationalist government in the name of supporting the strike. For instance, the silk filature manufacturers in Guangzhou closed their workshops in late May 1926 as a protest against the government's forced loan and unsecured bonds.[141] Furthermore, many Chinese merchants in Guangzhou were connected with Hong Kong either by business or by family ties. It was also commonly known that some major Guomindang leaders had direct capital investment in the colony; Song Ziwen and his friends, for instance, invested 1.5 million Hong Kong dollars in the colony in early 1926.[142] Thus, any economic crisis in the colony would directly or indirectly affect the business community in Guangzhou. It is not surprising that some Guangzhou merchants tried to settle the strike by sending a delegation to the Hong Kong government.[143]

Though the strike was an urban-based political movement, the boycott against Hong Kong also involved the deployment of about 2,000 armed pickets in the countryside along the southern Guangdong border. As discussed in the previous chapter, the Strike Committee also sent speech corps members to the countryside after they had received two weeks of training at the Peasant Movement Training Institute. The pickets deployed along the border regions also spread political propaganda among the peasants. Also, many returned Hong Kong strikers went back to their native villages, where they conveyed political messages from the Strike Committee to their fellow villagers. About forty returned Hong Kong teachers organized themselves into a propaganda team to launch a political movement in the countryside.[144] Some returned Hong Kong mechanics and seamen carried out similar activities in their native villages.[145]

141. *Hong Kong Daily Press,* 25 May 1926.

142. Brenan to Macleay, 16 Oct. 1926, F.O.371/11634 [F4951/1/10].

143. Clementi to Amery, 23 Dec. 1925, C.O.882/11. A similar visit undertaken by another group of delegates from the Guangzhou business community took place in June 1926. See Chinese newspaper cuttings, 9 June 1926, Guomindang Party History Archives, 447/39.2.

144. "Lishi ziliao huibian," vol. 1, no. 2, p. 21.

145. Interview with Liang Meizhi in Guangzhou, 28 Dec. 1984.

Political propaganda among the peasantry during this period was also directly related to the rapid expansion in the establishment of Communist Party cells in many parts of rural Guangdong under the instructions of the CCP Central Committee in October 1925. The primary function of this policy was to increase the Communists' influence among the peasantry and progressive youth with a view to creating an independent revolutionary force that would be separate from the Guomindang.[146] The CCP also simultaneously launched a labor movement in the countryside by establishing branch offices of the leading leftist trade unions in the major counties. Under this policy, the Chinese Seamen's Union established branch offices in Baoan and Zhongshan, which were the birthplaces of many seamen in south China. By maintaining close contact with its headquarters or with the Strike Committee, the branch offices of the Chinese Seamen's Union became a major channel between the strikers in Guangzhou and the peasants in the countryside.[147]

But for geographical and other reasons, it was impossible for the Communists or the strikers to spread their propaganda throughout the entire rural area of Guangdong. It appears that the peasants of only two major regions offered their support to the strike: Haifeng and the major counties near the Guangdong–Hong Kong border. Under the leadership of Peng Pai since 1922, the Haifeng peasants had become politically organized. They supported the strike with a contribution of $1,000 to the strikers in November 1925, and Peng Pai was twice invited to speak to the Strikers' Delegates Congress.[148] The reason that the peasants living in the Guangdong–Hong Kong border regions offered their support was related both to the deployment of pickets in these areas and to social factors.[149] The propaganda campaign organized by the Strike Committee in these regions was more intensive than in other rural areas because they were strategically important to the enforcement of the boycott. Numerous reports appeared in the *Gongren zhi lu* on the close collaboration between the pickets and the local peas-

146. Wilbur and How, eds., *Missionaries of Revolution*, pp. 187–88. For a report submitted by a Communist leader in Guangdong regarding their reaction to the Central Committee's directive, see *Guangdongqu dang tuan yanjiu shiliao, 1921–1926*, pp. 344–50. According to this report, the local Communists had successfully expanded their influence among the local youth.

147. *Gongren zhi lu*, 1 July 1925; Chen Yu, "Chen Yu zizhuan," p. 195.

148. *Gongren zhi lu*, 1 Nov. 1925. Peng addressed the Strikers' Delegates Congress on 7 Aug. 1925 and 18 Oct. 1925; see ibid., 8 Aug. and 19 Oct. 1925.

149. These counties included Zhongshan, Baoan, Dongwan, Shunde, Shantou, Huiyang, Leizhou, and Qiongyan Ya. See *Guangdongqu dang tuan yanjiu shiliao, 1921–1926*, p. 334.

ant associations to enforce the boycott against Hong Kong.[150] There were also strong clan connections between the peasants of these counties and the Hong Kong workers. Family ties certainly encouraged some Guangdong peasants to support the strike.

But this type of peasant-striker cooperation did not occur throughout rural Guangdong. No pickets were sent to the more remote areas. Even along the Guangdong–Hong Kong border, the local peasants sometimes resisted the boycott because it damaged their economic interests. The Strike Committee's regulations prohibiting the peasants from farming land located in these areas and from selling their agricultural and fishing products to the colony became main sources of discontent for many peasants. To overcome this problem, the Strike Committee eased some of the boycott regulations, allowing certain amounts of salted fish and preserved fruits to be exported to Hong Kong; and those farmers who had to cultivate their land located in the New Territories were allowed to cross the border to do so.[151] But these measures were only introduced in April 1926, nine months after the start of the strike, as a result of growing discontent among the peasants. The Strike Committee was later severely criticized by the CCP Guangdong Regional Committee for ignoring the economic interests of the peasantry:

The prohibition on the export of foodstuffs during the strike in order to besiege Hong Kong is quite good. But we should understand that these are the products of the peasantry; the prohibition on the export of foodstuffs also means cutting off their market. The strike should be supported; but to prohibit the export of agricultural products provokes discontent among the peasants, which in many locations they have continually expressed. At a peasants' congress [held] in Baoan, half of the members did not vote to support the strike. [When we] asked them why, the answer was that the pickets were bad. In fact, the pickets were not bad. It was in fact because they had prohibited them from exporting foodstuffs. Fertilizer and salted fish [produced] in [Luohu] are not allowed to enter Chinese territory, and the export of Chinese farmers' products is prohibited. All these measures have caused much suffering among the peasants. . . . The peasants in Hailufeng also feel discontent

150. See, e.g., *Gongren zhi lu*, 4, 8 Aug. 1925; 12, 13 Sept. 1925; 20 Dec. 1925; 23 Jan. 1926; 30 July 1926; and 24 Aug. 1926. For a printed documentary reference, see Guangdong zhexue shehui kexueyuan, ed., *Shenggang da bagong ziliao*, pp. 488–94.

151. Before 1949, some Guangdong farmers in Baoan in fact possessed some land in what is today called Luohu in the New Territories in Hong Kong. In the 1920s, there was no tight restriction on their crossing the border to cultivate their land. *Gongren zhi lu*, 9, 17 Apr. 1926.

toward the pickets because their pigs, cows, and fruits are not allowed to be shipped to Hong Kong.[152]

The Strike Committee was also criticized for causing unnecessary trouble to the peasants of Baoan because of some of the regulations concerning those who worked on farms located on the Hong Kong side. According to the regulations, each Baoan peasant had to present a passport with a photo of himself and his cow, if he had one, to the pickets whenever he crossed the border![153] The peasants' economic losses created poor relations between them and the pickets. Unlike the Guangzhou merchants who benefited from the boycott movement, the peasants generally became victims because the Strike Committee failed to protect their economic interests.

It would be wrong, however, to say that the strike leaders were not interested in the peasant movement. Indeed, Deng Zhongxia should be given credit for calling his comrades' attention to spreading political propaganda in the countryside. The major peasant movement leader, Peng Pai, was also an enthusiastic supporter of the strike. Both leaders regarded the alliance between the working class and the peasantry as the basis of the CCP revolutionary strategy. The lack of close collaboration between city and countryside in this period therefore was not because the strike leaders were oblivious to the countryside; rather, they regarded the peasants as an auxiliary force.[154] Nor was the problem caused by the personal attachment to the cities of many Communist leaders, "who undoubtedly felt most comfortable operating in the familiar setting of the cities."[155] The major source of this problem was the inability to devise a successful boycott policy in which the economic interests of the peasantry could be protected. Furthermore,

152. Guangdong zhexue shehui kexueyuan, ed., *Shenggang da bagong ziliao,* pp. 668–69. There is a serious typographical error in this printed document. Luohu, a small town in northern New Territories in Hong Kong that is connected to Guangdong by a bridge, is misprinted here as "Xinzhen."

153. For the terms of this regulation, see *Gongren zhi lu,* 9 Apr. 1926, or Guangdong zhexue shehui kexueyuan, ed., *Shenggang da bagong ziliao,* pp. 265–66. I am indebted to the late Professor Jin Yingxi of the Guangdong Provincial Academy of Social Sciences for reminding me of this interesting point.

154. Chesneaux, *Chinese Labor Movement,* p. 317.

155. Ying-mao Kau, "Urban and Rural Strategies in the Chinese Communist Revolution," in John W. Lewis, ed., *Peasant Rebellion and Communist Revolution in Asia* (Stanford: Stanford University Press, 1974), p. 258.

the problem was also deeply rooted in the Party's restricted organizational ability at the time.

There was a serious shortage of personnel within the local Party leadership. Deng Zhongxia explained this very clearly: "To speak the truth, in the present great current [of struggle], the Chinese Communist Party in fact is in a state of anxiety and uncertainty because [it] does not have sufficient manpower to support and lead the workers."[156] Though the CCP had launched a major campaign to recruit Party members by easing admission regulations and had expanded the cadres' training program starting in the winter of 1925, Deng still felt, after the end of the strike, that there was a serious problem of inadequate local Party leadership. For instance, there were only 300 Communists working among some 150,000 pro-Communist labor union members in the city of Guangzhou even by the summer of 1926.[157] In the countryside, the Communists had a similar problem. Shortly after the end of the strike in October 1926, the CCP Central Committee commented on the peasant movement in Guangdong as follows:

(I) In the past, the organization of our Party expanded from Guangzhou to the countryside; the peasant movement in the villages therefore developed accordingly. At present, the situation is vice versa. There has already been a great development in the peasant movement in the villages, but the Party has not expanded greatly. Now, the Party cannot lead the peasant masses [due to lack of manpower]. (II) There are 800,000 organized peasants, scattered over more than 60 counties. But we [have] organized fewer than 20 cell units with fewer than 600 [Party] members in these counties. Under the current objective conditions, it can only lead to a major danger in our Party; the peasants expose their weakness, [but] we cannot guide them. If the situation continues to develop like this, the peasant movement will definitely become very dangerous.[158]

Labor and peasant movement leaders were able to promote political activities only in the regions under their own control.

In concluding this chapter, certain observations are in order on the problems of the strike and its relationship to the Communist movement in the mid-1920s. The Shenggang General Strike was basically an anti-British movement, but its influence was mainly local. Its major contribution was to

156. Deng Zhongxia, *1926 nian zhi Guangzhou gongchao*, p. 79.
157. "Guangdong gonghui yundong de baogao (1926)," p. 346.
158. *Guangdongqu dang tuan yanjiu shiliao, 1921–1926*, p. 431.

consolidate the revolutionary base of the Nationalist Revolution. It failed, however, to spark a nationwide labor movement in support of the revolution. There was a serious lack of coordination between the Hong Kong strikers and the workers from the other major treaty ports; nor did the strikers receive massive support from the other social classes locally. Even worse, workers in south China, for reasons already discussed, engaged in a series of armed conflicts among themselves. There was, regretfully for the Communists, a class struggle within a class.

Moreover, the workers' political consciousness in south China generally did not go beyond the stage of antiforeign sentiment; only a few of them understood the meaning of socialist revolution. This study reveals, however, that the main cause of armed conflict among the workers in Guangzhou was not only their backward social and political consciousness but the reactionary labor policy of the right-wing Guomindang leaders. Poor CCP leadership exacerbated the problem of working-class division.

Although Deng Zhongxia, who was then supported by Su Zhaozheng, Yang Baoan, Yang Yin, and Huang Ping, had created a leadership composed of workers and Marxist intellectuals in the summer of 1925 for organizing a massive labor movement, the Communists encountered many unanticipated problems throughout the course of the strike. Most important was the problem of maintaining this shared leadership between workers and Marxist intellectuals. Different visions of the strike made this difficult. To the strike leaders, especially the south Chinese CCP members of intellectual background, men like Deng Zhongxia and Chen Yannian, the strike was part of the Nationalist Revolution. To the majority of the strikers, who were of working-class origin, however, it was an expression of their anti-British sentiment. The CCP leaders of intellectual background repeatedly, especially after the March Twentieth Coup, sacrificed the interests of the working class to their own vision of revolution.

The price for the Communists of their temporary success in urban mass mobilization during this period was high; it accelerated the growth of counterrevolutionary forces, which climaxed in the March Twentieth Coup. Though none of the Communists, either in Shanghai or in Guangzhou, approved Jiang's action on 20 March, they did not launch a military counteraction. The reason was related not only to the conciliatory policy formulated by the Russian advisors, as many Western historians have argued, but also to the Communists' inability to find a justification for action against Jiang at a time when the major objective of the revolution was stated to be anti-imperialism and anti-warlordism.

This study also demonstrates that the claim of Chinese Marxist historians regarding the Communists' ability to achieve support from the other social classes distorts the historical picture. Only in the early stages of the strike were the Communists able to rally support from the workers, petty bourgeoisie, and peasantry on the basis of their patriotic sentiment. The petty bourgeoisie and peasantry in particular supported the strike only to the extent that their personal economic interests were not disrupted. Deng Zhongxia and his comrades completely failed to satisfy the petty bourgeoisie and peasantry over this issue. Nor were they able to sustain working-class unity in the face of social tradition and party politics. As a result, the Communists were unable to create a strong and united revolutionary alliance between the various social classes that would be capable of challenging the growing reactionary power of Jiang Jieshi.

The contradiction between right-wing Guomindang power and the labor movement during the course of the strike was highlighted by the March Twentieth Coup. The fundamental issue of the coup was not merely a power struggle among the major political leaders; it was also directly related to a choice between party leadership and mass action. Jiang staged the coup out of fear of losing party control over the mass movement. Communist leaders in Guangzhou, including Deng Zhongxia, however, were to lose their sense of political direction after the March Twentieth Coup. They believed that the United Front policy must be maintained even if it meant sacrificing the interests of the working class. They agreed that the strike should be settled during the Northern Expedition in the interest of the Nationalist Revolution even though the original demands of the strikers had not yet been met. The sacrifice of the interests of the working class would compound their previous strategic errors by undermining further the social basis for revolution they had begun to put together during the Shenggang General Strike.

5

Imperialism and Nationalist Revolution

I*T IS CERTAIN* that none of the Chinese Commu-
nists, including Deng Zhongxia, expected the Shenggang General Strike to
continue indefinitely. Deng told the strikers during its early stages that they
were engaged in a protracted anti-British struggle, but he was well aware
that the strike would probably be settled after three months due to the
shortage of food. Although he was the chief strike organizer and leader,
Deng did not participate directly in the settlement negotiations; diplomatic matters were handled by the Guomindang Nationalist government.
However, he was a keen observer and perceptive analyst and wrote extensively on the problems relating to British policy on the strike. His writings
on diplomatic issues during this period were used as texts in the School
of Labor Movement Studies during the second half of 1926.[1] It has been
claimed that the leaders of the Guomindang Nationalist government conducting the strike settlement negotiations with the local British officials
frequently considered his diplomatic analyses and proposed tactics.[2]

1. Interview with Li Peiqun in Guangzhou, 28 Dec. 1984. These writings include *Shenggang
bagong gaiguan* and *Shenggang bagong zhong zhi Zhongying tanpan.*
2. Huang Ping, "Guanyu Shenggang da bagong de huiyi ziliao," p. 10.

Deng as Diplomatic Analyst

In his analysis of British military and diplomatic strength, Deng argued that Britain was not in a position to reintroduce gunboat diplomacy in dealing with the anti-British movement in south China.[3] He saw the decline in British overseas power as a consequence of the high rate of unemployment and the upsurge of the left-wing labor movement in England. He also saw the lack of international support as a decisive reason discouraging Britain from adopting gunboat diplomacy in seeking a strike settlement.[4] *Gongren zhi lu* was quick to report his observations. Under Deng's editorship, it issued a long article on 19 September 1925 that discussed the weaknesses of the British military and diplomatic position in China and that ascribed British weakness partly to lack of support from Japan and the United States.

Deng's analysis of the British position was largely valid. Although discussions on the use of force had been held among British officials between July and October, lack of support from the signatories of the Nine-Power Treaty of the Washington Conference prevented the British from sending gunboats to the Pearl River.[5] British officials were frustrated by the decline of British military power in the Far East after World War I; Sir Victor Wellesley, the deputy under-secretary of state for foreign affairs, complained that "from military and naval points of view, we are more or less powerless to deal with such an amorphous mass as China."[6] After vetoing the various measures proposed to deal with the strike and boycott,[7] the For-

3. Deng Zhongxia, *Shenggang bagong gaiguan,*pp. 59–61.

4. Deng Zhongxia, "Yingguo diguo zhuyi zhi weiji" [The Crisis of British Imperialsim], *Renmin zhoukan* 6 (19 Mar. 1926), pp. 3–8.

5. David C. Wilson, "Britain and the Kuomintang, 1924–1928: A Study of the Interaction of Official Policies and Perceptions in Britain and China" (Ph.D. thesis, University of London, 1973), pp. 278–80. John Pratt, advisor to the Far Eastern Department, commented in early 1926 that "we obviously cannot count on international cooperation in any retaliatory policy against Canton to stop the anti-British boycott." See "Minutes by Pratt, 25 Feb. 1926," F.O.371/11622 [F70/1/10]. Pratt's senior colleague completely concurred with his view. See "Minutes by Wellesley, 14 Oct. 1926," F.O. 371/1161 [F4239/1/10].

6. "Memorandum by Sir V. Wellesley, 28 Aug. 1925," F.O.371/11653 [F3456/8/10].

7. The various measures that had been considered and then vetoed by the Foreign Office between June 1925 and February 1926 were (1) to use force to attack Guangzhou; (2) to impose a blockade; (3) to offer assistance to an anti-Communist Chinese leader to overthrow the Nationalist government; (4) to put pressure on Moscow to try to discourage Comintern support to Guangzhou; (5) to adopt a policy of conciliation with the Guomindang; (6) to appeal to the League of Nations; and (7) to adopt a policy of patience and wait for the defeat of the radical elements in Guangzhou by internal causes. After several months of discussion

eign Office could only adopt a policy of "inaction" in February 1926. The only solution the British could hope for was that the Nationalist government would be defeated by internal causes.

This estimation was shared by British officials in China and London. In early September 1925, the British legation in Beijing predicted that the Nationalist government would soon be defeated by other warlords and that the strike would be settled without British intervention.[8] Three months later, the Foreign Office speculated that "the Strike Committee at Canton seems to be a Super Tammany Hall Party, which will be inevitably driven out sooner or later by the moderates."[9] The Hong Kong government was also pessimistic about British termination of the boycott. In January 1926, the governor predicted that "there is no means of ending the boycott except by holding out until the present Canton Government is overthrown either by internal disruption or by the attack of some hostile Chinese Generals."[10]

Deng's interpretation of the limitations of the British government in defending its interests in south China was fairly accurate. But he did not realize that the British were still in a position to use gunboat diplomacy if their patience ran out and if their economic interests were badly damaged. Besides, Deng also overestimated the strengths of the Chinese revolutionaries in Guangzhou. He even remarked on occasion that the Chinese were prepared to enter into a war with Britain![11] His misjudgment of the nature of the strike stemmed from a belief that the anti-British movement in Guangzhou would develop into a nationwide anti-imperialist movement.[12]

---

between the British officials in China and at Whitehall, the Foreign Office reluctantly followed a policy of patience and "inaction." For details regarding the raison d'être of the British diplomatic dilemma during this period, see the long printed confidential report "Memorandum Respecting Canton, 3 Feb. 1926," F.O.228/3153 [F513/1/10]. For scholarly interpretations, see Wilson, "Britain and the Kuomintang," chap. 5; William Roger Louis, *British Strategy in the Far East, 1919–1939* (Oxford: Clarendon Press, 1971), pp. 124–39; and Edmund S. K. Fung, *The Diplomacy of Imperial Retreat: Britain's South China Policy, 1924–1931* (Hong Kong: Oxford University Press, 1991), pp. 55–80.

8. Telegram, Palairet to Chamberlain, 5 Sept. 1925, F.O.228/3149.

9. "Minutes by Moss, 30 Dec. 1925," F.O.371/10950 [F6227/194/10].

10. Clementi to Amery, 14 Jan. 1926, C.O.882/11.

11. Deng Zhongxia, "Huanying yingguo diguozhuyi jingong Zhongguo de shiwan dabing" [Welcome the Attack of China by the 100,000 Soldiers of British Imperialism], *Renmin zhoukan* 4 (4 Mar. 1926), p. 4. At the beginning of the strike, Deng said that he did not believe the British would give up their treaty rights without a war with China. See *Gongren zhi lu,* 18 July 1925.

12. Deng Zhongxia, "Wo Shenggang bagong gongyu ying zhuyi de yige wenti" [Several Issues of Which Our Shenggang Strikers Should Be Aware], *Gongren zhi lu,* 24 Aug. 1925.

Deng's optimism contrasted with the views of Chen Duxiu. Two months after the start of the strike, Chen reminded his comrades in Guangzhou that, while seeking for a strike settlement, the strikers in Shanghai and Hong Kong should limit their demands to economic and local issues, and that they should leave the basic national issues such as the abolition of unequal treaties to the People's Convention (discussed below).[13] Ironically, Chen's views coincided with those of the British Foreign Office, which also regarded the strike as a local conflict between Hong Kong and Guangzhou that should be handled by local British officials.

Basically, the British legation was primarily concerned with the politics in Shanghai, Nanjing, and the Yangzi Valley, where the major British investments in China were located. The Foreign Office in London did not give much attention to political developments in south China until the Nationalist government had launched its Northern Expedition and had begun to upset the balance of power between the north and the south.[14] Indeed, as of March 1926, Whitehall was still indecisive as to whether to approach Guangzhou or Beijing to seek a strike settlement, since the Nationalist government was not recognized by the British or any major powers as the legitimate authority in China. Foreign Secretary Chamberlain claimed that a closer and more direct contact with Guangzhou regarding this matter would complicate the problem of the status of the Nationalist government.[15] Deng's optimism concerning the strike's potential for developing into a nationwide political movement was later to be criticized, though he was not named in any internal Party documents expressing this criticism. At the end of the strike, the CCP Guangdong Regional Committee issued the following declaration to the strikers: "Although you have struck a strong blow against British imperialism, we cannot expect the Shenggang General Strike or Guangdong to defeat British imperialism single-handed. To defeat them, we need to combine the power of the whole nation and the methods of the Shenggang General Strike."[16]

Though Deng Zhongxia had overestimated the impact and scope of the strike, his analysis of the methods used by the Hong Kong government in dealing with the anti-British movement in south China was perceptive. His view that Hong Kong served as the base for an anti–Nationalist government movement was shared by many contemporary Chinese. He accused

13. *Xingdao zhoubao*, 23 Aug. 1925.
14. Wilson, "Britain and the Kuomintang," pp. 335–37.
15. Telegram, Chamberlain to Macleay, 20 Mar. 1926, F.O.228/3153.
16. *Guangdongqu dang tuan yanjiu shiliao, 1921–1926*, p. 453.

the Hong Kong government, first, of allowing Hong Kong to be used as a base for the counterrevolutionaries, from which they organized their plots to assassinate Liao Zhongkai and to overthrow the Nationalist government. Second, he accused the colonial government of relying on the Chinese compradors in Hong Kong and Guangzhou and on right-wing Guomindang leaders to break the strike and boycott. Third, he accused the Hong Kong government of channeling funds to the warlords in south China, especially Chen Jiongming, for the overthrow of the Nationalist government.[17]

In view of the hostile attitude of the Hong Kong government toward the Guomindang, especially in the first half of the 1920s, Deng's accusations were not groundless. Although Whitehall had repeatedly emphasized a policy of nonintervention and neutrality in dealing with China after the Washington Conference,[18] it is doubtful that this policy was observed rigidly by the leading British officials in Hong Kong, who perceived the political developments in south China to be contrary to their interests. This was the general problem facing the governors of Hong Kong since, according to the Foreign Office, "the Governorship of Hong Kong should not be entrusted to anyone who does not possess the necessary qualifications to keep the balance between the domestic needs of the Colony and the exigencies of high policy."[19] However, both Governor Stubbs and Governor Clementi committed the similar mistake of overstressing the local interests of the colony, and both were severely criticized by the Foreign Office as a result. Sir Cecil Clementi's frequent requests to the home government for permission to introduce forceful measures, such as financing an enemy warlord of the Nationalist government or imposing a blockade, created embarrassment in the Foreign Office. In May 1926, John Pratt, now an advisor at the Foreign Office, could no longer restrain his irritation and criticized the governor severely:

The Chinese have a proverb that a frog at the bottom of a well sees only a narrow circle of the sky; and if in addition to this disadvantage the frog is suffering from nervous strain and loss of balance, then despatches like these are, I suppose, the natural result. That so able and scholarly a Governor as Sir C. Clementi can take such a narrow and prejudiced view and write what, without wishing to be disre-

17. Deng Zhongxia, "Women duiyu dongzheng de zeren," pp. 7–8; Deng Zhongxia, *Shenggang bagong gaiguan*, pp. 21–27, 40–43, 46–49; and Deng Zhongxia, *Jianshi*, pp. 242–46.

18. Macleay to Chamberlain, 23 Dec. 1925, F.O.228/3151.

19. "Memorandum on the Governorship of Hong Kong, 25 June 1924," F.O.371/10266 [F2086/169/10].

spectful, I can only describe as nonsense about China is an illustration of the spiritual isolation which is really the underlying cause of Hong Kong's troubles.[20]

This internal criticism did not prevent the governor from adopting other measures which caused further embarrassment to the British government. His proposal to issue an ultimatum to the Nationalist government if the strike and boycott were not settled by 10 October led to further concern in Whitehall. Wellesley commented, "I am beginning to feel a little uneasy about Clementi." Another member of the Far Eastern Department was annoyed by Clementi's suggestion and noted "an alarming tendency on the part of the Governor."[21]

The Hong Kong government's policy in dealing with the political situation in Guangzhou certainly diverged from the basic principle of nonintervention and neutrality that had been suggested by Whitehall. But how far and in what ways did the Hong Kong government depart from this principle? The answer we arrive at will allow us to assess the accuracy of Deng Zhongxia's analysis.

One of the sensitive issues was the relationship between Hong Kong and the anti-Guomindang warlords in south China. The major anti-Guomindang leader in this area, Chen Jiongming, had been on very friendly terms with the Hong Kong officials since the early 1920s. For instance, shortly after the Hong Kong Seamen's Strike was settled, there was a cordial exchange of views between A. G. E. Fletcher, the assistant colonial secretary, and Chen concerning the radicalism of the Guangdong government.[22] One month later the colonial government proposed offering a loan to Chen with a view to strengthening his army and restoring order in Guangzhou. Although Governor Stubbs's suggestion was turned down by his seniors in Beijing and London, he raised the same issue again several months later and received the same reply. During the Shenggang General Strike, the governor repeated his proposal to aid the enemies of the Nationalist government, again without gaining approval from London. After several requests by the Hong Kong government, in early October 1925 the Foreign Office reluctantly agreed that Whitehall would not disapprove of "any loans which

20. "Minutes by Pratt, 14 May 1926," F.O.3711/11625 [F1961/1/10].
21. "Minutes by Monnesy and Wellesley, 14 and 15 September 1926," F.O.371/11630 [F3776/1/10].
22. "A. G. E. Fletcher's Report on the Seamen's Strike," enclosed in Stubbs to Alston, 27 Mar. 1922, F.O.228/3527.

the Chinese merchants [in Hong Kong] may care to make to Chen [Jiong-ming]."[23]

Since the loan in the end did not come from government sources, some British scholars have argued that the Hong Kong government did not give any financial support to the anti-Guomindang warlord faction during this period.[24] But it is not quite true that the colonial government was not involved in the financing of Chen Jiongming or his colleagues. First, the activities of the Chinese community in raising funds for Chen Jiongming were strongly encouraged by the government. Second, government records released in recent years show that, as Governor Clementi admitted at the time, the Hong Kong government was directly involved in aiding the anti-Guangdong warlords financially.

In a strictly confidential dispatch, Governor Clementi reported, reluctantly and with embarrassment, to the Colonial Office that he had instructed the colonial secretary's account to pay $40,000 to the Donghua Charity Group, a major Chinese charity organization in Hong Kong, in January 1926, and he asked the Colonial Office to endorse his instruction. He also asked that the amount credited to the Donghua Charity Group "remain as an advance from the Trade Loan without interest until the political situation is clearer."[25] This financial arrangement was the result of aid given to an anti-Guomindang warlord, Wei Bangping, in mid-August 1925. According to this dispatch, the leading colonial officials, including the governor and the secretary for Chinese affairs, had held several meetings with the two Chinese representatives of the Legislative Council on matters relating to aiding Wei. The Hong Kong officials thought that $50,000 should be contributed to Wei by advancing cash from the Donghua Charity Group on the condition that the sum would be repaid by a small group of Chinese merchants, who had promised to take this financial responsibility. Wei's coup, however, met with defeat. When the Donghua Charity Group compiled its annual financial report and asked the concerned Chinese merchants for repayment, the governor stepped in to help them by offering a government

23. Telegram, Curzon to Clive, 4 Apr. 1922, F.O.228/2995; Jamieson to Alston, 23 Oct. 1922, F.O.228/2999; telegram, Curzon to Alston, 8 Jan. 1923, F.O.228/3000; telegram, Stubbs to Palairet, 22 Sept. 1925, F.O.228/3150; telegram, Palairet to Chamberlain, 24 Sept. 1925, F.O.228/3150; telegram, Stubbs to Palairet, 25 Sept. 1925, F.O.228/3150; telegram, Amery to Stubbs, 9 Oct. 1925, F.O.228/3150; telegram, Waterlow to Amery, 5 Oct. 1925, F.O.228/3150.

24. See, e.g., Wilson, "Britain and the Kuomintang," pp. 301–3.

25. Clementi to Amery, 24 Sept. 1926, C.O.129/498/23.

loan of $40,000 on 1 January 1926 to clear the balance. Although the concerned Chinese merchants were able to pay the first instalment of interest to the government on time, there was no further repayment of the loan. Due to financial difficulties in the colony, Clementi requested approval from the Colonial Office for exempting the debtors from paying interest until the colony recovered from economic chaos. The governor considered his request was justified because "to press them personally for payment would seriously embarrass them financially and would be impolitic."[26] It is therefore clear that the Hong Kong government not only encouraged Chinese merchants to raise funds for the anti-Guomindang movement but also served as a "consultant" for the local Chinese elite in matters relating to their fund-raising campaign for the anti-Guomindang warlords.

In his writings, Deng frequently emphasized that the Hong Kong government supported enemies of the Guangdong government by providing them with a shelter from which local anti-Guomindang leaders like Chen Jiongming, Chen Lianbai, and others could direct their anti-Guangdong movement.[27] His accusation that the Hong Kong government offered its support to Chen Jiongming was not groundless. In October 1925, the British consul general in Shantou wired the Hong Kong government after the Nationalist army had occupied that port as follows:

I should be greatly obliged if you would be so good as to cause representation, in such form as you see fit, to be made to General Chen Chiung-ming, urging him to issue instructions forthwith for the suppression of such intimidation. I venture to think that such action taken by the Hong Kong Government, under whose protection General Chen is living, would possibly have more effect than representations made by myself locally; and if it is possible to obtain from him a definite undertaking to deal suitably with the situation in which the British subjects are now placed, my hand will be correspondingly strengthened.[28]

The Hong Kong government responded to this request by "taking steps to induce General Chen Chiung-ming to restore normal conditions at that port."[29] The minutes of the Hong Kong government's Executive Council do not mention specifically what type of steps the colonial government took

26. Ibid.

27. Deng Zhongxia, *Shenggang bagong gaiguan*, pp. 16–18.

28. Telegram, Kirke to the Colonial Secretary of Hong Kong, 16 Oct. 1925, enclosed in Kirke to Palairet, 16 Oct. 1925, F.O.228/3529.

29. "Minutes of the Hong Kong Executive Council Meeting, no. 56, 22 Oct. 1925," C.O.131/65.

regarding this matter; but the reference is solid evidence of the close relation between the Hong Kong government and Chen Jiongming. It suggests Deng Zhongxia's accusation against Hong Kong for its use as a base and for channeling funds for the anti-Guangdong movement is well founded. There is no evidence, however, to support Deng's claim that the Hong Kong government was implicated in the assassination of Liao Zhongkai, even though some members of the colony's Chinese community may have contributed funds to the plotters.[30]

According to Deng Zhongxia, the Nationalist government contemplated settling the strike in early 1926 via a compromise with the Hong Kong government. There were informal negotiations between Hong Kong officials and some leading Guomindang leaders regarding this matter. In his writings, Deng named only Wu Chaoshu as a major right-wing Guomindang leader who had tried desperately to settle the strike by maintaining close contact with the Hong Kong government.[31] Others also involved in these contacts were Song Ziwen and Sun Ke; the former visited Hong Kong in mid-December and again in early January. During his second visit, Song met Sun Ke in the colony on the latter's home-bound trip from Shanghai. While they were in Hong Kong, they were kindly received by the governor and expressed their antipathy for the strike and their expectation for reaching an early strike settlement.[32]

Contrary to Deng's interpretation, the Hong Kong government favored Sun and Song over Wu Chaoshu, whom it viewed as the chief obstacle to ending the strike.[33] The Hong Kong governor wrote: "C. C. Wu was the chief obstacle to a strike settlement. . . . Wang Chingwei made a few half-hearted efforts to open negotiation and his departure is a loss from the British point of view. Sun Fo [Sun Ke] was a moderate element in the Canton Government. . . . Mr. Eugene Chen is more friendly to [Hong Kong] than his predecessor in office."[34] The Hong Kong Chinese elite also considered Song Ziwen as more "sympathetic and helpful" with regard to an early

30. Wilson, "Britain and the Kuomintang," p. 293.

31. Ibid., p. 41.

32. Clementi to Amery, 8 Jan. 1926, C.O.129/498/7.

33. For instance, after Wu was dismissed from his post as minister of foreign affairs, a leading Hong Kong official quoted an authoritative Chinese source that "[Wu] did his duty, according to his own light, on behalf of the Canton Government in connection with the strike and boycott. It is his misfortune to be somewhat cynical and subtle, and too legal." See "Memorandum by R. H. Kotewall, 4 June 1926," enclosed in Clementi to Amery, 8 June 1926, C.O.882/11.

34. Clementi to Amery, 11 June 1926, C.O.882/11.

strike settlement.[35] Sun Ke was also very friendly with the Hong Kong government. He visited the governor twice within three months in early 1926 and each time complained to the governor of his frustration with the Strike Committee.[36]

That Deng did not identify Song and Sun in his writings may have been due to their influential positions in the Nationalist government. Since Sun Ke was the son of the late Sun Yatsen, respect for his father probably led Deng to spare the son from open criticism. As for Song Ziwen, he was given credit by the local Communists for his financial support to the strikers in his capacity as the finance minister of the Nationalist government. Moreover, the close personal relations Song had with Borodin, for whom he acted as translator,[37] had created the impression that Song was sympathetic with the strikers. Partly because of this, Deng Zhongxia believed that the Guomindang remained a revolutionary party in spite of his suspicion of certain right-wing leaders. He was therefore willing to agree with the Guomindang's decision in calling off the strike and boycott in the interest of the Nationalist Revolution.

Early Attempts to Settle the Strike

On the day after the Shaji Incident, the American consul general in Guangzhou contemplated mediating the dispute between Guangzhou and Hong Kong; but his mission met with failure because the Chinese were unwilling to enter negotiations.[38] Thereafter, Britain stood alone in handling the antiforeign movement in south China; none of the major powers extended its assistance to Britain in finding a solution. Since the Foreign Office regarded the strike and boycott as a local issue, the responsibility for settlement rested on the British officials in the colony and Guangzhou. But great difficulties stood in the way of a settlement.

The Hong Kong governor, Sir R. E. Stubbs, whose term of office was due to expire at the end of June, took an uncompromising attitude toward

35. "A Report to Mr. Chow Shou-son and Mr. R. H. Kotewall, 2 Jan. 1926," enclosed in Clementi to Amery, 6 Jan. 1926, C.O.882/11.

36. "Memorandum of a Conversation with Mr. Sun Fu at the Government House, Hong Kong, by Clementi," enclosed in Clementi to Macleay, 29 Mar. 1926, F.O.228/3153.

37. *Guangdongqu dang tuan yanjiu shiliao, 1921–1926*, p. 421.

38. Jamieson to Macleay, 25 June 1925, F.O.228/3144.

the strikers.[39] He considered the anti-British movement to be the work of a small group of radical Communists whose activities did not receive mass support;[40] hence he was unwilling to negotiate with the Nationalist government. Instead, he introduced a series of suppressive policies in the colony in the hope of preventing further trouble. These included, *inter alia,* the introduction of press censorship and the right of the police to raid the premises of suspected lawbreakers. The intelligence service was strengthened by the employment of two Chinese who were responsible for obtaining political information from Guangzhou. The government also expanded its propaganda campaign by funding a Chinese newspaper, *Gongshang ribao* (Industry and Commerce Daily), and by organizing public street lectures.[41]

Governor Stubbs expected to solve the Guangdong problem by forceful measures instead of peaceful negotiation. He proposed putting diplomatic pressure on the Beijing government to deal with Guangzhou, cutting off the Russian supply of arms to the Nationalist government, and even using naval force. All these proposals were judged impractical by the Colonial and Foreign Offices.[42] In late September, Governor Stubbs even proposed that the Boxer Indemnity funds be used to aid an enemy of Guangdong such as Chen Jiongming and that Hong Kong serve as a naval base for the Beijing government to suppress the radical movement in Guangzhou. These suggestions too were vetoed by the British legation in Beijing, as well as by Whitehall.[43] His suggestions were clearly unrealistic and diverged from the

39. Because of the outbreak of the general strike, the Colonial Office extended Governor Stubbs's term of office so that he could deal with the crisis until the arrival of his successor, Sir Cecil Clementi, on 1 November 1925. Chan Lau Kit-ching, *China, Britain, and Hong Kong,* p. 184.

40. Telegram, Stubbs to Amery, 17 July 1925, C.O.129/448. See also Stubbs to Amery, 12 Sept. 1925, enclosed in Grindle to Foreign Office, 15 Sept. 1925, F.O.371/10949 [F4852/194/10].

41. "Memorandum by R. H. Kotewall, 24 Oct. 1925," enclosed in Stubbs to Amery, 30 Oct. 1925, C.O.882/11. In early September, Stubbs requested the Colonial Office for permission to subsidize the *Gongshang ribao* to the tune of $3,000 monthly for the purpose of anti-Communist propaganda. The request was granted. See Stubbs to Amery, 3 Sept. 1925, C.O.129/494. For a comprehensive account of the Hong Kong government's antistrike policy, see Chan Lau Kit-ching, *China, Britain, and Hong Kong,* pp. 184–93.

42. Stubbs to Amery, 12 Sept. 1925, enclosed in Grindle to Foreign Office, 15 Sept. 1925, F.O.371/10949 [F4582/194/10]. For details regarding the British legation's comments on Stubbs's suggestion, see the minutes written by A. L. Scott on 16 September 1925 attached to this dispatch.

43. Telegram, Stubbs to Palairet, 22 Sept. 1925, F.O.228/3150; Palairet to Chamberlain, 24 Sept. 1925, F.O. 228/3150.

general British policy toward China at the time. He left the colony on the last day of October 1925 without solving the problem.

James Jamieson, the British consul general in Guangzhou, was considerably shocked by the Shaji Incident. Since there were rumors that he would be assassinated, Jamieson, already an alcoholic, confined himself to Shamian most of the time and had little contact with the Chinese officials in the city. He was in fact criticized by the colonial officials for his inability to maintain proper contact, not only with the Chinese officials, but also with the Hong Kong government. When Jamieson's personal problem was brought to the attention of Whitehall and the British legation, they asked him whether he was able to carry out his normal duties and maintain contact with the Chinese officials. Although he cabled to Sir James Macleay in Beijing stating that there would be no difficulty in continuing his good service, his activity in seeking a settlement was limited to routine paperwork in his office.[44] In short, both the governor and the consul general failed to respond to the crisis by peaceful negotiation or by any other effective means.

On its part, the Nationalist government saw the diplomatic value of the Shaji Incident and demanded the abolition of unequal treaties.[45] The Guomindang felt that the time was ripe to call for a People's Convention for the purpose of spreading the anti-imperialist movement throughout the country.[46] The major strike leaders, Deng Zhongxia and Su Zhaozheng, were also eager to abolish unequal treaties, even though they had ideological differences with the Guomindang.[47] Deng Zhongxia agreed that the Guomindang should use this opportunity to convene a People's Convention in order to expand the Guomindang's influence and leadership throughout the coun-

44. Telegram, Chamberlain to Macleay, 2 Jan. 1926, F.O.228/3152; Clementi to Amery, 23 Dec. 1925, C.O.882/11; telegram, Macleay to Jamieson, 5 Jan. 1926, F.O.228/3152; telegram, Jamieson to Macleay, 7 Jan. 1926, F.O.228/3152. See also P. D. Coates, *The China Consuls: British Consular Officers, 1843–1943* (Hong Kong: Oxford University Press, 1988), p. 462.

45. The five major demands from the Guomindang were (1) an official apology; (2) punishment of those officials involved in the killing of the Chinese on 23 June; (3) withdrawal of all gunboats moored at Shamian; (4) compensation to those wounded and the families of those killed; and (5) return of administrative authority over Shamian to the Nationalist government. See Chinese newspaper cuttings, 14 July 1925, Guomindang Party History Archives, 445/13.2.

46. The idea of the People's Convention was suggested by Sun Yatsen in November 1924 with the aim of bringing all the democratic forces in China to bear against imperialism and militarism. See Cavendish, "Anti-imperialism in the Kuomintang," p. 27.

47. Dorothy Borg, *American Policy and the Chinese Revolution, 1925–28* (New York: Columbia University Press, 1968), p. 46.

try.[48] Although the Communists and the Guomindang both saw the need for convening a People's Convention, their motives were somewhat different. The Guomindang expected that the opening of a People's Convention in Beijing would help overcome the diplomatic isolation of the Nationalist government.[49] The Communists, however, regarded the convention as a means of rallying patriotic and anti-imperialist support from other major cities.[50] At any rate, both the Strike Committee and the Nationalist government were of the view that a delegation, consisting of Guomindang leaders and strikers' representatives, should be dispatched to Beijing with the mission of rallying nationwide support for anti-imperialism.

The delegation was initially headed by Hu Hanmin; but he was replaced by Zou Lu after the assassination of Liao Zhongkai, which also delayed the delegation's departure until 17 September.[51] Although it was well received by local merchant and labor organizations in cities like Nanjing and Shanghai, the delegation was unable to secure any concrete support. It arrived in Beijing on 14 October, but received a similar response. Indeed, while the delegation was in Beijing, its leader, Zou Lu, was dismissed by Wang Jingwei after the former had convened the so-called Western Hills Conference, in which he and his colleagues severely criticized the radicalism of the Guomindang in Guangzhou.[52] After this incident, the delegation ceased to function, and the Guomindang's effort to secure nationwide support for settling the strike met with complete failure.

Whereas the Hong Kong and the Nationalist governments were unwilling to take the initiative in entering negotiations for strike settlement, the local Chinese elite in the colony sought to break the deadlock. In the last week of September, a small group of representatives from the Hong Kong Chinese Chamber of Commerce visited Guangzhou to find a solution. Their complaints about their economic losses as a result of this anti-British movement were printed in the *Gongren zhi lu* during their visit.[53] They were received by Wang Jingwei to discuss the terms for settlement;

48. Deng Zhongxia, "Zancheng kai Guomin daihui yubei huiyi" [In Favor of Convening the Preliminary Meeting of the People's Convention], *Gongren zhi lu*, 16 July 1925.

49. Wilson, "Britain and the Kuomintang," p. 244.

50. *Gongren zhi lu*, 30 Aug. 1925.

51. The formation of the delegation was decided by the Political Council on 18 August 1925. See *Gongren zhi lu*, 19 Sept. 1925.

52. Ibid., 5, 9, 15, 20, and 21 Oct. 1925 and 22 Nov. 1925.

53. Ibid., 1 Oct. 1925. For a printed documentary source, see Guangdong zhexue shehui kexueyuan, ed., *Shenggang da bagong ziliao*, pp. 553–54.

afterward, Wang held a meeting with the Strike Committee, and nine representatives were elected to continue the negotiations.[54] Instead of accepting the Hong Kong Chinese merchants' proposed terms, the Strike Committee announced its own conditions to the Hong Kong government, demanding not only the reinstatement of strikers and payment of strike compensation but also political freedom and social equality in the colony.[55] The merchants did not have any authority to accept these terms. The Strike Committee also stated that the Hong Kong Chinese merchants were not in a position to negotiate for a strike settlement, because the anti-British movement was directly aimed at the Hong Kong government. The leaders of the Strike Committee and the Nationalist government expected to open negotiations only with the official representatives of the colonial government. This small delegation was later severely criticized by Deng Zhongxia for its unwillingness to support the strike in its early stage.[56] Humiliated, the Hong Kong Chinese merchants returned to the colony without any results.

The deadlock between Guangdong and Hong Kong was partially alleviated by the arrival of a new governor, Sir Cecil Clementi, in Hong Kong on 1 November. Officials both in the British legation and in the Foreign Office hoped that Clementi, with his knowledge of the Chinese language, could navigate the British out of troubled waters.[57] Unlike his predecessor, Clementi adopted a moderate policy in dealing with Guangzhou by opening wide contacts with the Nationalist government. When he spoke at Hong Kong University on Armistice Day, Clementi quoted the Chinese proverb "Within the four seas all are brothers" to show his intention of solving the problem by peaceful means.[58] Meanwhile, he also relied on the local Chinese elite, especially those with family or clan relations with the leaders of the Nationalist government, to establish contacts with Guangzhou. This policy was fairly successful, as it led to an exchange of visits by senior officials between Guangzhou and Hong Kong in mid-December.

Contact was initially arranged by a visit to Guangzhou in mid-December by Dr. Du Yingkun, who was the brother-in-law of Liao Zhongkai and practiced medicine in the colony.[59] He was instructed by Clementi to take

54. Company Correspondence, Hong Kong to London, 17 Oct. 1925, Papers of John Swire and Sons Ltd., box 62.

55. Guangdong zhexue shehui kexueyuan, ed., *Shenggang da bagong ziliao*, pp. 561–64.

56. *Gongren zhi lu,*2, 3 Oct. 1925.

57. Jamieson to Macleay, 20 Dec. 1925, F.O.228/3151.

58. *South China Morning Post,* 12 Nov. 1926.

59. Clementi to Amery, 23 Dec. 1925, C.O.882/11. The Hong Kong government also asked a

a personal letter to Wang Jingwei inviting him to open discussion with the Hong Kong government on matters relating to the strike settlement. Wang replied to Clementi by stating that the Nationalist government had agreed to send Song Ziwen to the colony for informal discussions.[60] Song visited Hong Kong government House on 19 December. In his discussions with the governor, he stated explicitly that it was impossible to settle the strike without payment to the strikers, and that the Nationalist government "would not last a single day, if it shot down the strike pickets."[61] The meeting was a disappointment for the Hong Kong government.

However, with a view to cultivating a better understanding with Guangdong, A. G. E. Fletcher, the assistant colonial secretary, went to Guangzhou with Song on the following day. Fletcher was well received by the leading members of the Nationalist government during his four-day visit. After holding several meetings with the leaders of the Nationalist government, he gained the impression that the Nationalist government was eager to settle the strike but expected great difficulty in persuading the strikers to accept terms. He explained: "They were a new Government, quite recently come into power, and they owed their position to the support of the laborers. They could not at the moment coerce the strikers—Mr. Sung [Song Ziwen] had interposed that if they shot down any strikers they would not last a day—but they would soon have to face the necessity for doing so."[62] Indeed, this was a sensitive issue between the Guomindang and the Strike Committee. Although the former was losing patience with the prolonged strike and boycott, it was unable to find an excuse to call off the political movement that had helped it to power.

Official representatives from both sides exchanged visits in late December, but the meetings were preliminary and *ad interim*. Although the Hong Kong government mentioned, during one of these informal meetings, that some senior officials from the colony would be dispatched to Guangzhou

group of merchants' delegates from Guangzhou who were visiting the colony in late November to convey its message to the Nationalist government inviting negotiation. In early December, the governor asked a semiofficial emissary of the Nationalist government to deliver a letter to Wang Jingwei indicating his willingness to discuss strike settlement. But these two attempts met with failure. For details, see the same dispatch.

60. Wong Ching-wei to Clementi, 1 Dec. 1925, enclosed in ibid.

61. Clementi to Amery, 24 Dec. 1925, C.O.882/11. See also "Record of an Interview . . . between the Governor and Mr. T. V. Sung at the Government House on 19 Dec. 1925," enclosed in Clementi to Amery, 23 Dec. 1925, C.O.882/11.

62. "Diary of Visit to Canton, 20 to 23 Dec. 1925," enclosed in Clementi to Amery, 24 Dec. 1925, C.O.882/11.

for formal negotiations, the governor withdrew this suggestion after he was informed that most of the Guangdong representatives would be members of the Strike Committee.[63] The governor insisted that formal negotiations be conducted between officials of the two governments with equal standing.

However, in the Executive Council's meeting held on Christmas Eve, Governor Clementi decided to make further use of the local Chinese elite to help him in obtaining a strike settlement. According to a decision made in the meeting, a team of respectable Chinese local elite would be dispatched to Guangzhou to bargain with the Guangzhou merchants and the Strike Committee. The governor also informed the delegation that he would not object to settling the dispute by paying money to the Strike Committee. But he insisted that, should such a payment be made, it would be the responsibility of the Hong Kong Chinese merchants.[64] Although a delegation consisting of eight well-known local Chinese personages was subsequently sent to Guangzhou for this purpose in late December, the mission turned out to be a total failure.[65] The Nationalist government and the Strike Committee both insisted that the negotiations be conducted between the Strike Committee and the Hong Kong government, with the Nationalist government serving as mediator. Prospects for ending the dispute became remote when Clementi decided that such an arrangement would cause loss of face to the Hong Kong government.[66]

This mission signaled the end of the role of the Hong Kong Chinese elite in seeking a strike settlement. By then, the governor had also decided that it was impolitic to rely upon merchant delegations. Furthermore, although he had informed Sun Ke during the latter's visit to the colony that Hong Kong would help Guangdong to modernize its port facilities and transportation system by supplying financial and technical aid,[67] there was no indication that the strike and boycott would soon be settled. The governor rested his hopes for an end to the strike on the defeat of Guangdong by an enemy warlord.[68]

By late January 1926, Governor Clementi modified his thinking and

63. Clementi to Amery, 23 Dec. 1925, C.O.882/11. See also Chinese newspaper cuttings, 28 Jan. 1926, Guomindang Party History Archives, 447/39.14; and *Gongren zhi lu,* 30 Jan. 1926.

64. Chan Lau Kit-ching, *China, Britain, and Hong Kong,* p. 204.

65. "A Report to Mr. Chou Shou-son and Mr. R. H. Kotewall, 2 Jan. 1926," enclosed in Clementi to Amery, 6 Jan. 1926, C.O.882/11.

66. Clementi to Macleay, 2 Feb. 1926, F.O.228/3152.

67. Chan Lau Kit-ching, *China, Britain, and Hong Kong,* pp. 206–7.

68. Clementi to Amery, 14 Jan. 1926, C.O.882/11.

began to consider seriously the use of force. He called a meeting to discuss strategic issues relating to the use of military action or to the imposition of a blockade. He invited not only some senior consular members, including James Jamieson from Guangzhou and Owen O'Malley, who was the newly appointed counselor at the British legation in Beijing, but also the naval commander in chief, Admiral Sir Edwyn Alexander Sinclair, and the military commander in Hong Kong, General Luard. The meeting was held on 25 January at the Hong Kong Government House. After lengthy discussion, the meeting reluctantly concluded that the policy of inaction and waiting for the collapse of the Nationalist government was the only means that the Hong Kong government could adopt.[69] It seemed that the colonial government was powerless to break the deadlock.

In Guangzhou, however, rumor was rife that the British would employ gunboat diplomacy in settling the anti-British movement. The "war scare" was highly publicized and it reached its climax when Deng Zhongxia published an article entitled "Welcome the Hundred Thousand Soldiers of British Imperialism to Attack China!" on 4 March in the local Communist organ.[70]

A few days before the publication of the article, R. Hayley Bell, the commissioner of Customs in Guangzhou, had closed down Customs for several days as a protest against the pickets, who, he claimed, had interrupted Customs inspections. Bell reopened Customs on 27 February after he had secured a guarantee from the Nationalist government that the pickets would no longer interfere.[71] Although there was no solid evidence to prove that the Hong Kong government had instructed the commissioner to take such an action,[72] Guomindang leaders feared that the British would send their gunboats to the Pearl River on the pretext of protecting the Customs Service.

69. See Clementi to Amery, 26 Jan. 1926, C.O.882/11.

70. Deng Zhongxia, "Huanying yingguo diguozhuyi jingong Zhongguo de shiwan dabing," pp. 2–5.

71. *Gongren zhi lu,* 28 Feb. 1926.

72. David Wilson has shown the lack of any documentary evidence to support a charge of collusion between Clementi and Bell on closing Customs and has argued that it was only coincidence that the incident occurred a few days after Bell's visit to the colony ("Britain and the Kuomintang," pp. 347–48). But there are good reasons to consider Deng Zhongxia's accusation that Bell was instructed by Clementi to close down Customs for a few days as a show of British power and influence. See Deng Zhongxia, *Shenggang bagong gaiguan,* pp. 43–45. First, there is evidence to prove that Bell was involved in arms smuggling to anti-Sun Yatsen forces in summer 1924. See Wilbur, *Sun Yat-sen,* p. 250. Second, the close relation between the governor and the chief commissioner was revealed by Governor Clementi; he reported to the Colonial

It was largely in response to this threat that the Nationalist government arranged another round of informal negotiation with the Hong Kong officials in early March. A secret meeting took place on 4 and 5 March in Macau. The Hong Kong government sent two Chinese members of the Legislative Council as its representatives, and the Nationalist government sent a commissioner for foreign affairs, Fu Bingchang, for informal negotiation. This meeting, too, failed to bring about any solution, due to disagreement over the question of strike payment from the Hong Kong government, which the colonial administration absolutely refused to consider. However, Fu Bingchang gave the impression to the Hong Kong representatives that the Nationalist government was ready to enter direct and formal negotiations.[73] This was an encouragement to Clementi, who subsequently invited Fu to visit the colony for further discussion. Wang Jingwei did not permit Fu to accept the invitation on the grounds that the latter was not a member of the Nationalist government's Executive Council; however, on 15 March, Wang in turn invited the Hong Kong government to send official representatives to Guangzhou for formal negotiations with Chinese officials of equal standing.[74] Before the meeting could take place, however, Jiang Jieshi successfully staged his coup, which led to a dramatic political change in Guangzhou.

The Northern Expedition and Gunboat Diplomacy

The March Twentieth Coup did not immediately affect the strike and boycott, and the Nationalist government continued the arrangement for negotiations with the Hong Kong official representatives as if nothing had happened. In early April, Wang Jingwei appointed a three-man committee, consisting of Song Ziwen, Chen Gongbo, and Wu Chaoshu, to enter into informal discussion with the Hong Kong government.[75] Apparently, Gover-

---

Office that he and Bell had held a meeting to discuss at great length the political situation in Guangdong in late August 1926. See Clementi to Amery, 21 Aug. 1926, F.O.228/3018.

73. Shouson Chow and R. H. Kotewall to E. R. Hallifax, 5 Mar. 1926, enclosed in Clementi to Amery, 8 Mar. 1926, C.O.882/11.

74. "Memorandum by R. H. Kotewall," enclosed in Clementi to Amery, 18 Mar. 1926, C.O.882/11.

75. Wong Shiu Ming to Clementi, 22 Mar. 1926, enclosed in Clementi to Amery, 28 Mar. 1926, C.O.882/11.

nor Clementi had by then been informed of the decline of the Guomindang leftists and the rise of conservative forces in Guangzhou after the coup, and his attitude became less conciliatory. He enjoined Hong Kong delegates to claim financial compensation from the Nationalist government for infraction of treaty rights if the Chinese raised the issue of strike payment.[76] But he was again disappointed; informal negotiations broke down on the same old question of strike payment. Also important was the Nationalist government's persistent refusal to serve in the formal negotiations in any capacity other than mediator.[77] The newly arrived Acting Consul General John F. Brenan, who replaced Jamieson, remarked bitterly that "prospects of ultimate settlement are remote and depend on political development of impending issue between moderates and Communists."[78] This comment was prophetic.

Internal political development in Guangzhou in the early summer of 1926 was marked by the consolidation of Jiang Jieshi's political and military power, on the one hand, and by the widespread propaganda in support of the Northern Expedition, on the other. The rise of Jiang after the coup has been discussed in the previous chapter. But what is significant in connection with the strike settlement was his decision to remove from office several Guomindang leaders who had previously sympathized with the strike and boycott movement. The most important change of personnel in the Nationalist government, as far as negotiation with Hong Kong is concerned, was the removal of Wu Chaoshu. He had been considered by the colonial officials to be "the chief obstacle to a strike settlement."[79] Wu was replaced by the moderate Eugene Chen. Also, Wu's former superior, Wang Jingwei, left Guangzhou for Shanghai in early May.[80] Along with the change of leadership in the Nationalist government, the drive to unify China by means of the Northern Expedition was the beginning of the end for the strike and boycott.

Although Jiang saw the Northern Expedition mainly as a military campaign, he also expected the strikers to serve as coolies for his soldiers.[81]

76. Clementi to Macleay, 25 Mar. 1926, F.O.228/3151.
77. Clementi to Amery, 11 Apr. 1926, C.O.882/11.
78. Brenan to Macleay, 10 Apr. 1926, F.O.228/3153.
79. Clementi to Amery, 11 June 1926, C.O.882/11.
80. Clementi to Amery, 8 June 1926, C.O.882/11.
81. Donald A. Jordan, *The Northern Expedition: China's National Revolution of 1926–28* (Honolulu: University Press of Hawaii, 1976), pp. 56–58.

Contrary to Donald Jordan's interpretation, the Strike Committee extended its unqualified support to Jiang's appeal.[82] Both the strikers and the Strike Committee were deeply concerned with the Northern Expedition, which they regarded as an essential step in the current stage of the anti-imperialist movement. The Chinese Seamen's Union had already expressed its support for the forthcoming Northern Expedition in mid-February 1926.[83] In late May of the same year, Deng Zhongxia spoke of the expedition enthusiastically at the Political Commission of the Huangpu Military Academy, where he stated that the whole responsibility for unifying the country and resisting imperialism rested on the soldiers who would be dispatched on the Northern Expedition.[84] When Jiang was appointed commander in chief of the Northern Expedition, the *Gongren zhi lu* reported that about 200,000 workers and strikers attended his inauguration ceremony, and that the Strike Committee had on the same day distributed 30,000 handbills to celebrate the event.[85] Although there were ideological differences between Jiang and the major Communist labor organizers in south China, both regarded the Northern Expedition as a means of unifying the country and resisting further foreign penetration.

The introduction of various regulations to limit the labor movement in the name of maintaining order in the revolutionary base after May 1926 doubtless caused great discontent among the strike leaders. On 31 May, the Nationalist government decided to reenter strike settlement negotiations with the Hong Kong government.[86] It also announced an eight-point program which aimed at paving the way for the Northern Expedition; the search for a strike settlement was part of this program.[87] The Strike Committee concurred with the Nationalist government's decision. Deng Zhongxia in fact regarded direct negotiations between these two governments as the beginning of a new diplomatic stage in which the Nationalist government would play a significant part.[88] But the outcome of the negotiations was another disappointment for both sides.

82. Ibid., p. 60.

83. *Gongren zhi lu*, 21 Feb. 1926.

84. "Gongjie daibiao Deng Zhongxia yanshuoci" [Speech by Labor's Representative, Deng Zhongxia], in *Jinian ce* [Commemorative Issue] (Guangzhou: Zhongyang junshi zhengshi xuexiao kanyin, 1926), pp. 8–10.

85. *Gongren zhi lu*, 10 July 1926.

86. Jordan, *Northern Expedition*, pp. 58–59.

87. Chan Lau Kit-ching, *China, Britain, and Hong Kong*, p. 212. See also Jordan, *Northern Expedition*, pp. 58–59.

88. Deng Zhongxia, *Shenggang bagong zhong zhi zhongyin tanpan*, p. 596.

The negotiations were held in Guangzhou between 15 and 23 July.[89] Apparently, the Nationalist government was still under pressure from the Strike Committee, which demanded a strike payment. The Hong Kong government in turn insisted that it would consider only loans to the Nationalist government for industrial development, a demand that probably stemmed from the colonial policy of divide and conquer. In addition, the Chinese also wanted a judicial inquiry into the Shaji Incident, which met with disapproval from the British representatives. These two major unresolved issues led to the adjournment of the negotiations *sine die* on 23 July.[90] During the discussions, Eugene Chen expressed the difficult position of the Nationalist government in dealing with the strikers:

The difficulty we have to face is this, that the Nationalist government must shoulder a financial burden by [calling off] the boycott. It is easy for us to destroy the boycott and end the whole thing, but that is no solution of the difficulties. The use of blind force might only end in driving the trouble under ground.[91]

In a personal meeting with Brenan in late August, Eugene Chen reiterated the awkward situation of the Nationalist government in settling the strike and boycott, stating plainly that

it was the general feeling in the [Guomindang] that while China was no match for the Western Powers when it came to armed conflict, the trade boycott was the weapon with which she would have to achieve her independence. Any action, therefore, which looked like an attempt to suppress the Strike Committee would be regarded as a betrayal of national aspirations, and was not to be contemplated.[92]

Although there was no prospect for ending the strike in August, Guangzhou was rife with rumors that the Nationalist government contemplated settling the strike regardless of the opinion of the Strike Committee. It was at this juncture that the major Guangdong Communists faced the difficult choice of maintaining the strike or terminating it in the interest of the

89. The Chinese representatives were Eugene Chen, Song Ziwen, and Gu Mengyu; Gu was the director of the Propaganda Department of the Nationalist government. The Hong Kong government was represented by Attorney General J. H. Kemp, Secretary for Chinese Affairs E. R. Halifax, and Acting Consul General in Guangzhou J. Brenan.

90. For details regarding the proceedings of these negotiations, see C.O.882/11, pp. 212–52.

91. "Notes of Proceedings, no. 4," enclosed in Clementi to Amery, 28 July 1926, C.O.882/11.

92. Brenan to Clementi, 29 Aug. 1926, enclosed in Brenan to Macleay, 29 Aug. 1926, F.O.228/3155.

Northern Expedition. There seems to have been a wide difference of opinion among the Communists on this issue. The CCP Central Committee stated in July that the strike must be settled soon.[93] The Strike Committee, however, stated that the strike would strengthen the defense of the revolutionary base.[94] The CCP Guangdong Regional Committee believed that any decision leading to the termination of the strike and boycott at this stage would encourage "the tiger to enter the house from the rear."[95] Deng Zhongxia and Zhang Tailei shared the view that the strike could only be settled if its goals were met.[96] Peng Pai suggested a more radical approach; he said that the boycott should be intensified in order to prevent the imperialists from attacking Guangzhou.[97] These divided opinions, however, did not significantly influence the policymakers of the Nationalist government, all of whom gave priority to the success of the Northern Expedition over the local victory of the anti-British movement; a view that was shared by Tan Pingshan, a leading Guangdong Communist and a senior official in the Nationalist government.[98]

The end of the Shenggang General Strike did not result from peaceful negotiations between Hong Kong and the Nationalist government. Instead, its termination came with a show of British naval power on the Pearl River on 4 September. After meeting repeated failures in negotiations, the British officials, both in London and in China, were losing patience. Even John Pratt, the liberal-minded advisor at the Foreign Office, commented in early September: "There are cases when, in dealing with the Chinese, force must be used and in those cases force is generally extremely effective."[99] Plans for a show of force, approved by Whitehall, were formulated by the newly arrived acting consul general in Guangzhou, John F. Brenan, who was an able young man. He not only possessed a good knowledge of Chinese poli-

93. *Zhonggong gongren yundong yuanshi ziliao huibian,* vol. 1, p. 183.

94. *Gongren zhi lu,* 23 Aug. 1926.

95. *Renmin zhoukan* 20 and 21 (8 Sept. 1926), p. 2.

96. Deng Zhongxia, *Shenggang bagong zhong zhi zhongyin tanpan,* pp. 631–32. Zhang Tailei, "Zhongying tanpan de jingge yu jieguo" [The Process and Consequence of the Sino-British Negotiations], *Renmin zhoukan* 17 (1 Aug. 1926), p. 14.

97. Peng Pai, "Chushi beifa yu Shenggang bagong" [The Launch of the Northern Expedition and the Guangzhou-Hong Kong General Strike], *Xiangdao zhoubao* 166 (6 Aug. 1926), pp. 1657–60.

98. Tan Pingshan, "Fanying yundong yu jieshu Shenggang bagong" [The Anti-British Movement and the End of the Guangdong-Hong Kong General Strike], *Xiangdao zhoubao* 166 (6 Aug. 1926), pp. 1657–60.

99. "Minutes by J. Pratt, 1 Sept. 1926," F.O.371/11629 [F3510/1/10].

tics but also knew how to persuade Whitehall to consider his suggestions favorably. Unlike his predecessor, Brenan combined diplomacy with force in dealing with Guangzhou.[100]

From the beginning, Brenan did not rule out the possibility of using armed intervention to settle the crisis.[101] In May, he proposed sending two British merchant ships from Hong Kong to Guangzhou to provoke conflict with the pickets and thereby provide an excuse for naval action. His suggestion, however, was turned down by his superiors.[102] Between June and July, he thought that the anti-British movement in south China could be solved by formal negotiations. But events proved otherwise. After the breakdown of the July negotiations, he informed the British legation in Beijing: "I do not believe that we shall secure settlement of the boycott unless [the] Canton Government are made to feel our patience is nearing an end and that [the] alternative to friendship is our active enmity."[103] A few days later, Brenan sent a long dispatch to Macleay asking approval for a naval plan which had been recently discussed with Clementi and the British senior naval officers in the colony. The proposed naval action would involve the seizure of the picket boats and, if necessary, an attack on the headquarters of the Strike Committee. After discussing the proposal with the British naval commander in chief in China, Macleay concurred with Brenan's modified plan, in which the naval action would be restricted to seizing the picket boats. He then cabled the plan to Whitehall for endorsement. On 2 September, Chamberlain sent his approval; but in order to justify the British naval action, he instructed British representatives in China to inform the Washington Powers that the action was taken because of "piratical outrages" in Guangzhou. Two days later, British gunboats appeared near Shamian. They did not have to fire a single shot, because all the picket boats had disappeared before their arrival; nevertheless, the gunboats did not sail away.[104]

The show of force on 4 September was regarded by the people of Guangzhou as a step toward the revival of British gunboat diplomacy. One day after the British naval demonstration on the Pearl River, Wanxian, a town

100. Wilson, "Britain and the Kuomintang," pp. 361, 696–701.

101. Brenan to Macleay, 17 May 1926, F.O.228/3154.

102. Company Correspondence, Hong Kong to London, 12 May 1926, Papers of John Swire and Sons Ltd., box 63.

103. Brenan to Macleay, 11 Aug. 1926, F.O.228/3155.

104. Brenan to Macleay, 16 Aug. 1926, F.O.228/3155; telegram, Macleay to Chamberlain, 30 Aug. 1926, F.O.228/3155; telegram, Chamberlain to Macleay, 2 Sept. 1926, F.O.228/3155. For an account of the naval demonstration, see Brenan to Macleay, 9 Sept. 1926, F.O.228/3156.

located on the Upper Yangzi, was bombarded by British gunboats as part of the British rescue operation following the seizure of two British merchant vessels on 31 August by the warlord forces of Yang Sen, an ally of Wu Peifu.[105] To the Guomindang leaders, the British naval action on these two days was evidence of the revival of gunboat diplomacy. They were also fully aware that, whenever conflict occurred between China and the West, the one who possessed the stronger naval force would be the victor.

The British naval actions on 4 and 5 September accelerated the strike and boycott settlement. A few days later, Eugene Chen invited Brenan to enter another round of informal negotiations. Although his first invitation was turned down by Brenan, they met on 17 September. In the meeting, Chen informed Brenan that the Nationalist government had secured agreement from the Strike Committee to end the strike and boycott on or before 10 October. But this decision was subject to the condition that the British would agree to the increase of certain customs dues. Chen also said that the British did not have to give an immediate answer. Brenan was satisfied that a settlement was finally in sight; but Governor Clementi thought otherwise. He proposed that Britain should issue an ultimatum, followed by a naval blockade of the ports of Guangzhou and Shantou, if the Nationalist government refused to settle the strike and boycott by a fixed date. Although this "warlike" decision was severely criticized by Whitehall, the rumor that the British would take another military action against Guangzhou was effective. Jiang Jieshi, upon receiving this new message in Hankou, immediately warned the officials in Guangzhou that the strike and boycott must be terminated at once because he could not afford trouble at his rear.[106]

Thus, by late September, it seemed that the time was ripe for settling the strike and boycott. The only issue that remained to be resolved was how to settle the dispute without causing loss of face to either side. The Chinese request for a surcharge of 2.5 percent on an import tax, which is said to have been suggested by Deng Zhongxia, was a sensitive issue.[107] The British considered it blackmail for calling off the strike and boycott. However, after careful consideration and exchange of views with his colleagues, John Pratt reluctantly recommended that the Foreign Office accept the request, as he

105. Fung, *Diplomacy of Imperial Retreat*, p. 132.

106. Brenan to Macleay, 27 Sept. 1926, F.O.228/3156; Chen Yu-jen to Brenan, 18 Sept. 1926, enclosed in Clementi to Amery, 25 Sept. 1926, C.O.882/11; telegram, Clementi to Macleay, 16 Sept. 1926, F.O.228/3018; Chamberlain to Macleay, 17 Sept. 1926, F.O.228/3018; "Minutes by Pratt, 21 Sept. 1926," F.O.371/11630 [F3896/1/10].

107. Huang Ping, "Guanyu Shenggang da bagong de huiyi ziliao," p. 21.

saw no other alternative. On 25 September, Chamberlain agreed to "shut our eyes [to] the new levy."[108] On 10 October, the Nationalist government, with the full agreement of the Strike Committee, officially called off the strike and boycott.

In conclusion, the CCP and the Guomindang, for different reasons, were prepared to sacrifice the success of a massive anti-British movement for the sake of other political objectives. For the Guomindang leaders, anti-imperialism embodied only their commitment to fighting for diplomatic equality and fair commercial competition with foreign countries. Therefore, the Guomindang leaders supported the anti-British movement in Guangzhou only within those limits. The Communists were also willing to call off the successful anti-British urban mass movement in the interest of the Nationalist Revolution. They remained, for the most part, coolies for the Guomindang.

Chinese workers in Shamian and Hong Kong made history in June 1925. The political significance of the Shenggang General Strike was incomparable, even though it failed to spark a nationwide working-class political movement. Its international implications were also considerable. By entangling Britain in a diplomatic dilemma, this massive anti-British movement caused Britain to lose prestige because of its inability to obtain an early strike settlement, even though Britain basically viewed the strike as a local movement and thought the problem should be dealt with by regional officials.[109] By the end of the strike, Britain had adopted a friendly attitude toward the newly established Chinese Nationalist government and released the so-called Christmas Memorandum in December 1926, which announced the British commitment to abolishing the unequal treaties in China. Such a diplomatic development, however, was due to Britain's response to the Northern Expedition. It was the success of this military campaign, rather than the prolonged period of strike and boycott, which convinced Britain that the Guomindang was no longer a local or regional authority but a party possessing the power and ability to maintain a stable and unified China.[110] The strikers, therefore, played mainly a supporting role in the Guomindang's revolutionary diplomacy of the period. They

108. Chamberlain to Macleay, 25 Sept. 1926, F.O.228/3156.

109. Wilson, "Britain and the Kuomintang," pp. 402–3.

110. "The Question of the Recognition of the Southern Government by W. Strang, 12 Dec. 1926," F.O.371/11663 [F5628/10/10].

were not, as many Chinese Marxist historians claim, the leading cause behind British abandonment of its traditional gunboat diplomacy.

In spite of their contribution to consolidating the revolutionary base of Guangdong and supporting the Nationalist government's revolutionary diplomacy, the strikers were in the end the losers because their interests were completely ignored by both political parties. After the strike and boycott were officially called off, the Strike Committee paid $100 to each of the remaining strikers for financial assistance.[111] But the strikers' original demands were never met. Even worse, the Nationalist army abandoned the strikers who served as coolies during the Northern Expedition; many were dismissed en route with almost no provisions.[112]

After the end of the strike and boycott, the Chinese authorities did not immediately demand that the British offer compensation for those who had been killed or wounded during the Shaji Incident. Although the Nationalist government did raise this issue in the early months of 1930, at a time when Sino-British relations were cordial, the British refused to pay any financial compensation for the Shaji Incident. Sir Miles Lampson, the British minister in Beijing, was in favor of paying compensation out of the Boxer Indemnity funds with a view to further cultivating Sino-British relations.[113] But the Foreign Office refused to entertain his idea because officials in London insisted that the British government bore no responsibility for the incident.[114] Eventually, the British agreed to pay £20,000 to the Chinese government as compensation for the bombardment of Wanxian. The offer was accepted, and no further demand for compensation for the Shaji Incident was made by the Chinese government.[115]

As for the major strike leader, Deng Zhongxia, it is certain that he was one of the best mass movement organizers of the time. But his understanding of diplomatic reality was far from complete. He suffered from excessive revolutionary optimism and underestimated the strength of British gunboat diplomacy. Although his observations on British policy in south China were basically accurate, he was wrong on important details, including, for instance, the relations between the Hong Kong government and the right-wing Guomindang leaders. But his fatal weakness, as indicated in the previous chapter, was his failure to create a lasting alliance between workers

111. Huang Ping, "Guanyu Shenggang da bagong de huiyi ziliao," p. 24.
112. Tsin, "Cradle of Revolution," p. 281.
113. Lampson to Foreign Office, 4 May 1930, F.O. 371/14677 [F2463/20/10].
114. "Minutes by Orde, 8 May 1930," F.O.371/14677 [F2594/20/10].
115. Lampson to Foreign Office, 22 Sept. 1930, F.O.371/14678 [F5326/20/10].

and the petty bourgeoisie after the March Twentieth Coup. His role in leading the labor movement in south China during the years 1925–26 was the greatest achievement of his revolutionary career. After October 1926, Deng never again captured another opportunity to build a powerful revolutionary leadership among Marxist intellectuals and workers.

6

The Tragedy of a Labor Hero

AFTER THE END of the Shenggang General Strike, the role Deng Zhongxia played in the Chinese Communist movement became less eventful. He was no longer the leading organizer in charge of the most important labor movement in Chinese history. Nevertheless, Deng contributed significantly to the development of a new revolutionary strategy in late 1927, although due to the collapse of the United Front, the Communists found it more difficult to mobilize the urban masses.

Deng's involvement in the formation of this new strategy, especially during the period when the Party was under the leadership of Qu Qiubai, sowed the seeds of confrontation with the Comintern leaders in Moscow in the aftermath of the CCP Sixth Congress. In 1929, he was accused by Moscow of being an anti-Comintern element and an associate of the Qu Qiubai faction. Ironically, just two years later, the Comintern once again condemned him for having committed serious strategic errors, but this time as a supporter of the "Li Lisan line." Deng was severely penalized: he was removed from all positions and duties in the Party leadership. Only in early 1932 was he assigned by the Party to take part in some minor underground activities in Shanghai. This did not last long. In May 1933 Deng was arrested, and four months later, he was secretly executed by the Guomindang at the age of thirty-nine.

The new element in his political activities after the general strike was certainly his close relationship with Qu Qiubai. Yet, as the following will demonstrate, he was neither anti-Comintern nor a supporter of the Li Lisan line; he was mainly a victim of factional struggle resulting from differences between Marxist intellectuals and workers within the Party leadership.

Reassessment of the Chinese Revolution

Deng continued working in Guangzhou for about four months after the Shenggang General Strike was officially called off. During this brief period, he continued his efforts to politicize the workers. On 25 October, the second session of the School of Labor Movement Studies took place under his directorship; 271 students were recruited and they were trained according to the previous curriculum.[1] Simultaneously, he engaged with right-wing Guomindang members in a debate about the role of the labor movement in Guangzhou. In response to their criticism that the labor movement was harmful to the Nationalist Revolution, Deng completed a manuscript entitled *1926 nian zhi Guangzhou gongchao* (Labor Disputes in Guangzhou in 1926), in which he analyzed the reasons for, and the political significance of, the upsurge of the labor movement in Guangzhou. The manuscript was finalized and published shortly before Jiang Jieshi launched his bloody suppression of the Shanghai labor unions in April 1927.[2]

In late March 1927 he left Guangzhou for Wuhan, where the headquarters of the ACLF had recently been relocated.[3] In Hankou, Deng actively participated in the organization of the Fourth National Labor Congress,

1. *Gongren zhi lu*, 25 Oct. 1926. See also Li Zhiye and Ye Wenyi, "Guangdong dangtuan huodong jiyao," p. 250.

2. According to an announcement published in *Renmin zhoukan*, his small booklet was ready for sale by late March 1927. See *Renmin zhoukan* 47 (18 Mar. 1927), p. 4

3. In September 1926, many leading Chinese Communist labor activists left Guangzhou for Wuhan. In February 1927, the ACLF formally relocated its headquarters to Hankou. See Zhonggong Wuhanshiwen dangshi bangongshi, "1927 nian zhonggong zhongyang jiquan you Shanghai qian Wuhan de jingge ji zai Han qingkuang" [The Transfer of the CCP Central Organs from Shanghai to Wuhan in 1927 and Their Conditions in Wuhan], in *Zhonggong dangshi ziliao*, vol. 21, p. 125. It is reported that most of the important leaders of the Guangdong Regional Committee, including Chen Yannian, Deng Zhongxia, Su Zhaozheng, Peng Pai, and Huang Ping, proceeded to Wuhan in late March. Party affairs in Guangdong were then managed by less important regional leaders like Yang Yin, Liu Ersong, and Li Sen, who had all been members of the Strike Committee. See Li Zhiye and Ye Wenyi, "Guangdong dangtuan huodong jiyao," p. 258.

the CCP Fifth Congress, and the First Pan-Pacific Labor Congress.[4] In the CCP Fifth Congress, he failed to gain a seat on the Central Committee, but he was elected secretary of the Party's Labor Committee, under the chairmanship of Li Lisan.[5] He also held important positions in the Fourth National Labor Congress; he was reelected to the Executive Committee and was appointed chairman of the Propaganda Department.[6] In the First Pan-Pacific Labor Congress, which was convened by the Profintern to strengthen class solidarity among workers in the Asian-Pacific region, he received the honor of addressing the congress as the representative of the CCP Central Committee.[7]

In late June, Deng regained his influence within the CCP leadership when he was appointed secretary to its newly formed Provisional Politburo. His appointment was a direct result of a shift of leadership within the Party due to Jiang Jieshi's suppression of the Communists on 12 April, followed by the resignation of Chen Duxiu from the CCP Central Committee.[8] Immediately after Chen's resignation, the Soviet advisor Michael Borodin instructed the Chinese Communist leaders to form a Provisional Politburo consisting of Zhang Guotao, Zhou Enlai, Zhang Tailei, Li Weihan, and Li Lisan.[9] Deng Zhongxia and Li Lisan were soon assigned by the newly formed Provisional Politburo to proceed to Nanchang to organize an armed uprising there; this uprising was a complete failure.[10] Deng then was instructed to take part in the preparation for an emergency meeting of the CCP leading members.[11] The outcome of the 7 August emergency meet-

4. Jiang Ping, *Deng Zhongxia de yisheng*, pp. 167–68.

5. Liu Jizeng, Mao Lei, and Yuan Jicheng, *Wuhan guomin zhengfu shi* [History of the Wuhan National Government] (Wuhan: Hubei renmin chubanshe, 1986), p. 436.

6. Jiang Ping, *Deng Zhongxia de yisheng*, p. 169.

7. Ibid.

8. Chen submitted his resignation on 15 July after refusing to implement the Comintern's policy of seizing political power during the Nationalist Revolution. See Hsiao Tso-liang, *Chinese Communism in 1927: City vs. Countryside* (Hong Kong: Chinese University of Hong Kong Press, 1970), pp. 30–35.

9. Li Weihan, "Guanyu Baqi huiyi de yixie huiyi" [Some Memories of the 7 August Meeting], in Zhonggong zhongyang dangshi ziliao zhengji wenyuanhui and Zhongyang danganguan, eds., *Baqi huiyi* [7 August Meeting] (Beijing: Zhonggong dangshi ziliao chubanshe, 1986), p. 183. See also Hsiao Tso-liang, *Chinese Communism in 1927*, p. 35.

10. Jiang Ping, *Deng Zhongxia de yisheng*, p. 171. For a fresh and vivid account of this abortive uprising, see Marcia R. Ristaino, *China's Art of Revolution: The Mobilization of Discontent, 1927 and 1928* (Durham, N.C.: Duke University Press, 1987), pp. 21–38.

11. According to a participant, the decision to call for an emergency meeting was made jointly by the newly arrived Comintern advisor to China, Besso Lominadze, and the members

ing was both significant and controversial and will be discussed in detail. But as far as Deng Zhongxia was concerned, the 7 August emergency meeting provided him with an opportunity to further strengthen his position within the newly elected Party leadership. During the meeting, the five-member Provisional Politburo was dissolved, and a new Politburo, headed by Qu Qiubai, was formed. Deng was elected as an alternate member of the Politburo and was reappointed secretary of the Jiangsu Regional Committee, a position that he had held since late July.[12] Thereafter, he worked closely with Qu Qiubai.

Prior to the rise of Qu to the CCP leadership, especially during the first few months of 1927, many Chinese Communists found themselves at a crossroads. In early 1927, Communists in Guangzhou and later on in Hankou witnessed growing tension between their party and the Guomindang while the Nationalist army under the command of Jiang Jieshi was swiftly moving to the north in a bid for national reunification. Many of them still expected that the United Front would be honored, though an increasing number of key Guomindang leaders had already begun to support an anti-Communist policy. Like all other Communists in the post–general strike period, Deng was frustrated by the increasingly reactionary Guomindang policy toward the laboring class.

Although the Shenggang General Strike was officially called off on 10 October 1926, its Strike Committee continued to function, but in a different capacity. It was mainly responsible for running relief programs for the strikers and helping them to look for employment.[13] Its organ, *Gongren zhi lu*, ceased publication on 21 January 1927.[14] On 6 November 1926, the headquarters of the Strike Committee was destroyed by fire. The Communists blamed the fire on right-wing Guomindang members. There were also rumors that the strike leaders had deliberately destroyed their own headquarters in order to cover up their financial corruption, which the Communists refuted by showing that all account books were saved from the

---

of the Provisional Politburo in late July. They both agreed that such a meeting was vital for reviewing the political situation and for formulating a new strategy. See Li Weihan, "Guanyu Baqi huiye de yixie huiyi," pp. 184–87.

12. "Guanyu Baqi huiyi ruogan qingkuang de diaocha baogao" [Research Report on the Several Issues Relating to the 7 August Meeting], in *Baqi huiyi*, p. 200; Zhao Piao, "Wuci dahui dao liuci dehui yinian zhong de zuzhi zhuangkuang" [The Condition of the Organization from the CCP Fifth Congress to the CCP Sixth Congress], *Dangshi yanjiu* [Research on Party History] 6 (1987), p. 150.

13. *Gongren zhi lu*, 11 Nov. 1926.

14. Xue Haozhou and Li Xiangjun, "Deng Zhongxia yu *Gongren zhi lu*," p. 8.

fire.[15] Although there was no verdict regarding responsibility for the fire, the incident caused further deterioration in the relations between the Guomindang and Communist labor leaders. The Guomindang intensified its criticism of labor movement activists and blamed them for hurting Guangzhou economically. On 6 December 1926 and again on 5 January 1927, the Nationalist government proclaimed two different regulations for controlling labor movement activity. The regulations stated that, in order to maintain the economic order of the revolutionary base, any form of labor movement in Guangzhou would be considered illegal.[16] Meanwhile, the unity of the labor movement in Guangzhou was deeply damaged by the anti-Communist movement launched by the yellow labor unionists, then headed by the Guangdong Mechanics' Union. Numerous cases of armed clashes between the two labor factions were reported.[17]

The growing Communist-Guomindang tension in Guangzhou thus caused much concern within the CCP and Comintern central leadership. In Moscow, Stalin and his associates reacted to the rapidly changing situation in China by convening the Seventh Plenum of the Executive Committee of the Communist International (ECCI) between 22 November and 16 December 1926. The plenum decided that, although the United Front policy should be maintained, it was necessary to reassess the role of the various social classes in the changing political situation in China. It adopted a resolution which proclaimed that the majority of the bourgeoisie were reactionary and should not be treated as reliable revolutionary partners. The driving force of the Nationalist Revolution was the proletariat, the peasantry, and the petty bourgeoisie. If the Communists maintained their alliance with the Guomindang, the latter would, as the ECCI argued, "provide effective channels for reaching the peasantry."[18] Thus, the CCP-Guomindang alliance was still valuable. Most important, the plenum also resolved that the

15. See Guangdong zhexue shehui kexueyuan, ed., *Shenggang da bagong ziliao*, pp. 411–30. The controversy over the Dongyuan (the name given to the headquarters of the Strike Committee) was further complicated by the claim of the French consul in Guangzhou that the site of the headquarters was the property of the Banque de l'Indo-chine; he demanded that the Nationalist government evacuate the Strike Committee from that site and return it to the bank. But the Nationalist government rejected this claim on the grounds that the ownership of the site of the Dongyuan had not yet been completely clarified. See *Guangzhou minguo ribao*, 11 Dec. 1926.

16. Cai Luo and Lu Quan, *Shenggang da bagong*, p. 149.

17. See, e.g., *Renmin zhoukan* 34 (11 Dec. 1926), p. 3; 39 (21 Jan. 1927), p. 3; 40 (30 Jan. 1927), p. 4.

18. Eudin and North, eds., *Soviet Russia and the East*, p. 294.

CHAPTER 6

Chinese Communists should henceforth radicalize the agrarian movement under the leadership of the proletariat:

The present situation is characterized by its transitional nature when the proletariat must choose between allying itself with a considerable section of the bourgeoisie or further consolidating its own alliance with the peasantry. If the proletariat does not put forward a radical agrarian program, it will fail to attract the peasantry into the revolutionary struggle and will lose its hegemony in the national liberation movement.[19]

Before receiving this ECCI resolution in January 1927, the CCP Central Committee was indecisive about whether the CCP-Guomindang alliance should be abolished. Some members in the Central Committee, including Zhang Guotao and Peng Shuzhi, strongly argued that the United Front policy should be terminated. But Chen Duxiu insisted that the alliance be maintained.[20] It was only on 26 January that differences between them were settled and the CCP Central Committee issued a lengthy directive to its members urging the Communists to launch a vigorous propaganda campaign with the purpose of "[convincing] the Guomindang that the Nationalist Revolution is still in the period of a most acute struggle, that it requires support of the masses of the people, and that the time of the final victory is yet to come."[21] It also instructed its members to urge the masses to render financial and military support to the Nationalist government. Although the directive did not present a new class analysis of the current revolutionary movement, it instructed the Chinese Communists that the middle bourgeoisie should not be "considered as belonging to the revolutionary class."[22] It is therefore clear that, as of early 1927, the CCP Central Committee and the ECCI differed over the role of the bourgeoisie in the Chinese Nationalist Revolution. To complicate matters, young Chinese Communist leaders in Guangdong had their own version of class analysis and revolutionary strategy. They argued that the Party should launch a counterattack against the right-wing elements of the Guomindang by mobilizing the petty bour-

19. "Theses on the Situation in China by the Seventh Extraordinary Plenum of the E.C.C.I., 23 Nov-16 Dec. 1926," in Robert North and Xenia Eudin, eds., *M. N. Roy's Mission to China: The Communist-Kuomintang Split of 1927* (Berkeley and Los Angeles: University of California Press, 1963), p. 138.

20. Li Lisan, "Dangshi baogao," p. 233.

21. "Political Report of the Central Committee, 26 Jan. 1927," in Wilbur and How, eds., *Missionaries of Revolution,* p. 808.

22. Ibid.

geoisie.[23] Thus, there was also a lack of consensus regarding class analysis and strategy among the CCP leaders as well as between the CCP and the Comintern. It was against this confusing background that Deng Zhongxia reexamined the problem of the Chinese Nationalist Revolution and proposed a new strategy.

Deng may have seen the resolution of the ECCI Seventh Plenum by early February 1927; his arguments were basically in accordance with the Comintern line. Deng firmly believed that, even though some Guomindang leaders had become more conservative, the United Front policy must be maintained. The roots of the current problems, as he analyzed them, lay in the fact that some opportunistic politicians, landlords, and big bourgeois had joined the Guomindang purely for reasons of personal interest after they had seen the initial victory of the Nationalist Revolution. He claimed that these new Guomindang party members were the troublemakers within the Nationalist Revolution because they were able to persuade some Guomindang leaders that success in the Nationalist Revolution depended on the suppression of any further development of labor and peasant movements.[24] In a spirit similar to that of the Guomindang leftists, he appealed to the Guomindang to maintain itself as a mass party:[25]

Any party that is revolutionary should organize mass movements, and no party has the authority to suppress mass movements. . . . The people are also willing to be led and directed by the revolutionary party, because they can achieve their immediate interests as well as their final liberation. But there is one condition; the revolutionary party must be sincerely cooperative [with the Communists]. Otherwise, there will be a split within the mass movement. A divided mass movement will lead to a split within the revolutionary force . . . and the revolutionary party will then be committing suicide.[26]

Deng viewed as groundless the criticism by some Guomindang leaders that the labor movement in Guangzhou had led to economic hardship in Guangdong. Citing statistics from Guangzhou Customs, he forcefully argued that Guangdong had enjoyed economic prosperity over the past three

23. Li Lisan, "Dangshi baogao," p. 230.
24. [Deng] Zhongxia, "Erqi yu guomin geming" [7 February and the Nationalist Revolution], *Renmin zhoukan* 41 (7 Feb. 1927), p. 1.
25. For a concise interpretation of the left-wing Guomindang's view on the nature of its party in 1927, see Arif Dirlik, *Revolution and History: Origins of Marxist Historiography in China, 1919–1937* (Berkeley and Los Angeles: University of California Press, 1978), p. 78.
26. [Deng] Zhongxia, "Erqi yu guomin geming," p. 4.

years, and that the merchants in Guangzhou had profited from the economic boom as well as from the recent development of local public transportation and utilities.[27] Therefore, he concluded, the Guangdong labor movement in recent years had not led to any deterioration in the economy of the province. Three factors, however, would mitigate against any further economic growth in Guangdong, as well as in other parts of China: imperialism, feudalism, and the economic backwardness of the Chinese peasantry with their low purchasing power.[28] In his social analysis of Guangdong, he did not consider this southern province a modern industrial society. Rather, it was only a modern *commercial* society, which was mainly dominated by foreign capital:

Guangdong certainly cannot be regarded as a modern industrial society. Nevertheless, it can be called a modern commercial society. But this commercial capitalist society is dominated by foreign investors, and it is also attached to the Hong Kong imperialistic economy. Therefore, the native industries in Guangdong cannot be developed, its agriculture is bankrupt, and its handicraft industries begin to deteriorate. At present, most of the handicraft industries [in Guangdong] survive only because their products have not yet been replaced by foreign goods.[29]

Because of heavy foreign capitalist investment in Guangdong and other provinces, China was a semicolonial society, and the main object of the Chinese revolution was to "completely overthrow imperialistic interests and privileges in China."[30] Thus, he proclaimed that the Chinese revolution was also a part of the world revolution.[31] His view on the relation between the Chinese revolution and the world revolution was certainly identical with that of his former ideological mentor Li Dazhao.

Because of foreign economic penetration in China, the Chinese bourgeoisie, in Deng's view, was an unreliable revolutionary partner. The ideal of the bourgeoisie was to develop China into a capitalist society. They would therefore rely on the support of foreign capitalists and betray the

27. [Deng] Zhongxia, "Guangzhou gongchao yu jingji fazhan yihui shuaitui" [Did the Labor Movement in Guangzhou Promote or Hurt Economic Growth?], *Renmin zhoukan* 39 (21 Jan. 1927), pp. 2–3.

28. [Deng] Zhongxia, "Guangdong jingji bu fazhan de yuanyin" [The Reasons for the Nondevelopment of Guangdong's Economy], *Renmin zhoukan* 40 (30 Jan. 1927), p. 2.

29. Deng Zhongxia, *1926 nian zhi Guangzhou gongchao*, p. 53.

30. Ibid., p. 94.

31. Deng Zhongxia, "Huanying guoji gongren daibiao tuan" [Welcome the International Labor Delegation], *Renmin zhoukan* 43 (23 Feb. 1927), p. 1.

Chinese revolution. He predicted: "If a bourgeois political power is realized in China, then the Chinese people will be living under an [indirect foreign rule]. How can China achieve independence and freedom, and how can the people of China be liberated?"[32] Deng feared that China would develop toward capitalism under foreign political enslavement if the Chinese proletariat failed to achieve revolutionary leadership. He believed that the Chinese revolution was neither a bourgeois revolution, as in the case of Turkey, nor a proletarian revolution, as in Russia. Instead, China had its own form of revolution, which would be based on the establishment of a democratic dictatorship under the united front of workers, peasants, and petty bourgeois. His proposed strategy was to prevent the bourgeoisie from seizing the revolutionary leadership and to maintain the proletarian hegemony for developing socialism in China.[33]

Although Deng's class analysis in early 1927 was similar to that of the resolution adopted in the ECCI Seventh Plenum, there were some major differences regarding the problem of the bourgeoisie and the policy of agrarian revolution. In Moscow, Comintern officials generally underestimated the influence of the Chinese bourgeoisie in the Nationalist Revolution. Some even mistakenly thought that there was a group of "liberal bourgeoisie" who would support the Nationalist Revolution.[34] The ECCI Seventh Plenum also considered that "the native bourgeoisie is comparatively undeveloped and weak as a class."[35] The newly arrived Comintern representative to China M. N. Roy even said in late February that "the Chinese bourgeoisie is young and weak. It is economically backward and politically immature."[36] Probably influenced by his experiences in leading the labor movement against capitalists, Deng Zhongxia thought otherwise. He saw the bourgeoisie as a major rival capable of capturing the revolutionary leadership. He was deeply worried that the imperialists might shift their support from the feudal warlords to the Chinese bourgeoisie in return for the protection of their special economic privileges in China. Because of this, he warned his comrades that the Chinese revolution was in danger. The only strategy to solve this problem was to mobilize the peasantry and the

32. Deng Zhongxia, *1926 nian zhi Guangzhou gongchao*, pp. 91, 94.
33. Ibid., pp. 93–94.
34. Eudin and North, eds., *Soviet Russia and the East*, p. 303.
35. North and Eudin, eds., *Roy's Mission*, p. 137.
36. Ibid., p. 149. The original version of this article translated into Chinese can be found in *Renmin zhoukan* 43 (23 Feb. 1927), p. 2.

petty bourgeoisie under proletarian leadership: "We need to do our best to compete with the bourgeoisie in seizing the [revolutionary] leadership. How do we capture the leadership? It is by achieving leadership among the middle classes [*zhongjian jieji*]. . . . The middle classes are the peasantry in the countryside and the petty bourgeoisie in the cities."[37] But he strongly opposed the idea of a radical agrarian policy in which all land would be confiscated. An extreme radical agrarian policy would only discourage the *zhongjian jieji* from supporting the Party. On the eve of the Nanchang Uprising, Deng Zhongxia proposed a tactic which was later labeled a "rich peasant policy." He claimed that in order to gain support from the middle and rich peasants, only landlord holdings of more than 200 *mu* should be confiscated.[38]

If Deng's agrarian policy at the time was not especially radical, his labor movement policy was also moderate. Following the directive of the CCP Central Committee in late January 1927, he appealed to the Guomindang to legislate a reform program for the improvement of industrial working conditions in the cities and called on the workers to support the Nationalist Revolution by joining the Guomindang as its party members.[39] His moderate view toward the Guomindang was similar to the policy adopted by the Comintern but differed from that of some members in the CCP Central Committee, as previously discussed.

Although Deng's class analysis in early 1927 was not as sophisticated as that of other Chinese Communists of the time, his insistence on the need for proletarian hegemony in the Nationalist Revolution, both in theory and in practice, was unique in the sense that it fully represented his confidence in the ability of the working class to achieve its own liberation. Thus, the policy of proletarian hegemony was not only an article of faith but served as the core of his operational guidelines. In this respect, Deng's view on the role of the Chinese working class was in line with the Comintern theoretical discussion on the Chinese revolutionary movement. Most important, his class analysis in early 1927 was fully appreciated by Chen Duxiu's successor, Qu Qiubai.

37. Deng Zhongxia, *1926 nian zhi Guangzhou gongchao*, p. 91.
38. Li Lisan, "Dangshi baogao," p. 268.
39. Ibid., pp. 359–60, 369–70.

Relations with Qu Qiubai

A week after Chen Duxiu had stepped down as the Party general secretary, Deng Zhongxia was appointed by the newly formed Provisional Politburo as its secretary on 24 June.[40] This appointment reflected his close relationship with the new Party leadership, which was soon to be headed by Qu Qiubai.[41] Although Qu was not a student of Beijing University, he participated in the Marxist Research Society organized by Li Dazhao in 1920. In October 1920, he went to Moscow, where he stayed until January 1923. While in Moscow, he joined the CCP and became its delegate to the Comintern Fourth Congress, which was held in late 1922. Probably due to his language and ideological training in Moscow, he emerged rapidly as a major young CCP leader.

Deng and Qu had a long and cordial working relationship. Politically, both were products of the New Culture Movement, in which they had transformed themselves from student radicals to Marxist revolutionaries. Intellectually, both shared a deep interest in modern literature as well as in Marxist literary thought. They were also gifted with editorial skill. When the organ of the Chinese Socialist Youth Corps, *Zhongguo qingnian* (Chinese Youth), was launched in Shanghai in early 1923, both were leading members of its editorial committee. Most significant, they shared a strong commitment to building a close link between Marxist intellectuals and factory workers. As teachers at Shanghai University in 1924, they emphasized the importance of organizing a labor movement. Qu was one of the earliest literary figures who advocated the development of a proletarian literature in China, an enthusiasm that Deng shared. They jointly took part

40. Cai Hesen, "Jihui zhuyi shi" [History of Opportunism], in *Gongfei huoguo shiliao huibian* [Selected Documents on Communist Troubles in China] (Taibei, 1961), vol. 1, p. 593.

41. This Provisional Politburo did not include Qu. Some of Qu's close comrades, such as Cai Hesen and Li Weihan, did not understand why Qu was not appointed. He was elected to the Politburo only at the 7 August Emergency Meeting. Although Qu did not formally establish his leadership before the 7 August Emergency Meeting, he was highly respected within the Party on the eve of the CCP Fifth Congress due to his severe criticism of Chen Duxiu, expressed in his booklet entitled *Zhongguo geming zhong zhi zhenglun wenti* [Controversial Issues in the Debate on the Chinese Revolution]. See Li Weihan, "Guanyu Baqi huiyi de yixie huiyi," p. 191. Therefore, although the "Qu Qiubai line" was not formally established before 7 August, his influence within the Party leadership was profound. For an analysis of the rise of Qu during this crucial period, see van de Ven, *From Friend to Comrade*, pp. 215–19; Benjamin I. Schwartz, *Chinese Communism and the Rise of Mao* (Cambridge: Harvard University Press, 1951), pp. 86–96.

in the establishment of the Workers' Part-time School, the West Shanghai Workers' Club, and the Workers' Association for the Promotion of Virtue for the cultivation of a better relation between intellectuals and workers.[42] Soon after the May Thirtieth Incident, Deng was assigned by the Party to lead the editorial committee of *Gongren zhi lu* in Guangzhou; Qu was responsible for editing a newspaper of similar nature, *Rexue ribao* (Hot Blood Daily), in Shanghai. Although they usually worked in different cities from mid-1925 to mid-1927, Deng in Guangzhou and Qu in Shanghai, they shared the view that the success of the Nationalist Revolution would be dependent on the participation of the Chinese working class. They were also extremely concerned with the problem of the bourgeoisie in the current stage of the political struggle, disagreeing with Chen Duxiu's class analysis, which emphasized the importance of the bourgeoisie in leading the Nationalist Revolution. When Chen's leadership came under severe criticism during the CCP Fifth Congress, held in April–May 1927, it was Qu Qiubai who took the lead in launching an anti-Chen movement.[43] Apparently, Deng sided with Qu in the intraparty debates during this period.[44]

After Chen had stepped down from the Party's leadership in mid-July, and Deng had become, not surprisingly, the secretary to the newly formed Provisional Politburo, Deng took a leading role in the initial planning for an uprising in Nanchang.[45] On 19 July he and Li Lisan, on the orders of the Provisional Politburo, arrived in Jiujiang of Jiangxi Province to study the feasibility of implementing this plan. Deng strongly supported the idea of agitation in the Twentieth Division Army, which was then under the command of He Long, and seizure of the weapons of the Third, Sixth, and Ninth Division Armies, which were stationed in Nanchang. The objective of this military operation was to establish a new government and oppose the Wuhan and Nanjing governments, then under the control of Wang Jingwei and Jiang Jieshi respectively. After the meeting in Jiujiang, Deng Zhongxia,

42. Paul G. Pikowicz, *Marxist Literary Thought in China: The Influence of Chu Chiu-pai* (Berkeley and Los Angeles: University of California Press, 1981), pp. 56–80.

43. Van de Ven, *From Friend to Comrade*, pp. 215–19.

44. There are very few records of Deng's activities during the CCP Fifth Congress. Even Deng's official biographer does not provide us with sufficient information. See Jiang Ping, *Deng Zhongxia de yisheng*, p. 167. For a brief account of different policies proposed by other leading CCP members during this congress, see North and Eudin, eds., *Roy's Mission*, p. 74.

45. Unless otherwise mentioned, the following discussion on the Nanchang Uprising is based mainly on the following sources: C. Martin Wilbur, "The Ashes of Defeat," *China Quarterly* 18 (Apr.-June 1964), pp. 9–24; Ristaino, *China's Art of Revolution*, pp. 21–27; Jiang Ping, *Deng Zhongxia de yisheng*, pp. 171–73.

together with Li Lisan and Yun Daiying, proceeded to Lushan, where they consulted with Qu, who completely endorsed their plan. On 24 July, Deng met the other Party leaders, including the newly arrived Comintern advisor Besso Lominadze, in Jiujiang for further discussion. At this second meeting in Jiujiang they unanimously agreed that the plan must be implemented. Following the meeting, Deng was instructed to present a report personally to the Provisional Politburo in Hankou, after which the Provisional Politburo called a secret meeting on 26 July mainly to discuss the Nanchang Uprising. Although there was some doubt about the chances of success, the Provisional Politburo ratified the plan for staging the Nanchang Uprising on 1 August. Deng, however, did not directly participate in this abortive uprising. In late July, he had been appointed secretary of the Jiangsu Regional Committee.[46] News of the Communists' defeat in Nanchang reached the Provisional Politburo in Hankou before he had left for Shanghai to take up his new assignment. The Communist leaders saw the urgent need to convene a Party meeting to review the political situation and to formulate a new strategy.[47] Since Deng was still in Hankou at that time, he was instructed to attend the Party emergency meeting held on 7 August in Hankou.

Contemporary Chinese Communists saw the 7 August emergency meeting essentially as an endorsement of a policy of uprisings because it approved the preparation for the Autumn Harvest Uprising.[48] Mainland Chinese historians since 1949, however, have attributed the significance of the meeting to its termination of the Chen Duxiu "rightist" leadership and its recognition of the importance of an agrarian policy in the Chinese revolution. They have also criticized the meeting for continuing the policy of "putschism" under the leadership of Qu Qiubai.[49] Deng Zhongxia was later to be accused by his opponents within the Party of having pursued a policy of putschism and of being an associate of Qu.

Although the 7 August emergency meeting was chaired by a leading Chinese Communist, Li Weihan, it was the Comintern representative,

46. Zhao Piao, "Wuci dahui dao liuci dahui yinian zhong dang de zuzhi zhuangkuang," *Dangshi yanjiu* 5 (1986), p. 62.

47. It must be clarified here that the decision to convene such a Party meeting was initially made on 23 July when Qu Qiubai held a planning session with Lominadze. See Li Weihan, "Guanyu Baqi huiyi de yixie huiyi," pp. 184–85; Ristaino, *China's Art of Revolution*, p. 40.

48. "Political Report of the Central Committee, 15 Sept. 1927," in Hyobom Pak, ed., *Documents of the Chinese Communist Party, 1927–1930* (Hong Kong: Union Research Institute, 1971), p. 76.

49. See Li Weihan, "Guanyu Baqi huiyi de yixie huiyi," pp. 1–2.

Lominadze, who gave the keynote speech. Lominadze stated clearly that the purpose of the meeting was to correct the mistakes of the previous CCP leadership under Chen Duxiu and to elect a new Politburo.[50] The previous errors, Lominadze claimed, were due to Chen himself. He denied that the Comintern might have been responsible for misguiding the Chinese Communists. He reminded his Chinese comrades: "The Comintern has much experience. We should believe and accept its guidance. Otherwise, we will lead ourselves along a non-Communist road."[51] But his speech contained many confusing political analyses. He recognized the importance of the agrarian revolution in the current stage of the political struggle, but he did not give sufficient attention to the role of the peasantry. Instead, he continued to emphasize the significance of the proletarian hegemony: "In the current stage of the class struggle, the Chinese proletariat is fighting against the native and foreign bourgeoisie on its own strength. No other class can match the strength and power of the proletariat."[52] His analysis of CCP-Guomindang relations was similarly confusing. He refuted the idea of breaking up the United Front and insisted that the Chinese Communists continue to cooperate with the Guomindang until the Nationalist Revolution had been successfully completed. But he also recognized that the Guomindang leaders had already betrayed the revolution. He therefore suggested: "Our policy is not to lean on the Guomindang leaders; [our strategy] is to rely on the Guomindang populace."[53]

Mao Zedong spoke immediately after Lominadze's confusing opening speech and put forward his slogan of "political power comes from the barrel of a gun."[54] Other leading Chinese Communist leaders expressed their views after Mao's brief statement. But no one criticized or questioned Lominadze's political analysis. They also supported his proposal to establish a new Politburo.[55] When Deng spoke, he completely concurred with Lominadze's judgment on Chen Duxiu's leadership. He also stated that the previous CCP Central Committee had not implemented the Comintern's instructions: "The seventh ECCI resolution contains two policies: (1) the unity of the working class, peasantry, and petty bourgeoisie; (2) agrarian

50. Ibid., pp. 49–50.
51. Ibid., p. 54.
52. Ibid., p. 50.
53. Ibid., p. 54.
54. "Mao Zedong guangyu gongchan guoji daibiao baogao de fayan" [Mao Zedong's Speech on the Report by the Comintern's Representative], in *Baqi huiyi,* pp. 57–58.
55. Li Weihan, "Guanyu Baqi huiyi de yixie huiyi," p. 189.

revolution. But our comrades did not fully understand these two policies. . . . the Central Committee did not fully understand the Comintern's resolution, and subsequently, [the Central Committee] regarded the petty bourgeoisie as more important than the agrarian revolution."[56] In criticizing the previous Party leadership, Deng Zhongxia also echoed the opinion of Qu Qiubai as expressed in the CCP Fifth Congress. Qu had complained that the Party was suffering from factionalism and opportunism. But Deng went further and asserted that the Party was, not a proletarian, but a petty bourgeois organization. He bitterly pointed out that "it can be said that our Party, from its date of foundation to the present moment, is petty bourgeois [in class identity]. . . . in dealing with problems, [some comrades] always prefer to use trickery [*shouwan*] instead of class standpoint."[57] As for current strategy in the Chinese revolution, Deng completely shared Lominadze's view that proletarian hegemony was the most important factor in seizing political power. He paraphrased the Comintern representative's statement by claiming that "we should know that the political consciousness of the Shanghai working class is a hundred times higher than that of the Party Central Committee."[58]

Of all the comments made by the Chinese Communists during the meeting, Qu Qiubai's concluding remarks were most striking. Calling for the radicalization of the agrarian revolution, he told the meeting: "The agrarian revolution has already entered its highest stage; it needs the support of our army for further development. . . . The peasants want to launch insurrections, and armed uprisings [will be] staged in many locations. . . . Under such circumstances, our strategy is to engage in independent worker-peasant class struggle."[59] Qu's proposed strategy met with no challenge in the meeting; moreover, he was elected a member of the Politburo. When the standing committee members were elected, Qu was appointed to take charge of the departments of peasant movement and propaganda, and in addition, he was made chief editor of the Party's organ, *Buerseweike* (The Bolsheviks).[60] Simultaneously, Deng Zhongxia was appointed an alternate

56. "Deng Zhongxia guangyu gongchan guoji daibiao baogao de fayan" [Deng Zhongxia's Speech on the Report by the Comintern's Representative], in *Baqi huiyi*, p. 59.

57. Ibid.; see also van de Ven, *From Friend to Comrade*, p. 231.

58. *Baqi huiyi*, p. 59.

59. "Zhongyang changwei daibiao Qu Qiubai de baogao" [Report by the Central Standing Committee's Representative, Qu Qiubai], in *Baqi huiyi*, p. 71.

60. Qu did not take the post of Party secretary general, which had been vacant since the resignation of Chen Duxiu. See *Baqi huiyi*, pp. 200–201.

member of the Politburo as well as retaining his post as the secretary of the Jiangsu Regional Committee. He was also appointed to the editorial committee of the Party's organ. Immediately after the meeting, the Politburo was transferred from Hankou to Shanghai,[61] and this relocation allowed Deng to maintain close contact with Qu Qiubai.

Although Deng Zhongxia played an active role in the 7 August emergency meeting and maintained close contact with the Politburo in Shanghai after the meeting, he did not immediately participate in the execution of the "Qu Qiubai line," which emphasized the organization of insurrections in the countryside and the establishment of soviets as political organs for leading China toward socialism.[62] Immediately after the meeting, Deng went to Shanghai, where he took charge of the Party's affairs in Jiangsu Province; this occupied his attention in the first two months after the meeting, ruling out his active involvement in the work of the Politburo.

The political situation in Shanghai when he arrived in late 1927 was tense. Many militant labor movement activists had been arrested by the Guomindang after April 1927, and in Jiangsu Province, including the city of Shanghai, 1,836 Communists had been executed between the April Twelfth Incident and the end of 1927.[63] Political suppression created a shortage of cadres to run the Party, which was then operating underground. The CCP was also seriously hindered in organizing the labor movement because of the Guomindang's tight control over labor union activities. But many Party leaders, including Deng Zhongxia, still regarded the mobilization of the working class in the cities as a cornerstone of the strategy for seizing political power. When he arrived in Shanghai on about 15 August,[64] the city was under political repression, and Deng recognized the urgent need to rebuild the local Party component and to reorganize the labor movement.

On 23 August, he chaired a Jiangsu Regional Standing Committee meeting in which a resolution was adopted to establish a Labor Movement Committee under the direct leadership of the Standing Committee. The Chinese Communists hoped this would improve relations between the Party and the

61. Zhao Piao, "Baqi huiyi yu dang de gaizu" [Party Organization and the 7 August Meeting], *Dangshi yanjiu* 4 (1985), pp. 61, 64.

62. For a lucid account of the formation of a new strategy under Qu Qiubai's influence in the aftermath of the 7 August Emergency Meeting, see Ristaino, *China's Art of Revolution*, pp. 48–55.

63. Jiang Ping, *Deng Zhongxia de yisheng*, p. 177.

64. Zhao Piao, "Wuci dahui dao liuci dahui yinian zhong dang de zuzhi zhuangkuang," *Dangshi yanjiu* 5 (1986), p. 62.

labor unions. A few days later, the Jiangsu Regional Standing Committee also appointed new leaders for the Shanghai labor movement. These leaders included not only experienced Party cadres but also some non-Communist, but militant, workers who had recently demonstrated their commitment to the Nationalist Revolution.[65] The recruitment of non-Communist workers directly into the Labor Movement Committee was due to the serious shortage of Party members in Shanghai at the time. This led Deng Zhongxia to recruit Party members not only from Shanghai but also from the rural areas and among the graduates of the Huangpu Military Academy.[66] His policy was quite successful; by early October, there were 1,164 Party members in Shanghai alone, working in six different districts of the city, and another 1,543 Party members working in different counties and villages throughout the province.[67]

Although he successfully created a new labor movement leadership and a new local Party component shortly after his arrival in Shanghai, Deng encountered serious difficulties in mobilizing workers because of the Guomindang suppression. The Politburo, however, did not recognize this problem. The 7 August emergency meeting adopted an unrealistic resolution on the labor movement, encouraging the Communists to promote struggle between the yellow and red unions.[68]

Starting in the summer of 1927, the Guomindang enacted a series of labor policies aimed at getting all workers under its control. To this end, an organization known as the Committee for Unification of Workers' Unions was set up in Shanghai. The Communists reacted by employing two tactics. One was terrorism: assassination of leading Guomindang labor movement activists. The other was to send pro-Communist labor activists into the yellow unions. The 7 August emergency meeting emphasized the latter tactic and condemned the former.[69] However, some Party cadres in Shanghai did not obey the Politburo, and several Guomindang labor activists were assassinated by the Communists. Reports of these incidents appeared in Shanghai's newspapers in October and November and were filed by the

65. Ibid.

66. Jiang Ping, *Deng Zhongxia de yisheng*, p. 177.

67. Zhao Piao, "Wuci dahui dao liuci dahui yinian zhong dang de zuzhi zhuangkuang," p. 63.

68. "Zuijin zhigong yundong yiyuean" [Resolution on the Recent Labor Movement], in *Baqi huiyi*, pp. 41–43.

69. Ibid., p. 43.

International Settlement's Shanghai Municipal Police.[70] Apparently, Deng Zhongxia did not oppose the policy of assassination. He is said to have organized a team of workers in October, with about fifty members, to assassinate reactionary yellow labor unionists and rural landlords.[71] This bloody tactic did not last long; by November, he decided to abandon the policy of assassination after discussing the matter with two other members of the Politburo, Qu Qiubai and Li Weihan.[72]

The policy of promoting struggle from within the yellow unions met with failure. During the last three months of 1927, the Communists in Shanghai organized several strikes, which were unsuccessful.[73] Even some Party historians in China in recent years have considered the organization of strikes and other Communist labor policies in the aftermath of the 7 August emergency meeting to have been completely unrealistic.[74] However, the Politburo adopted an even more radical labor policy during its enlarged meeting, held in Shanghai on 9–10 November. It was after this meeting that Deng Zhongxia became more actively involved in the Politburo.

Deng agreed completely with the political resolution of the November enlarged meeting, which called for radicalization of the labor movement. The resolution, drafted by the Comintern advisor Lominadze, clearly instructed the Chinese Communists that the center of Chinese revolution remained in the cities. It also repeatedly reminded them that "insurrections led by the urban working class constitute the most important strategy" and that "to underestimate the working class, and to treat it merely as a supportive force of the peasantry, is a major mistake."[75] Although the resolution concluded that the time for staging a general insurrection had not yet arrived, it contributed to the development of Qu Qiubai's policy of putsch-

70. "History of Disturbances in Shanghai Arising from Activities of Communists and Militant Labor," Shanghai Municipal Police Archives, D4820, box 38.

71. Jiang Ping, *Deng Zhongxia de yisheng*, pp. 182–83.

72. Li Weihan, "Guanyu Qu Qiubai zuoqing mangdong zhuyi de huiyi yu yanjiu" [A Retrospective Study of Qu Qiubai's "Leftist" Adventurism], in *Zhonggong dangshi ziliao*, vol. 5, p. 222.

73. "History of Disturbances in Shanghai Arising from Activities of Communists and Militant Labor," p. 27.

74. Liu Jingfang, "Ping Baqi huiyi guanyu zhigong yundong de celue" [Comment on the 7 August Meeting's Labor Strategy], *Dangshi yanjiu* 3 (1985), pp. 57–59.

75. "Zhongguo xianzhuang yu gongchandang de renwu jueyian" [Resolution of the Current Situation in China and the Duties of the Communist Party], in *Liuda yiqian dang de lishi cailiao*, pp. 924–25. See also Hsiao Tso-liang, *Chinese Communism in 1927*, pp. 105–14; Ristaino, *China's Art of Revolution*, pp. 75–96.

ism because Qu uncritically accepted Lominadze's theory of the "uninterrupted revolution."[76] The resolution also directly encouraged the Chinese Communists in Guangzhou to stage an insurrection on 11 December.

The planning for an uprising in Guangzhou was an outcome of the 7 August emergency meeting, and the uprising was initially discussed by Qu Qiubai and other Politburo members in Shanghai a week after the November enlarged meeting.[77] Both Zhang Tailei and Deng Zhongxia, who had experience in working with the Guangdong Regional Committee before the collapse of the United Front, also attended this planning session. Zhang was then the secretary of the Guangdong Regional Committee, and Deng's fine record in leading the workers in south China during 1925–26 was still fresh in the minds of many Chinese Communist leaders. The Communists felt that conditions in Guangdong at the time were favorable for staging an insurrection: Peng Pai had established the Hailufeng Soviet on 7 November, and in the city, a clash between two major Guomindang military factions under Zhang Fakui and Li Jishen on 17 November had weakened the opposition. The planners therefore concluded that the time was ripe for the Guangdong Communists to establish soviets by mobilizing workers and peasants and by encouraging mutinies and revolts among Guomindang soldiers. Immediately after the Politburo meeting held in Shanghai, Zhang Tailei rushed back to Guangzhou, where, on 26 November, he organized the Revolutionary Military Council, on which he served as chairman and Ye Ting as commander in chief.[78]

Although Deng Zhongxia was involved in the planning, he did not participate in the actual uprising because of his responsibilities in Jiangsu. The uprising on 11 December was led by a small group of Communists who had previously played leading roles in the Shenggang General Strike and included Zhang Tailei, Yang Yin, and Huang Ping.[79] Deng may have regretted being unable to fight alongside his comrades in a city in which he had mobilized half a million workers in a general strike. He believed that the workers in Guangzhou had strengthened their political consciousness through their participation in the general strike and that their anti-imperialist and revo-

76. Li Weihan, "Guanyu Qu Qiubai zuoqing mangdong zhuyi de huiyi yu yanjiu," p. 225.

77. Deng Zhongxia, "Guangzhou baodong yu zhongguo gongchandang de celue, 1930" [The Guangzhou Insurrection and the CCP Strategy], in *Deng Zhongxia wenji*, p. 405.

78. Ristaino, *China's Art of Revolution*, pp. 102–3; Hsiao Tso-liang, *Chinese Communism in 1927*, pp. 135–38.

79. Huang Ping, *Wangshi huiyi*, p. 47.

lutionary sentiment was still on the rise.[80] However, after only three days of street fighting, the uprising met with a bloody defeat. Zhang Tailei and some two thousand pro-Communist rebels lost their lives in the course of the struggle.[81]

The failure of the uprising brought Deng Zhongxia back to south China. After the death of Zhang Tailei, Li Lisan had become secretary of the Guangdong Regional Committee. But the Politburo was not satisfied with Li's leadership because of his views on the recent failure in Guangzhou. In early January, the Guangdong Regional Standing Committee, chaired by Li Lisan, adopted a resolution on the uprising after five days of discussion. The resolution had little good to say about the uprising and emphasized its strategic errors and organizational weaknesses. It criticized some of the leaders for stressing military tactics but neglecting the mobilization of the working class and peasantry. The resolution pointed out bluntly that the failure of the uprising was due to lack of support from the populace in both the city and the countryside and recommended to the Politburo that severe disciplinary measures be imposed on the leaders of the uprising: Huang Ping, Yang Yin, Ye Ting, Yun Daiying, and several other Guangdong Communists.[82]

The Politburo, however, was not satisfied with this resolution and believed that it was adopted mainly because of the Guangdong Communists' psychological instability caused by their defeat.[83] In fact, prior to receiving the resolution from the Guangdong Regional Committee, the Politburo in Shanghai had already adopted its own resolution on the Guangzhou Uprising on 3 January 1928. Unlike the Guangdong Regional Committee, the Politburo did not denigrate the role of the populace in the uprising; it repeatedly claimed that the workers and peasants had been ready to participate. The Politburo's resolution also glorified the achievements of the uprising and insisted on the significance of establishing soviets in the cities.

80. Zhonggong zhongyang dangshi ziliao zhengji wenyuanhui, Zhonggong Guangdong-sheng dangshi ziliao zhengji wenyuanhui, and Guangdong geming bowuguan, eds., *Guangzhou qiyi* [Guangzhou Uprising] (Beijing: Zhonggong dangshi ziliao chubanshe, 1988), p. 305.

81. Ristaino, *China's Art of Revolution*, pp. 102–8; Hsiao Tso-liang, *Chinese Communism in 1927*, pp. 138–42.

82. "Zhonggong Guangdong shengwei guanyu Guangzhou baodong wenti jueyian" [The CCP Guangdong Regional Committee's Resolution on the Guangzhou Insurrection], in *Guangzhou qiyi*, pp. 247–53.

83. Tang Chunliang, "Li Lisan zai Guangdong" [Li Lisan in Guangdong], in *Guangdong dangshi ziliao*, vol. 10 (1987), p. 190.

Thus, the Politburo continued to stress the importance of the city-centered strategy. It also believed that the powerful reactionary force rather than the strategic errors and organizational weaknesses of the Communists was the main reason for the failure.[84] When this Politburo resolution reached Guangzhou, Li Lisan became very upset. He complained that the Politburo did not understand the actual conditions in Guangzhou and that the resolution was adopted under the influence of the Comintern members who had bungled the uprising. He even suggested that the Politburo impose disciplinary measures on those Comintern members![85] By that time, the Politburo had decided to replace Li Lisan with Deng Zhongxia as secretary of the Guangdong Regional Committee. It also instructed Deng to submit a report to the Politburo on the uprising after a full investigation in Guangzhou.[86]

Disguising himself as a merchant, Deng went to Hong Kong in early February to talk with the Guangdong Communists, who were on the run.[87] After the suppression of the Guangzhou Uprising, it was too risky for any Communist to stay in Guangzhou, so the Communists had to hold their regional meetings secretly in Hong Kong. On 9 February, Deng chaired an Enlarged Guangdong Regional Standing Committee Meeting mainly to discuss the Guangzhou Uprising. In his opening remarks, he insisted that the basic principle of the resolution adopted by the Politburo was fundamentally correct and criticized the Guangdong Regional Committee for underestimating the significance of the event. He viewed the Guangzhou Uprising as "the beginning of a new age of soviet revolution."[88] One of the main reasons for its defeat, he argued, was the Party's failure to mobilize the populace, who were eager to participate. He repeatedly claimed that the Guangdong Communists' failure to mobilize the populace was the fatal weakness in the recent uprising. The main difference between the Politburo and

84. "Guangzhou baodong zhi yiyi yu jiaoxun: Zhongguo gongchandang zhongyang linshi zhengzhiju huiji tongguo de jueyian" [The Significance and Lesson of the Guangzhou Insurrection: Resolution Adopted by the CCP Provisional Politburo], in *Guangzhou qiyi*, pp. 255–86.

85. "Lisan tongzhi zhi zhongyang zhengzhiju xin" (16 Jan 1928) [Comrade Lisan's Letter to the Politburo], in *Guangzhou qiyi*, p. 300.

86. Huang Ping, *Wangshi huiyi*, p. 54; Tang Chunliang, "Li Lisan zai Guangdong," pp. 182–84.

87. Jiang Ping, *Deng Zhongxia de yisheng*, p. 185.

88. "Zhonggong Guangdong shengwei changwei kuoda huiyi jilu" (9 Feb. 1928) [Minutes of the Enlarged Meeting of the CCP Guangdong Regional Committee], in *Guangzhou qiyi*, pp. 302–3.

the Guangdong Regional Committee, as concluded by Deng, was that the former did not consider the failure a consequence of lack of mass support. During the discussion, even Li Lisan, with a view to keeping up the morale of the Communists, admitted that the resolution adopted by the Guangdong Regional Committee should be modified so that the significance of the Guangzhou Uprising could be recognized and appreciated by the Party. But he insisted that the Guangdong Communists had neglected to provide proper leadership in mass mobilization during the course of the uprising.[89]

Even though the meeting was able to narrow the gap between the Politburo and the Guangdong Regional Committee, it revealed the ambiguity of Deng Zhongxia, who, throughout the discussion, spoke uncritically of the Politburo's resolution. To defend the Politburo's position, he, perhaps intentionally, ignored many of the actual problems in mass mobilization during the uprising. Ironically, before 1927 he had challenged the CCP Central Committee's labor movement policy while mobilizing the workers in Shanghai and in Guangzhou. But now, serving in the Politburo, he had become a Party bureaucrat and overlooked the problems of his comrades at the local level.

Only two days after the meeting, as Li Lisan was preparing to leave Hong Kong for Shanghai, where he was instructed to report on the Guangzhou Uprising to the Politburo personally,[90] the secret Guangdong Communists' bureau in Hong Kong was searched by the police, and eight men were arrested, including Deng Zhongxia and three other Guangdong Communists.[91] Luckily, Deng was released because the police could not produce any solid evidence to support their charge against him as a Communist; in fact, the police failed to recognize his true identity.[92] After his release, Deng immediately proceeded to Moscow via Shanghai, where he attended the CCP Sixth Congress.

89. Ibid., pp. 320–22.

90. Tang Chunliang, "Li Lisan zai Guangdong," p. 189.

91. *South China Morning Post*, 28 Feb. 1928. Li Lisan also sent a report about this incident to the CCP Party Central; see Guangdongsheng danganguan and Zhonggong Guangdong shengwei yanjiu weiyuanhui bangongshi, eds., *Guangdongqu dang tuan yanjiu shiliao, 1927–1934* [Historical Materials on the CCP Guangdong Regional and Corps Committees, 1927–1934] (Guangzhou: Guangdong renmin chubanshe, 1986), pp. 120–23.

92. *South China Morning Post*, 29 Feb. 1928.

Power Struggle in Moscow

The CCP Sixth Congress was convened in order to review the recent Communist defeats and to formulate a new strategy after the complete collapse of the United Front. It was held between 18 June and 11 July 1928 in a village on the outskirts of Moscow, under tight security. A Chinese student interpreter at the congress later recalled that most of the young Chinese Communist members studying in Moscow at that time did not know anything about this important event.[93] Apparently, most of the Chinese Communists attending this congress were in a state of confusion because of the severe defeats they had recently suffered. Many were even uncertain about the future of the revolution and expected the Comintern to provide them with concrete guidance.

The CCP Sixth Congress was dominated by Comintern leaders, notably Joseph Stalin, Pavel Mif, and Nikolai Bukharin. At the beginning of the congress, Deng Zhongxia was nominated as a deputy secretary of the Presidium. But for some unknown reason, he did not accept this honor.[94] However, he accepted appointment to several working committees. Among them were the Review Committee on the Nanchang Uprising and the Review Committee on the Guangzhou Uprising, both of which were created on the seventh day of the congress. The main object of the committees was to review the strategic errors of these two unsuccessful revolts.[95] But in about two weeks, these two committees were dissolved by Pavel Mif, who proposed that the investigation should be directly conducted by the ECCI.[96] Apparently, Mif and his associates wanted to dominate every major review committee discussion about the recent abortive uprisings. The congress, without hesitation, accepted Mif's proposal. Deng, however, continued to serve on many other committees during the congress, including the Politburo, the Organizational, the Labor Movement, the Soviet Movement, and the Military Committees. He was also responsible for drafting the Congress Agenda and submitting the Party's resolution on the soviet movement to the congress for endorsement.[97]

93. Cheng Fou, *Mosike Zhongshan daxue yu zhongguo geming* [Moscow Zhongshan Academy and the Chinese Revolution] (Beijing: Xiandai chubanshe, 1980), p. 211.

94. Zhao Piao, "Diliuci quangguo daibiao dahui" [The CCP Sixth Congress], *Dangshi yanjiu* 1 (1986), p. 53.

95. *Dangshi yanjiu* 2 (1986), pp. 26–27.

96. Ibid. 4 (1986), p. 62.

97. Ibid. 2 (1986), pp. 21–24; and 4 (1986), p. 66.

Although he was an active member in the congress, Deng Zhongxia did not win a seat in the newly elected seven-member Politburo. Nor did he receive a place in the Central Committee, composed of twelve members. In the end, he was only elected as an alternate member of the Central Committee. With his revolutionary credentials, Deng may well have felt quite disappointed. But his nonelection might have been caused by Comintern policy, which now stressed the development of a new CCP leadership of men and women with working-class backgrounds. Of the twelve newly elected Central Committee members, seven were classified as workers and five were classified as intellectuals in terms of their class origins. Among the eleven elected alternate Central Committee members, there were six intellectuals, three workers, one peasant, and one of unknown class origins.[98] It is possible that Deng's failure to gain a seat in the Politburo was also due to his close association with Qu Qiubai and the former Comintern advisors to China in the years 1924–27, all of whom were now discredited.

One of the important items on the agenda of the CCP Sixth Congress was review of the strategic errors committed by the Chinese Communists. Although Bukharin accepted the fact that the Comintern should take some responsibility for the failure of the Chinese revolution, he insisted that the most at fault had been the individual Comintern advisors to China, notably Borodin, Roy, and Lominadze. Borodin was criticized for his failure to mobilize the Chinese peasantry, and Roy was condemned for informing Wang Jingwei about the details of the Comintern's instructions to the CCP at the most critical moment. Lominadze was criticized, prior to the Sixth Congress, as a Trotskyite because he advocated the theory of "uninterrupted revolution" in China and was responsible for promoting the policy of putschism under Qu Qiubai's leadership during the last two months of 1927.[99] Thus, Deng Zhongxia was in an awkward position at the congress because he had been closely associated with these former Soviet advisors and with Qu Qiubai.[100]

98. For a list of the names of the new Party leadership, see ibid. 4 (1986), p. 70. Of the 84 Chinese Communists who attended the Sixth Party Congress, about 52% were workers, 7% were peasants, and 40% were intellectuals. For details, see ibid. 1 (1986), pp. 53–56.

99. Xiang Qing, *Gongchan guoji he zhongguo geming quanxi de lishi gaishu*, pp. 95–98.

100. Even after Borodin had been purged by Stalin in 1928, it is said that Deng Zhongxia and Qu Qiubai still maintained their close contact with him by visiting him at his home in Moscow frequently. See Huang Ping, *Wangshi huiyi*, pp. 74–75. Their friendly relations with a "non-Stalinist" man certainly would have created tension between them and the Stalinist leadership.

Most important, there was also a major difference between Deng Zhong-xia and the leaders of the Comintern regarding the nature of the Chinese revolution before the congress was held. In early 1928, Deng frequently said, referring to the Guangzhou Uprising, that the Chinese Communists had already launched a soviet revolution in China. Yet Stalin and the other Comintern leaders in February 1929 adopted a resolution in the ECCI Ninth Plenum in which they indirectly criticized the CCP's "adventurous" policy under Qu Qiubai's leadership. The Moscow leaders claimed that the Chinese Communists' efforts during the previous year to skip over the bourgeois democratic stage was a major error in strategy. China, they insisted, had not yet entered the phase of soviet revolution.[101]

Although Qu Qiubai was elected to the Politburo at the end of the Sixth Congress, his influence within the Party declined sharply. The newly elected Politburo was headed by a Wuhan worker, Xiang Zhongfa, who had not taken part in the revolutionary movement in the years 1925–27 because he was then receiving Comintern training in Moscow. The appointment of Xiang as the secretary general of the CCP supreme organization indicated the Comintern's deep concern with creating a proletariat-led Communist Party in China. The Moscow leaders also wanted to put the CCP leadership back on the right track under the Comintern's guidance. Although the latter did not, during the CCP Sixth Congress, severely criticize Qu Qiubai and his associates, it did eliminate their influence within the Party leadership. One of the measures adopted to accomplish this was to keep them in Moscow rather than to send them back to China after the congress.

This idea originated from the announcement by Bukharin during the CCP Sixth Congress that, in order to prevent further strategic errors in the Chinese revolution, the Comintern had decided not to send any other advisor to China. Instead, he proposed that some leading CCP members should stay in the Soviet Union to serve as the liaison between the Comintern in Moscow and the CCP Politburo in China. Five Chinese Communist leaders were appointed to the Comintern's leading organizations. Among them were Qu Qiubai and Zhang Guotao, as CCP delegates to the Comintern; Deng Zhongxia and Yu Fei were representatives of the ACLF to the Profintern; and Wang Ruofei represented the Chinese Peasants' Association in the Red Peasant International. In the early period of their term of service, these five Chinese delegates maintained a cordial and cooperative

101. "Gongchan guoji zhixing weiyuanhui dejiuci kuoda huiyi guanyu Zhonggong wenti de yijiuan" (25 Feb. 1928) [Resolution on the Question of China Adopted by the ECCI Ninth Plenum], in *Liuda yiqian dang de lishi cailiao*, p. 931.

working relationship with the Comintern leadership. In fact, none of them had, at that time, opposed or criticized the fundamental policy laid down by the Comintern. Most of their opinions, expressed at different official functions, were identical with those recently endorsed by the Comintern.[102] Deng Zhongxia was no exception.

As a delegate of the ACLF to the Profintern, Deng was certainly delighted to have the opportunity to share his political experience with other Communist labor movement activists from different countries. He became a frequent guest speaker at official meetings hosted by the Comintern or by the Profintern. After the early tragic death of Su Zhaozheng in February 1929, Deng was invited to serve on the editorial committee of the *Pan-Pacific Monthly*, which was published by the Profintern. But his work on this international labor journal was to be brief, as he was assigned back to China in early 1930 (he was replaced by Xiang Ying).[103] During his two-year stay in Moscow, Deng emerged as a defender of the Comintern; and some of his ideas were accepted by the Comintern as policy for the reorganization of the Chinese labor movement.

In the Comintern Sixth Congress, Deng Zhongxia reported to his Moscow comrades that it was necessary to reestablish an effective system of political propaganda in China. He believed that there was an urgent need to reissue the two most important organs, namely the *Zhongguo gongren* of the ACLF and the *Bueerseweike* of the CCP Central Committee, so that a proper link between the Party leadership and the masses could be reestablished. In the same speech, he also appealed to the Comintern for a major research and publication project to be conducted by the Comintern, with the support of Chinese researchers, to analyze various social, economic, and political aspects of Chinese history as well as to study its recent revolutionary experiences.[104] This proposal was well received by the Comintern. In fact, Deng Zhongxia undertook some of this work himself; he began a project to analyze the history of the Chinese labor movement and, by the time he was posted back to China, had already completed a manuscript entitled *Zhongguo zhigong yundong jianshi* (A Brief History of the Chinese Labor Movement), first published in Moscow in 1930. During the Party Rectifica-

102. Ibid., pp. 106–7.

103. See the related issues of the Pan-Pacific Monthly, in the Library of Congress, Washington, D.C.

104. Deng Zhongxia, "Xiang gongchan guoji deliuci daibiao dahui zhuxituan de jianyi" [Suggestion to the Presidium of the Comintern Sixth Congress], in *Deng Zhongxia wenji*, pp. 375–76.

tion Campaign in Yanan, the CCP Central Committee reissued this book, which was widely circulated among Party cadres as compulsory reading.[105]

The Chinese labor movement strategy advocated by Deng Zhongxia during his two-year stay in Moscow was basically in line with that of the CCP Sixth Congress. He repeatedly emphasized the need to reformulate an effective strategy to mobilize the working class under CCP leadership. Although he suggested "taking steps without delay to organize the rural proletariat,"[106] he insisted that the center of revolution remained in the cities. He also completely agreed with the Party's policy in dealing with the yellow unions. In the face of the White Terror, Communist labor activists should penetrate the yellow unions in order to win the support of the working people. But Deng reminded the Communist labor activists that while working within the yellow unions, they should concentrate their efforts on winning over "the rank and file, the broad masses, and not the upper strata of the apparatus."[107]

In line with the resolution adopted in the CCP Sixth Congress, Deng disagreed with the idea of forming a united front with the yellow unionists. But he supported the policy of forming factory councils as a new strategy to promote the labor movement. However, he was unsatisfied with its progress because many Party cadres did not implement this important strategy on the grounds of practical difficulties. In early 1929, he emphasized that the "organization of the factory councils [is] the only means of assembling the workers under special circumstances. . . . if we don't do it, then we will have nothing."[108] His view on the organization of factory councils was well received by the Comintern; in fact, in late September 1929, the ECCI adopted a new resolution on Chinese labor movement strategy based on his suggestion.[109] Three weeks later, Deng returned to the same subject while speaking to the Tenth Plenum of the ECCI:

105. Apart from pointing out some minor factual errors of the book, the editorial committee of the CCP Central Committee in 1942 highly praised Deng's work for its in-depth analysis of the history of the Chinese labor movement under CCP leadership. See the preface of Deng Zhongxia, *Jianshi*, pp. 1–4.

106. "Speech to the Tenth Plenum of the ECCI," *International Press Correspondence*, 9 Oct. 1929.

107. Ibid.

108. Deng Zhongxia, "The Chinese Trade Unions after the Past Revolutionary Wave," *Pan-Pacific Monthly*, Apr. 1929, p. 21.

109. "Resolution of the ECCI on Communist Work in the Trade Unions of China," *International Press Correspondence*, 20 Sept. 1929. See also S. Bernard Thomas, *Labor and the Chinese Revolution*, Michigan Papers on Chinese Studies (Ann Arbor, 1983), p. 36.

The role of the factory councils in China would be different not only from that in the Soviet Union but also from that of Central Europe. The present political situation in China and the fierce White Terror make it inexpedient to lay down definite formalities and statutes for the factory councils or to establish bureaux and receive contributions. The main thing is that the factory councils be elected by the whole of the workers in a given factory. The central aim of the factory councils should be to take up the everyday demands of the workers. They should represent before the employers the interests of individual workers while waging the struggle for the general amelioration of the workers' conditions. The introduction of the factory councils should take place through the transformation of the fighting committees. The fighting committees (strike committees, wage committees etc.) should be set up for a short period and should be dissolved after the termination of the fight. The factory councils have the character of permanent organizations. Our most essential task is to have in our hands the leadership in the factory councils in order to set them up against the yellow trade unions. Although our Party Congress has already taken up the formation of factory councils as the new policy, no results are yet recorded because in many localities the significance and importance of the factory councils has not yet been grasped.[110]

At the end of his speech, Deng proclaimed the coming of a new revolutionary high tide in China and asked the Comintern for further instructions on Chinese labor movement strategy. It is clear that his prediction was the result of his acceptance of Bukharin's view that the struggle between the working class and the bourgeoisie would be intensified because of the recent international financial crisis.

Since his views were identical with those of the ECCI, it might be said that Deng Zhongxia was indeed a member of the pro-Comintern faction. Chinese Party historians nowadays criticize the policy of factory councils as a "leftist" strategy resulting from the Comintern's misunderstanding of actual conditions in China.[111] But in spite of the close and cordial relations between Deng Zhongxia and the Comintern during this period, he was soon criticized by the ECCI as a member of the anti-Comintern faction.

The criticism originated from a complicated power struggle that took

110. "Speech to the Tenth Plenum of the ECCI," *International Press Correspondence*, 9 Oct. 1929.

111. See, e.g., Gai Jun and Liu Jingfang, "Tudi geming zhanzheng shiqi de baiqu gongyun celue yu gongchan guoji" [The Comintern and the Labor Movement Strategy in the White Areas during the Land Revolutionary War Period], *Dangshi yanjiu* 2 (1987), p. 3. In his book-length study on Deng Zhongxia, the Nanjing historian Jiang Ping completely overlooks the close association between Deng's thinking and the Comintern's policy on the Chinese labor movement. See Jiang Ping, *Deng Zhongxia de yisheng*, pp. 196–200.

place at the Zhongshan Academy in Moscow, a Comintern-organized cadre training institute for the development of Chinese Communist leadership.[112] Starting in the summer of 1927, the struggle first involved the Trotskyite and Stalinist factions of the Soviet Party leadership. As soon as Trotsky was dismissed from the Party leadership, the pro-Trotskyite director of the Zhongshan Academy was replaced by Pavel Mif, who was a protégé of Stalin and a China expert. But the Comintern had to assign a temporary replacement for Pavel Mif while he was in China. The acting director, Agoor, was ambitious and wanted to establish his influence and overrule the Soviet Party secretary of the academy, Sednikov. Thus, the first thing Mif had to handle after his return to the academy was the struggle between Agoor and Sednikov. With the help of a small group of Chinese students, headed by Wang Ming, Mif rapidly eliminated the two factions within the academy. Wang Ming earned the trust of Mif.[113]

Soon after being appointed one of the ACLF delegates to the Profintern in Moscow, Deng Zhongxia found himself caught up in these factional struggles. In the spring of 1928, the anti-Trotskyite campaign paved the way for the Stalinist faction to discredit their opponents. In the Zhongshan Academy, Wang Ming and his associates saw the chance to eliminate those Chinese students who had previously supported Agoor, the former acting director. The pro-Agoor faction was accused of forming a so-called Jiangzhe faction. The criticism of this Jiangzhe faction was soon made official by the newly appointed general secretary of the CCP Politburo, Xiang Zhongfa, who, it is said, immediately announced his verdict on the accused without any investigation.[114] Members of the pro-Agoor faction, however, appealed to the CCP delegation to the Comintern. A working commit-

112. Price, *Cadres, Commanders, and Commissars,* pp. 89–90.

113. Wang Ming was sent to study at the Zhongshan Academy in 1926. After graduation in 1927, he remained at the academy as Mif's translator. During the CCP Sixth Congress, Wang served as Mif's secretary and helped organize the congress. He and a small group of Chinese students at the academy formed what was later called the "Returned Student Clique" or the "Twenty-eight Bolsheviks." At the academy, this small group identified themselves as faithful defenders of the Stalinist leadership. Above all, they offered their "doglike devotion to the Academy's director, Pavel Mif." See Schwartz, *Chinese Communism and the Rise of Mao,* p. 148. For a personal account by one of the members of the Twenty-eight Bolsheviks, see Cheng Fou, *Mosike Zhongshan daxue,* pp. 218–20. For a detailed account of the Agoor-Sednikov struggle and its impact on the relations between Wang and Mif, see Cheng Fou, *Mosike Zhongshan daxue,* pp. 226–27.

114. The few pro-Agoor Chinese students were natives of Jiangsu and Zhejiang. See Cheng Fou, *Mosike Zhongshan daxue,* pp. 230–31.

tee, composed of Qu Qiubai, Deng Zhongxia, and Yu Fei, was established
to investigate the conflict at the academy. Perhaps, Qu and Deng saw the
chance to take revenge on Xiang Zhongfa for his rapid promotion to the
Party leadership. According to one participant, there was serious tension
between the working-class and the intellectual Party leaders after the CCP
Sixth Congress. Qu Qiubai and his associates thought that it was completely unfair and unjustified to appoint Xiang Zhongfa as leader of the
Party simply because of his class origin and without considering his lack of
experience within the Party. Qu Qiubai, Deng Zhongxia, and Yu Fei thus
took the chance to mobilize some of the students of the academy who were
of proletarian origins but were also "politically ignorant"[115] and to challenge Xiang's verdict as well as to criticize the Wang Ming faction. Their
attempt met with failure due to lack of support. Instead, Qu, Deng, and Yu
were condemned by the ECCI for their failure to support Comintern policy
and for their unjustified criticism of the CCP leadership.[116] In April 1930,
they were also dismissed from their duties as CCP delegates to the Comintern.[117] But neither the ECCI nor the CCP Central Committee imposed
any severe disciplinary measures on Deng Zhongxia. When he left Moscow
for China in July 1930, Deng retained his good reputation within the Party;
he was appointed as the Central Committee's delegate to the West Hunan-
Hubei soviet area as well as the political commissar of the Second Division
of the Red Army, which was under He Long's command.[118] But the factional
struggle at the Zhongshan Academy marked the end of the close working
relationship between Deng Zhongxia and Qu Qiubai.

A Li Lisan Supporter?

While in Moscow, Deng Zhongxia frequently expressed optimism about
the revival of a revolutionary upsurge in China. In early 1929, he predicted
that the next revolutionary upsurge would occur in China within less than
ten years.[119] But a year and a half later, he doubted whether conditions in

115. Ibid., pp. 235–36.
116. A Chinese text of the ECCI resolution on this matter can be found in Tso-liang
Hsiao, *Power Relations within the Chinese Communist Movement, 1930–34* (Seattle: University
of Washington Press, 1967), vol. 2., pp. 336–37.
117. Xiang Qing, *Gongchan guoji he zhongguo geming quanxi de lishi gaishu*, p. 111.
118. *Zhongguo gongren yundong de xianqu*, vol. 2, pp. 121–22.
119. Deng Zhongxia, "The Chinese Trade Unions after the Past Revolutionary Wave," p. 22.

China were ripe for such a renaissance. The reason for his change in attitude was simply his lack of confidence in the ability of the working class to seize political power while under weak Party leadership.[120] His cautious attitude conflicted with that of Li Lisan, who had replaced Xiang Zhongfa as the general secretary of the CCP Politburo after the Zhongshan Academy affair.

When Li Lisan returned to China in late 1929, he bore a confused mandate from the Comintern. The ECCI instructed him to implement the agrarian revolution in order to develop the soviet areas in the country-side. But such a strategy had to be led by the proletariat in the city, a class which was then politically very weak. The ECCI also reminded him that the next revolutionary high tide in China would not be long delayed and instructed him to prepare for a new insurrection. Yet none of the ECCI instructions clearly indicated the exact timing of the next revolutionary upsurge. In June 1930, Li Lisan believed that conditions were ripe for staging a new armed struggle. He told his comrades in China that they should mobilize the revolutionary populace and achieve preliminary victory in one or more provinces. His thinking was influenced, on the one hand, by the Comintern's ambiguous instructions and, on the other hand, by his personal rivalry with Mao Zedong.[121]

As political commissar to the Second Division of the Red Army under He Long, Deng Zhongxia had to observe and implement the policy which had been decided by the Politburo. However, he was not in complete agreement with Li's policy as formulated in the CCP Politburo's meeting on 11 June 1930. In brief, the mid-June Politburo resolution instructed the Chinese Communists to organize a new revolutionary upsurge because the conditions were ripe due to the tension between the Nanjing regime and the Soviet Union and the imminent collapse of the capitalist system in the West. It also claimed that the forthcoming revolution in China would inspire anti-imperialist Communist movements throughout the world. Thus, Chinese Communists should take the lead in this movement by mobilizing workers in a political strike. Their most important task in the struggle was to capture cities and achieve victory in one or more provinces.[122]

120. Deng Zhongxia, "Pojin zhijie geming xingdong zhi zuzhi wenti" [The Question of Organization during the Direct Approach of Revolutionary Operation], *Hongqi ribao*, 26 Aug. 1930.

121. For a critical summary of the origins and development of the Li Lisan line, see Stuart Schram, "Introduction: The Cultural Revolution in Historical Perspective," in Stuart Schram, ed., *Authority, Participation, and Cultural Change in China* (Cambridge: Cambridge University Press, 1972), pp. 9–14.

122. "Xin de geming gaochao yu yisheng huo jisheng shouxian shengli" (11 June 1930)

Although Deng Zhongxia also encouraged his comrades to intensify preparations for a new political struggle, he was less optimistic than Li Lisan about the timing of a new revolutionary upsurge. About two months after the mid-June Politburo resolution was adopted, he made the following analysis:

We deeply believe that the revolutionary high tide will come even though the [Party] organization is weak. Yet the solidarity of the Communist Party, the strengthening of the red labor unions and all the other revolutionary organizations, and the powerful link between the Party and the mass organizations are essential conditions and primary factors for speeding up the onset of revolutionary high tide. [They are] the essential conditions for ensuring our Party leadership when the revolutionary high tide arrives; and they are also the indispensable conditions for our revolutionary victory.[123]

Implied here was a lack of confidence in the ability to launch a major revolutionary struggle at a moment when the Party organization was too weak either to lead the workers or to obtain their participation. He also said:

Under the bloody suppression of imperialism and the White Terror of the Guomindang, we know that it is *very difficult* to organize the majority of the masses. Even so, we will not neglect to organize [them] and we will give more effort to strengthening our organization. To be frank, the insurgent workers, if they lack a powerful organization, will not be able to seize all political power even if they overthrow the regime.[124]

Contrary to Li Lisan, Deng did not, in mid-1930, claim that the forthcoming revolution in China would influence the growth of the international Communist movement; his primary concern at that time was apparently the organizational weakness of the Party. He also did not express any hope that the Chinese Communists would be able to capture either one or more provinces when the Party was so weak. In view of his differences with Li Lisan, Deng Zhongxia was neither a Li supporter nor a member of Li's faction.[125]

[The New Revolutionary High Tide and the Preliminary Victory in One or Several Provinces], in *Zhonggong zhongyang wenjian xuanji*, vol. 6, pp. 115–35.

123. Deng Zhongxia, "Pojin zhijie geming xingdong zhi zuzhi wenti."

124. Ibid. (my emphasis).

125. Many historians in the West regard Deng as a supporter of the Li Lisan line. See, e.g., Jerome Ch'en, "The Communist Movement, 1927–37," in John K. Fairbank and Albert Feuerwerker, eds., *The Cambridge History of China* (Cambridge: Cambridge University Press,

Nevertheless, he complied, rather reluctantly, with the order from the Politburo to attack Wuhan in early October. This military campaign met with failure when the Second Division of the Red Army reached the outskirts of a small town called Shashi. Deng therefore reported to the Politburo that it would be a strategic error if the Second Division went on to Wuhan. Instead, he proposed that for the time being the Second Division should retreat southward and develop the soviet areas which had previously been brought under the Red Army's control. He also suggested that it was urgent to solve the problems in these soviet areas, one of which was the rise of a counterrevolutionary movement due to the mishandling of the rich and middle peasantry. Another problem was directly related to the poor Party discipline within the Red Army as a result of localism and traditionalism.[126]

To a certain extent, in 1930 Deng Zhongxia agreed with the policy of suppressing the rich peasantry; but he felt that the local Party cadres had mishandled this policy. From the outset, he disagreed with the extremely harsh measures, including extortion and kidnapping, the Party employed against this rural class. And although he thought that local Party cadres should mobilize the rural laborers and poor peasants against the rich peasants, he thought that local Party cadres did not have a clear understanding of class analysis in the countryside prior to launching the land revolution in the soviet areas. Many Party cadres could not distinguish between rich and middle peasantry. Thus, the middle peasantry were victimized because they were identified by the local Party cadres as counterrevolutionary elements. This misunderstanding, Deng claimed, created severe difficulty for the Party in attempting to rally support from the middle peasantry. Some of them, in fact, had shifted their support to the feudal counterrevolutionary forces because of the Party's mistakes.[127]

In regard to the disciplinary problem within the Second Division of the Red Army, Deng also reported to the Politburo that he had recently

1986), vol. 13, p. 173. Even some mainland Chinese historians also mistakenly identify Deng as a member of the Li Lisan faction. See Jiang Ping, *Deng Zhongxia de yisheng*, p. 215.

126. Deng Zhongxia, "Yaoqiu gaibian er juntuan xiang Wuhan jingong deng wenti gei zhangjiangju bing zhuan zhongyang de baogao, 15 Oct. 1930" [Report to the Central Committee via the Zhangjiang Bureau Regarding the Request for Modifying the Attack of Wuhan by the Second Division], in *Deng Zhongxia wenji*, pp. 640–45; Deng Zhongxia, "Guangyu zhengdun hong erliu jun deng wenti gei zhangjiangju bing zhuan zhongyang de baogao" [Report to the Central Committee via the Zhangjiang Bureau Regarding the Rectification of the Second and Sixth Divisions of the Red Army], in *Deng Zhongxia wenji*, pp. 645, 648–49.

127. Deng Zhongxia, "Yaoqiu gaibian er juntuan xiang Wuhan jingong deng wenti," pp. 641–43.

introduced measures to overcome it. His solution was the introduction of a compulsory military training program, which also emphasized the need for political education within all units. He also insisted that it was an urgent matter to simplify the administrative work within the army. However, he humbly claimed that it was still too early to assess the effectiveness of all these recently imposed measures.[128]

While serving as political commissar to the Second Division of the Red Army, Deng Zhongxia had successfully handled a complicated issue relating to a secret society. In Xiantao, a village near the soviet area under the Second Division's control, there was a powerful local secret society called Beijihui (the North Pole Society), which oppressed the local populace by extortion, murder, and burning of property. After the Red Army had approached Xiantao, Deng instructed his comrades to launch a major propaganda campaign to persuade people that the Beijihui was an enemy of the local people and an ally of the local landlord gentry. At the same time, he also imposed strict Party discipline on the Red Army to improve its image as a friend, instead of an enemy, of the local people. This policy was successful in winning the trust of the people in Xiantao, who forced the secret society to leave the area with the warning that the local people would appeal to the Red Army for support if it returned to the village.[129]

Deng's success in leading the Second Division was short-lived because of the rapid collapse of the Li Lisan line and the rise of the Wang Ming faction within the CCP Politburo. In January 1931, Deng advised the Second Division that it should retreat to the border region between the Hunan and Hubei areas. His strategy was to reorganize the Red Army and to consolidate the soviet areas in the mountainous region, where the Communists were facing a major counterattack by the Nationalist army.[130] But his strategy was rapidly condemned by the Wang Ming faction as a policy of escapism. In fact, as soon as Wang Ming had replaced Li Lisan as the general secretary of the Politburo in January 1931, Deng immediately became a victim to the factional struggle and was accused of opposing the Comintern. On 20 February 1931, the CCP Politburo adopted a resolution criticizing Qu Qiubai, Deng Zhongxia, and Yu Fei for disobeying the leadership while they were serving as the CCP's delegates to the Comintern in 1929. During the anti–Li Lisan campaign organized by the Wang Ming faction in March 1931, Deng was labeled a supporter of Li Lisan. He was also charged

128. Deng Zhongxia, "Guangyu zhengdun hong erliu jun deng wenti," pp. 648–49.
129. Ibid., pp. 647–48.
130. Jiang Ping, *Deng Zhongxia de yisheng*, p. 228.

with retreat, escape, pessimism, and failure to implement fully the struggle against the rich peasants.[131] Deng faced severe disciplinary punishment. By the end of the year, the CCP Politburo had deprived him of all his official Party titles, leaving only his Party membership. He was assigned to work in Shanghai as an ordinary Party member.[132]

In retrospect, although Deng's political activities after the end of the Sheng-gang General Strike had become less salient, he remained influential within the CCP leadership. Due to the need to reassess the Chinese revolution after the collapse of the United Front, Deng was forced to pay more attention to revolutionary theory and strategy. One of his striking contributions in this period was his class analysis; he predicted that a successful revolutionary strategy would be dependent on the establishment of a democratic dictatorship under the united front of workers, peasants, and petty bourgeois. He also realized the uniqueness of the Chinese revolution, which would have its own national form. In early 1927, Deng had already mentioned in passing that China could not follow uncritically the revolutionary experience of other countries. The vital problem of applying abstract Marxist-Leninist revolutionary theory to Chinese society was not fully recognized by other leading Communists until the early Yanan period. Deng was one of the few early Communists in 1927 who foresaw the problem, which was closely related to the development of Mao's theory of Sinification of Marxism. Not only did he make considerable theoretical contributions to Chinese Communism, but Deng was also one of the few Communists in the mid-1920s to speak about the fundamental Party problem resulting from factional struggle. Regretfully, he later became a victim of power struggle within the CCP leadership.

From the CCP Fifth Congress to its Six Congress, Deng Zhongxia executed a policy which could be easily identified with the Qu Qiubai line. There is sufficient evidence to claim, as the Comintern suggested, that Deng was a leading member of the Qu Qiubai faction. However, after the Sixth Congress, his class analysis and proposed labor movement strategy were closely in line with those adopted by the Comintern, and it was not accurate to classify him as anti-Comintern. ECCI criticism of Deng Zhongxia in April 1930 was therefore the product of personal conflict rather than difference of policy.

131. Hsiao, *Power Relations within the Chinese Communist Movement*, pp. 336–37, 486–89.
132. Jiang Ping, *Deng Zhongxia de yisheng*, p. 243.

Although Wang Ming was responsible for stirring up factional struggle within the Zhongshan Academy, Deng Zhongxia and Qu Qiubai were to blame for the conflict over Xiang Zhongfa, in which jealousy and personal interest played a large part. However, the class conflict between the Communist leaders of intellectual and working-class origin, as argued earlier, directly intensified personal tension and factional rivalry within the Party leadership.

Therefore, contrary to the view normally held by Chinese Marxist historians, the discrediting of Deng in Moscow should not be completely attributed to the Wang Ming line, which was then fully supported by the Comintern. The labor policy proposed by Deng during his stay in Moscow was identical with that of the Comintern: he was in fact a defender of ECCI policy. It seems that Chinese Marxist historians tend to avoid mentioning Deng's close association with the Comintern labor strategy after the CCP Sixth Congress, which is considered nowadays in China a leftist policy.[133] In fact, in the first few months after his return to China, Deng was closer to the Comintern than to the CCP Politburo, which was headed by Li Lisan.

Deng was not a supporter of the Li Lisan line in 1930. He became a victim of this factional struggle because of his close association with Qu Qiubai and the former Soviet advisors to China, especially Borodin, who had, by 1931, been purged by the Stalinist leadership. Moreover, his reservations about implementing a policy against the rich peasants in late 1930 was considered by Wang Ming to be completely un-Stalinist. As part of Wang Ming's attack on all his opponents, Deng Zhongxia was eliminated from the Party leadership. Without a doubt, the purge of Deng and many other Chinese Communists by the Wang Ming faction in the early 1930s was truly a tragedy of the Chinese revolution; and its detrimental consequences to the Chinese Communist movement were beyond measure.

133. See, e.g., Gai Jun and Liu Jingfang, "Tudi geming zhanzheng shiqi de baiqu gongyun celue yu gongchan guoji."

Epilogue

A MONTH after the Japanese Guandong Army had invaded Manchuria, Deng Zhongxia arrived in Shanghai. He could hardly mobilize the urban populace to launch an anti-Japanese campaign: he had no authority; he was only a low-level Party member, working secretly as a printer in a Communist cell in the eastern part of Shanghai.[1] Above all, the Guomindang was by then in complete control. Although some members of the Chinese bourgeoisie in Shanghai had staged an anti-Japanese boycott, they were led by the Guomindang.[2] For nearly half a year, Deng lived miserably; the Party extended no support to him and did not assign him any important duties. It was not until the autumn of 1932, due to a serious personnel shortage, that he was assigned by the Party to reorganize a local Party group called the Chinese Revolutionary Mutual Aid Association (CRMAA; Zhongguo geming huji zonghui).[3]

1. Shuai Mengqi, "Sanshi niandaichu Jiangsu sheng huxi quwei huodong pianduan" [Extract from the Activities of the Western Part of the Jiangsu Region during the Early 1930s], *Dangshi ziliao congkan* 2 (1983), p. 5.

2. Marie-Claire Bergère, *The Golden Age of the Chinese Bourgeoisie, 1911–1937,* trans. Janet Lloyd (Cambridge: Cambridge University Press, 1989), pp. 277–79.

3. Chen Nongfei, "Zhongxia tongzhi de zuihou yinian" [The Last Year of Comrade Zhongxia], *Shouhuo* [Harvest] 2 (1959), p. 91.

The CRMAA developed from another organization of similar nature, the Chinese Relief Society, which had been established in October 1925. The CRMAA was suspected by the Shanghai Municipal Police of being under the guidance of the Comintern and affiliated to the CCP.[4] This suspicion later proved to be valid. In late 1929, as a result of the White Terror in China, the Comintern gave specific instructions to the Chinese Communists for the formation of a society to help those comrades who had been arrested by the Guomindang. Thus, the former Chinese Relief Society was reorganized and renamed the CRMAA.[5]

Initially, the main responsibility of the CRMAA was to provide relief to Communists in need; but in the early 1930s when the Politburo was led by Wang Ming, the CRMAA radicalized its program. In addition to offering relief to Communists, it also organized political movements such as mobilizing workers to engage in class struggle and provoking the urban populace to launch antigovernment demonstrations.[6] Under this policy, Deng Zhongxia had to take the risk of organizing the labor movement. But most of these activities proved to be harmful to the Party, as many Communists were arrested. Besides, workers were discouraged by the political suppression, and only a few participated in the loosely organized labor movement.[7]

In such an unfavorable situation, Deng came under surveillance by the Shanghai Municipal Police, who identified him as one of the leading Communists who had, in April 1933, attended a secret meeting with a Comintern agent.[8] A month later, he was arrested by the Shanghai Municipal Police and was handed over to the Nationalist government. Some Chinese liberals appealed to the Nationalist government for his release; Madames Sun Yatsen and Liao Zhongkai commissioned the best lawyer in Shanghai to defend him.[9] The local Communists circulated handbills to demand the

4. Shanghai Municipal Police Archives, I.O. 4233, box 107.

5. Ni Moyan, "Cong jinanhui dao geming hujihui" [From the Relief Society to the Revolutionary Mutual-Aid Association], *Dangshi ziliao congkan* 4 (1983), pp. 103–11.

6. Ibid., pp. 112–14. A Chinese pamphlet entitled *Hujihui shi shenme* (What Is the Mutual-Aid Association?), written by a Shanghai Communist in 1933, provided much information relating to the political radicalization of the association. The document can be found in Shanghai Municipal Police Archives, D 4216, box 33.

7. Xue Shengshi, "1931 dao 1933 nian Shanghai zonggonghui de jiankuang" [Brief Account of the Shanghai General Labor Union from 1931 to 1933], *Dangshi ziliao congkan* 1 (1981), p. 106.

8. Shanghai Municipal Police Archives, D 5466, box 43.

9. Chen Nongfei, "Zhongxia tongzhi de zuihou yinian," p. 93.

release of their labor movement leader.[10] But all these efforts proved useless. Following a brief period of interrogation, he was executed secretly on 21 September 1933. At the age of thirty-nine, Deng Zhongxia gave his life for an ideology and a movement that he firmly believed would eventually liberate his country and people. During his last few days in prison, he left the following message for his comrades:

A man does not have to be afraid if he dies young; he only worries if he dies in the wrong place and at the wrong time. The Chinese people take death very seriously; some treat it as significant as the Mountain Tai [*taishan*], [but] some see it as light as a feather.

Someone who lives just to attain status and grow rich is not really living; he can be regarded as a dead person even when he is still alive. The meaning of his life is lighter than a feather.

Someone who dies for the interests of the majority of the Chinese people and for the interests of the industrious laboring people—his death is life; its meaning is more significant than the Mountain Tai.

A man lives and dies only once. But his life should be meaningful and his death should be valuable.[11]

Today, Deng Zhongxia is honored in the People's Republic of China as the greatest labor movement leader and political propagandist of the mid-1920s. Although he was basically a man of action, as evidenced by his success in mobilizing urban workers, he was no stranger to revolutionary theory. In recent years, Deng is credited for his contribution to the analysis of Chinese society during the period of the First United Front.[12] His proposal to establish a united front strategy consisting of workers, peasants, and petty bourgeois in early 1927 is now even considered a forerunner of Mao Zedong's theory of people's democratic dictatorship.[13] His numer-

10. A Chinese handbill entitled "A Declaration to Oppose the Arrest of Our Labor Movement Leader, Deng Zhongxia, and the Killing of the Peasant-Worker Populace by the Guomindang" can be found in the Shanghai Municipal Police Archives, D 4380/5, box 34.
11. *Geming lieshi shuxin* [Letters of the Revolutionary Martyrs], 2d ed. (Beijing: Zhonggong qingnian chubanshe, 1990), p. 78.
12. Jiang Ping, "Deng Zhongxia zai da geming shiqi dui Zhongguo shehui ge jieji de fenxi."
13. Li Ji, "Deng Zhongxia yanjiu Zhongguo geming wenti de tedian he chuangjian" [The

ous writings, especially his monograph *Zhongguo zhigong yundong jianshi* (A Brief History of the Chinese Labor Movement), are invaluable firsthand materials for our understanding of Chinese labor history during the 1920s.

His contribution in leading the Shenggang General Strike was certainly the greatest achievement of his entire political life. The source of his success in the mobilization of workers, especially in the mid-1920s, lay not only in his organizational ability and propaganda skill but also in his commitment to narrowing the gap between workers and Marxist intellectuals. Most important, after his first visit to Changxidian, he always believed that it was important to launch programs to politicize the working class. In terms of labor organizations, he considered that class unity could be achieved by the development of a modern form of labor union based on the Leninist concept of democratic centralism. In fact, the organizational structure Deng devised for the Strikers' Delegates Congress during the Shenggang General Strike is the earliest model of democratic centralism in the history of the Chinese Communist movement. Thus, he was a revolutionary in the Leninist tradition because he fulfilled the mission of Marxist intellectuals as the vanguards of the working class in his capacity as their ideological theoretician and organizational leader.

But his ideal of developing the political consciousness of the working class by ideological indoctrination under the guidance of Marxist intellectuals could not be fulfilled during his lifetime. For instance, one of the limitations of the Shenggang General Strike was the CCP's failure to maintain class unity among workers and strikers. In fact, due to the influence of the guild tradition and localism, strikers and workers in south China engaged in a protracted period of armed conflict among themselves. To be sure, this "class struggle within a class" was exacerbated by party politics during the uncertain period of rivalry between the CCP and the Guomindang. Nevertheless, the problem became so harmful to the Communist movement that Deng eventually had to admit, with deep frustration, that some workers were truly politically immature.[14] In December 1927, his disappointment was confirmed in the abortive Guangzhou Uprising when the majority of the working class in south China ignored the CCP's appeal for an urban insurrection.

The reasons for the CCP's failure to gain support from the urban work-

---

Uniqueness and Originality of Deng Zhongxia's Research on the Chinese Revolution], *Dangshi janjiu* 2 (1986), p. 20.

14. Deng Zhongxia, *1926 nian zhi Guangzhou gongchao*, p. 66.

ing class in the aftermath of the Shenggang General Strike were manifold. Some argue that the failure was related to suppressive Guomindang policy; others claim it was caused by the CCP's confusing strategies. The fundamental reason, as many would agree, was the Chinese working class's lack of commitment to a socialist revolution. If this general explanation is accepted, then we have to address ourselves to another important and related question. Why was the development of class consciousness among urban workers so limited despite the massive political indoctrination organized by Deng Zhongxia and his comrades during the Shenggang General Strike? The answer perhaps lies, *inter alia,* in the fundamental dilemma between Marxist intellectuals and workers.

As argued previously in an earlier chapter, the Chinese Marxist intellectuals were unable to channel a vision of socialist revolution to the workers and strikers for various reasons during the period of the First United Front. The ideological indoctrination of the working class during the Shenggang General Strike focused on anti-imperialism. While the labor leaders of Marxist intellectual origin saw the strike as the prelude to socialist revolution, the strikers regarded it mainly as an anti-imperialist movement. Thus, during the heyday of the labor movement in south China, Marxist intellectuals and workers each had different visions of revolution. As the CCP became more hierarchical, new contradictions between Marxist intellectuals and workers appeared due to the problem of identity.

Once the Marxist intellectuals became CCP leaders, they identified themselves with the Party instead of with the working class. Although the Party claimed it was the vanguard of the proletariat, it was fundamentally ruled by a small elite, many of whom were formerly Marxist intellectuals. Thus social stratification existed even within a revolutionary organization. Like the intellectuals in traditional China, whose main object was to serve the state as officials, Marxist intellectuals since the May Fourth period were Party bureaucrats and proclaimed loyalty solely to the Party. They even regarded the status of their Party as superior to the state and society. Therefore, as demonstrated earlier, Deng Zhongxia and the other CCP leaders were ready, especially for strategic reasons, to abandon the interests of the working class in the defense of their Party whenever they deemed it necessary. Perhaps this perspective best encapsulates the tragedy of the Chinese Communist revolution, especially before the Yanan period.

In spite of this dilemma between intellectuals and workers, the Shenggang General Strike has become a legend in modern Chinese history, representing the triumph of antiforeign sentiment over imperialism. Especially during its early phase, the strike has also shown that Marxist intellectuals and workers can unite and establish a new form of revolutionary leadership. Notwithstanding the CCP's limitations, especially in its failure to transform the Shenggang General Strike from a local anti-imperialist event into a nationwide revolutionary movement, this prolonged labor movement produced a group of local Party leaders of working-class origin. It is certain that many locally recruited Communists were killed by the Guomindang on 15 April 1927 or sacrificed in the Guangzhou Uprising in December of the same year. But of those who survived through the years of revolution, some became major Party leaders after liberation. To name only a few, Lin Jiangyun, who was the son of a Hong Kong worker and was a seaman by profession and a propagandist for the general strike, became the vice provincial governor of Guangdong during the 1950s. Another seaman, Feng Xin, who joined the CCP during the strike, was appointed the Guangdong provincial chairman of the ACLF after liberation. Chen Yun, another striker, remained influential among CCP policy decision makers up to the early 1990s.

But Deng Zhongxia was not to see the achievements of these strikers. Instead, by the time of his execution in 1933, the CCP was in crisis. The Party leadership suffered not only from the power struggle between the Maoist faction and the pro-Comintern faction headed by Wang Ming but also from lack of direct contact with urban workers because the Party could operate mainly in the countryside. Although a small number of Communists had shifted their activities to work underground in the cities, their influence, especially among the working class, was limited. For most of the Nanjing decade (1928–37), the urban working class was left alone and felt helpless. Even worse, their class interest was soon overshadowed by national interest as China entered a war with Japan in late 1937. The intellectuals, whether Marxist or liberal, were reluctant to raise the issue of class interest in their political discourses and social analyses at a time when China was confronting a full-scale Japanese military invasion.

Not until the years of the civil war (1945–49) did class interest become once again a major political issue. And it was also during these years that the Communists had to intensify their efforts at urban mobilization. Under such circumstances, the problem of unifying workers and intellectuals under the CCP banner reappeared as a principal concern among the Communist leaders. But could the CCP rebuild a strong leadership composed of workers and intellectuals, as happened during the Shenggang General Strike, in the major cities on the eve of the liberation? Most important, could the class interest of the workers be maintained in the face of a power-ful hierarchic Party bureaucratic system during the civil war? The search for answers to these questions, which will require another book-length study, is important because they may furnish us with new perceptions of the dilemma of the Communist leadership both before and after 1949.

Glossary

Aiguo renshi 愛國人仕

Baoding 保定
Beida 北大
Beihai 北海
Beijihui 北極會
Beijing daxue pingmin jiaoyu
　　jiangyantuan
　　北京大學平民教育講演團
Beijing daxue rikan 北京大學日刊
Beijing daxue xuesheng zhoukan
　　北京大學學生周刊
Buerseweike 布爾塞維克

Cai Hesen 蔡和森
Cai Yuanpei 蔡元培

Cao Rulin 曹汝霖
Changsha 長沙
Changxindian 長辛店
Chaozhou 潮州
Chen Bingsheng 陳炳生
Chen Duxiu 陳獨秀
Chen Gongbo 陳公博
Chen Jiongming 陳烱明
Chen Lianbai 陳廉伯
Chen Qitian 陳啟天
Chen Qiyuan 陳啟源
Chen Richang 陳日長
Chen Yannian 陳延年
Chen Yun 陳雲
Chen Zhiwen 陳志文
Chuannan 川南

Dai Jitao 戴季陶

Danshui 淡水

Deng Benyin 鄧本殷

Deng Dapao 鄧大炮

Deng Dianmo 鄧典謨

Deng Fa 鄧發

Deng Kang 鄧康

Deng Longbo 鄧隆渤

Deng Pei 鄧培

Deng Zhongxia 鄧中夏

Deng Zhongxie 鄧仲澥

Donghua 東華

Dongjiang 東江

Dongyuan 東園

Du Yingkun 杜應坤

Duan Qirui 段祺瑞

Feng Jupo 馮菊坡

Fu Bingchang 傅秉常

Fuzhou 福州

Gongchandang 共產黨

Gongren hezuoshe 工人合作社

Gongren julebu 工人俱樂部

Gongren yundong yanjiu xuexiao
工人運動研究學校

Gongren zhi lu 工人之路

Gongshang ribao 工商日報

Gongsheng tang 公勝堂

Gongtuan zonghui 工團總會

Gongzei 工賊

Guangdong gongren zhi lu
廣東工人之路

Guangdong jiqi gonghui
廣東機器工會

Guangdong zong gonghui
廣東總工會

Guangzhou gongren daibiao dahui
廣州工人代表大會

Guangzhou zong shanghui
廣州總商會

Guangzhoushi gongren yundong
weiyuanhui
廣州市工人運動委員會

Guomindang 國民黨

Guomin zazhi 國民雜誌

Guomin zazhishe 國民雜誌社

Haifeng 海丰

Hailufeng 海陸丰

Han Wenhui 韓文惠

He Long 賀龍

Henan-Anhui 河南安徽

Hu Hanmin 胡漢民

Hu Shi 胡適

Huagong zonghui 華工總會

Huang Huanting 黃煥庭

Huang Jinyuan 黃金源

Huang Ping 黃平

Huanghua gang 黃花岡

Hunan 湖南

Jiang Jieshi 蔣介石

Jiangzhe 江浙

Jiaotung xi 交通系

Jinghan 京漢

Jiujiang 九江

Junzhu guan 君主館

Juren 舉人

Kailuan 開灤

Kang Youwei 康有為

Kejia 客家

Laodong yin 勞動音

Li Dazhao 李大釗

Li Hongzhang 李鴻章

Li Jishen 李濟深

Li Langru 李朗如

Li Lisan 李立三

Li Sen 李森

Li Weihan 李維漢

Liang Bingxuan 梁冰弦

Liang Furan 梁复然

Liang Qichao 梁啟超

Liang Shuming 梁漱溟

Liao Zhongkai 廖仲愷

Lin Changzhi 林昌熾

Lin Weimin 林偉民

Lingdao 領導

Lingxiu 領袖

Liu Ersong 劉爾崧

Liu Shaoqi 劉少奇

Liu Shifu 劉師復

Luo Dengxian 羅登賢

Luo Yinong 羅亦農

Luo Zhanglong 羅章龍

Luohu 羅湖

Lushan 盧山

Ma Chaojun 馬超俊

Makesi xueshuo yanjiuhui
　　馬克思學說研究會

Mao Zedong 毛澤東

Mintuan 民團

Nanchang 南昌

Nanhai 南海

Nanjing 南京

Peng Pai 彭湃

Peng Shuzhi 彭述之

Qiaogang 僑港

Qingnian gongren yuekan
　　青年工人月刊

Qu Qiubai 瞿秋白

Quangang gongtuan lianhehui
　　全港工團聯合會

Quanguo zong gonghui 全國總工會

Rexue ribao 熱血日報

Shaji 沙基

Shamian 沙面

Shanghai 上海

Shantou 汕頭

Shashi 沙市

Shehui zhuji qingnian tuan
　　社會主義青年團

Shenggang 省港

Shi Bu 施卜

Shu Xincheng 舒新城

Shunde 順德

Sichuan 四川

Song Ziwen 宋子文

Su Zhaozheng 蘇兆征

Sun Ke 孫科

Sun Yatsen 孫逸仙

Tan Pingshan 譚平山

Tan Zhitang 譚植棠

Tianjin 天津

Tongyi gongye yundong
　　統一工業運動

Wang Jingwei 汪精衛

Wang Ming 王明

Wang minjian qu 往民間去

Wang Ruofei 王若飛

Wang Tao 王韜

Wei Bangping 魏邦平

Wenshe 文社

Wu Chaoshu 伍朝樞

Wu Peifu 吳佩孚

Wu Tiecheng 吳鐵城

Xiang Ying 項英

Xiang Zhongfa 向忠發

Xiangdao zhoubao 向導週報

Xianggang huaren jiqi hui
　　香港華人機器會

Xianggang jigong lianhe hui
　　香港機工聯合會

Xianggang jinshuye zong gonghui
　　香港金屬業總工會

Xianggang yangwu zong gonghui
　　香港洋務總工會

Xianggang yunshu gonghui lianhehui
　　香港運輸工會聯合會

Xianggang zong gonghui
　　香港總工會

Xianqu 先驅

Xiantao 仙桃

Xiao Chunu 蕭楚女

Xiao shangren 小商人

Xiaoshadu 小沙渡

Xie Yingbai 謝英伯

Xin qingnian 新青年

Xingzhong hui 興中會

Xiong Guangchu 熊光楚

Xiongdi guan 兄弟館

Xiyuan 曦園

Xu Chongzhi 許崇智

Xuesheng aiguohui 學生愛國會

Xuesheng jiuguohui 學生救國會

Yanan 延安

Yang Baoan 楊匏安

Yang Changji 楊昌濟

Yang Sen 楊森

Yang Yin 楊殷

Yangjiang 陽江

Yangwu gonghui 洋務工會

Ye Ting 葉挺

Yizhang 宜章

Yu Fei 余飛

Yu Jiaju 余家菊

Yu Youren 于右任

Yuan Shikai 袁世凱

Yun Daiying 惲代英

Zeng Ziyan 曾子嚴

Zhang Fakui 張發奎

Zhang Guotao 張國燾

Zhang Tailei 張太雷

Zhang Zuolin 張作霖

Zhexue yanjiuhui 哲學研究會

Zhigong yundong weiyuanhui
聯工運動委員會

Zhili 直隸

Zhongguo geming huiji zonghui
中國革命互濟總會

Zhongguo gongren 中國工人

Zhongguo laodong zuhe shujibu
中國勞動組合書記部

Zhongguo qingnian 中國青年

Zhongguo yanji shushu
中國研機書塾

Zhonghua gemingdang 中華革命黨

Zhongjian jieji 中間階級

Zhongshan 中山

Zhou Enlai 周恩來

Zhu Ziqing 朱自清

Zhuyi 主義

Zongzhihui 總指揮

Zongsiling 總司令

Zou Lu 鄒魯

Bibliography

Archival Records

Colonial Office. Public Record Office, London, England. Despatches from the Governor of Hong Kong. File C.O.129.

———. Minutes of the Hong Kong Executive Council. File C.O.131.

———. Despatches from the Governor of Hong Kong. File C.O.537. Documents in this file were regarded by the British officials as more sensitive than those in C.O.129.

———. Confidential Prints. File C.O.882/11. This file contains a unique collection of the Hong Kong governor's dispatches to the Colonial Office in 1925–27 about the strike and boycott movement in Hong Kong and Guangzhou.

Foreign Office. Public Record Office, London, England. Consular Archives. File F.O.228.

———. General Correspondence, China. File F.O.371.

———. Confidential Prints. File F.O.405.

Guomindang Party History Archives. Taibei, Taiwan.

Huston, Jay. Collection. Hoover Institution on War, Revolution, and Peace. Stanford University.

John Swire and Sons Ltd. Papers. School of Oriental and African Studies. University of London.

Shanghai Municipal Police Archives. National Archives, Washington, D.C.

Contemporary Journals and Newspapers

Gongchandang [The Communist Party]
Gongren zhi lu [The Road of Workers]
Guangzhou minguo ribao [Guangzhou National Daily]
Hong Kong Daily Press
Hongqi ribao [Red Flag Daily]
International Press Correspondence
The Pan-Pacific Monthly
Qingfeng [The Vanguard].
Renmin zhoukan [People's Weekly]
South China Morning Post
Times (London)
Xianqu [The Pioneers]
Xiaodao zhoubao [The Guide Weekly]
Xin qingnian [New Youth]
Zhengzhi zhoubao [Political Weekly]
Zhongguo gongren [Chinese Workers]
Zhongguo laogong tongmenhui yuekan [The Chinese Federation of Labor Monthly]
Zhongguo qingnian [Chinese Youth]

Other Works

Akatova, T. "Deng Zhongxia: A Leading Figure in the Chinese Labor Movement." *Far Eastern Affairs* 4 (1982).

Atwell, William S. "From Education to Politics: The Fu She." In William Theodore de Bary, ed., *The Unfolding of Neo-Confucianism*. New York: Columbia University Press, 1975.

Bastid-Bruguiere, Marianne. "Currents of Social Change." In Denis Twitchett and John K. Fairbank, eds., *Cambridge History of China*, vol. 11. Cambridge: Cambridge University Press, 1979.

Bergère, Marie-Claire. *The Golden Age of the Chinese Bourgeoisie, 1911–1937.* Trans. Janet Lloyd. Cambridge: Cambridge University Press, 1989.

Berkley, Gerald W. "The Canton Peasant Movement Institute." *Modern China* 11:2 (1975).

Boorman, Howard L., and Howard, Richard C., eds. *Biographical Dictionary of Republican China.* 5 vols. New York: Columbia University Press, 1967–71.

Borg, Dorothy. *American Policy and the Chinese Revolution, 1925–28.* Reprint. New York: Columbia University Press, 1968.

Brandt, Conrad. *Stalin's Failure in China*. Cambridge: Harvard University Press, 1958.

Cai Hesen. "Jihui zhuyi shi" [History of Opportunism]. In *Gongfei huoguo shiliao huibian* [Selected Documents on Communist Troubles in China], vol. 1. Taibei, 1961.

Cai Luo, and Lu Quan. *Shenggang da bagong* [The Guangzhou–Hong Kong General Strike]. Guangzhou: Guangdong renmin chubanshe, 1980.

Cai Luo, and Yuan Bangjian. "Guangyu diyici guonei geming zhanzheng shiqi zhonggong Guangdong quwei de jige wenti" [On Several Issues Relating to the CCP Guangdong Regional Committee during the First Revolutionary Civil War]. *Xueshu yanjiu* [Academic Studies] 4 (1981).

Canton Chamber of Commerce. *Industries in Canton*. Canton, 1933.

Canton: Its Port, Industries, and Trade. Canton, 1931.

Cavendish, Patrick. "The New China of the Kuomintang." In Jack Gray, ed., *Modern China's Search for a Political Form*. Oxford: Oxford University Press, 1969.

———. "Anti-imperialism in the Kuomintang, 1923–28." In Jerome Ch'en and Nicholas Tarling, eds., *Studies in the Social History of China and South East Asia*. Cambridge: Cambridge University Press, 1970.

Chan Lau Kit-ching. *China, Britain, and Hong Kong, 1895–1945*. Hong Kong: Chinese University Press, 1990.

Chan, Ming K. "Labor and Empire: The Chinese Labor Movement in Canton Delta, 1895–1927." Ph.D. diss., Stanford University, 1975.

———. *Historiography of the Chinese Labor Movement, 1895–1949: A Critical Survey and Bibliography*. Stanford: Hoover Institution Press, 1981.

Chan, Wai Kwan. *The Making of Hong Kong Society: Three Studies of Class Formation in Early Hong Kong*. Oxford: Clarendon Press, 1991.

Changxindian jiche cheliang gongchang changshi bianwenhui, ed. *Beifang de hongxing* [Red Star over the North]. Beijing: Zuojia chubanshe, 1960.

Chen Baqui. "Ji fandong de Guangdong jiqi gonghui shuishi" [On Several Reactionary Events of the Guangdong Mechanics' Union]. *Guangdong wenshi ziliao* [Historical Materials on Guangdong Culture and History] 12 (1964).

Chen Da. *Zhongguo laogong wenti* [Problems of Chinese Labor]. Shanghai: Shangwu yinshuguan, 1928.

Chen Duxiu. "Zhongguo nongmin wenti" [The Problem of Chinese Peasants]. *Qingfeng* 1:1 (July 1923).

———. "Zhongguo guomin geming yu shehui ge jieji" [The Chinese Nationalist Revolution and the Various Social Classes]. *Qingfeng* 1:2 (1 Dec. 1923).

———. "Zhongguo gongren yundong zhi zhuanji" [The Revival of the Chinese

Labor Movement]. *Xiangdao zhoubao* [The Guide Weekly] 58 (26 Mar. 1924).

———. "Zhongguo guomin geming yundong zhong gongren de liliang" [The Strength of the Workers in the Chinese Nationalist Revolution]. *Xiangdao zhoubao* 101 (7 Feb. 1925).

———. "Chen Duxiu guanyu shehuizhuyi wenti de jiangji" [Speech by Chen Duxiu Regarding the Problems of Socialism]. In *Liuda yiqian dang de lishi cailiao* [Historical Materials on the CCP before the Sixth Congress]. Beijing: Xinhua chubanshe, 1980.

———. "Chen Duxiu zai Zhongguo gongchandang diwuci quanguo daibiao dahui shang de baogao" [Chen Duxiu's Report at the CCP Fifth Congress]. In *Zhonggong dangshi ziliao* [Historical Materials on CCP History], vol. 3.

Chen Gongbo. *Kuxiao lu* [Matters of Wry Smile]. Hong Kong: Xianggang daxue chubanshe, 1979.

Ch'en, Jerome. "The Communist Movement, 1927–37." In John K. Fairbank and Albert Feuerwerker, eds., *The Cambridge History of China,* vol. 13. Cambridge: Cambridge University Press, 1986.

Chen Nongfei. "Zhongxia tongzhi de zuihou yinian" [The Last Year of Comrade Zhongxia]. *Shouhuo* [Harvest] 2 (1959).

Chen Tianjie and Chen Quitong. "Guangdong de yi jian zhengqi saosi chang Xu Chang Long ji qi chuangbanren Chen Qiyuan" [The First Steam-Engine Silk-Reeling Factory in Guangdong, Xu Chang Long, and Its founder, Chen Qiyuan]. *Guangzhou wenshi ziliao* [Historical Materials on Guangzhou Culture and History] 8 (1963).

Chen Yu. "Chen Yu zizhuan" [Autobiography of Chen Yu]. *Guangdong dangshi ziliao* [Materials on the Guangdong Party History] 1 (1983).

Chen Zhen, ed. *Zhongguo jindai gongye shi ziliao* [Historical Materials on Modern Chinese Industries]. 3 vols. Beijing: Sanlian shudian, 1961.

Chen Zhiling. *Xinbian diyici guonei geming zhanzheng shigao* [Draft History of the First Revolutionary Civil War, new ed.]. Xian: Shaanxi renmin chubanshe, 1981.

Chen Zhirang [Jerome Ch'en]. *Junshen zhengquan* [The Military-Gentry Coalition]. Hong Kong: Sanlian chubanshe, 1979.

Chen Zhiwen. "Zhongguo gongchandang zai Guangdong diqu jiandang chuqi de yixie shiliao" [Certain Historical Materials on the CCP Guangdong Regional Committee during Its Founding Period]. *Guangzhou wenshi ziliao* 17 (1979).

———. "Da geming shiqi de Guangzhou gongren yundong" [The Guangzhou Labor Movement during the Period of Great Revolution]. *Guangzhou wenshi ziliao* 21 (1980).

Cheng Fou. *Mosike Zhongshan daxue yu zhongguo geming* [Moscow Zhongshan Academy and the Chinese Revolution]. Beijing: Xiandai chubanshe, 1980.

Cherepanov, Alexander I. *As Military Advisor in China*. Moscow: Progress Publishers, 1982.

Chesneaux, Jean. *The Chinese Labor Movement, 1919–1927.* Translated by H. M. Wright. Stanford: Stanford University Press, 1968.

Chiang Yung-ching. "Borodin and the Re-organization of the Chinese National Party." In *Symposium on the History of Republican China*, vol. 3. Taibei, 1981.

Chow Tse-tsung. *The May Fourth Movement: Intellectual Revolution in Modern China*. Cambridge: Harvard University Press, 1960.

Clark, Peter. "Britain and the Chinese Revolution, 1925–27." Ph.D. diss., University of California, Berkeley, 1973.

Coates, P. D. *The China Consuls: British Consular Officers, 1843–1943*. Hong Kong: Oxford University Press, 1988.

Commercial and Industrial Hong Kong: A Record of 94 Years of Progress in the Colony, 1841–1935. Hong Kong: Bedikton Co., 1935.

Deng Zhongxia. "Jiehuo" [Enlightenment]. *Zhongguo qingnian* 3 (3 Nov. 1923).

———. "Shengli" [Victory]. *Zhongguo qingnian* 3 (3 Nov. 1923).

———. "Zhongguo xianzai de sixiangjie" [The Current Chinese Intellectuals]. *Zhongguo qingnian* 6 (24 Nov. 1923).

———. "Xinshiren de banghe" [A Criticism of the Modern Poets]. *Zhongguo qingnian* 7 (1 Dec. 1923).

———. "Geming zhuli de sange qunzhong" [The Three Social Classes as the Main Revolutionary Force]. *Zhongguo qingnian* 8 (8 Dec. 1923).

———. "Lun gongren yundong" [On the Labor Movement]. *Zhongguo qingnian* 9 (15 Dec. 1923).

———. "Gongxian yu xinshiren zhiqian" [A Contribution to the Modern Poets]. *Zhongguo qingnian* 10 (22 Dec. 1923).

———. "Zhongguo gongren zhuangkuang ji women yundong zhi fangzhen" [The Conditions of Chinese Workers and the Direction of Our Movement]. *Zhongguo qingnian* 10 (22 Dec. 1923).

———. "Lun nongmin yundong" [On the Peasant Movement]. *Zhongguo qingnian* 11 (29 Dec. 1923).

———. "Zhongguo nongmin zhuangkuang ji women yundong de fangzhen" [The Conditions of Chinese Peasants and the Direction of Our Movement]. *Zhongguo qingnian* 13 (5 Jan. 1924).

———. "Liening nianpu" [The Chronology of Lenin]. *Zhongguo qingnian* 16 (1924).

———. "Chise zhigong guoji zhi dongfang celue" [The Profintern's Labor Strategy in the East]. *Zhongguo gongren* 1 (Oct. 1924).

———. "Gongnongjun yu beifa" [Workers, Peasants, Soldiers, and the Northern Expedition]. *Zhongguo gongren* 1 (1924).

———. "Women de liliang" [Our Strength]. *Zhongguo gongren* 2 (Nov. 1924).

———. "Shanghai Riben shachang bagong suo delai de jingyan" [Experience from the Strike in the Shanghai Japanese Textile Factories]. *Zhongguo gongren* 4 (Apr. 1925).

———. "Laodong yundong fuxingqi zhong de jige zhuyao wenti" [Several Important Issues on the Labor Movement during Its Revival Period]. *Zhongguo gongren* 5 (May 1925).

———. "Xu Guomin zhengfu" [To Remind the Nationalist Government]. *Gongren zhi lu,* 2 July 1925.

———. "Zancheng kai guomin huiyi yubei huiyi" [In Favor of Convening the Preliminary Meeting of the People's Convention]. *Gongren zhi lu,* 16 July 1925.

———. "Shenggang bagong gongren de zuzhi" [Workers' Organization in the Guangzhou–Hong Kong Strike]. *Gongren zhi lu,* 16–17 July 1925.

———. "Zenyang shixing gongnong lianhe" [How to Implement Worker-Peasant Unity]. *Gongren zhi lu,* 28 July 1925.

———. "Wo Shenggang bagong gongyu ying zhuyi de yige wenti" [Several Issues of Which Our Shenggang Strikers Should Be Aware]. *Gongren zhi lu,* 24 Aug. 1925.

———. "Gonghui de zuoyong" [The Functions of Labor Unions]. *Gongren zhi lu,* 13–15 Dec. 1925.

———. "Wusa hou Zhongguo zhigong yundong de xin xianxiang" [The New Situation of the Chinese Labor Movement after 30 May]. *Renmin zhoukan* 1 (7 Feb. 1926).

———. "Xianggang shao you yi shu meng" [Another Fond Dream of the Hong Kong Young Master]. *Renmin zhoukan* 2 (1926).

———. "Ping Guangzhou gonghui zhi zheng" [On the Strife of Labor Unions in Guangzhou]. *Renmin zhoukan* 3 (24 Feb. 1926).

———. "Huanying yingguo diguozhuyi jingong Zhongguo de shiwan dabing" [Welcome the Attack of China by the 100,000 Soldiers of British Imperialism!]. *Renmin zhoukan* 4 (4 Mar. 1926).

———. "Zhongshan xiansheng shishi hou zhi Guomindang" [The Guomindang after the Death of Sun Yatsen]. *Renmin zhoukan* 5 (12 Mar. 1926).

———. "Zhongshan xiansheng zhi gongnong zhengce" [The Worker-Peasant Policy of Mr. Sun Yatsen]. *Renmin zhoukan* 5 (12 Mar. 1926).

———. "Yingguo diguo zhuyi zhi weiji" [The Crisis of British Imperialism]. *Renmin zhoukan* 6 (19 Mar. 1926).

———. "Gongren jieji de yishou gongke" [A Lesson of the Working Class]. *Gongren zhi lu,* 31 Mar. 1926.

———. "Deng Zhongxia tongzhi zhengzhi baogao" [Political Report by Comrade Deng Zhongxia]. *Gongren zhi lu,* 24 and 26 Apr. 1926.

———. "Jin nian wuji de mubiao" [The Objective of This Year's May Day]. *Renmin zhoukan* 10 (30 Apr. 1926).

———. "Gongnongshang lianhe zhanxian wenti" [Issues on the United Front of Workers, Peasants, and Merchants]. *Gongren zhi lu,* 12 June 1926.

———. "Jinlai po youxie huaiji jia" [There Are Certain Skeptics Recently]. *Renmin zhoukan* 19 (20 Aug. 1926).

———. *1926 nian zhi Guangzhou gongchao* [Labor Disputes in Guangzhou in 1926]. Guangzhou, 1926.

———. *Shenggang bagong gaiguan* [A General Account of the Guangzhou–Hong Kong General Strike]. Guangzhou, 1926.

———. *Shenggang bagong zhong zhi zhongying tanpan* [Sino-British Negotiations in the Period of the Guangzhou–Hong Kong General Strike]. Guangzhou, 1926.

———. "Guangzhou gongchao yu jingji fazhan yihuo shuaitui" [Did the Labor Movement in Guangzhou Promote or Hurt Economic Growth?]. *Renmin zhoukan* 39 (21 Jan. 1927).

———. "Guangdong jingji bu fazhan de yuanyin" [The Reasons for the Nondevelopment of Guangdong's Economy]. *Renmin zhoukan* 40 (30 Jan. 1927).

———. "Erqi yu guomin geming" [7 February and the Nationalist Revolution]. *Renmin zhoukan* 41 (7 Feb. 1927).

———. "Huanying guoji gongren daibiao tuan" [Welcome the International Labor Delegation]. *Renmin zhoukan* 43 (23 Feb. 1927).

———. "The Chinese Trade Unions after the Past Revolutionary Wave." *Pan-Pacific Monthly,* Apr. 1929.

———. "Pojin zhijie geming xingdong zhi zuzhi wenti" [The Question of Organization during the Direct Approach of Revolutionary Operation]. *Hongqi ribao,* 26 Aug. 1930.

———. *Zhongguo zhigong yundong jianshi* [A Brief History of the Chinese Labor Movement]. Beijing: Renmin chubanshe, 1951.

———. *Deng Zhongxia wenji* [Collected Works of Deng Zhongxia]. Beijing: Renmin chubanshe, 1983.

Dirlik, Arif. *Revolution and History: Origins of Marxist Historiography in China, 1919–1937.* Berkeley and Los Angeles: University of California Press, 1978.

————. *The Origins of Chinese Communism.* New York: Oxford University Press, 1989.

Diyici guonei geming zhanzheng shiqi de gongren yundong [The Labor Movement during the First Revolutionary Civil War]. Beijing: Renmin chubanshe, 1954.

Diyici Zhongguo laodong nianjian [The First Annual Report of the Chinese Workers]. Beijing, 1928.

The Dominions Office and Colonial Office List: 1939. London, 1939.

Duan, Zhimin. "Shi lun da geming shiqi Bao luoting dui Jiang Jieshi celue de xiangxiang fazhang" [On Borodin's Dual Strategy toward Jiang Jieshi during the Period of Great Revolution]. *Guangdong shehui kexue* [Guangdong Social Sciences] 3 (1989).

d'Encausse, Hélèn Carrère, and Schram, Stuart R., eds. *Marxism and Asia: An Introduction with Readings.* London: Allen Lane, Penguin Press, 1969.

Endacott, G. B. *A History of Hong Kong.* Oxford: Oxford University Press, 1958.

Eudin, Xenia J., and North, Robert C., eds. *Soviet Russia and the East, 1920–1927: A Documentary Survey.* Stanford: Stanford University Press, 1957.

Fairbank, John K. "The Creation of the Treaty System." In John K. Fairbank, ed., *Cambridge History of China,* vol. 10. Cambridge: Cambridge University Press, 1979.

Fang, Fu-an. *Chinese Labour: An Economic and Statistical Survey of the Labour Conditions and Labour Movement in China.* Shanghai: Kelly & Welsh Ltd., 1931.

Feigon, Lee. *Chen Duxiu: Founder of the Chinese Communist Party.* Princeton: Princeton University Press, 1983.

Feng He, ed. *Zhongguo nongcun jingji ziliao xupian* [Selected Materials on the Chinese Rural Economy]. Shanghai: Liming shuju, 1935.

Feng Zirong. "Deng Zhongxia de chusheng riqi ji qi mingzi" [The Names and Date of Birth of Deng Zhongxia]. *Dangshi yanjiu ziliao* [Sources of Party History] 6.

Fok, K. C. *Lectures on Hong Kong History: Hong Kong's Role in Modern Chinese History.* Hong Kong: Commercial Press, 1990.

Fung, Edmund S. K. *The Diplomacy of Imperial Retreat: Britain's South China Policy, 1924–1931.* Hong Kong: Oxford University Press, 1991.

Gai Jun and Liu Jingfang. "Tudi geming zhanzheng shiqi de baiqu gongyun celue yu gongchan guoji" [The Comintern and the Labor Movement Strategy in the White Areas during the Land Revolutionary War Period]. *Dangshi yanjiu* [Research on Party History] 2 (1987).

Galbiati, Fernando. *Peng Pai and the Hailufeng Soviet.* Stanford: Stanford University Press, 1985.

Geming lieshi shuxin [Letters of Revolutionary Martyrs]. 2d ed. Beijing: Zhonggong qingnian chubanshe, 1990.

Goals, Peter J. "Early Ching Guilds." In G. William Skinner, ed., *The City in Late Imperial China*. Stanford: Stanford University Press, 1977.

Gong Jun. *Zhongguo xin gongye shi* [History of China's New Industries]. Shanghai, 1933.

———. *Zhongguo dushi gongyehua cheng du zhi tongji fenxi* [Statistical Analysis of the Extent of Chinese Urban Industrialization]. Shanghai: Yinshuguan, 1934.

Guangdong geming lishi bowuguan, ed. *Huangpu junxiao shiliao, 1924–27* [Historical Materials on the Huangpu Military Academy]. Guangzhou: Guangdong renmin chubanshe, 1982.

Guangdong jingji yanjiusuo, ed. *Guangdong jingji gaiguan* [An Overview of Economic Conditions in Guangdong]. Guangzhou, 1935.

Guangdong renmin chubanshe, ed. *Nutao: Shenggang da bagong huiyi lu* [Furious Billows: Memoirs of the Guangzhou–Hong Kong General Strike]. Guangzhou: Guangdong renmin chubanshe, 1960.

Guangdong zhexue shehui kexueyuan, ed. *Shenggang da bagong ziliao* [Historical Materials on the Guangzhou–Hong Kong General Strike]. Guangzhou: Guangdong renmin chubanshe, 1980.

Guangdongsheng danganguan and Zhonggong Guangdong shengwei yanjiu weiyuanhui bangongshi, eds. *Guangdongqu dang tuan yanjiu shiliao, 1921–1926* [Historical Materials on the CCP Guangdong Regional and Corps Committees, 1921–1926]. Guangzhou: Guangdong renmin chubanshe, 1983.

———. *Guangdongqu dang tuan yanjiu shiliao, 1927–1934* [Historical Materials on the CCP Guangdong Regional and Corps Committees, 1927–1934]. Guangzhou: Guangdong renmin chubanshe, 1986.

Guangdongsheng zhengfu. *Guangdongsheng zhengfu gongbao 1925* [Guangdong Provincial Government Bulletin]. Guangzhou, 1925.

———. *Guangdongsheng zhengfu gongbao: faze* [Guangdong Provincial Government Bulletin: Legislation]. Guangzhou, 1926.

———. *Guangdongsheng zhengfu tekan 1926* [Special Issue of Guangdong Provincial Government]. Guangzhou, 1926.

———. *Guangdongsheng zhengfu tekan: jijuean* [Guangdong Provincial Government: Resolutions]. Guangzhou, 1926.

———. *Wunian de jianshe* [Five-Year Development]. Guangzhou, 1933.

"Guangzhou gonghui yundong de baogao (summer 1926)" [Report on the Labor Movement in Guangzhou]. In Zhongyang danganguan and Guangdongsheng danganguan, eds., *Guangdong geming lishi wenjian huiji* [Collected Documents on the History of the Guangdong Revolution], pt. 1, vol. 6. Guangzhou, 1982. Mimeographed.

Guangzhou wenshi yanjiu weiyuanhui, ed. *Guangzhou bainian dashi ji* [Chronology of Guangzhou in the Past One Hundred Years]. 2 vols. Guangzhou: Guangdong renmin chubanshe, 1984.

Guangzhoushi shizhengting. *Guangzhoushi shizheng gaiyao 1921* [Outline of Guangzhou Municipal Administration]. Guangzhou, 1921.

———. *Guangzhoushi shizhengting baogao 1925* [Report of the Guangzhou Municipal Administration]. Guangzhou, 1925.

———. *Shehui diaocha baogao: laogong wenti* [Report of Social Investigation: Labor Problem]. Guangzhou, 1926.

———. *Shehui diaocha baogao: renkou wenti* [Report of Social Investigation: Population Problem]. Guangzhou, 1927.

———. *Tongji nianjian* [Annual Handbook of Statistics]. Guangzhou, 1929.

He Qin. "Wusi shiqi de Deng Zhongxia" [Deng Zhongxia during the May Fourth Period]. In *Wusi shiqi de lishi renwu* [Historical Figures of the May Fourth Period]. Beijing: Zhongguo qingnian chubanshe, 1979.

Hershatter, Gail. *The Workers of Tianjin, 1900–1949*. Stanford: Stanford University Press, 1986.

Hiroaki, Yokoyama. "Ma Lin, Sun Zhongshan, guogong hezuo: yi Ma Lin dangan wei zhongxin" [Maring, Sun Yatsen, and Guomindang-CCP Cooperation, based on the Maring Archives]. Paper delivered at the International Conference on Sun Yatsen and Asia, Guangdong, China, 1990.

Ho, Ping-ti. *The Ladder of Success in Imperial China: Aspects of Social Mobility, 1368–1911*. New York: Columbia University Press, 1962.

Hobsbawm, E. J. "Class Consciousness in History." In István Mészáros, ed., *Aspects of History and Class Consciousness*. London: Routledge & Kegan Paul, 1971.

Hofheinz, Roy, Jr. *The Broken Wave: The Chinese Communist Peasant Movement, 1922–1928*. Cambridge: Harvard University Press, 1977.

Holubnychy, Lydia. *Michael Borodin and the Chinese Revolution, 1923–1925*. New York: East Asian Institute, Columbia University, 1979.

Hong Kong Government. *Hong Kong Administrative Report*. Hong Kong, 1919–27. Issued annually.

———. *Hong Kong Blue Book*. Hong Kong, 1919–27. Issued annually.

———. *Handbook on Conditions and Cost of Living in Hong Kong*. Hong Kong, 1921.

———. *Report of the Commission Appointed to Enquire into the Conditions of the Industrial Employment of Children in Hong Kong*. Government Sessional Paper. Hong Kong, 1921.

———. *Report on the Census of the Colony in 1921.* Government Sessional Paper. Hong Kong, 1921.

———. *Causes and Effects of the Present Trade Depression.* Government Sessional Paper. Hong Kong, 1931.

———. *Report on the Census of the Colony in 1931.* Government Sessional Paper. Hong Kong, 1931.

———. *Report on Labor and Labor Conditions in Hong Kong.* Government Sessional Paper. Hong Kong, 1939.

Honig, Emily. *Sisters and Strangers: Women in the Shanghai Cotton Mill, 1919–1949.* Stanford: Stanford University Press, 1986.

Hsiao, Tso-liang. *Power Relations within the Chinese Communist Movement, 1930–34.* Seattle: University of Washington Press, 1967.

———. *Chinese Communism in 1927: City vs. Countryside.* Hong Kong: Chinese University of Hong Kong Press, 1970.

Huang Ping. "Guanyu Shenggang da bagong de huiyi ziliao" [Memoirs of the Guangzhou–Hong Kong General Strike]. Guangzhou, 1963. Unpublished manuscript prepared by the Guangdong Provincial Academy of Philosophy and Social Sciences.

———. *Wangshi huiyi* [Memories of the Past]. Guangzhou: Guangdong renmin chubanshe, 1981.

Huang Yibo. "Wuzhengfu zhuyi zhe zai Guangzhou gao gonghui huodong huiyi" [Memories of the Anarchists' Labor Activities in Guangzhou]. *Guangzhou wenshi ziliao* 5 (1962).

Isaacs, Harold. *The Tragedy of the Chinese Revolution.* Stanford: Stanford University Press, 1951.

Jacobs, Dan N. *Borodin: Stalin's Man in China.* Cambridge: Harvard University Press, 1981.

Jiang Peinan, and Chen Weimin. "Zhongguo laodong zuhe shujibu shimokao" [History of the Chinese Labor Secretariat]. *Dangshi ziliao congkan* 3 (1980).

Jiang Ping. "Deng Zhongxia zai da geming shiqi dui Zhongguo shehui ge jieji de fenxi" [Deng Zhongxia's Analysis of the Role of the Various Chinese Social Classes in the Period of Great Revolution]. *Jindaishi yanjiu* [Modern Historical Research] 2 (1982).

———. *Deng Zhongxia de yisheng* [The Life of Deng Zhongxia]. Nanjing: Nanjing daxue chubanshe, 1985.

Jiang Ping, and Li Liangyu. "Deng Zhongxia tongzhi guanghui de yisheng" [The Glorious Life of Comrade Deng Zhongxia]. In *Jinian wusi yundong liushi zhounian xueshu taolunhui lunwenxuan* [Selected Essays from the Seminar Held on the Sixtieth Anniversary of the May Fourth Movement]. Beijing: Zhongguo shehui kexueyuan, 1980.

Jones, Susan Mann, and Kuhn, Philip A. "Dynastic Decline and the Roots of Rebellion." In John K. Fairbank, ed., *The Cambridge History of China*, vol. 10. Cambridge: Cambridge University Press, 1978.

Jordan, Donald A. *The Northern Expedition: China's National Revolution of 1926–28*. Honolulu: University Press of Hawaii, 1976.

Kau, Ying-mao. "Urban and Rural Strategies in the Chinese Communist Revolution." In John W. Lewis, ed., *Peasant Rebellion and Communist Revolution in Asia*. Stanford: Stanford University Press, 1974.

Ku, Hung-ting. "The Emergence of the Kuomintang's Anti-imperialism." *Journal of Oriental Studies* 16 (1978).

Lai Xiansheng. "Zai Guangdong geming hongliu zhong: huiyi 1922 nian–1927 nian de douzheng" [In the Current of Guangdong Revolution: Memoirs of the Struggle during 1922–1927]. *Guangdong dangshi ziliao* 1 (1983).

Lee, Leo Ou-fan, and Nathan, Andrew J. "The Beginnings of Mass Culture: Journalism and Fiction in the Late Ching and Beyond." In David Johnson et al., eds., *Popular Culture in Late Imperial China*. Berkeley and Los Angeles: University of California Press, 1985.

Levine, Marilyn A. *The Found Generation: Chinese Communists in Europe during the Twenties*. Seattle: University of Washington Press, 1993.

Levy, Marion J., Jr. "The Social Background of Modern Business Development in China." In *The Rise of the Chinese Business Class: Two Introductory Essays*. New York: Institution of Pacific Relations, 1949.

Lewis, Charlton M. *Prologue to the Chinese Revolution: The Transformation of Ideas and Institutions in Hunan Province, 1891–1907*. Cambridge: Harvard University Press, 1976.

Li Baiyuan. *Guangdong jiqi gongren fendou shi* [History of the Guangdong Mechanics' Struggle]. Taibei: Zhongguo laogong fulibu chubanshe, 1955.

Li Hongnuan and He Jinzhou. "Luo Dengxian" [Luo Dengxian]. In *Zhongguo gongren yundong de xianqu* [The Pioneers of the Chinese Labor Movement], vol. 4. Beijing: Gongren chubanshe, 1985.

Li Huang. "Wusi yundong yu shaonian Zhongguo xuehui" [The May Fourth Movement and the Young China Society]. *Mingbao yuekan* [Mingbao Monthly] 6 (1969).

Li Ji. "Deng Zhongxia yanjiu Zhongguo geming wenti de tedian he chuangjian" [The Uniqueness and Originality of Deng Zhongxia's Research on the Chinese Revolution]. *Dangshi janjiu* 2 (1986).

Li Lisan. "Dangshi baogao (Feb. 1930)" [Report on Party History (Feb. 1930)]. In *Zhonggong dang baogao xuanpian* [Selected CCP Reports]. Beijing: Zhonggong zhongyang danxiao chubanshe, 1982.

Li Weihan. "Guanyu Baqi huiyi de yixie huiyi" [Some Memories of the 7 August

Meeting]. In Zhonggong zhongyang dangshi ziliao zhengji wenyuanhui and Zhongyang danganguan, eds., *Baqi huiyi* [7 August Meeting]. Beijing: Zhonggong dangshi ziliao chubanshe, 1986.

————. "Guanyu Qu Qiubai zuoqing mangdong zhuyi de huiyi yu yanjiu" [A Retrospective Study of Qu Qiubai's "Leftist" Adventurism]. In *Zhonggong dangshi ziliao,* vol. 5.

Li Weishi. "Guangdongsheng cansiye de maoyi ji qi shuailuo" [The Silk Trade and Its Decline in Guangdong Province]. *Guangzhou wenshi ziliao* 16 (1965).

Li Xiaoyong. "Goumindang yu Shenggang da bagong" [The Guomindang and the Guangzhou–Hong Kong General Strike]. *Jindaishi yanjiu* 4 (1987).

Li Zhiye and Ye Wenyi. "Guangdong dangtuan huodong jiyao" [Chronology of the Guangdong Party's Activities]. *Guangdong dangshi ziliao* 5–7.

Liang Guozhi. "Guangzhou Shamian yangwu gongren de zuzhi ji bagong jing-guo" [The Organization and Experience of the Workers Employed in Foreign Firms in Shamian, Guangzhou]. In *Guangzhou da geming shiqi huiyilu xuanpian* [Selected Memoirs of the Great Revolutionary Period in Guangzhou]. Guangzhou: Guangdong renmin chubanshe, 1986.

Lin Jiayou and Zhou Xingliang. *Sun Zhongshan yu guogong deyici hezuo* [Sun Yatsen and the First Guomindang-Communist Cooperation]. Chengdu: Sichuan renmin chubanshe, 1988.

Liu Jingfang. "Ping Baqi huiyi guanyu zhigong yundong de celue" [Comment on the 7 August Meeting's Labor Strategy]. *Dangshi yanjiu* 3 (1985).

Liu Jizeng, Mao Lei, and Yuan Jicheng. *Wuhan guomin zhengfu shi* [History of the Wuhan National Government]. Wuhan: Hubei renmin chubanshe, 1986.

Liu Shaoqi. "Yi nian lai Zhongguo zhigong yundong de fazhan" [The Development of the Chinese Labor Movement over the Past Year]. *Zhengzhi zhoubao* 13 (1926).

Louis, William Roger. *British Strategy in the Far East, 1919–1939.* Oxford: Clarendon Press, 1971.

Lu Qi. "Ji zai Shenggang da bagong zhong de Deng Zhongxial tongzhi" [Memories of Comrade Deng Zhongxia in the Guangzhou–Hong Kong General Strike]. *Guangdong wenshi ziliao* 29 (1980).

Lu Quan and Zhe Qianhong. *Su Zhaozheng zhuan* [Biography of Su Zhaozheng]. Shanghai: Shanghai renmin chubanshe, 1986.

————. *Su Zhaozheng* [Su Zhaozheng]. Guangzhou: Guangdong renmin chubanshe, 1993.

Luk, Michael Y. L. *The Origins of Chinese Bolshevism: An Ideology in the Making, 1920–1928.* Hong Kong: Oxford University Press, 1990.

Luo Daming et al. "Da geming shiqi Guangdong gongren yundong qingkuang de huiyi" [Memoirs of the Guangdong Labor Movement during the Period of Great Revolution]. In *Guangzhou da geming shiqi huiyi lu xuanpian* [Selected Memoirs of the Great Revolution in Guangzhou]. Guangzhou: Guangdong renmin chubanshe, 1986.

Luo Hequn and He Jinzhou. *Liu Ersong* [Liu Ersong]. Guangzhou: Guangdong renmin chubanshe, 1986.

Luo Zhanglong. "Huiyi Beijing daxue Makesi xueshuo yanjiuhui" [Memories of the Marxist Research Society at Beijing University]. In *Wusi yundong hui-yilu* [Memoirs of the May Fourth Movement]. Beijing: Renmin chuhanshe, 1979.

————. *Chunyuan daiji* [Reminiscences in Garden Chun]. Beijing: Sanlian chu-banshe, 1984.

Ma, Chao-chun [Ma Chaojun]. *History of the Labor Movement in China*. Taibei: China Culture Service, 1955.

Ma Chaojun. *Zhongguo laogong yundong shi* [History of the Chinese Labor Movement]. Taibei: Zhongguo laogong fulibu chubanshe, 1958.

Ma Jianqun. "Deng Zhongxia tongzhi zai Changxindian" [Comrade Deng Zhongxia in Changxindian]. *Beijing ribao* [Beijing Daily], 7 Feb. 1959.

Macmillan, Allister. *Seaports of the Far East: Historical and Descriptive, Commercial, and Industrial Facts, Figures, and Resources*. London: W. H. & L. Collinbridge, 1925.

Marks, Robert. *Rural Revolution in South China: Peasants and the Making of History in Haifeng County, 1570–1930*. Madison: University of Wisconsin Press, 1984.

Meisner, Maurice. *Li Ta-chao and the Origins of Chinese Marxism*. Cambridge: Harvard University Press, 1967.

Minoru Takeuchi, ed. *Mao Zedong ji* [Works of Mao Zedong]. 10 vols. Tokyo: Hokubosha, 1972.

Nanyue yinlie chuan [Biographies of Martyrs in South Guangdong]. 6 vols. Guangzhou: Guangdong renmin chubanshe, 1983–89.

Nathan, Andrew J. *Peking Politics, 1918–1923: Factionalism and the Failure of Constitutionalism*. Berkeley and Los Angeles: University of California Press, 1976.

Ni Moyan. "Cong jinanhui dao geming hujihui" [From the Relief Society to the Revolutionary Mutual-Aid Association]. *Dangshi ziliao congkan* 4 (1983).

North, Robert, and Eudin, Xenia, eds. *M. N. Roy's Mission to China: The Communist-Kuomintang Split of 1927*. Berkeley and Los Angeles: University of California Press, 1963.

Pak, Hyobom, ed. *Documents of the Chinese Communist Party, 1927–1930*. Hong Kong: Union Research Institute, 1971.

Peng Pai. "Chushi beifa yu Shenggang bagong" [The Launch of the Northern Expedition and the Guangzhou–Hong Kong General Strike]. *Renmin zhoukan* 18 (12 Aug. 1926).

————. *Seeds of Revolution: Report on the Haifeng Peasant Movement*. Translated by D. Holoch. Cornell University East Asia Paper. Ithaca, 1973.

Peng Shuzhi. *Ping Zhang Guotao de "Wo de huiyi"* [Critique of Zhang Guotao's *My Memoirs*]. Hong Kong: Qianwei chubanshe, 1975.

Peng Zeyin. "Shijiu shiji houqi Zhongguo chengshi shougongye shangye hanghui de chongjian he zuoyong" [The Reestablishment and Function of the Guilds for Urban Handicraft Industry and Commerce in the Late Nineteenth Century]. *Lishi yanjiu* [Historical Research] 1 (1965).

Pennell, W. V. *History of the Hong Kong Chamber of Commerce, 1861–1961*. Hong Kong: Hong Kong Chamber of Commerce, 1961.

Perry, Elizabeth J. *Shanghai on Strike: The Politics of Chinese Labor*. Stanford: Stanford University Press, 1993.

Pikowicz, Paul G. *Marxist Literary Thought in China: The Influence of Chu Chiu-pai*. Berkeley and Los Angeles: University of California Press, 1981.

Porter, Robin. "Child Labor in Hong Kong." *International Labor Review* 5 (May 1975).

Price, Jane L. *Cadres, Commanders, and Commissars: The Training of the Chinese Communist Leadership, 1920–1945*. Colorado: Westview Press, 1976.

Qian Yizhang. *Shaji tongshi* [Painful History of Shaji]. Guangzhou, 1925.

Remer, C. F. *Foreign Investment in China*. Reprint. New York: Howard Press, 1968.

Rhoades, Edward. "Merchant Associations in Canton, 1859–1911." In Mark Elvin and G. William Skinner, eds., *The Chinese City between Two Worlds*. Stanford: Stanford University Press, 1974.

————. *China's Republican Revolution: The Case of Kwangtung, 1895–1913*. Cambridge: Harvard University Press, 1975.

Ristaino, Marcia R. *China's Art of Revolution: The Mobilization of Discontent, 1927 and 1928*. Durham, N.C.: Duke University Press, 1987.

Schram, Stuart. "Introduction: The Cultural Revolution in Historical Perspective." In Stuart Schram, ed., *Authority, Participation, and Cultural Change in China*. Cambridge: Cambridge University Press, 1972.

————. *The Thought of Mao Tse-tung*. Cambridge: Cambridge University Press, 1989.

Schwarcz, Vera. *The Chinese Enlightenment: Intellectuals and the Legacy of the*

May Fourth Movement of 1919. Berkeley and Los Angeles: University of California Press, 1986.

Schwartz, Benjamin I. *Chinese Communism and the Rise of Mao.* Cambridge: Harvard University Press, 1951.

Shaffer, Lynda. *Mao and the Workers: The Hunan Labor Movement, 1920–1923.* New York: Armonk, 1982.

Shenggang bagong weiyuanhui, ed. *Bagong yu dongzheng* [Strike and Eastern Expedition]. Guangzhou, 1925.

"Shenggang da bagong huiyiliu" [Memoirs of the Guangzhou–Hong Kong General Strike]. 4 vols. Guangzhou, Mar. 1962. Unpublished manuscript prepared by the Guangdong Provincial Academy of Philosophy and Social Sciences.

"Shenggang da bagong huiyiliu ziliao" [Memoir Sources of the Guangzhou–Hong Kong General Strike]. 2 vols. Guangzhou, Dec. 1962. Unpublished manuscript prepared by the Guangdong Provincial Academy of Philosophy and Social Sciences.

"Shenggang da bagong lishi ziliao huibian" [Collected Historical Sources of the Guangzhou–Hong Kong General Strike]. 2 vols. Guangzhou, May 1962. Unpublished manuscript prepared by the Guangdong Provincial Academy of Philosophy and Social Sciences.

Shuai Mengqi. "Sanshi niandaichu Jiangsu sheng huxi quwei huodong pianduan" [Extract from the Activities of the Western Part of the Jiangsu Region during the Early 1930s]. *Dangshi ziliao congkan* 2 (1983).

Skinner, G. William. "Introduction: Urban Social Structure in Ching China." In G. William Skinner, ed., *The City in Late Imperial China.* Stanford: Stanford University Press, 1977.

Slyke, Lyman Van. *Enemies and Friends: The United Front in Chinese Communist History.* Stanford: Stanford University Press, 1967.

Smith, Carl T. "The Chinese Church, Labor, and Elites, and the Mui Tsai Question in the 1920's." *Journal of the Hong Kong Branch of the Royal Asiatic Society* 21 (1981).

Stimson, Henry L. *The Far Eastern Crisis.* New York: Harper & Brothers Publishers, 1936.

Tan Pingshan. "Fanying yundong yu jieshu Shenggang bagong" [The Anti-British Movement and the End of Guangzhou–Hong Kong Strike]. *Xiangdao zhoubao* 166 (6 Aug. 1926).

Tang Chunliang. "Li Lisan zai Guangdong" [Li Lisan in Guangdong]. *Guangdong dangshi ziliao* 10.

Teng Ssu-yu and Fairbank, John K., eds. *China's Response to the West: A Documentary Survey, 1839–1923.* Cambridge: Harvard University Press, 1954.

Thomas, S. Bernard. *Labor and the Chinese Revolution.* Michigan Papers on Chinese Studies. Ann Arbor, 1983.

Tsai, Jung-fang. *Hong Kong in Chinese History: Community and Social Unrest in the British Colony, 1842–1913.* New York: Columbia University Press, 1993.

Tsin, Michael Tsang-woon. "The Cradle of Revolution: Politics and Society in Canton, 1900–1927." Ph.D. diss., Princeton University, 1990.

United Kingdom. *Memorandum by Governor Sir John P. Hennessy on Chinese Merchants in Hong Kong.* London, 27 Sept. 1877.

———. Parliament. *Papers Respecting the First Firing in the Shameen Affair of June 23, 1925.* Cmd. 2636. 1926.

van de Ven, Hans J. *From Friend to Comrade: The Founding of the Chinese Communist Party, 1920–1927.* Berkeley and Los Angeles: University of California Press, 1991.

Vishnyakova-Akimova, Vera V. *Two Years in Revolutionary China, 1925–1927.* Harvard East Asian Monographs. Cambridge, 1971.

Wang Jingwei. "Zhengzhi baogao" [Political Report]. *Zhengzhi zhoubao* 2 (1925).

Wei Wei and Qian Xiaohui. *Deng Zhongxia zhuan* [Biography of Deng Zhongxia]. Beijing: Renmin chubanshe, 1981.

Wilbur, C. Martin. "The Ashes of Defeat." *China Quarterly* 18 (Apr.–June 1964).

———. *Sun Yat-sen: The Frustrated Patriot.* New York: Columbia University Press, 1976.

———. *The Nationalist Revolution in China, 1923–1928.* Cambridge: Cambridge University Press, 1983.

Wilbur, C. Martin, and How, Julie, eds. *Missionaries of Revolution: Soviet Advisers and Nationalist China, 1920–1927.* Cambridge: Harvard University Press, 1989.

Wilson, David C. "Britain and the Kuomintang, 1924–28: A Study of the Interaction of Official Policies and Perceptions in Britain and China." Ph.D. thesis, University of London, 1973.

Wright, Arnold, ed. *Twentieth Century Impression of Hong Kong, Shanghai, and Other Treaty Ports.* London: Lloyd's Greater Britian Publishing Co., 1908.

Wright, Mary. "Introduction: The Rising Tide of Change." In Mary Wright, ed., *Revolution in China: The First Phase, 1900–1913.* New Haven: Yale University Press, 1968.

Wu Jialin and Xie Yinming. *Beijing dang zuzhi de chuangjian huodong* [The Activities and Establishment of the Beijing Party Organization]. Beijing: Renmin daxue chubanshe, 1991.

Wu, Tien-wei. "Chiang Kai-shek's March Twentieth *Coup d'Etat* of 1926." *Journal of Asian Studies* 27 (1967).

Wusi yundong huiyilu [Memoirs of the May Fourth Movement]. Beijing: Renmin chubanshe, 1979.

Xiang Qing. *Gongchan guoji he Zhongguo geming quanxi de lishi gaishu* [General History of the Relations between the Comintern and the Chinese Revolution]. Guangzhou: Guangdong renmin chubanshe, 1983.

———. "Gongchan guoji Sulian he Zhongshan jian shijian" [The Comintern, Soviet Union, and the S.S. *Zhongshan* Incident]. *Dangshi ziliao congkan* 2 (1983).

"Xianggang gongtuan zhi dalue diaocha" [A Rough Survey of Hong Kong Labor Unions]. In *Xianggang daguangbao gengshen zhengkan* [Supplementary Issue of Hong Kong Daguangbao]. 1920.

Xiao Chaoran. "Zhongshan jian shijian de qian qian hou hou" [The S.S. *Zhongshan* Incident]. In *Zhongguo jindaishi yanjiu luncong* [Collected Essays on Modern Chinese History]. Zhangchun: Jilin Renmin chibanshe, 1981.

Xue Haozhou and Li Xiangjun. "Deng Zhongxia yu Gongren zhi lu" [Deng Zhongxia and the *Road of Workers*]. *Xinwen yanjiu ziliao* [Research Materials of Journalism] 2 (1980).

Xue Shengshi. "1931 dao 1933 nian Shanghai zonggonghui de jiankuang" [Brief Account of the Shanghai General Labor Union from 1931 to 1933]. *Dangshi ziliao congkan* 1 (1981).

Yang Dajin. *Xiandai Zhongguo sheyi zhi* [History of Modern Chinese Industries]. Zhangsha, 1938.

Yi Long. "Jin nian wuyi Guangzhou zhi liang dai chengju" [The Two Outstanding Events in Guangzhou during This Year's May Day]. *Xiangdao zhoubao*, 10 May 1925.

Young, L. K. *British Policy in China, 1895–1902*. Oxford: Clarendon Press, 1970.

Yu Fuyuan. "Qingnian gongren yuekan" [Young Workers Monthly]. *Dangshi ziliao congkan* 4 (1982).

Yu Qizhong, ed. *Guangzhou gongren jiating zhi yanjiu* [A Study of Workers' Families in Guangzhou]. Guangzhou: Guoli zhongshang daxue, 1934.

Zhang Guotao. *Wo de huiyi* [My Memoirs]. Hong Kong: Mingbao yuekan chubanshe, 1971.

Zhang Hong. *Xianggang haiyuan da bagong* [Hong Kong Seamen's Strike]. Guangzhou: Guangdong renmin chubanshe, 1979.

Zhang Quan. "Guanyu Huxi gongyou julebu" [On the Huxi Workers' Club]. *Dangshi ziliao congkan* 3 (1980).

Zhang Tailei. "Bali gongshe jinianri" [Anniversary of the Paris Commune]. *Renmin zhoukan* 6 (19 Mar. 1926).

———. "Zhongying tanpan de jingge yu jieguo" [The Process and Consequence of the Sino-British Negotiations]. *Renmin zhoukan* 17 (1 Aug. 1926).

Zhang Yunhou et al., eds. *Wusi shiqi de shetuan* [Societies of the May Fourth Period]. 4 vols. Beijing: Sanlian chubanshe, 1979.

Zhao Piao. "Baqi huiyi yu dang de gaizu" [Party Organization and the 7 August Meeting]. *Dangshi yanjiu* 4 (1985).

———. "Diliuci quangguo daibiao dahui" [The CCP Sixth Congress]. *Dangshi yanjiu* 1 (1986).

———. "Wuci dahui dao liuci dehui yinian zhong de zuzhi zhuangkuang" [The condition of the Organization from the CCP Fifth Congress to the CCP Sixth Congress]. *Dangshi yanjiu* 5 (1986) and 6 (1987).

Zhonggong dangshi renwu yanjuihui, ed. *Zhongong dangshi renwu chuan* [Biographies of the Chinese Communists]. Xian: Shaanxi renmin chubanshe, 1982.

Zhonggong gongren yundong yuanshi ziliao huibian [Collected Primary Materials on the Chinese Communist Labor Movement]. 4 vols. Taibei: Sifa xingzheng bu diaochaoju bianyin, 1980.

"Zhonggong Guangdong quwei guanyu gongren yundong de baogao (Oct. 1925)" [Report on the Labor Movement by the CCP Guangdong Regional Committee]. In Zhongyang danganguan and Guangdongsheng danganguan, eds., *Guangdong geming lishi wenjian huiji*, pt. 1, vol. 6. Guangzhou, 1982. Mimeographed.

"Zhonggong Guangdong quwei guanyu Shenggang da bagong de baogao (July 1925)" [CCP Guangdong Regional Committee's Report on the Guangzhou–Hong Kong General Strike]. In Zhongyang danganguan and Guangdongsheng danganguan, eds., *Guangdong geming lishi wenjian huiji*, pt. 1, vol. 6. Guangzhou, 1982. Mimeographed.

Zhonggong Guangdong shengwei dangshi yanjiu wenyuanhui and Zhonggong Guangdong shengwei dangshi ziliao zhengji wenyuanhui, eds. *Zhonggong Guangdong dangshi dashi ji* [Chronology of the CCP History in Guangdong]. Guangzhou, 1984.

Zhonggong Guangzhou shiwei dangshi yanjiushi, ed. *Guangzhou yinlie chuan* [Biographies of Martyrs in Guangzhou]. Guangzhou: Guangdong renmin chubanshe, 1991.

Zhonggong Wuhanshiwen dangshi bangongshi. "1927 nian zhonggong zhongyang jiquan you Shanghai qian Wuhan de jingge ji zai Han qingkuang" [The Transfer of the CCP Central Organs from Shanghai to Wuhan in 1927 and Their Conditions in Wuhan]. In *Zhonggong dangshi ziliao*, vol. 21.

Zhonggong zhongyang danganguan, ed. *Zhonggong zhongyang zhengzhi baogao xuanji, 1922–1926* [Selected Political Reports of the CCP Central Committee, 1922–1926]. Beijing: Zhonggong zhongyang dangxiao chubanshe, 1981.

Zhonggong zhongyang dangshi ziliao zhengji wenyuanhui and Zhonggong danganguan, eds. *Baqi huiyi* [7 August Meeting]. Beijing: Zhonggong dangshi ziliao chubanshe, 1986.

Zhonggong zhongyang dangshi ziliao zhengji wenyuanhui, Zhonggong Guangdongsheng dangshi ziliao zhengji wenyuanhui, and Guangdong geming bowuguan, eds. *Guangzhou qiyi* [Guangzhou Uprising]. Beijing: Zhonggong dangshi ziliao chubanshe, 1988.

Zhonggong zhongyang dangxiao dangshi jiaoyanshi, ed. *Zhonggong dangshi cankao ziliao* [Reference Materials on CCP History]. 8 vols. Beijing: Renmin chubanshe, 1979.

Zhonggong zhongyang Malie zhuzho bianyiju, ed. *Wusi shiqi qikan jieshao* [Introduction to the Periodicals of the May Fourth Period]. 3 vols. Beijing: Renmin chubanshe, 1958.

Zhonggong zhongyang shuji chu, ed. *Liu da yiqian dang de lishi cailiao* [Party Historical Materials before the Sixth Congress]. Beijing: Xinhua chubanshe, 1980.

Zhonggong zhongyang wenjian xuanji [Selected Documents of the CCP Central]. 18 vols. Beijing: Zhonggong zhongyang dangxiao chubanshe, 1989.

Zhongguo dierci quanguo laodong dahui: Gongren jiaoyu de yijuean [The Second Chinese Labor Congress: Resolution on Workers' Education]. Guangzhou, 1925.

"Zhongguo gongchandang Guangdong zhixing weiyuanhui duiyu Guangdong shihu xuanyan, 13 June 1925" [The CCP Guangdong Executive Committee's Declaration on the Guangdong Situation]. In *Zhonggong dangshi cankao ziliao* [Reference Materials on CCP History], vol. 2. Beijing: Renmin chubanshe, 1979.

Zhongguo gongchandang Guangdongqu weiyuanhui. "Gei Guomindang zhongyang guomin zhengfu guomin gemingjun ji Guangdong renmen de yifeng gongkai xin" [An Open Letter to the Guomindang Central Nationalist Revolutionary Army and to the People of Guangdong]. *Renmin zhoukan* 7 (30 Mar. 1926).

Zhongguo gonghui lici daibiao dahui wenxian [Documents of the Various Chinese Labor Congresses]. Vol. 1. Beijing: Gongren chubanshe, 1984.

Zhongguo gongren yundong de xianqu [The Pioneers of the Chinese Labor Movement]. 4 vols. Beijing: Gongren chubanshe, 1983–85.

Zhongguo Guomindang dierci quanguo daibiao dahui huiji jilu [Minutes of the Second National Congress of the Guomindang]. Guangzhou, 1926.

Zhonghua quanguo zonggonghui. *Shenggang bagong weiyuanhui: zhiyuan yilanbiao* [Staff List of the Guangzhou–Hong Kong Strike Committee]. Guangzhou, n.d.

"Zhonghua quanguo zonggonghui wei 'wusa' canan zhi Xianggang ge gong-tuan de xin, 18 June 1925" [Letter from the All China Labor Federation to the Hong Kong Trade Unions on the May Thirtieth Tragic Case]. In *Zhonggong dangshi cankao ziliao*, vol. 2. Beijing: Renmin chubanshe, 1979.

"Zhonghua quanguo zonggonghui zuzhi Shenggang bagong weiyuanhui qushi, 13 June 1925" [The All China Labor Federation's Announcement for the Organizing of the Guangzhou-Hong Kong Strike Committee]. In *Zhonggong dangshi cankao ziliao*, vol. 2. Beijing: Renmin chubanshe, 1979.

Zhongyang danganguan, ed. *Zhonggong zhongyang wenjian xuanji* [Collected Documents of the CCP Central Committee]. 18 vols. Beijing: Zhonggong zhongyang dangxiao chubanshe, 1988.

Zhongyang danganguan and Guangdongsheng danganguan, eds. *Guangdong geming lishi wenjian huiji* [Collected Documents on the History of the Guangdong Revolution]. 60 vols. in pt. 1 and 2 vols. in pt. 2. Guangzhou, 1982. Mimeographed.

Zhongyuan [Deng Zhongxia]. "Gongchan zhuyi yu wuzhengfu zhuyi" [Communism and Anarchism]. *Xianqu* 1 (15 Jan. 1922).

Zhou Enlai. "Guanyu dang de liuda de yanjiu" [On the Study of the CCP Sixth Congress]. In *Zhou Enlai xuanji* [Selected Works of Zhou Enlai], vol. 1. Beijing: Renmin chubanshe, 1980.

———. "Guangyu 1924–26 nian dang dui Guomindang de guanxi" [On the Party's Relations with the Guomindang in 1924–26]. In *Zhou Enlai xuanji*, vol. 1. Beijing: Renmin chubanshe, 1980.

Index

Beijing (*continued*)
as China's capital, 97
dialect, 22
foreign legations in, 11
government, 32, 37, 207
National Assembly in, 74
mentioned, 14, 20, 23, 29, 35, 87, 95, 98,
104, 200, 202, 208, 209
Beijing Communist Group, 23, 24, 27, 33
n. 88
Beijing daxue rikan (Beijing University
Daily), 17
Beijing daxue xuesheng zhoukan (Beijing
University Students' Weekly), 20
Beijing-Hankou railway, 19, 54
Beijing University (Beida), 3, 14, 16, 17, 19,
20, 21, 23, 40, 85, 234
Beijing University Commoners' Education
Lecture Corps, 17, 19, 20, 21, 22
Bell, R. Hayley, 213, 213 n. 72
Blake, [Sir Henry], 95
Borodin, Michael
on boycott policy, 186
and CCP Guangdong Regional Committee, 116, 177
CCP Provisional Politburo, appointment
of, 226
criticism of, 247, 247 n. 100
criticized Guomindang, 89, 89 n. 146
relations with Deng Zhongxia, 247, 247
n. 100
on relocation of CCP Central Committee, 116
and Shenggang General Strike, 109, 115,
118, 137
mentioned, 88, 119, 158, 162, 164, 206,
259
bourgeois revolution, 184 n. 116, 232
Boxer Indemnity funds, 207, 222
Boxer Uprising, 11, 96
Brenan, John F., 159, 215, 217, 217 n. 89, 218,
219, 220
Britain
Colonial Office, 53, 96, 203
Foreign Office, 53, 56, 96, 198–99, 198
n. 7, 200, 201, 202, 206, 207, 210,
218, 222
Whitehall, 95, 200, 201, 202, 207, 208,
218, 219, 220

Buerseweike (The Bolsheviks), 238, 249
Bukharin, Nikolai, 246, 247, 248, 251
Butterfield and Swire Company, 61

Cai Hesen, 13, 36, 88, 234 n. 41
Cai Yuanpei, 14, 16
Cao Rulin, 18
Chamberlain, [Sir Austen], 200, 219
Changjiang, 25
Changsha, 13
Changsha Normal College, 13
Changxindian
labor journal (*Laodong yin*) in, 23
strike in, 33–35, 38, 39, 42
workers in, 20, 22, 27, 29
workers' school in, 22, 24
mentioned, 19, 21, 36, 130
See also Deng Zhongxia
Chaozhou, 54, 55, 137
Chen Bingsheng, 73–74, 78, 79, 94
Chen Duxiu
CCP Central Committee, resignation
from, 226 n. 8, 234
on "The Chinese Nationalist Revolution
and the Various Social Classes," 38,
40–42
on Chinese working class, 16, 21, 50
on Communist activities in Guangdong,
86
on Communist labor policy, 33, 34, 38,
39
condemned as "rightist" leader, 236, 237
criticized by Qu Qiubai, 234 n. 41
criticized Deng Zhongxia, 48
debate with Deng Zhongxia, 38–47
differences with Deng Zhongxia and Qu
Qiubai, 235
as father of Chen Yannian, 109
labor movement in Guangdong, promotion of, 85–86
and March Twentieth Coup, 164, 167, 168
on petty bourgeoisie, 184
on strike settlement, 200
on United Front, 229
mentioned, 21 n. 42, 46 n. 140
See also Deng Zhongxia
Chen, Eugene, 158, 205, 215, 217, 217 n. 89,
220
Chen Gongbo, 85, 214

Chen Jiongming, 77, 82, 83, 86, 87, 89, 97, 136, 137, 175, 201, 203, 204, 207
Chen Lianbai, 181, 181 n. 107, 204
Chen Qitian, 25
Chen Qiyuan, 58, 58 n. 24
Chen Richang, 108
Chen Sen, 181, 181 n. 107, 182
Chen Yannian
    biographical note on, 109 n. 29
    Borodin, relations with, 116
    and March Twentieth Coup, 164, 165, 168, 169, 176
    member of CCP Guangdong Regional Committee, 109, 111, 115
    mentioned, 114, 118, 186, 195, 225 n. 3
Chen Yu, 176 n. 87, 183
Chen Yun, 266
Chen Zhiwen, 108 n. 33, 178
Cherepanov, Alexander I., 89
Chesneaux, Jean, 4, 112 n. 46, 177 n. 91, 179 n. 100
China Institute for the Study of Mechanics (Zhongguo yanji shushu), 73
China Light and Power Company, 61
Chinese Communist Party (CCP)
    First Congress, 28, 29, 35
    Second Congress, 29, 32
    Third Congress, 38, 39, 46, 88
    Fourth Congress, 48, 101, 102
    Fifth Congress, 167, 226, 235, 235 n. 44, 238, 258
    Sixth Congress, 224, 245, 246–48, 247 n. 98, 250, 253, 258, 259
    Central Committee, 31, 36, 47, 48, 103, 104, 106, 107, 114, 115, 116, 133, 135, 164, 167, 168, 168 n. 50, 182, 191, 194, 226, 229, 233, 237, 238, 245, 249, 250, 250 n. 105, 253
    enlarged meeting of 1924, 46
    Guangdong Regional Committee, 86, 90 n. 150, 91, 93, 94, 107, 108, 109, 111, 114–17, 123, 129, 164–67, 182, 192, 200, 218, 225 n. 3, 242–45
    Guangdong Regional Standing Committee, 243, 244
    Jiangsu Regional Committee, 227, 236, 239
    Jiangsu Regional Standing Committee, 239

Labor Movement Committee, 102, 239, 240
Politburo, 227, 237–48, 252, 254–59
Provisional Guangdong Regional Executive Committee, 109, 109 n. 30, 110, 115
Provisional Politburo, 226, 226 n. 11, 227, 234, 234 n. 41, 235, 236
Shanghai Regional Executive Committee, 38
mentioned, 3, 4, 6, 7, 8, 26, 44, 50, 51, 74, 82, 84, 85, 87, 90, 94, 99, 156, 158, 169, 172, 174, 178, 193, 195, 221, 228, 230, 234, 237, 262, 264, 265, 266
See also Guomindang
Chinese labor history, 4–5, 5 nn. 5–6
Chinese Relief Society, 262
Chinese Restoration Society (Xingzhong hui), 82, 95
Chinese Revolutionary Mutual Aid Association (CRMAA; Zhongguo geming huji zonghui), 261–62
Chinese Seamen's Philanthropic Society, 74
Chinese Seamen's Union, 102, 191, 216
Chuannan Normal College, 24–25
Citizens' Press (Guomin zazhishe), 14
Clementi, Sir Cecil, 201–3, 207 n. 39, 210–12, 213 n. 72, 214–15, 220
Cock-crow Society (Huming xueshe), 75
Comintern (Communist International)
    Second Congress, 39, 86
    Fourth Congress, 39, 234
    Fifth Congress, 101
    and bourgeois democratic revolution, 30–31
    and CCP Sixth Congress, 246, 249
    Deng Zhongxia, as defender of, 237–39, 249, 251, 259
    directive from, 169
    Executive Committee of (ECCI), 228–29, 230, 232, 258
    Li Lisan, criticism of, 244
    and Sun Yatsen, 87–88
    mentioned, 23, 49, 49 n. 154, 89, 90, 104, 224, 232, 233, 236, 241, 252, 253, 262
Commitment Club (Jueran julebu), 75
Communication Clique (Jiaotong xi), 30
Conference of the Transport Workers of the Pacific, 90

Dai Jitao, 156
Dairy Farm Company, 61
Danshui, 127, 127 n. 113
democratic centralism
    Leninist concept of, 7, 33, 264
    and Shenggang General Strike, 119, 122,
        264
    mentioned, 103
Deng Benyin, 137
Deng Dapao, 22
Deng Dianmo, 9
Deng Fa, 91
Deng Kang, 9
Deng Pei, 103, 178
Deng Zhongxia
    ACLF, role in, 103, 117–18, 249, 252
    and anarchism, 19, 28
    armed labor conflicts, views on, 182
    arrest by Hong Kong Police, 245
    arrest by Shanghai Municipal Police, 3,
        262
    and 7 August emergency meeting,
        237–38
    Beijing University, graduation from, 23
    and Beijing University Commoners'
        Education Lecture Corps, 19–20
    biography on, 46 n. 140, 251 n. 111
    Borodin, Michael, relations with, 247,
        247 n. 100
    boycott policy, views on, 186–87
    British diplomacy, views on, 197–99, 197
        n. 1, 199 n. 11
    CCP organizational weaknesses, views
        on, 194, 238, 255
    and CCP Sixth Congress in Moscow,
        246–48
    Chen Duxiu, debate with, 38–47
    Chinese Marxist historians' comments
        on, 34, 34 n. 98, 251 n. 111, 255
        n. 125, 259, 263
    Chinese revolution, class analysis and
        reassessment of, 231–33
    and Comintern, 237–39, 249, 251, 259
    as Communist labor activist among
        railway workers, 29–30, 33–34
    early life of, 9–15
    execution of, 3, 263
    and Gongren zhi lu, 106, 106 n. 16, 160,
        235

Guangzhou Uprising, planning for, 242
Guomindang, views on, 160–61, 170, 170
    n. 62, 171, 183, 205, 206, 230
    Hong Kong government, views on, 201,
        202, 204
    Hong Kong Chinese merchants, criti-
        cism of, 189–90
    Jiang Jieshi, policy toward, 169, 170 n. 62
    labor issues, increased concern with, 21
    labor movement (1924), on reorganiza-
        tion of, 90
    in Labor Secretariat, 28–29
    and labor unions, 172, 178
    last message of, 263
    Lenin, views on, 43–44
    and Li Lisan, 243, 255
    marriages of, 12, 12 n. 7
    and Marxism, 21, 23, 24, 27, 28
    in May Fourth Movement, 14–18
    in Moscow, 249–53, 259
    and Nanchang Uprising, 235–36
    National Labor Congress, involvement
        in
        First, 31–33
        Second, 102–3
        Fourth, 225
    Nationalist government, views on, 160
    Northern Expedition, support for, 216
    other names of, 9
    petty bourgeoisie, views on, 44, 184–85
    politicizing young students, role in,
        24–25
    problems in the study of, 4
    and Qu Qiubai, 234–35, 242, 258
    Red Army, political commissar to, 254,
        256, 257
    Shanghai, political activities in, 35–38,
        239–42, 261–62
    Shanghai labor movement, influenced
        by, 18, 19, 27
    at Shanghai University, 35–36
    and Shenggang General Strike
        aftermath of, 225–27, 225 n. 3
        appeal to the peasantry, 131, 193
        leader of, 114–18
        preparation for, 106–11
        role in politicizing strikers, 128–35
        strike organization, creation of,
            121–22, 126

right wing of, 73, 77, 92, 130, 157, 161, 173, 181, 195, 196, 201, 205, 206, 222, 225, 227, 229

Second National Congress of, 163

Shanghai Executive Branch of, 36, 38, 114

and Shanghai University, 36

and Shenggang General Strike, 109, 110, 111, 115, 123, 125, 126, 135, 157, 159

and Soviet advisors, 89, 118

and Special Court, 124, 127

United Front with CCP, 3, 31, 32, 34, 35, 36, 39, 46, 48, 88–89, 93, 94, 133, 160, 161, 167, 228, 229

and Western Hills faction, 158, 208

workers, influence on, 31, 32, 73, 75, 78, 82, 83, 85, 89, 92, 93, 94, 105, 135, 175, 177

mentioned, 171, 177, 179, 190, 191, 197, 211, 213, 215, 217, 221, 224, 230, 237, 239, 242, 255, 261, 262, 265

See also Deng Zhongxia; Shaji Incident; Sun Yatsen

Haifeng, 191

Hailufeng, 192, 242

Halifax, E. R., 217 n. 89

Han Wenhui, 172

Hankou, 54, 75, 83, 220, 225, 227, 236, 239

Hanyeping General Union, 102

He Long, 235, 253, 254

Hennessy, Sir John P., 62

Hobsbawm, Eric, 7

Hong Kong

anti-Guomindang activities in, 202–5

as British colony, 52, 53

British officials' comments on, 53, 54

Communist activities in, 94

Guangdong, relations with, 54–57, 70–71

industrial relations in, 69–70

investment in, 58, 60–62

labor exploitation in, 69

labor force in, 64

labor organizers in, 73–74, 75

labor unions in, 79–81

secret societies and labor activists in, 79, 80 n. 117

Shenggang General Strike in, 112

women and children as laborers in, 67–68, 68 n. 68

workers leaving, 113

working conditions in, 65–66

See also Deng Zhongxia; Guangzhou; Hong Kong government; Hong Kong Seamen's Strike

Hong Kong and Shanghai Banking Corporation, 57

Hong Kong and Whampoa Dock Company Limited, 61

Hong Kong Chamber of Commerce, 188

Hong Kong Chinese Mechanics' Union (Xianggang Huaren jiqi hui), 80, 81, 172

Hong Kong Electric Company, 61

Hong Kong Federation of Labor, 103

Hong Kong General Union (Xianggang zong gonghui), 172, 174, 177, 178, 178 n. 94

Hong Kong government

Executive Council in, 204, 212

Legislative Council in, 203, 214

and Shenggang General Strike, 207, 210–14, 210 n. 59, 216, 217

tension between local Chinese and, 95–98

mentioned, 57, 66, 70, 79, 82, 96, 97, 98, 106, 111, 128, 136, 164, 188, 190, 199–205, 208, 222

Hong Kong Mechanics' Federation (Xianggang jigong lianhehui), 174, 177

Hong Kong Police, 77 n. 98, 83, 105

Hong Kong Postmen's Labor Club, 84

Hong Kong Seamen's Strike

class solidarity in, 84

Communists' participation in, 86

development of, 83

mobilized workers in, 78

mentioned, 30, 48, 69, 91, 202

See also Guomindang

Hong Kong Seamen's Union

in Hong Kong Seamen's Strike, 78

in Shenggang General Strike, 175, 176, 177

mentioned, 74, 79, 81

Hong Kong Tramway Company, 61, 112

Hong Kong University, 210

Hu Hanmin, 157 n. 5, 158, 159, 161, 209
Hu Shi, 25, 40, 40 n. 122
Huang Huanting, 76, 78, 180
Huang Jinyuan, 80 n. 117, 121
Huang Ping
  in Guangzhou Uprising, 243
  in Shenggang General Strike, 107, 109,
      116 n. 62, 117, 133, 134, 242
  mentioned, 94, 106 n. 17, 108, 165, 195,
      225 n. 3
Huangpu Military Academy
  and Jiang Jieshi, 162, 164 n. 30
  student-cadets of, 112, 126
  mentioned, 25, 89, 117, 165, 216, 240
Huiyang, 191 n. 149
Hunan, 9, 13, 18, 25, 46, 52, 57, 172
Hunan First Normal College, 25
Hunan-Hubei, 253, 257
Hunanese, 16, 19, 20
Hundred Days Reform, 11

International Settlement
  in Shamian, 118–19
  in Shanghai, 33, 105
  and Shanghai Municipal Police, 3, 37
      n. 11, 241, 262
  mentioned, 184

Jamieson, James
  criticized Governor Stubbs, 98
  and Governor Clementi, 213
  and Shaji Incident, 113, 208
  mentioned, 164, 215
Japan
  cotton mills in Shanghai, 106, 120
  Guandong Army of, 261
  influence in China, 14, 18
  investment in Guangdong, 59
  Sino-Japanese Military Mutual Assis-
      tance Convention, 14
  and Twenty-one Demands, 13
  war with China, 266
  mentioned, 10, 11, 17, 74, 75, 187, 198
Jiang Jieshi
  and Deng Zhongxia, 3
  and March Twentieth Coup, 162–64, 169,
      183, 195, 196, 214
  and Northern Expedition, 215–16

planned to attack Shamian, 119
  regarded as Guomindang leftist, 137, 161
  regarded as revolutionary leader, 168
  and Shenggang General Strike, 157, 220
  and Soviet advisors, 167, 168, 169, 180
  suppressed Communists, 225, 226
  mentioned, 165, 182, 227, 235
  See also Guomindang
Jiang Ping, 46 n. 140, 251 n. 111
Jiangsu, 38, 242, 252 n. 114
  See also Chinese Communist Party
Jiangzhe faction, 252
Jinghan railway, 30
Jiujiang, 235, 236
Jordan, Donald A., 216
junzhu guan (Master's Lodge), 69

Kailuan, 33
Kang Youwei, 11, 53, 95
Kejia, 55
Kemp, J. H., 217 n. 89
Kowloon, 54, 61, 64
Kowloon Wharf and Godown Company, 61

Labor Federation of Hong Kong Metallur-
      gical Industries (Xianggang jinshuye
      zong gonghui), 176–77
Labor Movement Committee of Municipal
      Guangzhou (Guangzhoushi gongren
      yundong weiyuanhui), 180
Labor Secretariat (Zhongguo laodong zuhe
      shujibu)
  establishment of, 28–29, 29 n. 73
  journal issued by, 129
  mobilized workers, 29–30
  organized First National Labor Con-
      gress, 31–32
  retreat of, 34, 35
  weakness of, 33
  mentioned, 26, 48, 102
Lampson, Sir Miles, 222
Laodong yin (The Voices of Workers), 23
Legge, James, 53
Leizhou, 191 n. 149
Lenin
  and bourgeoisie democratic revolution,
      39, 41, 86–87

Deng Zhongxia's views on, 43–44
and elite party leadership, 6
Leninist, 7, 32, 33, 34, 264
See also democratic centralism
Li Dazhao
as Deng's ideological mentor, 3, 231
recommended Deng, 35
recommended Su Zhaozheng, 48
mentioned, 16, 17, 21, 23, 25, 30, 44, 234
Li Hongzhang, 95
Li Huang, 25
Li Huixin (Xia Ming), 12 n. 7
Li Jishen, 242
Li Langru, 185
Li Lisan
chairman of CCP Labor Committee, 226
condemned by Wang Ming, 257
criticized the Comintern, 244
and Deng Zhongxia, 243, 255
on Guangzhou Uprising, 244–45
member of CCP Provisional Politburo,
226
and Nanchang Uprising, 235–36
on revolutionary upsurge (1930), 254
secretary of CCP Guangdong Regional
Committee, 243–44
mentioned, 224, 225, 245 n. 91, 253, 259
Li Peiqun, 166 n. 40, 197 n. 1
Li Qihan, 29 n. 73
Li Sen, 111, 118, 123, 124, 133, 134, 172, 174
Li Weihan, 226, 234 n. 41, 236, 241
Liang Bingxuan, 75
Liang Furan, 94
Liang Meizhi, 172 n. 70, 190 n. 145
Liang Qichao, 11, 40
Liang Shuming, 40
Liang Zhiguang, 80 n. 117
Lianyi Society, 74
Liao Zhongkai
assassination of, 158, 161, 162, 201, 205,
209
left-wing Guomindang leader, 89, 92, 157
supporter of Shenggang General Strike,
109, 117, 118
wife of, 262
mentioned, 85, 157 n. 5, 163, 210
Lin Changzhi, 106, 106 n. 18
Lin Jiangyun, 266

Lin Weimin
admitted to CCP, 84, 91
as organizer of Shenggang General
Strike, 111, 114
on Strike Committee, 121, 123, 123 n. 92
mentioned, 6, 103, 118
Lin Yunan, 29 n. 73
liquidation faction, 38
liquidationism, 46
Liu Ersong
biographical note on, 92 n. 155
as Communist labor activist in Guangzhou, 92, 93, 108
in Shenggang General Strike, 111, 179
mentioned, 118, 225 n. 3
Liu Shaoqi, 103, 135, 162, 175, 177 n. 89
Liu Shifu, 73, 75
Lominadze, Besso, 226 n. 11, 236, 236 n. 47,
237, 238, 241, 242, 247
Luo Dengxian, 90
Luo Yinong, 109
Luo Zhanglong, 9 n. 2, 19, 29
Luohu, 192, 192 n. 151, 193 n. 152
Lushan, 236

Ma Chaojun, 73, 78, 77, 79, 83, 94, 173
Macau, 214
Macleay, Sir James, 188, 208, 219
Manchuria, 261
Mao Zedong
and 7 August emergency meeting, 237
and Deng, 13, 18, 25, 263
and Li Lisan, 254
mentioned, 5, 10, 29 n. 73, 165, 184
March Twentieth Coup
Chinese Communists' response to,
164–68
impact of, 169–71, 176, 181
and Jiang Jieshi, 162–64, 169, 183, 195,
196, 214
Soviet advisors' response to, 168–69
Strike Committee's announcement after,
166
mentioned, 134, 163, 170 n. 62, 173, 175,
183, 195, 196, 214, 223
Maring, H., 30, 39, 40, 87, 88
Marxism, 5, 19, 21, 23, 24, 27, 28, 35, 50, 258

Qu Qiubai
and 7 August emergency meeting, 238
criticized by CCP Politburo, 257
criticized Chen Duxiu, 234 n. 41
and Deng Zhongxia, 234–35, 242, 258
in Moscow, 247, 248, 253
at Shanghai University, 36
mentioned, 224, 225, 227, 236 n. 47, 238
n. 60, 241, 242, 247 n. 100
Queen's College (Hong Kong), 112

Rand School (New York), 74
Red Army, 253, 254, 256, 257
Red International, 49 n. 154, 103, 132
See also Profintern
Red International of Transport Workers'
Federation, 175
Renmin zhoukan (People's Weekly), 128,
129, 162
Republican Revolution (1911 Revolution),
13, 41, 74, 75, 82, 85, 87, 93, 94, 96, 184
Rexue ribao (Hot Blood Daily), 235
Roy, M. N., 39, 232, 247

Safarov, G., 39
Scramble for Concessions, 54
Sednikov, 252
Shaji Incident, 112–13, 118, 206, 208, 208
n. 45, 217, 222
Shamian
anti-British demonstration in, 99, 112,
113
Chinese workers in, 69, 93, 173, 221
Jiang Jieshi's plan to attack, 119
representatives to Strike Committee, 121,
123
women workers' union in, 131
mentioned, 92, 187, 208, 219
Shanghai
British investment in, 57–58
CCP members in, 240
labor movement in, 18–21, 27, 74, 77, 120,
239–40, 241, 245
May Thirtieth Incident in, 101, 105–7
as treaty port, 53
mentioned, 14, 30, 32, 33, 35, 36, 38, 46,
47, 48, 67, 69, 72, 75, 87, 97, 99, 104,
111, 115, 116, 156, 165, 167, 168, 183,

184, 195, 200, 205, 209, 215, 224, 225,
234, 235, 236, 238, 239, 242, 243, 258,
261, 262
See also CCP; Deng Zhongxia; Guomin-
dang
Shanghai Federation, 102
Shanghai University, 35–36, 37, 37 n. 113,
234
Shantou, 75, 126, 137, 175, 204, 220
Shenggang (Guangzhou–Hong Kong)
General Strike
Accounting Division in, 125, 126
Advisory Committee in, 117, 121
Business Department in, 124
diplomatic achievement of, 221–22
economic impact of, 186–88
end of, 218–21
Financial Committee in, 124, 125
foreign workers' donations to, 126 n. 107
overseas Chinese donations to, 126, 127
Picketing Department in, 126
pickets of, 125–28, 128 n. 118, 129, 131, 211,
213, 219
political significance of, 136–37, 194–95
preparation for by Communists, 106–12
Propaganda Department in, 130, 131
Provisional Strike Committee in, 109,
120
Recreation Department in, 125
and Shaji Incident, 112–13
Special Court in, 124, 127, 128
Special Transport Committee in, 124
Stores and Auction Department in, 125,
127
Strike Committee in, 110, 113, 114, 117,
120, 122–25, 125 n. 98, 126–29, 131–
36, 157, 159, 159 n. 13, 160, 164, 166,
177, 181, 185–87, 190–93, 199, 206,
209–12, 216–22, 225 n. 3, 227
Strikers' Delegates Congress in, 121, 122,
123, 159, 191, 264
Transport and Communication Department in, 125
mentioned, 6, 51, 81, 86, 91, 101, 114, 118,
135, 156, 159, 167, 173, 194, 196, 197,
200, 202, 218, 221, 224, 225, 227,
242, 258, 264, 265, 266
See also Borodin, Michael; Deng Zhong-